COUNTERINSURGENCY
IN
MODERN WARFARE

COUNTERINSURGENCY
IN
MODERN WARFARE

EDITORS
DANIEL MARSTON
CARTER MALKASIAN

First published in Great Britain in 2008 by Osprey Publishing,
Midland House, West Way, Botley, Oxford OX2 0PH, United Kingdom.
443 Park Avenue South, New York, NY 10016, USA.
Email: info@ospreypublishing.com

A CIP catalog record for this book is available from the British Library

ISBN: 978 1 84603 281 3

Sergio Catignani, Bruce Gudmundsson, Richard Iron, Peter Lieb, Anthony James Joes, Carter Malkasian,
Daniel Marston, John A. Nagl, Douglas Porch, Richard Stubbs, Charles Townshend, Jonathan Walker and
J. R. T. Wood have asserted their right under the Copyright, Designs and Patents Act, 1988, to be identified
as the authors of this book.

Index by Alan Thatcher
Typeset in ITC Stone Serif, Monotype Gill Sans, Bembo, MT Grotesque, Sabon and Univers
Maps by Peter Bull Art Studio and The Map Studio
Originated by PDQ Media, Bungay, UK
Printed and bound in China through World Print Ltd

08 09 10 11 12   10 9 8 7 6 5 4 3 2

For a catalog of all books published by Osprey please contact:

NORTH AMERICA
Osprey Direct c/o Random House Distribution Center
400 Hahn Road, Westminster, MD 21157, USA
E-mail: info@ospreydirect.com

ALL OTHER REGIONS
Osprey Direct UK, P.O. Box 140, Wellingborough, Northants, NN8 2FA, UK
E-mail: info@ospreydirect.co.uk

www.ospreypublishing.com

Acknowledgments

The editors would like to thank many people for their help with this project. Firstly, we would like to thank the authors of the chapters who have agreed to be involved with this project. Secondly, we are grateful to the many military and civilian practitioners of COIN who have been kind enough to offer their opinions on current and past operations. Thirdly, we would like to thank our editor Ruth Sheppard for all the professionalism and organization that saw the project through. Finally, we are grateful to Nancy Owens for her excellent copyediting.

Dedication

To Robert O'Neill, veteran of Vietnam and mentor to many.

CONTENTS

Contributors   8

Introduction   13

Chapter 1   IN AID OF THE CIVIL POWER: 19
            Britain, Ireland and Palestine 1916—48
            Professor Charles Townshend

Chapter 2   COUNTERINSURGENCY IN THE PHILIPPINES   37
            1898—1954
            Professor Anthony James Joes

Chapter 3   THE FIRST OF THE BANANA WARS: US Marines in   55
            Nicaragua 1909—12
            Major Bruce Gudmundsson (ret)

Chapter 4   FEW CARROTS AND A LOT OF STICKS: 70
            German Anti-Partisan Warfare in
            World War Two
            Dr Peter Lieb

Chapter 5   FRENCH IMPERIAL WARFARE 1945—62   91
            Professor Douglas Porch

Chapter 6   FROM SEARCH AND DESTROY TO HEARTS   113
            AND MINDS: The Evolution of British Strategy
            in Malaya 1948—60
            Dr Richard Stubbs

Chapter 7   COUNTERINSURGENCY IN VIETNAM: American   131
             Organizational Culture and Learning
             Lieutenant Colonel John A. Nagl

Chapter 8   RED WOLVES AND BRITISH LIONS: 149
             The Conflict in Aden
             Jonathan Walker

Chapter 9   BRITAIN'S LONGEST WAR: Northern Ireland   167
             1967–2007
             Colonel Richard Iron

Chapter 10   COUNTERING THE *CHIMURENGA*:   185
             The Rhodesian Counterinsurgency
             Campaign 1962–80
             Dr J. R. T. Wood

Chapter 11   THE ISRAEL DEFENSE FORCES AND   203
             THE *AL-AQSA INTIFADA*: When Tactical
             Virtuosity Meets Strategic Disappointment
             Dr Sergio Catignani

Chapter 12   LESSONS IN 21ST-CENTURY COUNTERINSURGENCY: 220
             Afghanistan 2001–07
             Dr Daniel Marston

Chapter 13   COUNTERINSURGENCY IN IRAQ: 241
             May 2003–January 2007
             Dr Carter Malkasian

             Endnotes   260
             Bibliography   287
             Index   296

CONTRIBUTORS

Dr Sergio Catignani is a Max Weber Fellow at the European University Institute, Florence, where he is conducting a comparative study on Western approaches to low-intensity conflicts. Prior to the EUI, Dr Catignani was a Lecturer in the Department of War Studies, King's College London, where he also obtained his Ph.D. in War Studies under the supervision of Professor Sir Lawrence Freedman. His publications have appeared in *The Journal of Strategic Studies*, *Terrorism & Political Violence*, *Parameters*, and *The Royal United Services Institute Journal*. His Ph.D. thesis has been published as *The Israel Defense Forces and the Two Intifadas* (2008).

Major Bruce Gudmundsson, USMCR (Retired) is a historian who specializes in tactical innovation – the way that military organizations respond to radical change. The author of four major books and several hundred articles, he has taught at the Marine Corps Command and Staff College, the Royal Military Academy Sandhurst, and Oxford University.

Colonel Richard Iron OBE was originally commissioned into the British Army in 1975. He has served in Germany, Kenya, the Falkland Islands, the Sultanate of Oman, the Balkans, and in several tours in Northern Ireland. He attended both the British and US Army staff colleges. His appointments include chief of staff of an armored brigade and command of an armored infantry battalion. He has a wide background in joint and land doctrine, leading the British Army's doctrine branch from 2001 to 2004; he was also responsible for overseeing the development of NATO land doctrine for six years. He led a US-UK planning team for the 2003 invasion of Iraq and was responsible for the British Army's subsequent analysis of the Iraq war. He was an expert military witness for the prosecution in the Sierra Leone war crimes tribunal. In 2007 he was appointed as mentor for the senior Iraqi Army commander in Basra.

Dr Peter Lieb is a Senior Lecturer at the Royal Military Academy Sandhurst, Department of War Studies, and Research Fellow at the European Studies Research Institute, University of Salford. Prior to this he was a Research Fellow at the Institut für Zeitgeschichte in Munich, and the German Historical Institute in Paris. He holds a Ph.D. and an M.A. from the University of Munich. His research interests are the German Army in both world wars, and insurgencies and counterinsurgencies in the 20th century, as well as war crimes throughout history. He has published a book on the radicalization of warfare in the West in 1944 entitled *Konventioneller Krieg oder NS-Weltanschauungskrieg? Kreigführung und Partisanenbekämpfung in Frankreich 1943–44* (2007). Furthermore, he has written several articles in German, French and English about the German Army and war crimes in both world wars.

Professor Anthony James Joes has a Ph.D. from the University of Pennsylvania, and an A.B. from Saint Joseph's University, where he is now Professor. He was Director of the International Relations Program 1972–2002 and Visiting Professor of Political Science at the US Army War College, 2001–03. He has presented on the subjects of insurgency and counterinsurgency to the CIA, the Center for Army Analysis, the US Marine Corps Concepts and Plans Division, the United States Air Force, the National Defense University, the Foreign Policy Research Institute, and the RAND Insurgency Board. He is the author of eleven books and has edited or contributed to several others including *Urban Guerrilla Warfare* (2007), *Resisting Rebellion: The History and Politics of Counterinsurgency* (2004), *America and Guerrilla Warfare* (2000), *Saving Democracies: U.S. Intervention in Threatened Democratic States* (1999), and *Guerrilla Warfare: A Historical, Biographical and Bibliographical Sourcebook* (1996). He has also published many articles.

Dr Carter Malkasian directs research on stability and development at the Center for Naval Analyses (CNA) in Alexandria, Virginia. Prior to this job, he was assigned to the I Marine Expeditionary Force as an adviser on counterinsurgency. He deployed with I MEF to Iraq from February to May 2003, February 2004 to February 2005, and February 2006 to August 2006. He has written a number of articles, including "Signaling Resolve, Democratization, and the First Battle of Fallujah," in *The Journal of Strategic Studies*; "The Role of Perceptions and Political Reform in Counterinsurgency," in *Small Wars & Insurgencies*; and "Toward a Better Understanding of Attrition," in *Journal of Military History*. He has also written two books, *A History of Modern Wars of Attrition* (2002) and *The Korean War, 1950–1953* (2001).

Dr Daniel Marston is a Research Fellow at the Strategic and Defence Studies Centre at the Australian National University and a Visiting Fellow with the Oxford Leverhulme Programme on the Changing Character of War. He was previously a Senior Lecturer in War Studies at the Royal Military Academy Sandhurst. He has focused on the topic of how armies learn and reform as a central theme in his academic research. Dr Marston was responsible for overseeing the counterinsurgency modules for Royal Military Academy Sandhurst and the British Army. He has lectured widely on the principles and practices of counterinsurgency to units and formations of the American, Australian, British and Canadian armed forces, as well as serving as a reviewer of and contributor to counterinsurgency doctrine for all of the above. He continues academic research in this area, and is a Fellow of the Royal Historical Society. He completed his doctorate in the history of war at Oxford University.

Lieutenant Colonel John A. Nagl is a West Point graduate who holds a D.Phil. from Oxford University. He led a tank platoon in Operation *Desert Storm* and served as the operations officer of Task Force 1-34 Armor in Khalidiyah, Iraq in 2003–04. Nagl is the author of *Learning to Eat Soup with a Knife: Counterinsurgency Lessons from Malaya and Vietnam* (2005) and was on the writing team that produced *Field Manual 3-24, Counterinsurgency* (2006).

Professor Douglas Porch earned his Ph.D. from Corpus Christi College, Cambridge University. He has been a Senior Lecturer at the University College of Wales, Aberystwyth, the Mark Clark Chair of History at the Citadel in Charleston, South Carolina, and Professor of Strategy at the Naval War College in Newport, Rhode Island. He is now Professor and Chair of the Department of National Security Affairs at the Naval Postgraduate School in Monterey, California. A specialist in military history, Professor Porch's books include *The French Foreign Legion: A Complete History of the Legendary Fighting Force* (1991), which won prizes both in the United States and in France; *The French Secret Services: From the Dreyfus Affair to Desert Storm* (1995); and *The Path to Victory: The Mediterranean Theater in World War II* (2004), which was awarded the US Army Historical Foundation Prize.

CONTRIBUTORS

Dr Richard Stubbs is Professor of Political Science and former Chair of the Department of Political Science at McMaster University, Canada. He has published widely on the security and political economy issues in East and Southeast Asia. He is author of *Hearts and Minds in Guerrilla Warfare: The Malayan Emergency 1948–1960* (1989; repr. 2004), and *Rethinking Asia's Economic Miracle: The Political Economy of War, Prosperity and Crisis* (2005). He is also co-editor (with Paul Rich) of *The Counter-insurgent State* (1997) and (with Geoffrey R. D. Underhill) of *Political Economy and the Changing Global Order* (3rd ed., 2006).

Professor Charles Townshend is currently Professor of International History at Keele University, UK. He was formerly Fellow of the National Humanities Center, North Carolina, and of the Woodrow Wilson International Center for Scholars, Washington, D.C. His first book was his doctoral thesis, *The British Campaign in Ireland 1919–1921* (1975). Since then he has written *Political Violence in Ireland: Government and Resistance since 1848* (1983), *Britain's Civil Wars: Counterinsurgency in the Twentieth Century* (1986), *Making the Peace: Public Order and Public Security in Modern Britain* (1993), and *Ireland: The Twentieth Century* (1999). He was editor of the *Oxford Illustrated History of Modern War* (1997), and was co-editor (with Richard English) of *The State: Historical and Political Dimensions* (1999). His *Terrorism: A Very Short Introduction* (2002) has been translated into German, Italian, Japanese, and four other languages. He was awarded a Leverhulme Senior Research Fellowship in 2002–05 and his most recent book, *Easter 1916: The Irish Rebellion*, was published in 2005.

Jonathan Walker was born in 1953 and educated at Clifton College, UK. He is a member of the British Commission for Military History and is an Honorary Research Associate at the University of Birmingham Centre for First World War Studies. He is author of *Aden Insurgency: The Savage War in South Arabia 1962–1967* (2005). His other publications include *The Blood Tub: General Gough and the Battle of Bullecourt, 1917* (2000), and he was editor of a new edition of *War Letters to a Wife* (2001). Pursuing his interest in insurgency warfare, his forthcoming book *Poland Alone* is a study of the Polish Home Army during World War Two. He has broadcast on various aspects of military history and contributes to historical journals.

Dr J. R. T. Wood was born in Bulawayo and raised in Salisbury, UK. He was educated at St George's College, Rhodes and Edinburgh University. He was a Commonwealth scholar and is a Fellow of the Royal Historical Society. He was the Ernest Oppenheimer Memorial Research Fellow at the University of Rhodesia and a Professor of History at the University of Durban-Westville. He has spent 35 years researching the history of Rhodesia and is author of numerous articles and four books: *The Welensky Papers* (1983), *The War Diaries of André Dennison* (1989), *So Far and No Further! Rhodesia's Bid for Independence During the Retreat from Empire 1959–1965* (2005), and *A Matter of Weeks Rather than Months: Sanctions and Abortive Settlements: 1965–1969* (2007). He is researching a fifth book covering the period 1970–80. As a territorial soldier, he served in the 1st and 8th Battalions, The Rhodesia Regiment and in the Mapping and Research Unit of the Rhodesian Intelligence Corps.

INTRODUCTION

The Ideas and History Behind Counterinsurgency

After being neglected in the aftermath of the Vietnam War, the study of counterinsurgency returned to prominence in the early years of the 21st century as a result of the wars in Iraq and Afghanistan. On one side of the Atlantic, Rupert Smith's *The Utility of Force*, published in 2005, offered the proposition that wars among the people were now the dominant form of warfare. On the other, John Nagl's *Learning to Eat Soup with a Knife: Counterinsurgency Lessons from Malaya and Vietnam*, first published in 2002, brought the lessons learnt in these countries back into US military discourse. Both of these works were closely followed in 2006 by the new counterinsurgency field manual of the US Army and Marine Corps.

This book looks at the history of individual counterinsurgency campaigns. The focus is on how different strategies were developed and how they did, or did not, contribute to the ultimate success or failure of the campaign.

Ideas of Counterinsurgency

The history of the study of counterinsurgency begins in the late 19th and early 20th century. Scholars and military officers began to reflect on campaigns between colonial powers, such as Great Britain and the United States, and insurgent opponents, such as the Boers and the Filipinos. These experiences were encapsulated in writing by officers and militaries. The best examples are C. E. Callwell's *Small Wars*, Charles Gwynn's *Imperial Policing*, and the US Marine Corps' *Small Wars Manual*.

With the Cold War, counterinsurgency took on a new importance as the West battled a series of insurgencies, most notably in Malaya, Algeria, and Vietnam. There are three "key" theorists from this period, whose works are still influential: Colonel David Galula, Sir Robert Thompson, and General Sir Frank Kitson.

Colonel David Galula was a French officer who served from 1956–58 in the Algerian War of Independence. His book, *Counterinsurgency Warfare: Theory and Practice*, was written in 1964, based upon his experiences in Algeria. Galula described two themes of counterinsurgency that have defined its study.

First, for Galula, counterinsurgency was about protecting the population, not killing the enemy: "Destroying or expelling from an area the main body of guerrilla forces, preventing their return, installing garrisons to protect the population, tracking the guerrilla remnants – these are predominately military operations."[1]

Second, Galula declared political power to have primacy over military power in counterinsurgency. As he put it: "[that] the political power is the undisputed boss is a matter of both principle and practicality. What is at stake is the country's political regime, and to defend it is a political affair."[2]

Sir Robert Thompson wrote *Defeating Communist Insurgency* in 1966, outlining the lessons of his experiences in the Malayan Emergency. *Defeating Communist Insurgency* outlines five principles for COIN operations:

1. The government must have a clear political aim
2. The government must function within the law
3. The government must have an overall plan
4. The government must give priority to defeating the political subversion, not the guerrillas
5. In the guerrilla phase of an insurgency, it must secure its base first.

These principles had wide influence as a basic framework for conducting counterinsurgency. Like Galula, Thompson emphasized the importance of politics in counterinsurgency. In terms of military operations, he also looked to protect the population. He invented the term "clear and hold," which has been used to describe the best tactical approach for conducting military operations against an insurgency, particularly in Iraq and Afghanistan (classed as the clear, hold, and build approach in these two campaigns). As Thompson stated:

> For clear operations...the first essential is to saturate it with joint military and police forces... "Clear" operations will, however, be a waste of time unless the government is ready to follow them up immediately with "hold" operations... The objects of a "hold" operation are to restore government authority in the area and to establish a firm security framework... [T]his hold period of operations inevitably takes a considerable time and requires a methodical approach and a great attention to detail. It never really ends and overlaps into the stage of

winning the population over to the positive support of the government. "Winning the population" [akin to the "build" stage of a clear, hold, and build approach] can tritely be summed up as good government in all its aspects... When normal conditions have been restored, and the people have demonstrated by their positive action that they are on the side of the government, then, as the government advance has been extended well beyond the area...[it] can be called "white"[or won].[3]

General Sir Frank Kitson (British Army) wrote *Low Intensity Operations* in 1971. Kitson served in the anti-Mau-Mau, Malayan Emergency, Oman, Cyprus, and Northern Ireland operations. In *Low Intensity Operations*, Kitson covered many of the same issues as Galula and Thompson, but in greater detail. More than any other theorist, he explained the importance and methods of intelligence collection and training. Indeed, he is the first to articulate intelligence collection as key to success, rather than assuming it to be an unstated and integral aspect of other principles. He wrote: "If it is accepted that the problem of defeating the enemy consists very largely of finding him, it is easy to recognise the paramount importance of good information."[4] In his chapter entitled "Handling Information," Kitson outlines how the military can best set out to gather information about insurgent groups. He stated that "two separate functions are therefore involved in putting troops into contact with insurgents. The first one consists of collecting background information, and the second involves developing it into contact information."[5] For Kitson, the responsibility for developing background information lay not with the intelligence organization but the operational commanders. In his words:

> Basically the system involves a commander in collecting all the background information he can get from a variety of sources including the intelligence organisation, and analysing it very carefully in order to narrow down possible whereabouts of the enemy, the purpose being to make deductions which will enable him to employ his men with some hope of success as opposed to using them at random in the hope of making contact.[6]

He also points out the need to rely on local police in gathering this information.

Themes Arising from the History of Counterinsurgency Campaigns

Focusing on the history of different examples of counterinsurgency rather than the theory, each chapter in this book examines a strategy for fighting an insurgency, from the US campaign in the Philippines to the present conflicts in Afghanistan and Iraq. The intent is not to provide a comprehensive history of each case but to examine how counterinsurgency strategy was devised and why it was or was not successful.

Naturally, these questions cannot be answered by focusing solely on military decisions or the development of doctrine. Insurgencies, more than any other form of war, draw in the social and political landscape. To borrow from Rupert Smith, they are a "war amongst the people." Consequently, politics and society form an important subtext to the study of counterinsurgency.

In the cases examined in this book, political compromise rather than seeking a total military victory characterizes several successful strategies. In these situations, counterinsurgents addressed the grievances that motivated people to become insurgents. Strategies that failed to do so allowed the insurgency to retain popular support against all but the most brutal military tactics. Counterinsurgency failures in France, Russia, Indochina, Algeria, Rhodesia, and Israel are all related to strategies that neglected to attempt a political compromise with the insurgents. For example, the French continued with colonialist goals of retaining control of Algeria and consequently could never come to any compromise agreement with the FLN. Similarly, the neglect of Pashtun concerns between 2001 and 2005 in Afghanistan contributed to a resurgence of the Taliban in 2006.

Another way that politics and society affect counterinsurgency is in terms of ethnic or sectarian divisions. Conflicts in Malaya (Malay versus Chinese), Rhodesia (white versus African), Northern Ireland (Catholic versus Protestant), Afghanistan (Pashtun versus Uzbek and Tajik), and Iraq (Sunni versus Shi'a) were all due in part to a sectarian divide. Counterinsurgency strategy needed to address the concerns of the aggrieved sect or ethnic group, through providing them with political representation, economic assistance, or positions within the country's military forces. Otherwise, no political compromise could occur and locals tended to back the insurgency.

Tactical brilliance at counterinsurgency translates into very little when political and social context is ignored or misinterpreted. Time and time again tactical military successes have not deterred a local population from supporting or joining an insurgency if its concerns are not addressed. In such circumstances, military successes only bring an end to the conflict when the local population becomes exhausted.

In looking at how counterinsurgency strategies are devised, one of the central issues is how states fail to adapt. Why do they often fail to pay attention to politics and society? Why are overly militarized strategies often employed? The book tries to provide insight into this problem.

One simple explanation is bad leadership, meaning that the officers commanding a counterinsurgency operation or the politicians guiding the strategy have made poor decisions. Under this argument, a different leader, or set of leaders, would have made better choices. This explanation comes to mind for the Iraq War. It has often been argued that the poor decisions of the Bush administration or Ambassador Paul Bremer led to a quagmire. Similarly, a popular argument regarding Vietnam is that the war would have turned out better if Creighton Abrams had commanded US forces in 1965 instead of William Westmoreland.

Culture provides a different explanation. In this argument, the history, structure, and ideology of a military affect success in fighting insurgencies. As John Nagl has argued in his book *Learning to Eat Soup with a Knife*, the culture of the US military in the 1960s, with its emphasis on fighting big battles, played an important role in inhibiting US adaptation in Vietnam. On the other hand, he shows that the British military's history of fighting small colonial wars allowed it to adapt successfully in Malaya. To take another example, the contemporary culture of the Germans in World War Two led to a brutal but ultimately ineffective counterinsurgency strategy.

Even when the military adapts effectively to fighting an insurgency, its efforts can be restricted by the domestic political situation. If the home government lacks the political support to field a large military, budget war expenditures, or suffer steady casualties over several years, then the counterinsurgency campaign may not succeed. This was the case for France in Indochina and Algeria, where the conflicts were promoted by a minority of politicians. When the costs of both conflicts rose, political support declined and France lost the wars.

A final explanation is that, in some cases, the gap between the aims of the government and the aims of the insurgents may be too great for any political compromise and the conflict can only be resolved once one, or both, sides are militarily exhausted. For example, the conflict in Rhodesia could never be resolved as long as the white government insisted on holding onto power. This explanation would also seem to fit the most recent intifada, in which, after five years of fighting, Israeli Prime Minister Ariel Sharon decided that it was better to pull out of certain occupied territories and wall them off rather than continue to hope that military measures might some day quell the violence.

This book does not endorse any single explanation. The chapters demonstrate the different ways in which states have failed to adapt to fighting an insurgency, as well as how they have succeeded. We hope that this book can serve as a starting point for those looking to understand the principles and history of counterinsurgency, an understanding that is an essential starting point when devising successful counterinsurgency strategy for current and future campaigns.

1

IN AID OF THE CIVIL POWER

Britain, Ireland and Palestine 1916–48

Professor Charles Townshend

Introduction

In the first half of the 20th century, Britain was confronted for the first time with modern armed resistance movements, which proved very different from the sporadic, incoherent resistance to its imperial expansion in the previous century. It faced them without a doctrine of counterinsurgency, or indeed a concept of insurgency itself. At the start of the century, the business of fighting irregular opponents remained as unattractive to regular soldiers as it had always been. The first survey of the wide British experience of attempting to pacify "remote regions peopled by half civilised races or wholly savage tribes," C. E. Callwell's book on "small wars," soberly judged that "such campaigns are most difficult to bring to a satisfactory conclusion."[1] This was a Victorian understatement of the real message – don't go there, if you can possibly avoid it. British soldiers could not entirely avoid it, but they could avoid thinking too much about it. Callwell's book was thoughtful, but it could not match the appeal of tracts on regular warfare.

The experience of war in South Africa at the turn of the century showed just why irregular war was so uninviting. The second "Boer War," which the Afrikaners themselves called the "war for freedom," dragged on for almost three increasingly frustrating years. It took Britain less than a year to achieve what should have been a decisive military victory, but 18 months to wear down the irregular campaign of the Boer commandos. Faced by opponents who, after losing the conventional military battle, resorted to guerrilla tactics, Britain responded first by psychologically belittling the enemy, turning them from fellow Europeans into enemies of civilization, and second by applying overwhelming military force. The process revealed the special difficulty of establishing, in the British system, the kind of legal regime – martial law – that soldiers believed necessary to deal with diffuse resistance. It also left uncertainty about which of the two principal military techniques employed against the Boer guerrillas had determined the final outcome – the depopulation and devastation of the country, involving the concentration of civilians in camps to deprive the guerrilla fighters of their support structure, or the vast system of blockhouses and fences constructed to inhibit the mobility of the Boer commandos and enable the country to be controlled. It was, conveniently, possible to sideline this uncertainty with the argument that the situation in South Africa had been unique, so that its "lessons" would not be relevant elsewhere. It was true that nothing quite like the Boer War would happen again, but the phenomenon of armed resistance resting on public support, and the problem of applying military force to suppress it, would recur all too soon.

The end of World War One, which had seen the British army reach an unprecedented scale of conventional operations, immediately brought sharp reminders of the alternative military world of peacetime, when action took place "in aid of the civil power." The reception of General Dyer's deliberately intimidatory action at Amritsar in 1919 sharply demonstrated the constraints imposed by British legal and political culture.[2] Dyer believed that he had used the level of force that was absolutely required to prevent the situation in Punjab getting out of control, but British opinion condemned it as excessive. All British officers were aware of the doctrine of necessary force, spelled out in King's Regulations, and given memorable form in the cashiering of the military commander called in to suppress the Bristol riots of 1831. He was convicted of not using sufficient force – the opposite of Dyer's offense – in a judgment that pointed out the daunting challenge faced by a commander who had to apply exactly the degree of force necessary to control the situation, and face the prospect of his decision being raked over in court. Despite many requests, the government had resisted the idea of codifying the criteria to be applied in the form of some kind of "state of emergency" or "state of siege."

Identifying "the kind of war on which they are embarking" is, as Clausewitz noted, "the most far-reaching act of judgment that the statesman and commander have to make."[3] Identifying an emergent insurgency is among the most difficult of all such judgments. In any case, the obscurity and ambiguity of the low-level actions that constitute the early stages of a resistance campaign render clear analysis impossible. In the British case, the working assumptions of liberal democratic culture tend to delay any supposition that opponents will step outside the realm of politics into that of violence. Law and orderliness are regarded as normal and natural. Violent action is likely to be viewed as aberrant or indeed deviant. "Extremism" is by definition marginal.

Ireland

Such was certainly the case in early 1919 when, with the benefit of hindsight, the shape of the Irish republican campaign can be seen to have emerged. The Sinn Fein Party, having practically annihilated the formerly dominant Irish Nationalist party in the December 1918 general election, constituted an independent national assembly, Dail Eireann, in January 1919, and issued a unilateral declaration of independence. Simultaneously, the first shots were fired in anger by a local unit of the Irish Volunteers, killing two policemen in an ambush. The simultaneity was accidental, however, and the meshing of the organizations that would come to constitute the republican counter-state was barely beginning. This emphasizes the magnitude of the challenge faced by British intelligence. The British authorities had little understanding of Sinn Fein. Although it had been in existence for some 15 years, it had only taken its final form as a political party in 1917. Persistent branding of "Sinn Feiners" throughout the war as fringe fanatics, antiwar agitators, and even German agents made it almost impossible to recognize the party as a potential mainstream nationalist grouping. The potential of the Irish Volunteers was similarly hard to gauge. Although the Volunteers had mounted a striking challenge to British power by staging a rebellion in 1916, they had made the British Army's task easier by confining themselves to defensive positions in Dublin. Isolated evidence of the potential of guerrilla action appeared in 1916, but was not taken seriously. Fixated, inevitably, on the stupendous battles of the Western Front, military intelligence took a comfortable view of the Volunteers' capacity.

The initial British reaction to the events of early 1919 was frankly one of bafflement. When action was finally taken, eight months after the first meeting of the Dail, it was indiscriminate: not only the quasi-military organizations such as the Volunteers (now becoming known as the Irish Republican Army or IRA) and the women's organization Cumann na mBan, but Sinn Fein and Dail Eireann itself were proscribed. Strategically, the banning of a political party was a highly questionable step, since the government's key line was to demand a "return to constitutionalism" as a prelude to a political settlement. British political and legal strategies were determined by the postwar situation. Home Rule for Ireland had been enacted at the start of the war, but was suspended for its duration. Partly because the "Home Rule" party had been wiped out in the 1918 election, the government showed no desire to bring in a new measure immediately. There was a political stand-off: Sinn Fein refused to accept Home Rule, and the government refused to grant any more substantial measure of autonomy (such as "dominion status"), much less full independence. A new Home Rule measure (the Government of Ireland Bill, establishing separate parliaments for Southern and Northern Ireland) was only introduced in late 1920.

In the interim, Ireland was ruled under the wartime emergency legislation, the Defence of the Realm Act (DORA), with some methods – for instance "Special Military Areas" in which the army had powers to regulate assembly and movement – drawn from the older Irish Crimes Act. Not until the summer of 1920 was DORA replaced by a new emergency powers law, the Restoration of Order in Ireland Act (ROIA). At that point, the Cabinet provided a significant insight into the assumptions of British political culture when it worried about "utilising machinery intended for time of war in time of peace."[4] The war/peace framework was ill-adapted to dealing with the situation that had developed in Ireland by that point: Ireland had become effectively ungovernable, but the government could not admit this. Military forces were increased, but the official line was, as the prime minister would later put it, that "the Irish job was a policeman's job supported by the military."[5] If it became a "military job," Lloyd George believed it would fail. The key assumption underpinning this was that the republican fighters (labeled "gunmen" or "thugs" by the government) were extremists whose ideas were being forced on the Irish public by terrorist methods.

A new policing policy was gradually put together between mid-1919 and mid-1920; whether it was coherent is open to question. Crucially, the main Irish police force, the Royal Irish Constabulary (RIC), had always been a counterinsurgency force of a sort, designed to neutralize the threat of armed insurrection by nationalist groups like the Fenians (Irish Republican Brotherhood or IRB). Unlike the British police and the metropolitan police in Dublin, it was armed, and received some elementary military training. After 1916, however, the Fenian preference for open insurrection was abandoned by a new generation of IRB men, led by Michael Collins.

Adapting the RIC to cope with the new challenge of insurgency was problematic. The force had long been threatened with abolition once Home Rule came into effect, and its morale was low. Falling recruitment triggered a historic decision to open the RIC's ranks to non-Irish recruits. The possible implications of this were not well understood or considered. An influx of English ex-soldiers in early 1920 was a propaganda gift to the republicans, who had always denounced the RIC as an "army of occupation" – a charge which now looked more plausible. As the Sinn Fein-led public boycott of the police was followed by IRA attacks, the military background of the new recruits (christened "Black and Tans" in Ireland because, as a temporary expedient, they were initially given a mixture of police and military uniforms) created discipline problems that the old RIC code was too weak to contain. These problems were foreseen by the incoming military commander, General Nevil Macready, who argued that rather than continue to expand the RIC (which he saw as a lost cause), a new set of special "garrison battalions," subject to military law, should be created. Instead, a new chief of police, Henry Tudor, was appointed, who pushed on with expanding and rearming the RIC. It became clear that Tudor's attitude to the RIC's discipline problem permitted a kind of unavowed counter-terror to develop as policemen responded to IRA attacks with violent reprisals that intimidated the public. Tudor's policy – clearly also tacitly approved at Cabinet level – was most notoriously enshrined in the words allegedly used by one of his senior commanders: "The more you shoot the better I shall like you, and I assure you that no policeman will get into trouble for shooting any man."[6] The RIC *Weekly Summary* was, as one Black and Tan recalled, the most "fatuous, childish and lying Government publication" ever; "its methods of attempting to rouse our blood were laughable had they not been so dangerous."[7] Tudor's most dramatic creation, the Auxiliary Division of the RIC, became a byword (in the jaundiced military view) for unofficial reprisals. Recruited from ex-officers, known as "Temporary Cadets," and organized in motorized companies of about 100, the "Auxies" were the nearest approach to a dedicated counterinsurgency force that Britain was to set up. Their objective was to get to grips directly with the "gunmen;" in Lloyd George's vivid phrase, getting "murder by the throat."

The actual nature and operating methods of the IRA, however, were rather different from the prime minister's image of them. The republican forces were more closely embedded in their local communities than government propaganda suggested. The most effective republican units, notably those in Dublin and Cork, and across the southwest more generally, constructed intelligence networks dependent on public cooperation, which minimized the chance of unplanned contact with the police or British troops. As the Dublin District General Officer Commanding (GOC) put it, "a 'bow wave' of suspicion"[8] preceded every raiding party. On the British side, the decline of the RIC atrophied its key local intelligence function, which the Black and Tans were, as foreigners, unable to rebuild. Shorn of reliable police information, the army was slow to see and implement the need for consistent, systematic intelligence work. The "intelligence gap" was certainly perceived as an issue, but the appointment of a specialist intelligence director in Dublin had only limited effects. It may be suggested that intelligence failures, exacerbated by weak cooperation between military and police, allowed the IRA to build itself into a formidably resilient and (irregularly) effective guerrilla force.

The turning point for the republican campaign came in the summer and fall of 1920. The process of turning the imaginary republic of 1919 into a counter-state with real governing pretensions was decisively advanced by Sinn Fein victories in the local government elections, after which many local authorities formally transferred loyalty from the British administration to Dail Eireann. At the same time, a system of republican courts was established, while the IRA brought the British judicial system to a standstill by the systematic intimidation of jurors and witnesses. By the late summer of 1920, when the Assizes broke down, effective British rule in many parts of the country had ceased. Britain responded by strengthening the Irish government (Dublin Castle) and passing the ROIA. The latter seemed successful initially, since the surge of military action drove many IRA men to go "on the run." Its long-term consequences were catastrophic for British prestige, however, as these men formed themselves into "flying columns" (Active Service Units) capable of carrying out more ambitious operations. Though they varied greatly in strength, ambition, and capacity, several of them, especially in the southwest, became quite formidable. During the fall, the most visible British response to this heightened military challenge took the form of reprisals – most notoriously on "Bloody Sunday" in Dublin on November 21 and in Cork after an ambush of Auxiliaries in December – that triggered a hemorrhage of public support for the government's repressive strategy in Britain itself.

The Cork events provoked the final stage in the British response: the application of martial law. This deeply problematic concept was disliked by General Macready, a former Adjutant General with a strong suspicion that the political will to back up a policy of real toughness would evaporate – a judgment borne out by events. Martial law was confined to the southwest, and clearly seen by the prime minister as a political weapon to persuade republicans to enter negotiations. Its operation was hampered by the persistent intrusion of civil courts of appeal into the martial law system, culminating in the Chancery Court judgment of July 8, which ruled that habeas corpus applied to martial law cases. Had the conflict been prolonged beyond that month, this would have brought martial law to a standstill. Just as bad, from the military viewpoint, martial law did not deliver the one thing that Macready expected from it – military control of the police. Military–police cooperation had reached a new low point in the winter of 1920–21, with senior officers openly deprecating the conduct of the Auxiliaries. Even in the "martial law area" (the eight southwestern counties), the GOC remained at loggerheads with the RIC Divisional Commissioner, and elsewhere no regular mechanism of cooperation was established. While the counterinsurgency strategy stalled, negotiation with Sinn Fein was quietly explored by Lloyd George's agents in Dublin. There were certainly some Sinn Feiners who were anxious to end what was becoming an increasingly grim and destructive conflict, but the prime minister's insistence on a surrender of IRA arms made any agreement impossible at this stage.

In the longer term, the British military response became more effective. While martial law was probably not worth the political costs it incurred, the gradual development of more flexible operational methods, together with the incremental improvement in military intelligence, led to significant results in the spring of 1921. The impulse to conduct large-scale operations, notably "drives," never disappeared, but it was accompanied at unit level by the acceptance of the need to adopt tactics mirroring those of the enemy: one- or two-platoon-strength foot columns able to move undetected for several days at a time. IRA reports – which became more comprehensive as a new organizational structure, including the formation of divisional commands, was established in April 1921 – reveal a mounting frustration at local level, and something approaching collapse for many "flying columns." A series of major arms seizures in Dublin demonstrated that the "intelligence gap" was at last being closed.

All this came too late in political terms, however. Until the spring, the government could still hope that its constitutional proposal, the 1920 Government of Ireland Act (GIA), might work. The triumph of Sinn Fein in the GIA elections eliminated that possibility, and drove ministers to the conclusion that repression was not going to succeed. Both carrot and stick had failed. In an extraordinary public comment in June 1921, Lord Birkenhead admitted that what was going on in Ireland was "a small war," and that British military methods had failed to "keep pace with, and overcome" those of their opponents.[9] Under the cover of the King's speech opening the Northern Ireland parliament that month, peace talks were accelerated, and in July a formal truce was agreed, followed by extended negotiations that produced the Anglo-Irish Treaty of December 1921.

In strictly military terms, Britain had, of course, not been defeated. As the IRA Chief of Staff reminded the Dail during the debate on the Treaty, the republican forces were still not strong enough to drive their enemy from anything bigger than a medium-sized police station. And in political terms, the threat of restarting the war with bigger military forces and wider repressive powers – though it contained a hefty element of bluff – undoubtedly exerted an influence on the treaty negotiations. The operational successes of 1921 had certainly impressed Michael Collins. Still, the British Army could not but be aware that it had fallen far short of expectations. It might also have been aware that it had been given a priceless preparatory experience in what would become the most difficult military challenge of the coming century. There were some signs of such awareness. Two of the three divisions that had been engaged in sustained contact with the insurgency drafted substantial assessments of their experience. The General Staff of Irish Command produced a full-scale systematic analysis (*Record of the Rebellion in Ireland*) clearly designed to allow the lessons of the conflict to be widely absorbed. Significantly, a full half of this analysis was devoted to the problem of intelligence. But there is no sign that any of these were read outside Ireland, and certainly the original idea of producing a general pamphlet on partisan warfare was not realized. An intelligence officer of the 6th Division, A. E. Percival, delivered lectures on the Irish experience at the Staff College, but then returned to a conventional military career (ending in the command and surrender of an army 100,000 strong at Singapore in 1941).

Perhaps most remarkably, Ireland was not included among the case studies that Sir Charles Gwynn chose for his book *Imperial Policing* (1934), a kind of empirical codification of good practice. Gwynn cryptically explained that he had "thought it inadvisable" to draw on Irish experiences, however "instructive from a military point of view" they were.[10] It seems certain, though, that Irish experience reinforced the last of his four key principles (the first three being the need for government policy to make military sense, the need to use minimum force, and the need for timely action) – the need for "close cooperation and mutual understanding" between the civil and military forces. Still more was it reflected in his emphasis on the crucial role of intelligence. Gwynn's case studies included the 1929 crisis in Palestine, even though it was not technically part of the British Empire: presumably it did not appear quite so politically sensitive, odd as this may seem. Five years after his book appeared, Palestine was absorbing as much military attention as Germany. Had he ever produced a further edition of his book, Palestine might well have swamped it.

Palestine

Superficially, there were some similarities between Ireland and Palestine – both smallish countries with salient religious divisions – but the differences were far more significant. Although Palestine existed as a conceptual entity before World War One, it was not an administrative entity; and, most importantly, there was no Palestinian national movement. Insofar as Arab nationalism had emerged at all in this area, it was focused on Damascus, not Jerusalem; Palestine, in Arab eyes, was simply southern Syria. The situation was radically transformed by British military conquest, and the issuance of the Balfour Declaration[11] a month before General Edmund Allenby's capture of Jerusalem in December 1917. It was this undertaking to "view with favour the establishment in Palestine of a national home for the Jewish people"[12] that kick-started the Palestinian nationalist response. Fatefully, however, the country was not placed under an administration geared to implementing the Declaration. For three crucial years, Palestine was under military rule – Occupied Enemy Territory Administration (South), also known as OETA(S). OETA(S) was, by international law, obliged to remain studiously neutral in regard to any political development of the country. But its neutrality had a particular cast. In October 1921, a year or so after OETA(S) was replaced by a civil administration, the General Staff in Cairo produced a remarkable memorandum admitting that "[w]hile the Army officially is supposed to have no politics, it is recognised that there are certain problems, such as those of Ireland and Palestine, in which the sympathies of the Army are on one side or the other." The effect of this explosive admission in Palestine was far-reaching.

It might, indeed, be thought to be the basis for the highly noticeable removal of the military garrison from Palestine during the 1920s, with the dire consequences that Gwynn would elucidate in his study of the 1929 disorders. However, the reason was more normal: troops were expensive, and Palestine, in common with other areas of the Middle East, was placed under the new (and cheap) system of "air control" after 1922. The only problem was that, as even the greatest enthusiasts for air power clearly saw, Palestine was more urbanized than Trans-Jordan and Iraq, and much less amenable to the special techniques developed to compel submission there. In Palestine, everything would hinge on the quality of the semi-military police forces. In the first serious disorders of 1920 and 1921, the local police failed; the question of how to render them effective would occupy the next two decades. As remarkable as the high-level admission of military politics in connecting Ireland and Palestine was the decision – taken by Winston Churchill – to ship General Tudor and 500 of his former Black and Tans to Palestine to form the backbone of the internal security system.

As Director of Public Security, and GOC as well as Inspector General, Tudor had overall strategic control of the police and two new "gendarmeries," Palestinian (cavalry) and British (motorized). The key issue was to create an ethos of policing in a society with no local tradition of self-government, and a high level of arms-carrying by individuals. The police were mainly Arab (because of the reluctance of Jewish immigrants, especially from Russia, to join the police); the Palestinian Gendarmerie overwhelmingly so. The British Gendarmerie was intended to stiffen the riot-control rather than crime-solving capacity of the police, and it was rapidly wound down under a mixture of financial stringency and declining disorder. First it was halved in size, then in 1925 abolished, leaving a small British section attached to the ordinary police. The Palestinian Gendarmerie became the Trans-Jordan Frontier Force, a unit mainly paid for by Palestine but with an ambiguous cross-border role and identity: a later High Commissioner regretted that "the desirability of preventing too much of the cost falling upon Palestine, caused the Palestine Government to lay more stress than had originally been contemplated upon the needs of Trans-Jordan" (detached from Palestine by Churchill in 1921).[13] At the same time, the remaining military forces were withdrawn to Egypt.

The first High Commissioner, leaving Palestine in 1925, expressed disquiet at these developments. He urged that some British infantry units, however small, should stay, because they were worth much more than Palestinian cavalry. He also worried about the "bad effect on the people"[14] of transferring the Black and Tans to ordinary police duty. (He politely mentioned only their ignorance of Arabic, and this was indeed a huge problem, but not the only serious one.) Over the next decade, these concerns were to be proved all too prescient. They were, however, ignored. The 1929 disorders might well have been choked off had military forces been available. Their long-term effects on Jewish attitudes to Britain, and the overriding need for security, were profound. The problem was recognized, to the extent that a full-scale reassessment of policing was carried out by Dowbiggin, and two battalions of troops were retained in Palestine, though the AOC remained in charge of security. The obvious numerical weakness of the police (barely 1,500 strong in 1929) was partly rectified (its strength rising to 2,500 by 1936) and such arrangements as the sealed armories at Jewish settlements – the removal of which shortly before the 1929 bloodbath was a major Zionist complaint – were restored. A new Inspector General, Colonel R. G. B. Spicer ("a ridiculous man called Spicer,"[15] in the unkind view of the High Commissioner's private secretary), was brought in from Kenya in 1931. He was certainly as dedicated to the values of British policing as he was to hunting, and tried to get his British and Arab constables to work together, but there is little sign that he really understood the scale of the cultural problem he was confronting. Despite five years of efforts to establish a Criminal Investigation Department (CID), when the 1936 crisis broke, police intelligence remained totally inadequate to cope with the situation.

This was foreshadowed in the police response to the first signs of hardening Arab-Muslim nationalist militancy under the leadership of Shaykh Izz al din al-Qassam in 1934. The police dismissed al-Qassam as a rabble-rousing charlatan, and his followers (always called a "gang") as ignorant and credulous fanatics in the pay of foreign powers. Although they succeeded in killing him in a gunfight in 1935, this outcome was fortuitous for Qassam's cause. His martyrdom became a potent spur to guerrilla activity, which accelerated after the declaration of a national strike in April 1936 in protest against the collapse of the proposed legislative council.

The response to the heightening violence in the summer of 1936 provided a classic illustration of the conflict between civil and military priorities. The High Commissioner, Sir Arthur Wauchope (himself a Lieutenant General, who thus outranked his security chief), was dedicated to conciliatory methods, and repeatedly turned down the AOC's advice that martial law should be declared. Military reinforcements poured in, but were dispersed on local protective duties. Wauchope resisted the army's demand for more aggressive operations, and continued to do so even after the need for martial law was accepted by the Cabinet in London and Lieutenant General Sir John Dill was sent to Palestine with a reinforcing division. (The sole, and quite spectacular, exception was the assault on Jaffa in July, carried out under the guise of public health improvements – two wide highways were blasted east–west and south–north through the maze of streets that had stymied all military searches thus far.) When the Higher Arab Committee called off the strike, and insurgent activity died down pending the arrival of a Royal Commission of Inquiry, the army was convinced that the rebellion had been "scotched not killed."[16]

When armed action resumed in the fall of 1937 after the Royal Commission recommended the partition of Palestine, the civil–military balance of power was eventually reversed. In late 1937, military courts were established. Early in 1938 Wauchope was replaced, and in the fall of that year his successor accepted the idea of "military control," a kind of undeclared martial law giving the army authority over the police. With two infantry divisions and the British police expanded to 3,000, supplemented by 5,500 (Jewish) Supernumerary Police – the Arab police had been effectively given up as unreliable – the forces available were significantly larger than ever before. An ambitious "village occupation" policy was adopted, with 18 mutually supporting garrisons in place by July 1938. An even more ambitious scheme was launched by the newly arrived police adviser, Sir Charles Tegart, in late 1938: the construction of a wire fence to seal the border between Palestine and Syria (to prevent the supposed influx of "foreign" forces), supported by a system of concrete

"Tegart forts" extended along the eastern frontier as well. The effect of this massive investment (by Palestine budget standards) was hard to assess. The insurgents, operating in small bands, continued to become noticeably more active and effective through 1938. Some of their operations, notably the systematic sabotage of the Iraq Petroleum Company (IPC) pipeline, had international impact. By October the GOC, Lieutenant General Robert Haining, accepted that "civil administration and control of the country was to all practical purposes non-existent"[17]: as in Ireland, the insurgents challenged the legitimacy of the state head-on by establishing their own law courts, and the High Commissioner recognized that "the Arab movement has recently become more of a national one."[18]

The most concise analysis of the reasons for this failure of control was produced by Captain Orde Wingate in June 1938. Government operated in daytime only: "on the approach of darkness, the virtual control of the country passes to the gangsters. They are free to move without danger anywhere."[19] Police and troops seldom moved at night, and then only in motor vehicles on the main roads, where they could be easily ambushed. When they were, "the practice has been to return fire, a useless proceeding by night, and to allow the gangs to withdraw unpursued."[20] Wingate developed a policy of "moving ambushes" by small, well-trained units, which would immediately close with the rebels "by bodily assault with bayonet and bomb."[21] These were the famous (or notorious) Special Night Squads (SNS), designed to demoralize the rebels and convince the civilian population that "terror by night will in future be exercised, where necessary, by Government."[22] Based near the IPC pipeline at Ein Harod, Wingate's mesh of SNS units extended across northern Palestine. The units (totaling some 100 men in July 1938) were basically British, but Wingate's own political agenda – he became an ardent Zionist – was to use the system to train Jewish forces drawn from the Supernumerary Police. The possible political costs of this hardly need to be stressed, and it is not clear how far Wingate's superiors (who flatly refused to countenance any open creation of Jewish military units) understood what was going on. General Haining certainly approved of the "offensive night work,"[23] although the High Commissioner and Colonial Secretary believed they had only approved defensive operations.

The impact of the SNS was noticeable, especially around the IPC pipeline, but the precise nature of its "offensive" actions remains contentious. This relates to the wider question of the reasons for the eventual petering out of the Arab insurgency in early 1939. Although military operations became more intense in late 1938, the methods – sweeps by mobile columns, raids and searches, curfews, collective punishments – remained essentially those that had been employed before. What changed, it may be suggested, was the psychological atmosphere of "military control." Some writers have suggested that in Palestine and elsewhere, the British Army successfully held to the policy of "minimum force" advocated by Gwynn and required by British law. It seems beyond question, however, that not only the SNS but also other military units – notably the 16th Brigade, in whose area Wingate himself operated – habitually used what may be called "exemplary force," if not indeed counter-terror. The brigade Officer Commanding (OC), Brigadier John Evetts, the longest-serving commander in the country (he had been there since before the 1936 outbreak) had consistently urged tough action and was the first to encourage Wingate. The northern divisional commander, Bernard Montgomery, backed him unreservedly, but Richard O'Connor of the southern division took the opposite view, that "harshness and unnecessary violence on the part of our soldiers"[24] must be curbed. (He wrote privately in November 1938 that "Jack Evetts has always encouraged his men to be brutal."[25]) The fact that Haining himself thought it necessary to urge his divisional commanders in December to punish "unnecessary violence, vindictiveness which is un-British, killing in cold blood"[26] speaks volumes.

The fact was that the army's pro-Arab partisanship had been eroded by the frustrations of pursuing small bands of men regarded as unworthy opponents. The "Oozlebarts" of 1938[27] were another species from the romantic Bedouin of the Lawrencian legend. For instance, the use of "Oozle minesweepers" – Arab hostages placed on the front of trains, or forced to run ahead of military convoys on mined roads – was happily approved by Haining himself. Probably few British officers followed Wingate into open support of Zionism, but freed of political restraint and anxious to extricate its forces from the quagmire of Palestine, the army destroyed such military potential as the Arab community possessed. The appearance towards the end of the rebellion of Arab "peace bands" on the government side attested to the breakdown of national spirit (and of course Montgomery resolutely insisted that the insurgents were not nationalists but criminal bandits). The British Army thus unwittingly shaped the outcome of the ultimate showdown between Arabs and Jews in 1948–49.

Ironically, when it faced a Jewish armed revolt after the end of World War Two, its capacity to inflict damage was much more sharply restricted.

Even the optimistic Montgomery painted a dismal picture of governmental paralysis and police uselessness in Palestine in 1939. (The High Commissioner also lamented the "Black and Tan tendencies"[28] shown by the rapidly enlarged British police force.) The Arab rebellion was certainly ended as much by political concession as by military repression. The British White Paper of May 1939 was a clear recognition (heralded in the fall of 1938) that the basic demand of the Arab Higher Committee had been conceded. Self-government – an Arab-controlled Palestine – would be implemented within 10 years, and in the meantime Jewish immigration would cease after five years. Zionists fiercely denounced this as a surrender to violence. Only World War Two delayed the inevitable response of Revisionist Zionists, who had always believed that a Jewish state could only be established by force.

Jewish "terrorism" after 1945, spearheaded by the Revisionist Irgun Zvai Leumi (IZL), had to be confronted in political conditions that were very different from those of the 1930s. Britain's already constricted options (following the rejection of the partition proposals of the 1936 Royal Commission) were further reduced by a new American interest in Palestine, added to immense post-Holocaust pressure to allow in Jewish refugees. As before, however, the gulf between the political caution of the High Commissioner (vigorous repressive measures would entail "a serious risk of violent Jewish reaction amounting to a general conflagration which would destroy all hope of a political settlement"[29]) and the gung-ho military view expressed by Montgomery, now Chief of the Imperial General Staff [CIGS] (a re-run of his intensive 1938 methods would mean "no real harm would be done to the population and in time they would tire of being upset and would cooperate in putting an end to terrorism"[30]) could not be bridged. Once again, as in Ireland, this led to the development of a "third force," a militarized police. Although yet another expert adviser (Sir Charles Wickham of the Royal Ulster Constabulary) was called in, and issued a strong warning against the creation of specialized anti-terrorist units, his advice was set aside. The fire-brigade style operations of the Police Mobile Force (PMF) directly defied Wickham's dogma that "an armoured car performs no useful police duty,"[31] and though the PMF was disbanded in mid-1946, this was for manpower rather than for doctrinal reasons. The creation of another

Wingate-inspired set of (nameless) "undercover squads," led by Wingate's deputy, Bernard Fergusson, to take on the terrorists directly, was a hazardous step. The crisis provoked by the actions of one of these secret units in 1946 did not in itself invalidate what was coming to be known as the "counter-gang" method, but it suggested how limited its relevance was in a sensitive political environment such as that of Palestine.

The key issue in the growing ungovernability of Palestine, however, was the failure of even large-scale military measures to produce the kind of results that Montgomery had predicted. This was as much the case with rural "cordon and search" operations as with the huge collective punishments in the form of isolation and curfew imposed on cities like Tel Aviv, such as Operations *Elephant* and *Hippopotamus* in 1947. The forces available in 1946 and 1947, totaling some 100,000, appeared significantly larger than those employed in the 1930s, and the police, at some 20,000, were vastly enlarged (mainly through expanding the Supernumerary Police to nearly 13,000). But in terms of effectives available for military operations, the total probably never exceeded 25,000. Though their "terrorist" opponents were, as in the 1930s, small in number, they were tightly organized and, most crucially, enjoyed real support among the Jewish population. The difficulties of conducting searches in the tightly knit Jewish settlements – not merely the passive resistance "so determined that it could only be broken by force"[32] but also the morally daunting sense of fierce public hostility – were virtually insuperable. The outcome of larger-scale operations such as the massive combing-out of Tel Aviv (Operation *Agatha*) in June 1946 was equally frustrating, in that the damage inflicted on the infrastructure of the Zionist military organizations was not followed by a reduction in violence. The IZL responded with the bombing of the King David Hotel in Jerusalem in July. Its targeting was designed to provoke the maximum retaliation, and though the military response was probably less brutal than in the Arab rebellion, the struggle degenerated into a grim vendetta. Its climax was the hanging and booby-trapping of the bodies of two British NCOs by the IZL in July 1947 – a response to the biggest military operation of all, the sealing-off under martial law of Tel Aviv and Jerusalem, which broke down prematurely as a result of the suspension of all essential services.

Throughout this increasingly desperate struggle, the army was acting formally in aid of the civil power. Insofar as Gwynn's principle of unified control was implemented, it was done negatively, by excluding the GOC

Palestine from formal membership of the High Commissioner's Central Security Committee. Civil supremacy was thus maintained. Nonetheless, although the High Commissioner was consistently opposed to it, the British government seemed to be attracted by the idea of imposing martial law. The Cabinet was, for instance, dissatisfied by the rapid abandonment of the *Elephant*/*Hippopotamus* martial-law regime,[33] and urged the Palestine authorities to work on making the system more adaptable. Palestine in fact remained under an updated version of the old 1930s Defence Order in Council (still used today by Israel to administer the West Bank), with the enhanced military powers of the October 1938 model, regarded by many people as a form of statutory martial law. Interestingly though, the government prohibited use of the term "statutory martial law," insisting on the term "controlled areas" instead. It wanted to preserve the potential impact of declaring martial law "proper," although as the Colonial Office noted, such a declaration would be "tantamount to throwing in our administrative hand in Palestine."[34]

By the end of the year, however, that hand had been thrown in; in May 1948 Britain quit Palestine in humiliating circumstances of widespread anarchy. Britain's counterinsurgency strategy, such as it was, had failed. The situation was exceptionally difficult, but it would be hard to argue that an effective military doctrine had been developed since the Irish experience. In both Ireland and Palestine, the army had been slow to adjust its perspectives and attitudes from the recent major wars: in Palestine after 1945 in particular, the dominant military figure, Montgomery, insisted that the army stand apart from "politics" and (as the High Commissioner reported) "visualise matters from a purely military angle." The result was a reluctance to adapt to the situation, and a persistence in conventional large-scale military operations. The problem of intelligence was never fully addressed, and the increasingly crucial issue of propaganda was neglected. While the civil and military authorities did develop a working relationship for planning local security operations through the Central Security Committee, there was, as David Charters has noted, "no similar meeting of minds at the strategic level."[35] The traditional distinction between war and peace hampered the recognition of a new kind of "gray area" conflict. In 1938 Brigadier Simpson, who had been Chief of Staff in Palestine, in a sharp critique of the British response to rebellion, called for a new category – "sub-war" – to be recognized. But his demand that "a new system of emergency rule"[36] be devised to deal with it had not been met by 1948.

Conclusion

Lessons had been learned by individual units rather than by institutions, and if Palestine had been followed by 20 years of quiet it seems likely that all the lessons would have been lost again.[37] As it was, some individuals (such as the Chief of Police in Palestine) went directly to Malaya: imperial networking provided a kind of doctrinal continuity. The next generation would experience a military revolution: a rapid succession of insurgencies that shifted perspectives decisively away from the focus on big-war fighting. In the 30 years from 1918 to 1948, the British Army had conducted three difficult modern counterinsurgency campaigns, and had reluctantly amassed a formidable bank of experience. It might have drawn the conclusion that excessive force was counterproductive, and that accurate intelligence was crucial. Whether it did is a matter of debate, since no official evaluation was generated at this stage. Later writers have detected an institutional commitment to the principle that was becoming known as "minimum force." But if this was so, it was due not to military preferences but to the constraints of British law and the ingrained British political determination to maintain the supremacy of the civil power. Only where they were far distant from the sources of political control – as, notably, in the Sudan – were British military forces free to experiment with the ruthless use of force. In Ireland and Palestine, they were effectively freed of civil control only once, in the last six months of the Arab rebellion. They might conclude – as Montgomery did – that the result then was success, whereas the other two campaigns were lost. In Ireland in 1921 the outcome was perhaps equivocal in a military sense; in Palestine in 1947 it was unequivocally humiliating.

Ultimately, though, these campaigns indicated that success or failure would result not from military methods, but from political circumstances. It was not that all nationalist movements were inherently undefeatable: the Arabs in Palestine were definitely defeated. The key question was one of accurately grasping their ideological and organizational dynamics – a task far outside the military remit and capacity. It was, and remains, the task of governments, not armies, to assess the feasibility of applying military force to solve a political problem.

2

COUNTERINSURGENCY IN THE PHILIPPINES 1898–1954

Professor Anthony James Joes

This chapter analyzes two insurgencies in the Philippines. The first, waged by the followers of Emilio Aguinaldo against the United States and its indigenous allies, broke out shortly after the conclusion of the Spanish-American War and lasted until 1902. The second, by the Communist-led Huks against the Republic of the Philippines supported by the US, began in 1946 and ended, for all practical purposes, in 1954.

The American Counterinsurgency 1899–1902

A Forgotten Victory

Many powerful factors have long linked the peoples of the Philippines and the United States: trade, military alliance, and memories of a victorious struggle against a common foe in World War Two. The Filipinos modeled their constitution upon that of the United States, and most of them speak the language that their forebears learned during a half-century of American tutelage. Paradoxically, this long and intimate relationship began in a military conflict waged by American troops, in a locale and against people of whom they knew very little, but which turned out to be "the most successful counterinsurgency campaign in US history."[1]

The Spanish Philippines

Located between the Philippine Sea and the South China Sea, named for Philip II of Armada fame, the Philippines occupy the maritime crossroads of the Pacific and Indian Oceans. The country has an area of 115,000 square miles, about the size of Italy or the state of Nevada. The 7,000-island archipelago, of volcanic origins, extends over a thousand miles north to south, the distance between Madrid and Vienna or Seattle and Los Angeles. Only 3,000 of the islands have names, and only 400 are permanently inhabited. Except in highland areas, the climate is hot, humid, and enervating.

Magellan reached the islands in 1521, and the Spanish established fairly effective control by the 1560s, founding Manila in 1571. Spanish rule created the first unity the islands had known; today's Republic is the direct geographical heir of the Spanish colony. Christian missionaries brought Filipinos into the orbit of the Western world, and consequently the Philippines remain the only East Asian society consistently and profoundly influenced by Occidental culture. But few Spaniards settled in the islands; as late as 1898 only 10 percent of the native population of perhaps 10 million knew Spanish. The majority spoke many local languages and dialects, a reflection of the ethnic and tribal divisions, often of a violent nature, that characterized Philippine society and would play an important role in the American counterinsurgency effort. Incomparably the most important division was that between the Christian majority and the Muslims on Mindanao and the Sulu archipelago. Called Moros ("Moors") after the Saracens who had invaded Spain from North Africa centuries earlier, their society was based on Islam, piracy, and slavery: as late as 1936 women were openly bought and sold in their territory. The Moros violently resisted the Spanish, the Christian Filipinos, and the Americans, as they would resist the Japanese occupation and, finally, the Philippine Republic. At the time of the Spanish-American War, Spain's authority over the Moro regions was largely nominal. Another serious faultline in Philippine society was between the Tagalog, dominant on Luzon, and other ethnic and tribal groups there and elsewhere in the archipelago. These tensions would play an important role in the fighting after 1898.

Spain promoted neither economic development nor self-government. Filipinos of education and social prominence, the "ilustrados," resented discrimination against them in appointments to government and Church offices. Late in the 19th century they founded the Katipunan, a secret society aiming at independence.[2] Emilio Aguinaldo, born in 1869, became head of the Katipunan on Luzon and eventually in the whole archipelago.

The Americans Arrive

The Katipunan launched a major rebellion in the summer of 1896. It lasted about a year, until Aguinaldo and other leaders went into exile in

Hong Kong in return for a substantial cash payment from the Spanish authorities. Rebellion broke out again in March 1898. Two weeks after that the US and Spain were at war. The origins of the war had little to do with the Philippines, but its effects there would be lasting and profound.

The US Asiatic Squadron, under Commodore George Dewey on his flagship *Olympia*, sailed from Nagasaki to Manila Bay, where, on May 1, it destroyed the entire Spanish fleet, while losing one man (from heatstroke).[3] Having been brought back to Luzon by Dewey, Aguinaldo proclaimed himself dictator of a Provisional Philippine Republic. By the end of June, he controlled most of Luzon outside the capital city. Nevertheless, many Spanish garrisons held out, and Manila did not fall to the Americans until August 13. Aguinaldo believed that Washington would recognize his government, and American troops stood by while Aguinaldo's followers subdued numerous small Spanish posts, but they would not allow Aguinaldo to enter Manila in strength.

The Position of President McKinley

The war with Spain had been about Cuba, and Dewey's unexpected victory in Manila found the McKinley administration with no policy for the Philippines. President McKinley came to believe that returning the islands to Spain would be dishonorable, but most officials in Washington thought the Filipinos were not ready for independence. The islands would dissolve into ethnic civil wars, inviting other powers present in the Western Pacific (especially Germany and/or Japan) to occupy them. Thus McKinley adopted the policy of temporary US possession of the whole archipelago, with promises of future independence that he hoped would be satisfactory to most of the islands' inhabitants.[4] Accordingly, the US bought the archipelago from Spain for $20 million.

In February 1899, about 15,000 US troops held Manila under command of General Elwell S. Otis. Many of them were volunteers. Surrounding the capital were 30,000 armed Filipinos, loyal in varying degrees to Aguinaldo. Actual fighting began on February 4. President McKinley sent a distinguished civilian commission to the islands promising good administration, protection of rights and customs, and steps toward democratic self-government and eventual independence. Many Filipinos, even in Aguinaldo's party, wished to accept these terms, and some eventually joined US-sponsored police units or acted as scouts and interpreters for the US Army.

The Philippines

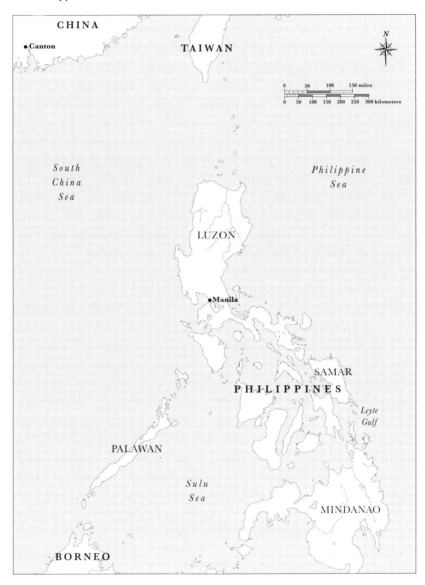

While Aguinaldo commanded a substantial armed force and a far-flung political organization (the Katipunan), it would be highly anachronistic to view him as the head of a full-fledged Filipino nationalism. Large elements of the social elite remained aloof from his movement. More importantly, the deeply embedded ethnic divisions and hostilities that characterized

Philippine life affected the Katipunan as well, with bitter rivalries sometimes bursting into fatal confrontations. Aguinaldo and most of the other major leaders were Tagalog, only one of many large ethnic groups. The Americans quickly learned to take advantage of these rivalries by employing non-Tagalog Filipinos in their paramilitary force. These eventually numbered 15,000, a figure that does not include thousands of other Filipinos and local Chinese who formed part of the US intelligence network in the main islands. Thus terms such as the "Philippine-American War" are quite misleading. In addition, not a single foreign power recognized Aguinaldo's authority.

Guerrilla War

In November 1899, following the acknowledged defeat of his regular forces by American troops, Aguinaldo proclaimed guerrilla war as the dominant strategy. From the beginning, guerrillas were active on Luzon, often under the very eyes of American forces. The scope and tempo of conflict varied greatly from one region or island to another; in half the provinces no fighting ever occurred. Because of the existing level of communications technology – no radios, no helicopters – and the great number of islands, the American counterinsurgency of necessity developed in a decentralized manner: local US commanders, down to the level of captain, were free to adjust their tactics to the local situation. Units remained in the same area for extended periods, a condition that Frederick Funston, who would eventually capture Aguinaldo, described as essential for intelligence gathering. The course of the fighting showed that the long rainy seasons were as hard on the guerrillas as on the US troops; besides, the Americans built all-weather roads to increase their mobility. Very notably, the Americans would achieve their final complete victory without the technology so essential to later counterinsurgency campaigns.

Of course, good intelligence became a key to victory. Close observation, bribery, and offers of amnesty eventually produced much information. Prisoners obtained their freedom if they would identify former comrades or lead US troops to their hideouts. And the growing numbers of indigenous recruits from ethnic groups hostile to the Tagalog proved increasingly valuable.

Guns were relatively scarce among the guerrillas, partly because no supplies for them were coming in from the outside. The Americans concentrated on finding, capturing, or buying rifles. A Philippine civilian

41

could obtain cash, or even the release of a prisoner, for turning in a rifle, no questions asked. General Arthur MacArthur, successor to General Otis (and father of Douglas), called this prisoners-for-rifles trade one of his "most important policies."[5]

Disrupting the enemy's food supply is of course a venerable stratagem of warfare, and American forces soon adopted this practice in the Philippines. Frequent patrolling uncovered guerrilla food-growing areas and hidden stores. The US Navy impeded the insurgents' inter-island communications, thereby aggravating their food shortage. Life for many of the guerrillas was difficult enough in the best of times; now their attention had to shift to obtaining enough food to stave off disease or death.

Food denial programs inevitably suggest population concentration. Such a measure came late in the conflict, in areas where the guerrillas seemed determined to fight on even after their cause had been clearly lost despite American offers of honorable surrender. Concentration generally worked in this way: the military authorities instructed the civilian population in a given region to move with their family members, animals, and foodstuffs into a designated town by a specific date. After that time, any goods or animals found outside the town would be subject to confiscation, and men would be liable to arrest as guerrillas. Food shipments between towns were strictly controlled. (British forces would employ similar methods 50 years later during their textbook-quality counterinsurgency campaign in Malaya.[6])

Among the regrouped populations, the Americans carried out vaccination on a large scale, and tried to provide adequate employment and living conditions. Nevertheless, hardships existed in many places, with sanitation a severe problem. Perhaps 11,000 Filipinos died as a result of poor hygiene levels in the concentration areas. (At almost the same time, similar problems were arising during British efforts to concentrate the Boer population in the South African War.)

Events correctly or incorrectly labeled war crimes occur in every war. The Philippine conflict was no exception. American troops in the islands were mostly under 25 years old. Many, perhaps most, had never been outside their home states before. They were operating in a maddeningly unhealthy climate, among local populations to whom they were racially and often religiously alien, and whose languages they could not understand, against an enemy whom they found almost impossible to distinguish from ordinary civilians.

During the first year of the war, the American watchword was eventual reconciliation. Hence, once US soldiers had disarmed prisoners, they released them; they did not punish villagers, except for overt acts; and they accepted compulsion or intimidation as excuses for having aided the insurgents. Essentially, they offered inducements for supporting the US side, but no real penalties for opposing it. As the war went on, many Americans began to realize that most Filipinos feared them less than they feared the rebels – with reason. Hence arose the new policy of benevolence for those who submitted, but severity for those who persisted in useless resistance.[7]

During General Otis's command, some serious American misbehavior had occurred, including the looting of several churches. Otis took pains to see that such acts were punished. Brigadier General Bell went so far as to forbid his soldiers to enter civilian homes. Beginning in 1900, some US units burned *barrios* (neighborhoods) in or near which an ambush or act of terror had occurred. Soldiers stationed in towns for extended periods had much less trouble with civilians and prisoners than did those on field duty. No doubt American abuses increased in more remote areas as time wore on. And of course, rebel propaganda depicting American soldiers as soaked in innocent blood reached the US.[8]

The insurgents also committed incontestable war crimes, more frequent and more ferocious than those of their American opponents. Some of these actions reflected ethnic hostilities, others probably involved the settling of scores from before the war. The rebels engaged in widespread indiscriminate pillaging, and sought to dissuade cooperation with the Americans by putting entire villages to the torch. Toward the end of 1900, when the tide had unmistakably turned against the guerrillas, they greatly increased assassinations of officials in local governments established by the Americans, murdered individual members of the pro-cooperation Federal Party, and threatened to execute all male inhabitants of any village that displayed friendliness to the Americans. Naturally, actions of this sort provoked a hostile reaction to the guerrillas.

Whatever the final scoresheet of violations, either of the laws of war or of simple humanity, it was clear that good relations between Filipinos and Americans were flourishing in many areas, even while the conflict was at its height. Emilio Aguinaldo himself later wrote admiringly of his former American foes, and expressed the belief that US rule over the Philippines saved them from partition among several less benevolent foreign powers.[9]

The Policy of Attraction

General Otis understood that his task was not only to defeat the rebels, but also to prepare the ground for reconciliation and eventual independence. He and the other Americans occupying the Philippines came from a US going through the Progressive Era, with its belief in the possibility and duty of good government to uplift the general society. The Manila that they found, with its 400,000 inhabitants, was a mess: the port was not operating, the schools were shut, uncollected rubbish and garbage clogged the streets, and the Aguinaldo forces had cut off the city's water supply. Manila verged on epidemic and anarchy. In response, the Americans cleaned the streets. They appointed municipal health officers to give free medical care to the many indigent people, and vaccination reduced smallpox from a scourge to a problem. They provided the same medical attention to prisoners as to their own soldiers. They released numerous persons who had languished in jail for years without charges. They built or rebuilt schools and appointed soldiers as instructors, one of their most popular endeavors. This general "policy of attraction" deeply disconcerted the insurgent leaders.

The War at Home

Aguinaldo intelligently decided on a strategy of protracted war: he believed that as the Philippine climate decimated American forces in an obscure conflict far from home, opinion in the US would inevitably turn against the war (the Hanoi Politburo would develop a variant of this strategy 60 years later). American antiwar activists engaged in correspondence with guerrilla leaders, and sent pamphlets to US troops in the islands, urging them to abandon "this brutal war."[10] But the insurgents invested their greatest hopes in the presidential candidacy of William Jennings Bryan, immortalized in later years by the "Scopes Monkey Trial." Bryan made "US imperialism" the centerpiece of his 1900 campaign against President McKinley. Two years earlier, Bryan had gone to Washington and ordered Democratic senators to vote for McKinley's annexation treaty, so that he could make the war an issue. In the event, Bryan suffered a decisive electoral repudiation (his second but not his last). Many Filipinos who had wished to make peace, but feared a US abandonment if Bryan won, were heartened. Money and food for guerrillas declined noticeably, but the mass surrenders that Americans had hoped for did not materialize.

President McKinley's victory was the signal for MacArthur to bring the conflict to a conclusion. The objective was to isolate the guerrillas more completely from the civilian population. In December 1900, MacArthur's 70,000 troops garrisoned more towns, and concentrated an increased share of the civilian population into those towns. To persuade guerrillas to give up the fight rather than be captured, the US Army stopped its practice of releasing prisoners, instead sending large numbers of them to camps on Guam. Then, on March 23, the Americans achieved a great coup: improved intelligence led to the capture of Aguinaldo himself.[11] In the weeks following this signal event, about 13,000 insurgents surrendered; Aguinaldo swore an oath of allegiance to the US and urged his remaining followers to lay down their arms. From May 1900 to June 1901, US forces had sustained only 245 fatal casualties. By mid-1901, thousands of Filipinos (almost all non-Tagalog) were serving with US forces, and on July 4, 1901 William Howard Taft, one day to be US President, took the oath as civil governor of the Philippines.

All this good news contrasted sharply with events on the island of Samar. In September 1901, near the town of Balangiga, an insurgent force was able, through treachery, to massacre a company of the US Ninth Infantry. Such an act, coming at a time when it was obvious to all that the guerrillas had no hope whatsoever of victory, infuriated the American troops on the island, who launched a severe punitive campaign totally at variance with the broader US policy of attraction. US local commanders often failed to distinguish friend from foe, burning houses and executing prisoners. Such acts resulted in courts martial, and condemnation by President Theodore Roosevelt. Unfortunately, some authors have turned the Samar episode into a microcosm of the whole conflict, thereby perpetuating "one of the great historical fallacies of the war."[12]

Nevertheless, another amnesty offer went forth on July 4, 1902, and by the end of that year US force levels decreased from an average of 24,000 to about 15,000 (compared to Aguinaldo's 80,000–100,000 armed followers not long before).[13]

Fighting the Moros

Distinct and remote from Aguinaldo's insurgency was the conflict between the Americans and the Moros on Mindanao and some adjacent areas. Many Moros assisted US forces against Aguinaldo's followers. But General Leonard Wood, appointed governor of the Moro Province in

1903, refused to countenance the slavery that was intrinsic to Moro culture; hence, fighting broke out that lasted at least a decade. The Moros were brave; the US Army had to replace the .38 caliber pistol with the .45 because the former would often prove inadequate against a charging Moro sworn to give his life in exchange for that of a Christian (which all Americans were in Moro eyes). But the Moro cause was hopeless: they had no outside friends. Christian Filipinos hated and feared them, and their usual tactic when confronted with US regulars was to withdraw into fortified buildings, where they were vulnerable to artillery. Captain John "Black Jack" Pershing, one day to command US forces in war-torn France, played a key role in the eventual pacification of the Moros by convincing them that, unlike the Spanish, the Americans would not try to impose Christianity upon them.[14]

A Clear Counterinsurgent Victory

In their contest with Aguinaldo's guerrillas, US military forces suffered 4,200 fatal casualties, a greater number than during the war with Spain. Aguinaldo was operating on his home territory, in terrain almost ideal for guerrillas, under the banner of national independence. In contrast, the Americans were foreign in every way: lacking colonial experience; untrained in counterinsurgency methods; without adequate protection against numerous local maladies; deploying insufficient numbers in a vast archipelago with whose geography they were unfamiliar; and generally reliant on communications in no way superior to those of the Napoleonic era. Nevertheless, the Americans won a complete victory over the insurgents and laid the foundations for the enduring Philippine–American friendship.

How was this possible? In the first place, Aguinaldo suffered from serious weaknesses. He received no outside assistance, while ethnic antagonisms limited his actual and potential support. The Philippine upper class generally stayed aloof from his movement, and, as members of that upper class themselves, Aguinaldo and his commanders made no move toward trying to incite a class war among the country's numerous poor peasants against the wealthy and the Americans.

Second, the Americans employed sensible counterinsurgent methods. Their campaign was generally one of small units, armed with rifles and aided by indigenous elements. It concentrated on isolating the guerrillas from food and recruits, and on protecting the civilian population from guerrilla terrorism. Equally importantly, the Americans unlimbered their policy of attraction, making undeniable improvements in the lives of many Filipinos, and repeatedly offering written, solemn promises of eventual complete independence. Thus the conflict between Aguinaldo and the Americans revolved around the question of *when*, rather than *if*, the Philippines should become independent, hardly an issue to sustain a protracted and widespread insurgency in a deeply divided society. This combination of sound military tactics and an intelligent political program proved decisive. After, and even during, the conflict, reconciled insurgent leaders received appointments to office under the US civil administration. Indeed, the man elected in 1935 as the first President of the Philippine Commonwealth was the ex-insurgent Major Manuel Quezon; the opponent he roundly defeated was Emilio Aguinaldo.

The Huk Rebellion 1946–54

By their acquisition of the Philippines, the Americans placed themselves squarely between the empire of Japan and the rich and weakly defended colonial territories of Southeast Asia which it coveted. Thus a blazing red line ran from Manila to Pearl Harbor. The Japanese occupation of the Philippines (1942–44) was one of the most destructive and brutal episodes of World War Two. Further, it established the foundations for a major Communist-led attempt to take over the country by force. Partly as a result of US assistance, that attempt failed, and the Philippine Republic became the first Asian country to defeat a Communist insurgency.

After they concluded their conflict with Aguinaldo, the Americans began to make good on their promises to prepare the Philippines for independence. Major steps along that road included the creation in 1907 of the first popularly elected legislature in Southeast Asia, and admission to the vote of all literate males in 1916. At the time of the 1941 Japanese invasion, Filipinos occupied most of the civil service positions, including some at the highest level.

The Philippines achieved their independence on the first Fourth of July following the end of the Pacific War. At that time, the population of the Republic was approximately 20 million. American and Filipino troops had suffered severely together during the battle of Corregidor and the Bataan Death March. Under the occupation, the civilian population endured great hardship as well, from Japanese atrocities and economic disruption. The islands had been the scene of the largest naval engagement in history, at

Leyte Gulf in 1944. The Japanese occupation ended at the price of widespread death, atrocity, and destruction; 70 percent of Manila, liberated in February 1945, lay in ruins. Thus the newly independent Republic was devastated physically and morally.[15] A noted Philippine statesman wrote that the Japanese had been particularly cruel to the Filipinos because, while Japan viewed the Pacific War as a crusade to expel the arrogant whites from East Asia, the Philippine population had remained overwhelmingly loyal to the US.[16] (The Japanese commander in the Philippines, Lieutenant General Yamashita, was hanged as a war criminal.[17])

The Huks

During the Japanese occupation several guerrilla organizations arose, and approximately 260,000 persons served in one or another of these groups. Local Communists helped to found the People's Army Against Japan, whose Tagalog acronym – Hukbalahap – yielded the nickname Huks. By 1943, 10,000 Huks were fighting both the Japanese and also other guerrilla movements organized by American military personnel, the latter preparing to gain control after the war's end. At the time of the liberation, the Huks were well supplied with weapons taken or purchased from the Japanese or shipped in to them from the US. Their stronghold was the island of Luzon, 40,000 square miles in area, about the size of Cuba, or four times the size of Sicily. The central districts of that island had been the scene of agrarian unrest for generations, the result of overpopulation, absentee landlordism, and a deplorable record of peasant exploitation by Philippine government officials. General Douglas MacArthur famously observed that "If I worked in those sugar fields, I'd probably be a Huk myself."

Many Luzon landlords had collaborated with the Japanese occupation. Luis Taruc, the most well-known of the Huk leaders, wrote that "when we dealt with [the landlords] harshly, it was because they were betraying our country to the Japanese and oppressing the common people. This knowledge of the period is essential to an understanding of Huk activities."[18] The Huks bitterly opposed leniency toward these collaborators, but it was US policy to draw a curtain over the events of those terrible occupation days, except in the most flagrant cases. Thus Manuel Roxas, who served in the Cabinet of the collaborationist Jose Laurel's government, was saved from prosecution by MacArthur, and was elected first President of the Philippine Republic by the Liberal Party.

Open conflict between the Roxas administration and the reorganized Huks broke out in late 1946.

The Huks were not a self-consciously Maoist movement, because Mao Tse-tung had not yet achieved victory. The Huk leadership, like that of the Philippine Communist Party, was overwhelmingly urban, and included several former university professors. Their chief military commander was Luis Taruc, an ex-medical student and politician. These leaders were for the most part sympathetic to the peasantry, but did not really understand them. The Communists wanted Stalinist-style forced industrialization and the uprooting of the traditional family structure; most peasants wanted not revolution but rather a return to the prewar system of stable tenant farming, cushioned by patron–client relations.

The primary Huk activities were robbing banks, payroll offices, and trains. The Republic's main defense against the Huks was the paramilitary Philippine Constabulary, with 25,000 members on paper. This force was not well trained or well equipped, and suffered from political interference with promotions and assignments. Their principal tactics consisted of wide sweeps and encirclements, easily evaded by the Huks. Abuse of civilians by the Constabulary became common and systematic. Indeed, Taruc later cited this provocative behavior as the main fuel that kept the rebellion going.

The death of President Manuel Roxas in 1948 brought to power Vice President Elpidio Quirino. His administration soon proved to be both incompetent and corrupt. Consequently, when he ran for re-election in 1949, the Huks cynically supported him. But Quirino did not need their help. He held onto the presidency by buying and stealing votes and intimidating the electorate.

These "dirty elections of 1949" seemed to prove once and for all that the Huks were right: there was no road to reform except revolution. By 1950, when the Korean War broke out, the Huks had close to 24,000 fighters. They began staging some spectacular operations on the very outskirts of Manila. But in this dark hour the tide was about to turn.

In violation of approved Leninist strategy, the Huks had failed to bring other discontented groups into a broad political front. On the contrary, as the conflict went on, Huk leaders became more open about their Communist aims, and after Mao's triumph in 1949, they changed the name of their movement to the People's Liberation Army.

Their actions also became more self-destructive. Huk guerrilla commanders wore better clothes and smoked better cigarettes than the peasants among whom they operated. The movement's leaders often entrusted the task of opening up a new military front to criminals, or those who soon behaved like criminals. The Huks executed men who fell asleep on duty or who asked for home leave (because they viewed such requests as a prelude to desertion), and sometimes demanded that a member kill one or more of his noncombatant relatives as proof of loyalty. None of this endeared the Huks to the peasant population, while senseless acts such as the murder of the widow and daughter of the popular ex-President Manuel Quezon in August 1949 appalled almost the entire nation. Luis Taruc later accused the Communist leaders of needlessly prolonging the rebellion after 1950, when it had clearly been defeated.

But above all these factors, the key to the Huk defeat was the appointment by President Quirino, in September 1950, of Ramon Magsaysay as Secretary of Defense.

Magsaysay Defeats the Huks

Ramon Magsaysay was born in 1907. The son of a high-school carpentry teacher, he was of pure Malay stock, in contrast to most of the Philippine ruling elites. During the Japanese occupation, he had led a guerrilla unit organized by US forces. Thus he understood at first hand the strengths and weaknesses of the Huk insurgency. While Secretary of Defense, he had as his close friend and adviser Colonel Edward Lansdale, USAF, who would later fill a similar role for South Vietnamese President Ngo Dinh Diem.[19]

Magsaysay acted vigorously and imaginatively to reduce military abuse of civilians. Drawing on his experiences with American soldiers during World War Two, Magsaysay provided Philippine Army units with candy to distribute to village children. The army provided medical help to numerous peasants. In a brilliant move, Magsaysay had army lawyers litigate on behalf of peasants against oppressive landlords, and they won several notable cases. And for a nominal fee, any citizen could send a telegram to the Secretary of Defense.

Magsaysay also changed the army's approach to counterinsurgency, which had previously consisted mainly of fruitless sweep operations. In their place, he organized so-called Battalion Combat Teams, whose purpose was to invade hitherto undisturbed Huk areas, disrupting their food supply and depriving them of rest.[20] Huk bands had to retreat into the swamps, where many became seriously ill.[21] He organized small, specially trained hunter groups to target guerrilla leaders. And to ensure that local commanders were actually carrying out his orders, Magsaysay flew about in a small plane, descending on military units or installations without notice to bestow praise or punishment.

A former guerrilla himself, Magsaysay was of course keenly aware of the supreme value of intelligence – the numbers, weapons, morale and intentions of the enemy – in counterinsurgency. Better relations between civilians and the security forces had increased the amount of information available to the latter. More humane treatment of prisoners was another rich source of intelligence. In a notable move, Magsaysay offered sizeable monetary rewards for information leading to the arrest of particular guerrilla leaders, not because they were insurgents per se, but because they stood accused of specific criminal acts in specific places against specific persons. Aside from producing some valuable captures, the effort to criminalize the guerrilla leadership undermined the Huks' Robin Hood image. A spectacular consequence of these converging intelligence flows was the arrest in Manila of most of the members of the Politburo of the Philippine Communist Party, along with literally truckloads of important documents.

Magsaysay advocated amnesty, but he realized that many Huks had joined the movement in the early days of the Japanese occupation or shortly thereafter, when they were very young. Since they had literally grown up as guerrillas, amnesty per se would mean little to such persons; they had no other life to return to. Thus, to guerrillas who would accept amnesty, Magsaysay additionally offered resettlement in areas far from the fighting, plus a grant of 20 acres, army help to build a house, and a small loan. This program transformed enemies of the state into productive citizens.

Most of all, Magsaysay was determined that the approaching mid term Congressional elections of 1951 would be clean. He used the army to discourage intimidation and eliminate ballot-box stuffing. Consequently the opposition Nacionalista Party won a landslide victory. Years later, Ernesto Guevara would write that it is impossible to make a successful insurgency against a government that is democratic, or even pretends to be such. This certainly proved to be the case in the Philippines: "to all intents and purposes the 1951 elections sounded the death knell of the Hukbalahap movement."[22]

Magsaysay to the Presidency

In 1953 President Quirino was seeking re-election. Magsaysay declared his candidacy against him, and, running as the Nacionalista candidate, carried a presidential campaign into remote villages and rural areas for the first time in Philippine history. Luis Taruc predictably urged his followers to support Quirino once again. To run for president, Magsaysay had to give up his office as Secretary of Defense, presenting Quirino with the opportunity to corrupt the elections as in 1949. But this time the Philippine press was much more vigilant. US Army officers urged their friends in the Philippine Army to keep the elections clean. The US State Department made sure that numerous American and other foreign journalists covered the election at first hand; US government funds were secretly funneled to the Magsaysay campaign. Aware of Washington's opposition to his administration, Quirino tried to stir up anti-American sentiment, but after the Japanese occupation, this was very weak tea. (Similarly, Huk slogans denouncing American imperialism had never made a noticeable impact.) Finally, the Philippine bishops reminded their numerous followers of their duty to go to the polls and prevent the triumph of dishonest men. In the event, Magsaysay thrashed Quirino with 2.4 million votes to 1.15 million (the 1949 results purportedly showed Quirino with 1.6 million, against 1.5 million for several opponents).[23] Now Magsaysay would be in full control of the army and of anti-insurgent policy. In May 1954, Luis Taruc surrendered (eventually to receive a 12-year prison sentence); his abandonment of the struggle is conventionally accepted as the end of the Huk insurgency. Between 1946 and 1954, 12,000 Huks died, 4,000 were captured, and 16,000 surrendered.[24] Regrettably, while campaigning for re-election in March 1957, President Magsaysay died in a plane crash not far from where Magellan the Circumnavigator had lost his life.

The US, of course, had an emotional as well as a political stake in the success of Philippine democracy. President Truman sent US officers to help train the Philippine Army. As the Huk challenge mounted, President Quirino repeatedly requested US combat troops, but without effect. Washington was preoccupied with civil wars in China and Greece, launching the Marshall Plan and erecting NATO (the North Atlantic Treaty Organization). Then, in June 1950, the North Korean Army roared into South Korea. In the same year, the US began a massive financial underwriting of French efforts to hold on to Vietnam. Many in Washington, including General George Marshall, were convinced that the roots of the Philippine insurgency were poor leadership and the maldistribution of land. Secretary of State Dean Acheson deeply disliked President Quirino. Most importantly, the Department of Defense adamantly opposed sending ground combat troops to the Philippines. According to the Joint Chiefs of Staff, the essential problem in the country was not military but political. Besides, by the end of 1951 the defeat of the Huks was clearly looming. Hence the question of dispatching US combat troops was closed. (Nevertheless, between 1951 and 1954 the US provided the Philippines with $95 million in non-military assistance.)

Why the Huks Lost

The most obvious weakness of the Huks was their inability to receive outside assistance. Certainly, such aid is no guarantee of insurgent success: witness the Greek Communists, the Viet Cong, and the IRA. But help for the insurgent side from foreign sources played an important and sometimes determining role in conflicts such as the American War of Independence, the Spanish revolt against Napoleon, the anti-Nazi insurgency in Yugoslavia, and the Afghan struggle against the Soviets. Men and munitions from Communist China turned the tide in favor of the Viet Minh against the French, and might have done the same for the Huks but for the intractable impediments of Philippine geography and American sea power.[25] For the same reasons, indirect (or unintentional) assistance, such as the Japanese gave to Mao Tse-tung by mauling Chiang Kai-shek's Kuomintang armies, and to Ho Chi Minh by humiliating the French, was unavailable. Thus, like Aguinaldo before them (as well as the Vendeans of revolutionary France, the Boers in South Africa, the Cristeros in Mexico, the Home Army in Poland, the Communists in Malaya, the Resistance Army in Tibet, and Sendero Luminoso in Peru, all of whom came to an unhappy end), the Huks were on their own.[26]

That factor in itself might have proved decisive in the long run, although the Huks were doing well enough without such aid up until 1951. But, beginning that year, they encountered the effective policies of Ramon Magsaysay. In contrast to the failed methods of the Japanese Army and Quirino's Constabulary, he greatly improved the military's treatment of civilians, put into practice a workable amnesty program – both of which steps led to invaluable intelligence – and increased military pressure on guerrilla areas. Above all, by cleaning up the electoral process, Magsaysay restored a peaceful alternative to armed revolution. Little collateral damage occurred during the counterinsurgency campaign, in vivid and instructive contrast to American efforts in Korea and Vietnam. Magsaysay's program provides a striking example of the essential links between effective military tactics and intelligent political strategy.

Some Conclusions

In contrast to the Napoleonic forces in Spain or the Soviets in Afghanistan, the foreignness of American soldiers in the post-1898 conflict was not a decisively negative factor, since they were replacing the Spanish, compared to whom, as almost everyone readily admitted, they were a vast improvement. Besides, amid the ethnic tensions of the islands, Aguinaldo's upper-class and Tagalog forces were never able to establish a valid claim to embody a Philippine national movement; to many Filipinos, the Tagalog were in no way preferable to the Americans.

Almost half a century later, the Huks were doing well against an ineffective and corrupt indigenous regime until Magsaysay's reforms succeeded both in narrowing the gap between security forces and the civilian population, and in widening that between Communist insurgent leaders and their peasant followers.

The most obvious, and perhaps the most decisive, characteristics shared by both wars were the isolation of the insurgents from outside assistance and the impossibility of establishing a cross-border sanctuary. Such conditions made a solution to Aguinaldo's severe shortage of weapons impossible. The isolation of the Huks resembled that of the Communist insurgents in Malaya. Both Philippine conflicts suggest that, where outside assistance to the insurgents can be prevented or severely limited, sound political reforms and sensible military tactics constitute an unbeatable counterinsurgent formula.

Finally, the Huk conflict indicates that, despite the cloud of myth that has surrounded the techniques of Communist, and especially Maoist, guerrilla insurgency for so long, these could prove quite ineffective when the Communists were not able to present themselves as the spearhead of a burgeoning or outraged nationalism, or to receive abundant cross-border assistance.[27]

3

THE FIRST OF THE BANANA WARS

US Marines in Nicaragua 1909–12

Major Bruce Gudmundsson (ret)

In the century leading up to 1909, United States Marines took part in 50 or so minor operations on the shores of Central America and the islands of the Caribbean Sea. These small expeditions, which were invariably carried out by landing parties drawn from the crews of warships, tended to be short-term affairs. In all but a handful of cases, the Marines and Bluejackets who made up these landing parties spent less than a week ashore.[1] Between 1909 and 1912, however, the pattern of American involvement changed. For most of the quarter-century that followed, the raids, rescues, and local displays of force that had so long been the bread and butter of the American naval presence in the Caribbean gave way to operations of a different sort. Described as "small wars" by the Marines who carried them out and "banana wars" by subsequent generations, these enterprises involved the deployment of substantial expeditionary forces, occupations that lasted for years, and efforts at nation-building that, for good or for ill, had a profound effect on the future development of the peoples concerned.[2]

The naval forces of the United States began to operate in the Caribbean during the American War of Independence (1775–83). Nevertheless, they did not establish a permanent presence in the region until the spring of 1823, when President James Monroe ordered the creation of the West India Squadron. The initial purpose of this "Mosquito Fleet" (as it was sometimes known) was to suppress an epidemic of piracy in the Florida Straits and the Gulf of Mexico. Once this was accomplished, the West India Squadron took on the mission that would define the role of American naval forces in the region for nearly a hundred years: protecting American citizens, whether afloat or ashore, from the side effects of the political violence endemic to the region. In fulfilling this mission, these forces also provided a concrete reminder of the policy that would eventually become known as the "Monroe Doctrine."[3]

At first, the focus of American interest in the Caribbean lay in places that were adjacent to American territory and, in particular, the sea-lanes that ran from the mouth of the Mississippi to the Straits of Florida. After the US acquired California in 1848, however, Americans began to pay much more attention to Central America. The most obvious product of that increased attention was the Panama Railway. Funded entirely by American investors and completed in just five years (1850–55), this 49-mile-long railroad reduced the time it took to travel from the Caribbean to the Pacific Ocean from four days to four hours, eliminated most of the hardships and (frequently fatal) dangers associated with that trip, and added greatly to American interest in the possibility of a canal that would allow seagoing ships to pass directly from the Pacific to the Caribbean.[4] This, in turn, encouraged Americans of a maritime frame of mind to think about the places where a ship that had entered the Caribbean by means of such a canal would pass into the open Atlantic, and thus the islands of Hispaniola and Puerto Rico. It also excited interest in the western coast of Central America.

The American Civil War (1861–65), which put a temporary halt to all schemes for transoceanic canals and overseas naval bases, had the paradoxical effect of elevating the Monroe Doctrine from an informal understanding between two powers into an unquestioned article of faith for American statesmen. While the US was distracted, Spain regained possession of the Spanish-speaking parts of Hispaniola, thereby converting the Dominican Republic into the colony of Santo Domingo, and France sent an army to Mexico, where it fought on behalf of an imported monarchy against the forces of an indigenous republic. These incidents, and the speed with which the Spanish and French governments restored the status quo at the end of the Civil War, convinced contemporary American statesmen that a powerful US was the only significant obstacle to the recolonization of Latin America. The Civil War, which saw the extensive use of islands throughout the Caribbean as bases for Confederate blockade runners and commerce raiders, also convinced many American naval officers that the interests of the US in the region extended well beyond the coastal waters of the Gulf of Mexico and the Florida Straits. It is thus not surprising that the following decade saw the earnest exploration of such possibilities as the establishment of American naval bases on Hispaniola, the American purchase of the Danish West Indies, and the granting of American statehood to the Dominican Republic, as well as expeditions to survey possible routes for a transoceanic canal.[5]

By 1875, none of the American projects to obtain naval bases, acquire territory, or begin the construction of transoceanic canals in the Caribbean had achieved the slightest degree of success. While some of these failures were the result of poor management, technical difficulties, or political obstacles of the local variety, the chief reason was the disappearance of the factors that had previously motivated American interest in the region. Transcontinental railroads (the first of which was completed in 1869) solved the transportation problems of many Americans who would otherwise have clamored for a transoceanic canal. The relative weakness of France, Russia, and Spain (the powers that had inspired the original Monroe Doctrine), and the continuation of the traditionally benign attitude of Great Britain, reduced fears of an expansion of European influence in the Western Hemisphere. This development coincided with a considerable reduction in the activity of US naval forces in Central America and the Caribbean. Between 1866 and 1890, only three American landing parties went ashore in the region. Two of these (in 1873 and 1888) were dispatched to protect the American residents of the Caribbean terminus of the Panama Railroad (what is now the city of Colón) from becoming the unintended victims of local civil wars. The third landing party, which went ashore in the Haitian capital of Port-au-Prince in 1888, served as escort to Rear Admiral Stephen B. Luce, who was on a mission to secure the release of an American ship that had been seized on the high seas by participants in one of Haiti's many intramural conflicts. While Luce had been authorized to use force to recover the ship, he was able to fulfill his mission without firing a shot.[6]

The next revival of intense American interest in Central America and the Caribbean, which began in the 1890s, took place within the context of "navalism." Codified in the writings of Captain Alfred Thayer Mahan of the US Navy, navalism held that the secret to success in naval warfare, and thus the contest for predominance among seafaring nations, was a large fleet of powerful warships that, in the event of war, could be rapidly concentrated in order to fight decisive battles. While the most obvious effect of navalism was to encourage states to expand and modernize their navies, the movement also created a number of secondary effects, which varied from one country to the next. In Germany and Japan, navalism provided the justification for ambitious programs to transform modest navies of purely local significance into world-class fleets, as well as the acquisition of overseas colonies of doubtful economic value. In Great Britain, it led to a reduction in those overseas commitments that inhibited the ability of the Royal Navy to concentrate its forces. This, in turn, led to an explicit recognition on the part of Great Britain that the US was the dominant power in Central America and the Caribbean.

In the US, navalism resulted in a renewed desire for the acquisition of permanent naval bases in the Caribbean and the Pacific, as well as the development of a capability to establish temporary naval bases in the course of a naval campaign. It also convinced many Americans that the US, which maintained fleets in both the Atlantic and the Pacific, needed a canal that, in case of war, would be open to US warships and closed to those of hostile nations. The most obvious products of the renewal, intensification, and "navalization" of American interest in a transoceanic canal were the American assumption (and subsequent completion) of the ill-fated French project to build a canal across the Isthmus of Panama; sponsorship of the revolution that separated Panama from Colombia; and the Anglo-American agreements that replaced the ideal of a neutral, essentially demilitarized transoceanic waterway with one that was, quite literally, under the guns of American fortresses.[7]

American victory in the Spanish-American War of 1898, which provided the US Navy with two naval bases in the Caribbean (Guantánamo Bay in Cuba and Culebra in Puerto Rico), satisfied the essential elements of the longstanding American desire for such facilities.[8] Similarly, the annexations of Hawaii, Puerto Rico, the Philippines, and Guam effectively put an end to American enthusiasm for the acquisition of additional territories. At the same time, the rise of Germany and Japan as global naval powers led to considerable concern about the possibility that Germany might obtain naval bases in the Caribbean, that Japan would acquire naval bases off the Pacific coast of Central America, and that either power would gain control of a trans-isthmian canal or find some other means of interfering with the rapid transit of American warships from one ocean to the other. In the years leading up to World War One, such fears were fueled by the Japanese victory in the Russo-Japanese War (1904–05), a Japanese attempt to acquire a naval base in Baja California, the rapid expansion of the German Navy, frequent expressions of disdain for the Monroe Doctrine on the part of prominent Germans, and German endeavors to acquire naval bases on Hispaniola and in the Danish Virgin Islands.[9]

In the aftermath of the Spanish-American War, emerging American concerns about grand strategy, naval operations, and the security of the soon-to-be-completed Panama Canal coincided with a development that, for want of a better name, might well be called the "crisis of kleptocracy." Over the course of the 19th century, the combination of extractive economics and strongman politics created a number of traditions in which the lion's share of entrepreneurial energy in the independent republics of Central America and the Caribbean was channeled into attempts to capture the income stream produced by customs duties. In some cases, these exercises in armed entrepreneurship resulted in struggles between regional warlords (who desired control over discrete slices of the governmental revenues) and ambitious centralizers (who coveted the entire pie). In others, it resulted in endemic struggles that pitted regional warlords against each other, or short-lived changes of national government that, if only for a while, left all the customs revenues of a given republic in the hands of a single person or party.

Though the crisis of kleptocracy and American worries of the navalist variety were separate developments, they overlapped in one area. For nearly a century, European investors had been in the habit of making substantial loans to the national governments of the various Caribbean and Central American republics. Though they sometimes took the form of mortgages on particular mines or pieces of land, these loans were usually advanced against customs duties in general, the duties collected on particular items, or the duties collected in a specific place. While the governments that took out these loans were notoriously unstable, European investors continued to make them. One reason for this was the universal practice of holding each regime responsible for the debts of its predecessors. Another was the willingness of European governments to employ their navies as collection agencies. Thus, whenever a Caribbean or Central American government fell behind on the payments on its international debt, it had to deal with the threat of foreign warships in its harbors, foreign landing parties on its soil, and the seizure of its custom houses. This had the secondary effect of exciting American fears about foreign influence in the region, fears that were exacerbated on those occasions when the German Empire proclaimed itself the champion, not merely of German creditors, but of those of other European nations as well.

The inability of a Caribbean or Central American republic to keep up with its international financial obligations was often the result of a breakdown in local arrangements for the distribution of national revenue. Thus, the dispatch of European warships to a Caribbean or Central American republic often coincided with outbreaks of political violence in that country. This, in turn, led to situations where the European warships put landing parties ashore to protect their diplomats, their expatriates, or the local international community as a whole from the worst effects of civil strife. In this way, many Caribbean countries found themselves caught in constantly escalating (and seemingly endless) cycles of insolvency, insurrection, and international intervention.

On December 13, 1901, the German government announced that, in order to collect debts owed by Venezuela to German nationals, it planned to send ships to blockade Venezuelan harbors and, should this not achieve the desired result, take control of customs houses on the Venezuelan littoral. Thus began the Venezuelan Claims Crisis of 1902–03. In the 15 months that followed, Germany convinced Great Britain and Italy to participate in an international naval expedition to Venezuelan waters; German and British warships seized four Venezuelan gunboats and blockaded the port of Caracas; Great Britain withdrew its ships; the US Navy conducted ostentatious maneuvers in the southern Caribbean; and, in the end, the parties concerned agreed to submit their dispute to international arbitration.[10] On December 6, 1904, the threat of a similar crisis over the international debts of the Dominican Republic led President Theodore Roosevelt to announce the policy that has since become known as the "Roosevelt Corollary to the Monroe Doctrine." Roosevelt argued that, as attempts by European powers to ensure the payment of debts would necessarily violate the Monroe Doctrine, the US would have to take measures to ensure that its sister republics in the New World honored their international financial obligations.

The mechanism for the implementation of the Roosevelt Corollary in the Dominican Republic was similar to the sort of regime that might be imposed upon a bankrupt corporation. Financial experts arranged for new loans that allowed both debt consolidation (replacing multiple European creditors with a single American one) and a much lower rate of interest. At the same time, American officials took charge of the Dominican customs service, supervised the collection of duties, and ensured that revenues were divided (in accordance with a pre-established formula) between debt service and the legitimate expenses of government. Lest it be tempted to interfere with the operation of this arrangement, the Dominican leadership also agreed to give up the right to change its customs duties without American permission.

In some respects, the situation in the Dominican Republic was highly amenable to the "customs receivership" imposed by the US. Traditionally more concerned about the threat of Haitian aggression than the danger of recolonization, Dominican leaders at the national level were less reluctant than most of their Caribbean counterparts to sacrifice significant portions of sovereignty on the altar of security. Thus, there was little immediate resistance to the imposition of the new arrangement. The vast majority of the Dominican bonds, moreover, were held by American, French, and Belgian investors, who, as a rule, were much happier with an American customs receivership than the prospect of a debt-collection regime managed from Berlin. At the same time, Dominican geography (which was characterized by poor overland communications and a multitude of natural harbors), politics (which were controlled by powerful regional warlords) and customs duties (which were higher than they should have been) were all highly favorable to smuggling. Nonetheless, the short-term results of the American customs receivership were encouraging. Consequently, Roosevelt's successor as president of the US, William Howard Taft, decided to extend the techniques of customs receivership and debt consolidation (an approach that he would soon begin to describe as "dollar diplomacy") to other places in Central America and the Caribbean.

Ironically, the first application of Taft's "dollar diplomacy" took place in Nicaragua, which was not only one of the more stable states in the region (with a dictator who had been in power since 1893), but also one of the few Caribbean republics that had managed to make regular payments to its international creditors during the first decade of the 20th century (though only at the cost of inflating the national currency). In the eyes of the US, however, these virtues (such as they were) did little to mitigate the many offences of the regime of José Santos Zelaya. In the previous few years, Zelaya had done much to undermine the traditional autonomy of the Mosquito Coast, thereby making many enemies among the people who lived there, a number of whom were American citizens. At the same time, he had been involved in a number of thinly veiled attempts to overthrow the governments of Guatemala, Costa Rica, Honduras, El Salvador, Colombia, and Ecuador. Worst of all, Zelaya had invited both Germany and Japan to build a second transoceanic canal. In peacetime, such a waterway would have threatened the economic viability of the Panama Canal, thereby depriving the US of the revenue needed to offset the cost of construction. In the event of war, a Nicaraguan canal under the control of Germany and Japan would have done much to complicate American naval operations.

The most successful of the many extraterritorial maneuvers conducted by Zelaya was the Nicaraguan invasion of Honduras in 1907. Though

Zelaya himself described the resulting war as a struggle between sovereign states, the presence of many Hondurans on his side, and many Nicaraguans and Salvadorans on the other, gave the conflict the character of a Central American civil war.[11] President Roosevelt responded with a diplomatic initiative that made the US and Mexico joint sponsors of a Central American peace conference, as well as joint guarantors of a treaty that created a framework for the peaceful resolution of disputes in the region.[12] Unfortunately, as Mexico was suffering from many of the same ills as its smaller neighbors to the south, and the problem at hand was less a matter of inter-state disputes of the traditional kind than of Zelaya's exploitation of domestic unrest on the territory of his neighbors, Roosevelt's attempt to craft a multilateral response won him little more than the half-hearted approval of contemporary idealists.

The Fighting

In the spring of 1909, the recently inaugurated administration of President Taft found itself faced with yet another attempt by Zelaya to take control of a nearby country, an enterprise that, among other things, involved the sending of ships full of armed men and supplies from ports on the Pacific littoral of Nicaragua to points on the coast of El Salvador. Taft's response made use of the diplomatic framework created by his predecessor, but did not depend upon it. Thus, while the Mexican Navy made a token contribution of two aged gunboats to the flotilla stationed in the Gulf of Fonseca, the lion's share of the business at hand (which included intercepting ships carrying arms or revolutionaries, strengthening the resolve of the Salvadoran government, and discouraging Zelaya from further adventures of this type) was carried out by four armored cruisers of the US Navy and a battalion of US Marines.

While the Marines deployed to the Gulf of Fonseca spent most of their time in enforced idleness, their inclusion in the expedition of 1909 reflected a significant change in organization, capabilities, and self-conception that had taken place in the Marine Corps during the previous decade. Throughout the 19th century, the vast majority of Marines had either been assigned to the ships' companies of armed vessels (where they kept order among the sailors, provided crews for some of the shipboard guns, and served in landing parties) or to naval installations on land (where they served as guards and trained for duty at sea). Though Marines from ships' detachments and barracks were sometimes formed into military-style field units, the units so created had no permanent existence. After the Spanish-American War, however, some of the temporary field units cobbled together by the Marine Corps began to take on a more permanent character. Thus, rather than sending out provisional companies and battalions made up of detachments from various barracks and warships, the Marine Corps began to assemble provisional battalions and regiments from permanently constituted companies. (As a rule, companies consisted of a hundred or so men, battalions of three or four companies, and regiments of two or three battalions.)

The frustration of Zelaya's ambitions in the Gulf of Fonseca convinced several of his lieutenants that Nicaragua was ripe for a change of government. In October of 1909, Juan J. Estrada, who had commanded the Nicaraguan forces that had recently fought in Honduras, and had consequently been rewarded with the governorship of the Department of Zelaya, raised the banner of rebellion. While Estrada's ambitions were national, the greater part of the impetus behind his movement came from the ethnically mixed (and largely English-speaking) population of his province, which encompassed the Mosquito Coast and its hinterland. In particular, residents of this area, which had long enjoyed a high degree of independence and had few commercial, traditional, or cultural connections with people in other parts of Nicaragua, resented the restrictions that Zelaya had imposed upon them. They were particularly incensed by Zelaya's practice of granting (or selling) trade monopolies, which greatly interfered with the international commerce that played such an important role in the local economy.

The immediate American response to the rebellion on the Mosquito Coast was very much in keeping with the way that the US had traditionally dealt with outbreaks of political violence in the Caribbean: the State Department proclaimed strict neutrality and the Department of the Navy dispatched a warship with orders to protect the lives and property of American expatriates. Within a few weeks, however, the execution of two American citizens who had been captured by government forces while serving in the ranks of Estrada's rebel army proved to be the straw that broke the camel's back. On December 1, 1909, the US broke off diplomatic relations with Nicaragua and, while declining to offer direct support to the rebels, made it very clear to all concerned that it had lost all patience with Zelaya. Nine days later, Zelaya resigned his office and went into voluntary exile, hoping thereby to keep his supporters in positions of power.[13]

For four months, it seemed as if Zelaya's act of political self-sacrifice had had its intended effect. The nationwide revolution that Estrada had hoped to spark failed to materialize, and what remained of his army had taken refuge in Bluefields, a city that had long served as the commercial capital of the Mosquito Coast. Before the government troops could deliver the *coup de grâce*, however, the US consul in Bluefields requested reinforcements for the hundred-man landing party that an American cruiser had put ashore to protect the many Americans who lived there. On May 31, 1910, elements of the same battalion of Marines that had recently been deployed to the Gulf of Fonseca landed in Bluefields and began to do things that, while described as measures to prevent harm to American citizens, had the effect of protecting the remnants of Estrada's rebel army from the government troops. On one occasion, for example, the senior Marine ashore (the soon-to-be-famous Major Smedley D. Butler) informed the commanders of both sides that, as projectiles landing in Bluefields might endanger American citizens, he would take action against any soldiers who fired into the city, but had no objection to bullets that flew in the other direction.[14] The actions of American warships, which prevented each side from interfering with commercial traffic, were also of greater benefit to Estrada's rebel army, which was able to collect customs duties at Bluefields and obtain supplies purchased overseas, than to the government forces, which, being far away from their sources of supply in the cities of western Nicaragua, were forced to live off the land.[15]

While the government forces cooled their heels outside Bluefields, forcing their countrymen to accept increasingly worthless paper money in exchange for food, fodder, and other supplies, Zelaya's old enemies in other parts of the country launched uprisings of their own. By the end of the summer of 1910, Zelaya's successor was out of power and a fragile coalition of rebel leaders had taken the reins of government. While maneuvering against each other in a variety of ways, these leaders agreed that the resources of the state should be used both to compensate their supporters for their losses and reward them for their loyalty. This policy, which left Nicaragua without the foreign currency needed to pay its international debts, but with far too much of its own paper money, created a financial and monetary crisis that quickly brought the economic life of the country to a standstill.

The remedy provided by the US, which combined a debt-consolidation loan with a customs receivership and a new currency, solved the worst of Nicaragua's fiscal and monetary problems. At the same time, the abolition of the many monopolies and special concessions that Zelaya had granted during his long dictatorship did much to stimulate trade. Unfortunately, progress in the realm of economics led directly to problems in the political sphere. Many Nicaraguans resented the loss of sovereignty inherent in both the customs receivership and the monetary reform. At the same time, the abolition of monopolies and special concessions created a class of influential people who, having paid for such advantages with money and political support, tended to view them as their private property.[16]

The Rebellion

In the summer of 1912, the fragile power-sharing arrangement fell apart and the government in Managua found itself faced with separate rebellions in the two largest cities in the country. The leader of the first revolt was Benjamin Zeledón, who had previously served Zelaya as Minister of War, while that of the second was Luis Mena, a founding member of the ruling coalition who had recently been maneuvered out of office. Once again, the US responded with an ostensibly neutral intervention that tipped the balance in favor of one side. This time, however, it was not rebels who benefited from the actions of American forces, but the national government of President Adolfo Díaz. (A former employee of an American mining concern on the Mosquito Coast, Díaz had played a key role in the financing of Estrada's rebellion.)

The forces deployed in the American intervention of 1912, which included sizeable landing parties from several warships and three battalions of Marines, were much larger than those sent out to the Mosquito Coast in 1910. The task they faced, however, was much more difficult. Whereas the American forces landed at Bluefields were concentrated in that city, those put ashore in 1912 had to operate along a very large portion of the Pacific Railway of Nicaragua, a stretch of track some 190 kilometers (119 miles) long that connected the Pacific port of Corinto (where the American forces came ashore) with the cities of León (where Zeledón's rebellion had broken out), Managua (which was still under the control of President Díaz), and Granada (which served as the base for Mena's rebel army.)

At first, neither of the rebel commanders wanted to risk his forces in an attack against the Americans. Instead, each waged a separate campaign of petty harassment (which often involved damage to the railroad) and low-stakes confrontation. This, each of the rebel commanders believed, would allow his particular side to maintain its nationalist credentials while preserving its forces from the losses that would inevitably result from a clash of arms. Zeledón, the more inventive of the two rebel commanders, seems to have taken this logic a step further. He maneuvered his forces in a way that suggests that he may well have attempted to orchestrate a battle between the Americans and the forces led by his competitor. Whether or not this was the case, the reluctance of the rebels to engage in open battle created an opportunity that was well suited to American purposes.

The overall commander of the American forces in Nicaragua, Admiral William H. Southerland of the US Navy, was as eager as the two rebel commanders to avoid a clash of arms. This was particularly true in the early days of the intervention, when the bulk of the forces allocated to him were still in transit and the strengths of the three contending parties were still uncertain. At the same time, Southerland was obliged to protect the American citizens in western Nicaragua (who were concentrated in Corinto, Managua, and Granada) and remind all concerned that 51 percent of the Pacific Railway was American property. To these ends, he established small garrisons at several points between Corinto and Managua, and employed a train full of Marines and machine guns to maintain communications between them. (As might be expected, this train was placed under the command of the seemingly ubiquitous Major Butler.)

For the most part, the struggle for control of the Pacific Railway was a game of bluff and bluster, with rebel leaders attempting to intimidate, impede, or embarrass Butler, and Butler making various displays of force and resolve, but little in the way of battle. The exception to this took place late in the evening of September 16, 1912, when forces loyal to Zeledón ambushed the American train near the town of Masaya. In the brief exchange of fire that followed, the Zeledónistas managed to wound five Marines while American bullets (many of which were fired by the 16 Colt machine guns mounted on the train) struck 128 of the attackers. The following morning, Zeledón sent a letter to Butler, claiming that the ambush had been a mistake. As proof of his good faith, Zeledón returned the three Marines his men had captured during the firefight.[17]

The two-month "war of nerves" for control of the railroad ended when Butler's train reached Granada. Though he had only intended to convince the Menista rebels in control of that city to refrain from interfering with traffic on the railroad and return some American property they had seized, Butler discovered that their leader Mena, who was suffering from a highly debilitating disease, had lost all desire for power. He therefore traded the promise of a safe passage out of Nicaragua for Mena and his son for the dissolution of the Menista army and the surrender of its weapons. Shortly thereafter, Zeledón decided that, with his chief rival out of the way and the government forces growing stronger by the day, it was time to make a stand. He blocked all rail traffic between Managua and Granada, deployed his forces on a pair of hills near the town of Masaya, and challenged the Americans to dislodge him.

In many respects, the fight for the two hills was a combat typical of the decade that preceded the outbreak of World War One, and, in particular, bore a strong resemblance the smaller engagements of the wars that were then taking place in the Balkans, Mexico, and Libya. Zeledón's forces consisted largely of men armed with bolt-action magazine rifles, but also included a small number of rifle-caliber machine guns, several 1-pounder (37mm) guns and three or four 3-inch (76.2mm) field guns. The Marines and Bluejackets lacked the 1-pounders, but were otherwise armed in a similar fashion, with bolt-action magazine rifles, quite a few Colt machine guns and six 3-inch (76.2mm) field guns. The American attack began with a desultory artillery bombardment that lasted for 21 hours. This served the triple purpose of giving the untrained Marine artillerymen an opportunity to learn the rudiments of the gunner's art, providing Zeledón with one last opportunity to withdraw his forces and preventing the Zeledónistas from firing on the Marines and Bluejackets who were forming up for the assault. Though plagued by faulty fuses and a shortage of shells, the Marine artillerymen quickly got the better of the defenders of the two hills, causing the crews of artillery pieces and machine guns, as well as a high proportion of the riflemen, to seek shelter on the reverse slope of the two hills.

Shortly before dawn on October 4, 1912, the Marines and Bluejackets began to advance up the taller of the two hills, a feature known as El Coyotepe. Because the officer commanding the Marine artillery lacked confidence in the skills of his men and the reliability of his ammunition, the American guns had stopped firing several minutes before the assault began. Thus, the attacking infantry had to rely upon their own rifles to suppress the fire of Zeledónistas, with one part of each company firing while the other rushed forward. On the whole, this sufficed to keep the defenders from making effective use of their weapons. The crew of one of Zeledón's machine guns, however, refused to be intimidated by the American rifle fire, and managed to kill four Marines before falling prey to the bayonets of the dead men's comrades.[18]

Once the Marines and Bluejackets had taken El Coyotepe, they made use of the machine guns and artillery pieces they found there to drive the Zeledónistas off the second hill. Once that second hill was secure, and the

Stars and Stripes were seen to be flying over it, 400 Nicaraguan soldiers in the service of the Díaz government, who were supposed to have taken part in the attack upon the two hills but had somehow missed the rendezvous, burst into the nearby town of Masaya. There they engaged in a three-hour battle with the Zeledónista garrison, during which Zeledón himself was killed. Once the firing died down, the government troops celebrated their victory by looting the town.[19]

Though sporadic resistance continued for a day or two, the battle of Coyotepe (as the fight for the two hills became known) marked the end of Zeledón's rebellion. Within four months, the landing parties had returned to their warships and the three Marine battalions had returned to their bases in Panama and the US. Soon thereafter, the US concluded a set of agreements with the Nicaraguan government that gave the US the exclusive right to build a transoceanic canal on Nicaraguan territory, established a customs receivership modeled on the one adopted by the Dominican Republic, and permitted the permanent presence of a company of Marines at the American legation in Managua. Though it consisted of only 100 or so Marines, this legation guard provided a concrete reminder of American determination to keep the peace, not merely within the borders of Nicaragua, but also within Central America as a whole.

Conclusion

The de facto American protectorate that followed the intervention of 1912 brought 12 years of uninterrupted peace to Nicaragua and its neighbors, a government that was more respectful of the rights of its citizens than any of its predecessors and a period of unprecedented prosperity. At the same time, the protectorate put the US in the awkward position of sponsoring a government that enjoyed little in the way of support from traditional political elites. This situation, in turn, made it easy for anyone who opposed the American-backed government to wrap himself in the mantle of patriotism. It also ensured that self-serving warlords like Zeledón and Zelaya would enter the pantheon of national heroes and that, rather than being remembered as the last major engagement of a multi-sided civil war, the battle of Coyotepe would be remembered (at least in some circles) as the Nicaraguan equivalent of the battle of Bunker Hill.[20]

In the two decades that followed the intervention of 1912, US Marines became involved in four additional "small wars" in Central America and the Caribbean. One of these, the seven-month occupation of the Mexican city of Veracruz (April 21–November 23, 1914), bore a close resemblance to the landing at Bluefields in 1910. While the American forces landed at Veracruz were larger than those put ashore at Bluefields, and the American occupation of the Mexican city lasted much longer than that of the Nicaraguan town, both operations combined the explicit goal of protecting the lives and property of American citizens with the effect of tipping the balance in a local civil war. The other three interventions had little in common with what had gone before. In Haiti (1915–34), the Dominican Republic (1916–24) and Nicaragua (1927–33), US Marines operated against forces using classic guerrilla tactics, conducted sustained counterinsurgency campaigns, formed local constabularies, and engaged in various nation-building programs. Indeed, these three occupations were so different from the Nicaraguan interventions of 1910 and 1912 that a recent (and otherwise comprehensive) book on the development of small wars doctrine in the Marine Corps in the first half of the 20th century does not refer to them.[21]

Strictly speaking, the Nicaraguan interventions of 1910 and 1912 do not qualify as counterinsurgency campaigns. The forces that fought against the Marines did not operate as guerrillas. Neither did the Marines make any attempt to separate those forces from the inhabitants of the areas in which they operated, provide security, build local institutions or attempt to redress political or economic grievances. Nonetheless, it makes little sense to characterize the two interventions as "conventional" operations. Rather, the Marines found themselves involved in a multi-sided conflict in which direct negotiation, intricate political maneuvers, the movement of troops and exchanges of gunfire, not to mention a great deal of bluff and bluster, were intermixed in a highly promiscuous fashion.

Viewed from the perspective of subsequent small wars in Central America and the Caribbean, the American interventions in Nicaragua were transitional events, undertakings that eased the metamorphosis of the Marine Corps from a seagoing force that specialized in the work of landing parties to a land-based constabulary that developed considerable competence in counterinsurgency operations and nation-building. From the point of view of the preceding century, however, the American expeditions to Nicaragua of 1910 and 1912 were little more than oldfashioned landing operations that had been carried out on a somewhat larger scale, served a more ambitious purpose, and lasted for a longer period of time. After all, the combination of tactical maneuver with retail diplomacy had been part and parcel of the work of landing parties from the days of the Mosquito Fleet.

4

FEW CARROTS AND A LOT OF STICKS
German Anti-Partisan Warfare in World War Two

Dr Peter Lieb

During World War Two, the Wehrmacht and the German police faced large partisan groups in most of the countries under Nazi occupation. Although its military character was the same as that of other insurgencies of the 20th century, the partisan war differed in one essential point: integrated in a huge war, its military importance was always overshadowed by the events on the front line. Nonetheless, the Allies considered the partisans a valuable asset in the fight against the Axis. Thus, the Soviets supported the Communist partisan movement in the rear of the German Eastern Front with large amounts of materiel and men. The same was true for the Western Allies, especially the British, who saw the nationalist partisans in Western Europe and the Balkans as a relatively cheap weapon with which to harass the Axis. Additionally, supporting partisans offered the British the opportunity to maintain political influence in these areas and to contain local Communist resistance movements.

The partisan war was also characterized by harsh German countermeasures, not only against the insurgents themselves, but also against the local civilian population. Some scholars have argued that German anti-partisan warfare served as a pretext for the annihilation of "undesirable elements" in Nazi ideology, namely Jews, Communists, and members of "inferior races."[1] Although this view is far too simplistic for the entire partisan war, it is true that ideology and military measures often went hand in hand. It is thus one of this chapter's aims to show the extent of the impact ideology had upon German partisan warfare.

The main purpose is, however, to analyze the tactical and operational evolution between 1941 and 1944 in German anti-partisan warfare or, to use the modern term, counterinsurgency.[2] What were the reasons that enabled the Germans to achieve military victories, but never really to tame

The Partisan War in the Occupied Soviet Union 1941–44

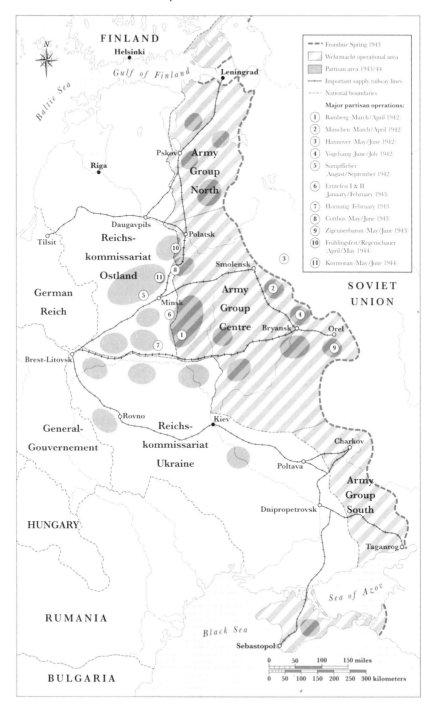

FINLAND

Helsinki

Gulf of Finland

Baltic Sea

Leningrad

Riga

Pskov

Army
Group
North

Daugavpils

Tilsit

Reichs-
kommissariat

Ostland

Polatsk

Smolensk

German
Reich

Minsk

Army
Group
Centre

Bryansk

Orel

SOVIET
UNION

Brest-Litovsk

Rovno

Kiev

General-
Gouvernement

Reichs-
kommissariat

Ukraine

Poltava

Charkov

HUNGARY

Dnipropetrovsk

Army
Group
South

Taganrog

RUMANIA

Sea of Azov

Black Sea

Sebastopol

BULGARIA

Legend:
- Frontline Spring 1943
- Wehrmacht operational area
- Partisan area 1943/44
- Important supply railway lines
- National boundaries

Major partisan operations:
1. Bamberg (March/April 1942)
2. München (March/April 1942)
3. Hannover (May/June 1942)
4. Vogelsang (June/July 1942)
5. Sumpffieber (August/September 1942)
6. Erntefest I & II (January/February 1943)
7. Hornung (February 1943)
8. Cottbus (May/June 1943)
9. Zigeunerbaron (May/June 1943)
10. Frühlingsfest/Regenschauer (April/May 1944)
11. Kormoran (May/June 1944)

0 50 100 150 miles
0 50 100 150 200 250 300 kilometers

or master the partisan threat? The final question, therefore, is: who won this bloody struggle, the Germans or the partisans? This chapter will attempt to answer this question by considering the history of anti-partisan warfare in the German Army before 1939 and case studies of partisan warfare in the Soviet Union and France during World War Two.

German Anti-Partisan Operations in World War One

The German Army has often been admired for its military professionalism, its efficiency, and its discipline, all of which contributed to astonishing victories against numerically far superior opponents.[3] This assessment is certainly not untrue, but it neglects the other side of the coin: a military culture which favored a broad interpretation of the term "military necessity" and that paved the way for an extreme use of violence. In particular, most forms of civilian resistance were countered with drastic measures, including shooting hostages and burning down houses. To put such actions in historical context, it is important to note that the laws of armed conflict were vague at this time, and allowed considerable freedom of interpretation.

In the early days of World War One, the invading German Army spread violence among the civilian populations in Belgium and northern France. With the memory of the so-called Francs-Tireurs ("Free-Shooters") of the Franco-Prussian War (1870–71) still fresh,[4] German soldiers overreacted against mostly imagined ambushes and took drastic countermeasures: up to 6,000 Belgian and French civilians are believed to have been killed in these first few weeks of the war. However, these events were short-lived; they stopped as soon as the front line stabilized in early fall 1914.[5]

It was only in 1918 that the German Army was confronted with a large-scale partisan war in the occupied Ukraine. In this largely forgotten chapter of history, the Germans faced a Bolshevik insurgency supported by small landowners. The initial German response to this threat was fairly similar to the tragic days of summer 1914 on the Western Front: harsh orders were issued to shoot all captured "bandits," burn down houses, impose contributions on villages, and seize hostages. At the first stage, the Germans tried to put down this Moscow-sponsored Bolshevik revolution by sheer force alone. However, soon understanding that these methods lacked a long-term perspective, they started developing a more sophisticated approach. The German authorities built up an effective network of agents in the communities and a locally recruited self-defense force. The drastic early orders were now replaced by moderate tones in an attempt to build a feeling of trust among the population. German troops were instructed to cooperate closely with the Ukrainian administration in order to identify real partisans and supporters; fatal mistakes could therefore be avoided. On the political level, the Germans tried to stabilize the de jure independent Ukrainian government by fostering close economic bonds between the two states. However, neither the first socialist government, nor its nationalist-authoritarian successor from May 1918, ever found much acceptance among the Ukrainian population.

Despite this lack of political support, the Germans were able to suppress the Bolshevik insurgency by early summer 1918, and a time of relative calm reigned in the Ukraine until the withdrawal of German troops in November 1918. The Ukraine in 1918 is thus one of the rare examples of a successful counterinsurgency campaign in modern history. However, it must remain uncertain if this achievement would have been of lasting duration in a long-term German occupation. Nonetheless, it is noteworthy that the Germans were able to stabilize the country, despite impending defeat on all other fronts of the war. And it is also indisputable that they took the right path towards a relatively modern counterinsurgency strategy.[6]

In the interwar years, the German militaries forgot all the positive lessons learned in the Ukraine in 1918. In the 1920s the Reichswehr, having been cut down to 100,000 men by the Treaty of Versailles, planned a conventional defensive war; in the 1930s the Wehrmacht experimented with armored mobile warfare. The image of a more or less clear-cut front-line war between two mass armies dominated German military thinking. Aside from short-lived ideas in the mid-1920s about a people's war on home territory, irregular warfare played no role in the German concept of a future war.

However, the mentality of the officers' corps underwent a drastic radicalization in the aftermath of World War One. When revolution broke out in Germany in November 1918, monarchy was swept away, and the democratic government immediately concluded a ceasefire. For most officers, more than four years of fighting and dying on the Front seemed to have been in vain. In their perception, this shame was due to socialist agitation on the home front; the German Army had remained undefeated in the field and was "stabbed in the back." Besides, Communist insurgencies at home, Polish usurpations in Upper Silesia, and the Bolshevik advance in the Baltic States all challenged the stability of Germany. Irregular warfare played a vital role in these conflicts, and all were fought with extreme brutality on both sides. Many German officers of the so-called Freikorps ("Freecorps") suspected that socialists and Jews were behind all these upheavals. The traditional fear of Francs-Tireurs had been enriched with a new ideological element, and the fervor of the struggles further enhanced this paranoia. All these elements were grim predictors of the coming devastations of World War Two.

German Anti-Partisan Warfare in World War Two

The resistance movements in World War Two were not restricted to certain countries, but were a European phenomenon. Hurt national feelings, ideological fervor, brutal oppression, or the sheer struggle for survival triggered revolt against the German yoke. The form of resistance chosen varied from country to country, region to region, and period to period. Similarly, German occupation policies and countermeasures against resistance were by no means standardized.

German Anti-Partisan Warfare in the Soviet Union 1941–44

Of all the partisan movements in World War Two, the Soviet movement was the largest.[7] After the war, the Soviet regime claimed that its partisans had contributed considerably to the Allied victory in the "Great Patriotic War." This ideologically inspired view of a people's war against a fascist invader is more myth than reality, but it is nevertheless true that the Germans never managed to defeat the partisans completely. Their strongholds, mainly in the rear of German Army Group Center, constantly posed a serious threat to the German supply lines.

It will always remain a point of academic debate whether the harsh and often indiscriminate German countermeasures against partisans and civilians were driven by the situation or by Nazi ideology.[8] It was most likely a combination of the two. Certainly the most important situational factor for the Germans was their lack of manpower in the rear. At the start of Operation *Barbarossa*, the German invasion of the Soviet Union (June 1941), the three Army Groups (North, Center, South) received only three Security Divisions each. The two civil-administered Reichskommissariate (Imperial Commissariats), Ostland and Ukraine, which were responsible for establishing administration in the occupied areas, received another Security Division each. All five divisions were small (5,000 to 10,000 men), poorly equipped, and recruited from overage men. Nonetheless, these third-class divisions, reinforced by a number of Landesschützenbataillone (Territorial Battalions) of even lower combat power, were entrusted with securing long communication lines and vast areas in the rear of the Eastern Front. Furthermore, 26 German police battalions (some 12,000 men in total) waged the ideological war against Jews and Communists in the rear of the front.[9] Later, in 1942, units from Allied countries, especially Hungary and Slovakia, were sent to fill manpower gaps behind the front lines; they behaved with brutality equal to that of the Germans.[10]

The 707th Infantry Division serves as an example of the flaws and the low quality of these Security Divisions. This division was much smaller than an ordinary infantry division and had only 5,000 men. Apart from the division commander, the entire officer corps initially consisted of reserve officers. The average age of a platoon commander was 30, of a company commander, 42, and of a battalion commander, 53. The regular soldier of the 707th Infantry Division was far beyond his 30s. The division was further hampered by a severe lack of transport vehicles, which made a fast deployment to troubled areas virtually impossible. Nonetheless, an area twice the size of Belgium was allocated to the 707th Infantry Division during its deployment in Belorussia over the fall and winter of 1941–42.[11]

Given the quality of these troops and the large area it was necessary to secure, the Germans were never able to apply an ideal, but only a feasible approach to solving the partisan problem in the occupied territories of the Soviet Union. Throughout the years of occupation, the German aim was never really to pacify the country, but merely to secure the communication lines in an attempt to ensure the undisrupted supply of the front-line troops.

In order to achieve their goals, the Germans initially relied upon the application of violence and terror. They hoped, by using deterrence, to keep the civilian population from supporting the partisans. The basic principles underlying such a strategy had been set down before the start of the campaign in the Kriegsgerichtsbarkeitserlass of May 13, 1941. The Kriegsgerichtsbarkeitserlass was a decree on the military jurisdiction for Operation *Barbarossa*. Military courts no longer had to deal with crimes perpetrated by German troops against civilians, thus denying occupied populations all legal protection against arbitrary acts. Guerrillas were to be relentlessly liquidated, either in combat or after capture, and officers with the powers of at least a battalion commander were authorized to impose collective reprisals against civilian populations, such as the burning down of entire villages.[12]

This Kriegsgerichtsbarkeitserlass fitted well into the *Weltanschauungs-krieg* (ideological war) concept on the Eastern Front. The High Command of the German Armed Forces, along with many field officers, issued various orders to explain to their soldiers the necessity of waging a war against Judeo-Bolshevism.[13] The Jews were defined as the bogeymen for all possible, alleged, and real acts of resistance against the Germans. "Where the Jew is, is the partisan" became a frequent slogan in military decrees. Hence, the first year of Operation *Barbarossa* saw a combination of the Holocaust with the struggle against partisans.

This peculiarity of German anti-partisan warfare was not restricted to the Soviet Union – Serbia in 1941 constituted a similar case[14] – but it was in the occupied East that it reached horrendous dimensions and paved the way for the "final solution." Weeks before the start of the campaign, the Chief of the Reichssicherheitshauptamt (Reich Security Main Office) and the Sicherheitspolizei und Sicherheitsdienst (Sipo/SD) (Security Police and Security Service), SS-Obergruppenführer Reinhard Heydrich, and the General Quartermaster of the army, General Eduard Wagner, concluded an agreement which regulated the tasks of the Sipo/SD and the Wehrmacht in the hinterland: the army carried out the military part of the campaign, while Sipo/SD took responsibility for the execution of the political tasks.

This arrangement gave the green light to the infamous Einsatzgruppen of Sipo/SD, as well as two SS brigades and more than two dozen police battalions. From the onset of *Barbarossa*, they all commenced killing Jews and other "undesirable elements" behind the front, and very soon rationalized their murderous actions in the guise of anti-partisan operations.[15] A climax was the major anti-partisan operation *Sumpffieber* (Marsh Fever) in Belorussia in August and September 1942, which ended with the liquidation of the Jewish ghettos in the operational area. Within slightly more than one year, the four Einsatzgruppen (of battalion strength), two SS brigades, and some regular German police regiments, supported by local collaborators, killed about 500,000 Jews on occupied Soviet territory. A number of Wehrmacht officers felt uneasy, especially when it came to the indiscriminate killing of Jewish women and children. But the desire for a calm hinterland with secure communication lines kept official protests very limited, as most of them really believed in this allegedly direct association between Jews and partisans. In the special case of Belorussia, the 707th Infantry Division even organized mass murder on its own initiative, resulting in the death of more than 10,000 Jews within its security area during the fall of 1941.[16] The link between Holocaust and anti-partisan operations was especially apparent in the first months of the campaign, but did not play a major role later, as by the second half of 1942 most Jews had been exterminated or deported to the concentration and death camps.

In general, the harsh and brutal German measures in 1941 were aimed at a potential rather than a real partisan threat in the rear. At this point, theory and practice of the partisan war differed enormously in parts. Despite some crude prewar concepts and Stalin's appeal for a people's war shortly after the start of the German onslaught on June 22, 1941, the fast retreat of the Red Army resulted in a chaotic rout of the Soviet administration and left no time for a proper organization of a partisan movement in the occupied territories. Institutional quarrels impeded the organization further as the Communist Party, the NKVD, and the Red Army all claimed their leadership role in such a movement. The majority of the partisans encountered in the first month of the German–Soviet clash were in fact individual Red Army soldiers or entire units up to battalion strength cut off from the main body of the retreating forces. They were the remains of the huge cauldron battles in which the Germans were never able to take all Red Army soldiers as POWs. These soldiers, adding up to tens of thousands, were wandering around in remote areas such as large forests or swamps, trying to escape the German clutches.

Although they seldom attacked Wehrmacht communication lines in 1941, these soldiers nevertheless constituted a great potential danger in the German-occupied hinterland; this partly explains the brutal German approach in the first months of the war. Their harsh measures, in concert with the winter of 1941–42, hit the Soviet partisan movement very hard and almost annihilated it. However, supported by some substantial air supply and reinforced by units infiltrated through the front line, the movement survived the winter and emerged again in early spring 1942, motivated by the successful offensives of the Red Army in the previous months.

By early winter 1941 it had become clear that the Soviet Union had not been subjugated in a *Blitzkreig* campaign, and that the war in the East would continue. New concepts for a long-lasting occupation policy seemed to be unavoidable. Various German Army field commanders voiced criticism of the anti-partisan approach practiced so far and drew up memoranda.[17] The general tone was a timid "hearts and minds" policy: the occupied people would need a perspective for life under German rule. They should earn a living wage through a boost of the stagnating economy, and no longer be victims of an indiscriminate German anti-partisan policy. "Rigor and justice" became one of the key phrases.[18] Propaganda was to motivate partisans to go over to the Germans, where they could expect to be treated as POWs.

A cornerstone of the new concept was the integration of indigenous forces. Cautious about the prospects for indirect rule in the East, the Germans had initially deployed only a very limited number of collaborators, mainly in the Baltic States for local policing duties, the poorly armed and equipped *Selbstschutz* (self-protection) units. In spring 1942 the Germans started to build up self-defense units recruited from the local population. Racial factors still played a role, as ethnic minorities from the Baltic States or the Caucasus and, to a lesser degree, the Ukraine, enjoyed more trust than the Russians.

They also launched the experimental Selbstverwaltungsbezirk (Local Self-Government District) in Lokot.[19] In this area, south of Bryansk (in Russia), the Commander of 2nd Panzer Army, Generaloberst Rudolf Schmidt, allowed the local population to take their fate into their own hands. Under its governor, Bronislav Kaminski, schools, police, administration, and the economy were all autonomously built up, free of German interference. Indigenous forces, the Miliz (Militia), or later Volkswehr (People's Defense), undertook fighting as required against the local partisans; the occupiers contented themselves with a liaison staff and by making military reinforcements available as needed. Generally it was seen as enough if the Miliz "[learned] how to [shoot] and to chase partisans out of a penetrated village."[20] In summer 1942, the German Army also began to establish regular units of Red Army prisoners under the slogan "Combat against Bolshevism."[21] It remains more than doubtful if these *Osttruppen* (Eastern Troops) believed in this idea, as most of them just wanted to escape from the horrible conditions in the camps where, in fall and winter 1941–42, almost two million prisoners had perished.[22]

The year 1942 saw a change in the perception of anti-partisan warfare not only on a political, but also a tactical level. Combat against partisans began to achieve a certain professionalism. Hitherto it had been a task of the Ic officer and his staff (equivalent of G2 in NATO), but in the summer of 1942 it became the responsibility of the Ia (equivalent of G3 in NATO).[23] Furthermore, the institutional rivalry between the police and the SS on the one hand, and the Wehrmacht on the other, was solved by a division of the territory of responsibility: the army led all anti-partisan operations in the operational area, while the SS was at the head of all anti-partisan operations in the Reichskommissariate Ukraine and Ostland. Of all the German-occupied territories in the East, it was in Ostland that the struggle against the partisans, and the accompanying measures, reached their peak in brutality and had the most dramatic impact on the local population.[24] As the head of the SS and the German police, Himmler later created a new post: the Bevollmächtigter der Bandenkampfverbände (Plenipotentiary of the Bandit Combat Formations), established to centralize all future efforts and analyze the information gathered.

From 1942, two forms of fighting the partisans prevailed: one was passive and one active. "Passive" combat consisted of securing the railway lines and roads in the hinterland, using a system of strongpoints with patrols in between. This system was not particularly successful, because chronic lack of manpower meant that potential targets could never be fully protected. In the rear area of 2nd Panzer Army alone, 1,100 sabotage acts (demolition and attacks against guards) occurred over a six-month period from May to October 1942.[25]

The Germans grasped very quickly that only the "active" form of chasing the partisans was likely to lead to success. This involved supporting the passive protection of the communication lines with small and flexible *Jagdkommandos* (hunting detachments), mostly consisting of a reinforced platoon.[26] These *Jagdkommandos* were not new – they had formed the basis of the anti-partisan operations in 1941 – but in 1942 they received more professional training tailored to their tasks. The basic idea was that the *Jagdkommandos* should themselves behave and act like partisans by setting traps and laying ambushes. They would make all their movements far away from villages and roads, to maximize the element of surprise. Although the *Jagdkommandos* model points precisely to modern military counterinsurgency practices, and despite the successes they achieved everywhere, they were never more than a local remedy, and never succeeded in hindering the partisan movement from spreading further. Here again, the lack of manpower took its toll; each division had only one *Jagdkommando*.

In the fall of 1941, the Oberkommando des Heeres (OKH, High Command of the German Army) had explicitly advised against large-scale "cauldron" operations;[27] despite this warning, the cauldron maneuver became a favorite of German troops in 1942 and 1943. During quiet times, whole regiments or even divisions could be withdrawn from the front line for some days or weeks at a time. They were sent to reinforce security forces in the hinterland, giving the Germans greater scope in targeting partisan groups. It was only on these occasions that the Germans could employ ordinary combat infantry or even elite tank units in anti-partisan operations. The large-scale operations commenced in spring 1942 in the rear areas of Army Group Center; the largest operations included *München* (March–April), *Bamberg* (March–April), *Hannover* (May–June) and *Vogelsang* (June–July).[28]

These operations normally consisted of three phases. In the first phase, troops from different starting points were assembled in order to create a cauldron around the suspected partisan area. This cauldron was, of course, only rarely unbroken, considering the huge operational area. In the second phase, the Germans tightened up the cauldron by a concentric advance from all sides. Specific daily targets were allocated to each participating unit or battle group; villages located on major roads were searched for partisans and their supporters. In the third and last phase, the area was overhauled again for a few days. This maneuver was in use until late 1943, when the Germans developed a new tactic in the Balkans involving a slowly approaching front which tried to press the partisans onto a cordon line.[29]

Drastic and brutal measures always accompanied these large-scale pacification operations. The Germans were aware that their insufficient manpower made it difficult both to catch the quickly dispersing partisans during the operation, and to hold the ground afterward. Thus they tried to uproot the partisans from their living bases: entire regions were transformed into "desert zones." Villages were burned down, the local population was evacuated, and all cattle and agricultural products were looted.[30] The units – especially the police – sometimes did not waste time on the complicated evacuation process; instead they just shot the civilians on the spot. Having said this, the behavior of the German troops was not homogenous, but could differ dramatically from one unit to another.[31] When the Germans withdrew, the partisan counterterror operations against the remaining population began. Their actions were, however, directed against a specific group: collaborators and suspected collaborators.

Of course, the "active" German strategy was the opposite of a "hearts and minds" policy. The tender seedling of a new, softer occupation policy was doomed to fail from the beginning through these operations and their effect on the population. The reality was that many officers and men could not overcome their initial disrespect and disdain for the occupied Slavic population. Neither Germans nor partisans ever really sought to win the "hearts" of the population; winning "minds" seemed to be sufficient, and this was done by demonstrating superiority over the enemy with sheer violence. The population, squeezed between the hammer and the anvil,[32] was often left with no choice but to support whichever was the stronger side in the area at any moment.

By late 1942, the prospect of a softer approach in anti-partisan operations had receded, at least for the time being. In a central order sent on December 16, 1942 Hitler and the Oberkommando der Wehrmacht (OKW, High Command of the German Armed Forces) decided:

> If we do not wage this struggle against the bandits in the East and in the Balkans by most brutal means, our available resources will not last in the foreseeable future to control this pestilence. Therefore, the troops are allowed and obliged to apply every mean without exceptions in this fight, also against women and children, as long as it is successful. Considerations, no matter in what way, are a crime against the German people and the soldiers on the front, who have to bear the attacks of the bandits and who cannot have any understanding for giving mercy to the bandits and their collaborators.[33]

The following year, 1943, saw a continuation of large-scale operations, mainly in the Reichskommissariat Ostland, but also in the operational area. Among them was Operation *Zigeunerbaron* (Gypsy Baron) during May–June, in which six divisions took part. Its aim was to cleanse the rear area of 9th Army and 2nd Panzer Army for Operation *Zitadelle* (Citadel), the last big German offensive on the Eastern Front at Kursk-Orel. As had been the case with most previous anti-partisan operations, the Germans were once again unable to score a sweeping success. The bulk of the partisans escaped the cauldron and when the operation was over the area resembled a "desert zone."

By mid-1943, the partisan war had practically been decided by the situation on the front line and the lack of a real alternative German occupation policy. German propaganda efforts were counteracted and doomed to fail by their own brutal actions and the continuous advance of the Red Army. More and more civilians supported or even joined the partisans in 1943 and 1944,[34] and the irresolute ones did not want to expose themselves as possible collaborators with the "fascists" in the face of the Red Army's imminent arrival.

Despite repeated setbacks, German attempts to solve the partisan problem continued. The OKH ordered that all partisans should be treated as prisoners and no longer be shot after capture.[35] Locally, similar orders had already been issued in 1942,[36] but as of July 1943 they became official guidelines. The German war economy desperately needed laborers, and captured partisans promised a steady supply. The same rules applied to civilian populations evacuated from the "desert zones": they were deported to the Reich for labor according to orders from Hitler and Himmler in summer and fall 1943.

Next, the staff of Army Group Center and the Reichskommissariat Ostland almost simultaneously conceived an identical project promising lasting success: the *Wehrdörfer* (fortified villages).[37] In a number of selected villages relatively safe from partisan threat, the reliable civilian population was armed to protect itself and enjoyed a certain autonomous administration. The first step of this new project was to halt the losing of ground, the second to stabilize the situation. In the third and final step, the *Wehrdörfer* expanded into areas hitherto dominated by partisans. A mixture of military action and propagandistic attraction of these villages was considered key to success. By the time the project gained full pace in spring 1944, however, it was already too late; the last important German-occupied territory in the East was lost with the annihilation of Army Group Center in June and July 1944.

As a result, it is difficult to measure the success or failure of the *Wehrdörfer* project. Three points should be noted: first, the central and official guidelines for anti-partisan combat issued by the OKW in May 1944 stressed that the *Wehrdörfer* concept should become the pivotal point of all future anti-partisan policy.[38] Second, the partisans feared the *Wehrdörfer* more than any other German approach; it is revealing that post-1945 Communist historiography often described it as the most dangerous weapon of the "fascists" in the "people's war." And third, other armies showed a huge interest in the *Wehrdörfer* after 1945, particularly the French in Algeria and the

US Army and Marines in Vietnam, all of whom experimented with similar projects.

It remains debatable whether the Germans could have achieved better success in their anti-partisan war in the Soviet Union with a more moderate occupation policy. Even if this had run against national socialist ideology, scholars have recently argued that the relentless and brutal German approach did in fact hinder the partisan movement from spreading any further.[39] However, the Soviet regime could also interpret its partisan war as a success. With relatively few people and little effort, it was possible to unnerve the Germans in the rear areas. The costs for the Soviet population were of course disastrous,[40] but civilians were a disposable item in this ideological struggle between Nazism and Bolshevism.

German Anti-Partisan Warfare in Occupied France 1943–44

In contrast to its harsh and inflexible approach in the Soviet Union, Germany displayed a better understanding of occupation policies in the West, at least until 1942–43. The first years of the German occupation of France were a period of relative calm, due primarily to two factors. First, the French population lapsed into a state of shock following its unexpectedly swift and decisive defeat by the Wehrmacht in May–June 1940. Into the void, ultra-conservative groups emerged to take power under Marshal Philippe Pétain as head of Vichy France. They saw their opportunity to settle accounts with the detested political left from the interwar years, which meant that Vichy France was willing to collaborate with the German occupier in order to realize the *Révolution nationale*, an attempt to redirect French society towards the values embodied in its slogan *"Travail, famille, patrie"* (work, family, homeland).[41] The majority of the French did not really commit themselves to either collaboration or resistance, but rather awaited the outcome of the war – an attitude named *attentisme*.

Second, the Germans' occupation policies were adaptable to this special situation.[42] Initially, they placed only northern and western France under military administration.[43] The south, under the so-called Vichy government, remained formally independent until November 1942, although the government was never dissolved even in the later years of occupation. Vichy France was allowed to keep its administration and police forces active throughout the whole of France, which gave the population a false feeling of independence. The Germans were satisfied with installing only Feldkommandanturen (Field Garrison Headquarters) as the local occupation authorities in every French *département*. These Feldkommandanturen, consisting of only a handful of officers, controlled the French administration and police by personal contact with the administrative head of each *département*, the *préfet* (prefect); persons unreliable in German eyes were replaced with more loyal ones. The French police were eager to chase the hated Communists, and also cooperated with the Germans in the deportation of the Jews.[44] This occupation system, called Aufsichtsverwaltung (Supervision administration), worked in favor of the Germans until at least 1942, and could still be maintained in its core functions until their withdrawal in August 1944. It allowed the Germans to save administrative personnel as well as occupation troops: before the German retreat in August 1944, no more than 1,000 administrative personnel, along with 80,000 occupation troops, were needed to run a country of 40 million people.

The French resistance played a negligible role in the first years of the occupation. It consisted of two different branches: the Free French, the "outer resistance," who fought under the leadership of Charles de Gaulle as regular troops side by side with the Allies in North Africa, and later in Italy; and the "inner resistance" in metropolitan France, which is commonly referred to as the Résistance.[45] The Résistance was initially split up into dozens of different movements, but over the years two major groups prevailed: the Communists and the Gaullists (who can also roughly be described as the nationalists). The two groups disagreed about which tactics were most effective in a guerrilla campaign. The Communists advocated terrorist-like tactics, involving many small and immediate violent actions, irrespective of consequences. The Gaullists, however, preferred a more conventional approach. They wanted to build up gradually an effective resistance network all over France, acquiring weapons from Allied container air drops or from stocks of the dissolved French army. They felt that real combat against the occupier should not commence until Allied forces landed in France. De Gaulle, who in 1943 became the acknowledged leader of all resistance forces in France, tried to control the strategy from London, but in practice the Résistance followed both the Communist and Gaullist approaches. In February 1944 all armed resistance movements were united in the Forces Françaises d'Interieur (French Forces of the Interior, or FFI). The Communists, with their Francs-Tireurs et Partisans Français (French Free-Shooters and Partisans, or FTPF), managed to retain a certain amount of independence, which led to political quarrels in the provinces.

The Partisan War in Occupied France 1944

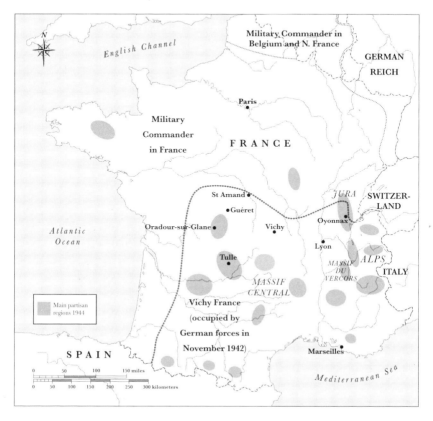

The first real acts of French resistance began in August 1941, following the German invasion of the Soviet Union. French Communists launched a bombing campaign against German soldiers, mainly in Paris. The effects were very limited; only a handful of people were killed or wounded. The German Militärbefehlshaber in Frankreich (Military Commander in France) wanted to shoot a limited number of hostages, but Hitler personally intervened. He considered this too "soft" a punishment, and ordered 100 hostages to be shot for every dead German soldier. The resulting quarrel, between the militaries in France on one side and Hitler and the OKW on the other, lasted for some months before it was decided that Communists and Jews should be deported to the East as future reprisals.[46] Furthermore, a new post of a Höherer SS- und Polizeiführer (Higher SS and Police Leader) was installed in France, and the tasks of the hitherto very small Sipo/SD branch in France were expanded. They became responsible for dealing with all questions involving Jews, reprisals, and hostages, undercutting the authority of the military administration. Until the end of the German occupation, the allocation of responsibilities in the struggle against the French resistance remained unclear and chaotic, especially after this combat became a military as well as a police task.[47]

In the fall of 1943, the Germans deployed military units in small quantities against the Résistance for the first time. A big stimulus for its growth was the Service du Travail Obligatoire (STO or Obligatory Labor Service), a mandatory service introduced in early 1943 by the Vichy Regime to funnel young Frenchmen to Germany to work in the war industry. Many of them tried to escape the STO by fleeing into remote areas, mainly in southern France. Their name, Maquisards or Maquis (meaning "scrub"), derives from the Corsican language and described their hideouts. Once outlaws, these youngsters did not automatically become resistance fighters,[48] but the Résistance was increasingly successful in gathering and organizing the Maquisards, a label which later became a synonym for the Résistance or the FFI. The British Special Operations Executive (SOE) and the American Office of Strategic Services (OSS) were also involved,[49] parachuting in military instructors such as "Jedburghs" to train the young men in guerrilla warfare. However, these efforts were too few and training circumstances prevented them from forming a fearsome partisan force. The military training of the French resistance remained inadequate throughout the German occupation, and the FFI was no match for the Germans when they met in combat.

The German Sipo/SD was able to set up a particularly effective counter-network and to slow the growth of the Résistance considerably. Their agents, recruited from French collaborators, regularly penetrated the Résistance cells. Their methods of collecting information were often inhumane, and brutal torture in their prisons was commonplace. They were also supported by the Milice Française (French Militia), an armed fascist and Vichyiste organization, although from spring 1944 onward the Germans rated them as ineffective and used them only for auxiliary tasks such as the execution of prisoners.

The first major military operations against the French resistance started in early 1944 in the French Alps and the French Jura. They were mainly carried out by the 157th Reserve Division, a training unit of low combat power.[50] The French resistance forces in the Jura dispersed immediately after the German attack, but came out of their hideouts as soon as the operation was over and the Germans had disappeared. In contrast, the battle on the Plateau de Glières in Savoy in late March 1944 ended with a heavy defeat for the local resistance forces. Here the FFI had tried to hold their positions, but it rapidly became obvious that they could not withstand major German forces in a conventional battle. The Résistance, however, ignored the lesson to be learned from this disastrous engagement.

When the Allies landed in Normandy on June 6, 1944 most resistance groups ignored all warnings from London to avoid an overhasty general uprising and attacked German convoys and garrisons with enthusiasm. The resulting conquest of some provincial towns in central France and the Jura, including St Amand, Guéret, Oyonnax and, most important, Tulle, was a short-lived victory. By mid-June the FFI had suffered heavy casualties and received the general order from London to consolidate and refrain from larger actions.

The swift suppression of this premature uprising was partly due to harsh German countermeasures.[51] As in the East, the Germans lacked troops to control vast areas in the hinterland, and settled on terror tactics as the best means of keeping the population submissive. Pushed by the OKW, the Oberbefehlshaber West (Supreme Commander West) issued the following order on June 8, 1944:

> In order to restore law and security, most stringent measures must be applied as a warning to the entire population. The population of the constantly infested areas must be deterred and lose all interest in accommodating resistance groups. Ruthless severity is imperative in this critical moment in order to ward off the danger in the back of our fighting troops [in Normandy] and to avoid larger sacrifices of our troops and the population in future.[52]

This exaggerated fear of getting cut off from supplies in Normandy, combined with a feeling of uncertainty in the face of a perceived national insurgency, led to a brutality hitherto unseen in France. Hence, the majority of significant atrocities against the French civil population happened in the week after D-Day.

When other factors were added to these fears, particularly ideological indoctrination or previous experience on the Eastern Front, the result was especially devastating. The infamous 2nd SS-Panzerdivision "Das Reich" committed numerous massacres on their march from southern

France to Normandy in June 1944.[53] In Tulle, the SS hanged 99 residents after they had retaken the town from the Résistance, and on June 10, 1944 a company of this division perpetrated the worst bloodbath of the German occupation. In Oradour-sur-Glane, in central France, they slaughtered 642 men, women, and children and set the small village on fire. By measures such as these, the Germans were able to restore order by mid-June, but the struggle seemed endless as the FFI had consolidated and emerged again by mid-July.

Between July 21 and early August, the Germans and the Résistance fought their biggest battle of the occupation in the mountain massif of the Vercors, near Grenoble.[54] Tactically similar to operations in Russia, almost 10,000 German soldiers encircled the plateau. Four battle groups consisting of mountain infantry, paratroopers, and armored infantry attacked and annihilated the 4,000 resistance fighters. As had happened on so many other occasions, this operation was accompanied by atrocities against the civilian population. Defeating the enemy was not enough, since the Germans did not have the manpower to hold the ground once the area was cleansed from resistance fighters, and they were well aware that the resistance movement could only survive with the support of the population. Thus, they used terror to deter the local farmers from delivering food to the Résistance.

In fairness, it should be noted that the Germans, thanks to their relatively effective intelligence service provided by the Sipo/SD, very often hit the "right" targets – that is, hidden Maquisards or their supporters. Generally speaking, the partisan war in the West was less indiscriminate and bloody than that in the East; only SS troops killed women and children, and only on rare occasions. The absence of a Nazi-ideological component in this struggle partly explains the more "moderate" form of anti-partisan warfare in the West.

After the war, General Eisenhower declared in his memoirs that the FFI had the combat value of 10 Allied divisions.[55] When the Allies broke through the Normandy front in early August, followed by their landing in southern France on August 15, the FFI was indeed able to take some isolated garrisons prisoner, often in concert with advancing Allied forces. They also succeeded in liberating some small territories by mid-August 1944, but this was mainly due to German withdrawals from remote areas, as every soldier was desperately needed on the crumbling Normandy front. Eisenhower's statement was hence more than exaggerated and the overall military effect of the FFI remained very limited. It is estimated that the FFI killed some 2,000 Germans, compared to the approximately 12,000 to 14,000 French, roughly one-third of them civilians, killed by the Germans.[56] In addition, the 6,000 French collaborators killed before the liberation demonstrates that France, as in so many insurgencies in history, also experienced a civil war.[57]

Conclusion

Who won the partisan war in World War Two – the Germans or the partisans? It can be best described as a stalemate. The partisans were able to create liberated areas, both in the East and (to a much lesser extent) the West, but they could never hold their territory once the Germans attacked. Thus, the partisan war was mainly decided by external factors, primarily the war on the front line. On both the Eastern and Western Fronts, the partisan war remained a sideshow for both sides, only a part of the larger military campaign. This was true even in Yugoslavia, the only place where the partisans, under Tito, achieved some lasting success. Their gains were facilitated by the strategic situation on other fronts, which demanded the withdrawal of German troops.[58] Thus, the political aspects of those insurgencies mostly played only a secondary role.

In German planning, short-lived victories against the partisans were generally enough to relieve the front for a certain period. Though the partisans never posed a serious threat to German rule, they were perceived as a constant danger. This psychological impact and a political legitimacy were perhaps their greatest achievement. On the other hand, German rule failed to offer an alternative to the population. A long-lasting substantial occupation policy was never tried and the policy applied in the East was based on suppression or even annihilation of certain sections of the population. The Germans were clearly able to defeat the insurgents militarily, but their lack of a deeper political understanding of the insurgencies hindered them from achieving a lasting success. Only the relatively moderate official guidelines of the *Merkblatt 69/2 Bandenbekämpfung* (Instructions 69/2 Bandit Combat) from spring 1944 pointed in the right direction for a modern counterinsurgency campaign, but they came far too late for the Eastern Front and did not show much effect in France.

Nevertheless, some Allied commanders considered the harsh German approach effective. In early 1945, the British, American, and French forces issued orders that, in the event of an insurgency in occupied Germany, all captured German partisans were to be shot on the spot.[59] Western countries also referred to German tactics after 1945.

In the case of the French, the struggles of the Résistance also shaped the mentality of many officers who later served in Indochina or Algeria. In an interview given more than 40 years later, one member of the feared Service Spéciaux (Special Services), General Aussaresses, confessed to the systematic torturing of prisoners in Algeria. His explanation was revealing: "In the [French] Résistance and within the Services [Spéciaux] friends told me that it is impossible to resist torture and that there would be a moment when it is legitimate to talk."[60] Likewise, Americans who later held key positions in the Vietnam War, such as Aaron Bank or William E. Colby, had been involved in guerrilla warfare as "Jedburghs" in France 1944. The influence of German anti-partisan warfare on Western counterinsurgency after 1945 has possibly been underestimated or neglected for a long time and hence will offer a wide field for academic research in future.

5

FRENCH IMPERIAL WARFARE 1945–62

Professor Douglas Porch

Although the French Army demonstrated commendable ability to adapt to the battlefield environment in the post-World War Two wars of independence in Indochina and Algeria, ultimately it lost these conflicts because its strategy was overly militarized, and its insurgent enemies produced a more compelling political scenario. Defeat was not pre-ordained, however. Paris might have avoided these long and costly colonial wars had it seized opportunities to craft policies aimed at the establishment of stable, independent countries with interests allied to those of France. Instead, a colonization project anchored in military conquest and occupation, and maintained through inflexible mechanisms of political and economic dependency, allowed a minority of disaffected activists to question the legitimacy of French rule.[1] Once challenged, France could offer no ideology to counter successfully that of indigenous nationalism. As the last French commander of Algeria noted, French psychological action failed "because it was incapable of finding a sentiment to exploit" that could match that of "the desire to see the departure of Europeans and achieve independence."[2] As a consequence, from the mid-1940s until the early 1960s, France was reduced to pursing wars of "reconquest" in Indochina and Algeria,[3] an over-militarization of strategy that played into the hands of determined nationalists who, although initially lacking means and organization, captured the political high ground by framing their rebellions as struggles for "national liberation."

In this and other respects, the wars in Indochina and Algeria shared common characteristics. Both the Viet Minh and Front de Libération Nationale (FLN) are paradoxical examples of the weak prevailing over the strong. Each used the defeat and occupation of France between 1940 and 1944 to question the right of the French to rule. Each took advantage of an absence of French presence or inattention to firmly establish their rebellion before Paris could react. Each war challenged the French military to innovate and adapt, which it did with some success. But each insurgency compensated for military weakness by internationalizing its cause, a task made easier by the bipolar, Cold War world of the 1950s. Each war presented a complex, multi-sided conflict in which both the insurgents and the French counterinsurgents contained competing factions.[4] And in each case the insurgents won, but with victory scenarios that were radically different.

Wars of Decolonization

Indigenous nationalism, which had been growing in both Indochina and North Africa in the interwar years, received an enormous boost from France's 1940 collapse. France's inability to defend either country called into question the legitimacy of rule from Paris. While colonialists subsequently blamed the weakness and defeatism of the Fourth Republic for debacles in both Indochina and Algeria, the truth was that imperialists forced their wars on a Republic whose citizens were never sold on the imperial project, not vice versa. Imperial lobbies, a catchbag of pro-imperial journalists, politicians, military, and occasionally business interests, were able to exercise influence beyond their numbers in a fragmented, multi-party parliament to sabotage political concessions that might have avoided long and bloody conflicts and produced outcomes more favorable to French interests. While popular support for these wars was increasingly eroded as the costs multiplied, resources devoted to the war effort were consistent with French capabilities and legal constraints. Paris was not defeated because its policies were confused or its political class divided, but because its strategies were overly militarized and anchored in visions of French grandeur out of place in the emerging Cold War world.

Indochina

The First Phase 1946–50

By the time General Leclerc de Hauteclocque disembarked at Saigon on October 5, 1945, at the head of a depleted division of French troops, the political dynamic in Indochina had already escaped the French. A coalition of nationalist groups known as the Viet Minh, led by the Communist Ho Chi Minh, had seized Hanoi and declared Vietnamese independence on September 2, 1945. British troops had managed to end the mayhem that had broken out in Cochinchina, Vietnam's southernmost province, while Chinese nationalists, invited by the Potsdam Agreement to restore order in the north, systematically plundered Tonkin. By February 1946, Leclerc had reestablished a semblance of French control south of the 16th parallel, as well as in Cambodia. Ho agreed to the reoccupation of Tonkin by 15,000 French troops in exchange for the departure of 180,000 rapacious Chinese, the recognition by Paris of Vietnam as a free state within the French Union, and the promise of a gradual withdrawal of French troops over five years. "It is better to sniff French dung for a while than eat China's all our lives," Ho is alleged to have said of this compromise.

This cohabitation was probably destined to be a tense one, even had hard-line colonialist Admiral Thierry d'Argenlieu, High Commissioner and commander-in-chief of French forces in Indochina from August 1945, not been determined to undermine it by encouraging regional secessionist movements, sabotaging negotiations, and escalating the small skirmishes between Viet Minh and French troops into full-scale warfare at Haiphong, the harbor city of Hanoi, from November 20, 1946. By December 21, with fighting spreading throughout the Red River Delta, the French and Ho Chi Minh were formally at war.

The French Army entered the Indochina War with serious handicaps. Disorganized by defeat in 1940, the army had only begun to rebuild itself, with US assistance, in 1943. Many of the units that had acquitted themselves best under Allied tutelage were North African units, serving under French officers. The rehabilitation of a logistical and support structure had been neglected in favor of raising combat units to strengthen French muscle in Allied councils of war. Consequently, the French in Indochina were short of mechanics and logisticians. These shortcomings were especially problematic as their hybrid army had complex logistical requirements, while they were forced to fight with an assortment of surplus weaponry which required different ammunition and spare parts. The fact that the Viet Minh weaponry steadily became more uniform and more lethal hardly boosted French morale. The Fourth Republic's first defense priority in 1945 was to create a force to occupy southwestern Germany. Members of the French Résistance who had been folded into the army that invaded France on the coattails of Anglo-American forces in 1944 were ill received and mostly expelled by 1946, leaving the officer corps under strength.

Indochina

French presence in Indochina had to be reconstructed from the ground up. Old Indochina hands had perished during the Japanese occupation, and with them went the repository of historical wisdom on the culture and languages of Vietnam. The army's older officers, veterans of World War One and the Riff War in Morocco (1924–25), and even younger ones who had served their apprenticeship in the Allied armies from 1943, brought to Indochina a strong professional tradition of adapting with imagination to tactical and operational problems. Unfortunately, the challenges of innovation using what was essentially a 19th-century force structure parachuted into a difficult operational environment of the post-colonial and atomic age, would prove overwhelming.

The French force in Indochina, whose numbers rose from 145,000 in 1950 to 235,000 by the war's end in 1954, combined North African and Senegalese colonial units whose enthusiasm to defend French imperialism was definitely on the wane, mixed with French *troupes de marine* and the Foreign Legion. This force was gradually augmented by a further 261,000 men from the "Associated States" of Vietnam, Laos, and Cambodia, forces of dubious provenance. This was a constabulary army adapted for imperial policing and was not an instrument well suited to fight a war of attrition against an elusive, resilient, and politically sophisticated foe. While the French adapted specialized commando, paratroop, and mechanized units for combat in Indochina's diverse and challenging environments, these became "wasting," or less effective, assets as cadres were killed off, recruitment dried up, training was curtailed, and the French lost the strategic initiative.

Initially at least, the French maintained an imperious sense of racial and martial superiority over the Vietnamese, whom they viewed as diminutive, effete, and querulous. Underestimating the enemy was hardly wise, given the weakness of French capabilities: with the priority placed on Europe, the army in Indochina was forced to scatter 80 percent of its troops in defensive positions across large swaths of territory – in 1951, for example, 82,000 French troops were immobilized in 920 posts to defend the Tonkin delta against an estimated 37,000 Viet Minh. Limited French air power was further compromised by poor meteorological conditions, Viet Minh camouflage, and eventually the acquisition of antiaircraft artillery; a small inventory of planes compromised paratroop operations and hampered the successful support of air bases. Intelligence was scarce because the Viet Minh, lacking radios, offered few opportunities for signals intelligence, while human intelligence suffered from the fact that anyone who cooperated with the French was murdered. As a result, units patrolled blind, making them vulnerable to ambushes and, hence, to casualties by a Viet Minh very well supplied with human intelligence, and eventually, with Chinese help, signals intelligence.

None of this might have been fatal had the French possessed a more realistic policy, for in 1946 Ho Chi Minh's Viet Minh numbered roughly 30,000 indifferently armed troops who had been driven into the mountainous redoubt of northern Tonkin. Viet Minh strengths included a smart and patient political leadership, superb organizing skills and the ruthlessness to apply them, deep political indoctrination that served as the foundation for iron discipline, and a blueprint for victory anchored in Mao's theories of revolutionary warfare. In Vo Nguyen Giap the Viet

Minh possessed one of the greatest strategic minds of the 20th century. The organizational structure of main-line, reserve, and militia forces allowed the Viet Minh to maintain the strategic initiative throughout a very geographically diverse campaign environment.

Hoping to avoid a pinprick war of raids and ambushes, the French reasoned that if they captured the Viet Minh leadership, the movement would shrivel, or at least be seriously disrupted. Decapitation strategies offer a popular option for counterinsurgents, who reason that the removal of a few leaders will disorganize and de-motivate the insurgency. When, on October 7, 1947, sticks of French paratroops floated out of recycled Junker 52s down on the Viet Minh "national redoubt" of Bac Can – a network of workshops, depots, and military headquarters in the Tonkin highlands near Tuyen Quan – the Viet Minh were caught by surprise. They fled into the jungle without a fight, leaving significant stocks of arms and munitions behind. But the Viet Minh leadership, whose capture had been the objective of Operation *Lea*, eluded them.

That might have defined the war for some time. Faithful to Mao's first phase of insurgency warfare, the Viet Minh restricted themselves to small raids and ambushes, while extending their political network. The French maintained superiority in firepower, were able to control the major population centers, keep main roads open, and occupy the vital rice growing areas in Cochinchina and the Red River delta of Tonkin. Politically, they established alliances of convenience with minority groups in Cochinchina, and convinced Catholics in Tonkin to abandon outright support for the nationalists. In 1948, Paris tried to seize the political initiative by reinstating the abdicated emperor of Vietnam, Bao Dai, with his own government.

But the long-term trends were unfavorable. The French lacked the manpower to be strong everywhere, and a surge in one region came at the cost of opening another to Viet Minh attack. Bao Dai claimed no constituency in Vietnam, and, to deflect charges that he was Paris' puppet, adopted a position of practical neutrality in the war. Therefore, no matter how aggressively the French Army patrolled, French strategy lacked a pacification dimension that should have been supplied by strong Vietnamese allies. The French Communist Party (PCF), which commanded roughly a quarter of the electorate, came out in open support of Ho Chi Minh in April 1947. The government, trying to reconstruct a France devastated by war, occupation, strikes, and inflation, was reluctant to dispatch troops to the other side of the world when it feared a civil war at home. Paris sought a political compromise with Ho, which put it at odds with the army, who argued that the Viet Minh were on the ropes. *Lea* had taught Ho Chi Minh the value of dispersing and entrenching his forces. Worse for Paris, the triumph of Chinese Communists to the north in 1949 offered the Viet Minh a powerful ally and patron. Viet Minh units traveled to southern China to be trained and equipped with mortars, artillery, and radios. They returned to put pressure on the isolated French garrisons strung along the Route Coloniale 4 (RC4) that paralleled the frontier with China from Lang Son to Cao Bang. When, in October 1950, the French decided to evacuate Cao Bang – the garrison lying at the extreme limit of the RC4 – along the tortuous road that wound through mountains and steep, limestone canyons, the Viet Minh mounted a huge ambush which cost the French 4,800 dead and threw the imperial forces away from the frontier and back to the Tonkin delta.

1950–53

The setback on the RC4 seemed to completely unhinge the French commander, General Marcel Carpentier, who prepared to evacuate Hanoi. The army's casualties mounted, and morale hit rock bottom. The Viet Minh now had a solid redoubt in northern Tonkin that backed on to a friendly China. In France, defeat inflamed a strident, PCF-led campaign against the "dirty war" that included demonstrations around trains carrying wounded and strikes at ports and military installations. The truth was that the war had become unpopular across the spectrum of left and center-left parties. The problem was that no one could figure out how to walk away from it – talk of withdrawal led to predictions of the massacre of loyal Vietnamese and elicited comparisons with the shame of 1940.

On the plus side, the outbreak of the Korean War in 1950 allowed the French to reframe Indochina as a front in the global struggle against communism to elicit US aid. The French also replaced Carpentier with World War Two hero General Jean de Lattre de Tassigny, who successfully thwarted a January 1951 Viet Minh offensive against the Tonkin delta, and then created the "de Lattre line," a ring of blockhouses and fortified positions to steel the delta against future offensives. Giap unwisely took this as a challenge. In March and again in May 1951, Viet Minh offensives were repulsed with heavy casualties as de Lattre organized a flexible defense backed by air reconnaissance and naval gunfire from river craft.

De Lattre's death in January 1952 left Raol Salan in command. Salan's arrival coincided with three innovations crafted to increase the size and the legitimacy of French Union forces, improve their strategic mobility, and get the French back on the offensive: Vietnamization, the *base aéroterrestre* (air-land base), and the *groupes mobiles* (mechanized infantry battalions). Vietnamization was an idea pushed by de Lattre as a force multiplier, as a way to legitimize the Bao Dai government, and as a vehicle to entice aid from Washington, eager to help as long as the war against communism could be divorced from the stigma of imperialism. Bao Dai declared a "general mobilization" of the Vietnamese population in July 1951. Vietnamese battalions were initially given French officers and NCOs, and paired with a French battalion. While this virtually doubled French strength in Vietnam, Vietnamization proved a disappointment: recruitment stalled; the best and most dedicated nationalists had been enlisted by the Viet Minh; and training and developing motivated, professional cadres proved to be difficult in the midst of fighting a war. Many of these Vietnamese units were consigned to isolated posts where morale plummeted and desertion skyrocketed.

The *base aéroterrestre* was inspired by the experience at Hoa Binh, a town east of the Tonkin delta taken by the French in 1951. Salan realized that Giap was perfectly content to allow the French to thrust forward, seize a territory, and then attack their supply lines and invest the garrison. The fight to extract forces from Hoa Binh had been far more difficult than the one to take the town, which was the point.

The remedy, or so it seemed, was to create air-supplied bases in the Viet Minh "rear" strong enough to withstand insurgent attacks. The first of these created at Na San was a resounding success – Giap took heavy casualties trying to overrun the interlocking defensive positions in November and December 1952. The French concluded that these *bases aéroterrestres* would be invulnerable, mainly because the Viet Minh lacked the logistical capability to bring heavy weapons and enough munitions against them in a sustained siege. After an attack lasting barely a few days, the insurgents were obliged to withdraw.

This was the defensive part of the strategy. The offense was to be supplied by *groupes mobiles*. A concept transferred from North Africa, *groupes mobiles* (GM) were essentially mechanized infantry battalions placed in Dodge trucks and half-tracks that motored along the roads of Vietnam to attack Viet Minh forces and relieve beleaguered garrisons. An amphibious version utilizing Alaska "weasels" and Mississippi "alligators" was developed for Cochinchina. De Lattre expanded the GMs as part of his mobile defense of the Tonkin delta in 1951. Service in the GMs was considered preferable to the intolerable boredom of static posts. Unfortunately, they were most useful in areas with developed road networks, like the Tonkin delta. Elsewhere, the GMs became strung out and vulnerable to ambush, and lacked mechanics to keep them efficient, while heavy personnel demands were a drain on other units.

The End Game in Indochina

By 1953, the French government was desperate to exit Indochina. The death of Stalin and the end of the Korean War found Beijing looking for a *détente* with the West. The Americans were complaining about the lack of French commitment to the war. When, in December 1953, Ho Chi Minh offered to negotiate a settlement, the French took the bait. Talks were to begin on April 26 in Geneva to end the war. The time seemed propitious: the French had scored some tactical successes with an airborne raid on Lang Son, and some spoiling operations around Hué in Annam and in the Tonkin delta. The French wanted a thumping success to capture the momentum in the negotiations. By creating a *base aéroterrestre* at Dien Bien Phu, the French commander General Henri Navarre sought to protect indigenous allies in upper Tonkin, deny the opium crop to the Viet Minh, and repeat the success of Na San in 1952.

It proved a desperate mistake. Dien Bien Phu would be no repeat of Na San. Giap was able to muster significant Chinese support to acquire artillery and antiaircraft guns. He also created a logistical structure to resupply munitions once the initial allotment had been expended. Furthermore, with the outcome of the negotiations at stake, the Communists were prepared to bet everything on a final throw of the dice. Consequently, the French overreached by placing themselves in a remote location 300 kilometers from Hanoi that they could not support, in an extremely disadvantageous tactical position. Neither General René Cogny, the regional commander, nor Colonel Christian de Castries, the garrison commander, were up to the task, and some of the imperial units were distinctly unwilling to die for the French Empire. At 12 battalions, the garrison was too small to hold back a 60,000-man Viet Minh force supported by trucks, a massive mobilization of porters, and artillery.

When Giap's artillery opened fire from the hills above the French base on March 13, 1954, the French were astonished by its volume and accuracy. One by one the base's strong points were submerged by human wave attacks. Artillery soon prevented planes from landing, so that supplies, parachuted from ever higher altitudes, benefited the Viet Minh more than the French. At huge costs, Giap overwhelmed the final strong point, Isabelle, on May 7. France's US and British allies did nothing on the tactical and operational level to aid a relief of the siege, and the French raised the white flag. On June 24, 1954, GM 100 was ambushed and lost 1,200 men, plus all of its artillery and vehicles, near An Khé. On June 17, Geneva had divided Vietnam at the 17th parallel, making way for the subsequent Americanization of the war there by the end of the decade.

Algeria

Hardly had the Geneva accords concluded than the French faced another, more fateful challenge in North Africa. Algeria became the cauldron of two civil wars other than the main event between the FLN and France that was initiated by the bombings of November 1, 1954 and continued beyond the Evian accords of March 19, 1962 that officially ended the conflict.[5] While battling the French, Algerian nationalists simultaneously engaged in an often murderous fratricide for political ascendancy, one that continued after independence in orgies of score settling with political rivals, minority political factions, and Algerian Muslims reckless enough to have supported France. Likewise, diehard proponents of *Algérie française* – whose core constituencies were anchored by colonial, special forces, and intelligence units of the French military, and in the roughly one million European settlers in Algeria known colloquially as *pieds noirs* – contributed to the overthrow of the Fourth Republic in 1958, violently opposed Charles de Gaulle's policy of "self-determination" for Algeria, and continued a terrorist war against the Fifth Republic as part of the Organisation armée secrète (OAS).

The surprise offensive launched by the newly formed FLN on November 1, 1954, comprising 70 bombings throughout Algeria that left 10 dead, was a declaration of war on the French state. It also represented a leap of faith, if not folly, by a handful of militants impatient with the hesitations of moderate nationalists in the Mouvement nationalist Algérienne (MNA) and eager to unite nationalists around the idea of armed struggle. Violent acts calculated to strike the imagination aimed to rekindle a spirit of resistance to the French conquest and to recall memorable precursors: 19th-century leader Abd el-Kader; the Sétif uprising of May 1945; and a popular folklore of *jihad* and banditry.[6] Therefore, the legitimacy of the FLN, in its own eyes, sprang from the lineage of resistance to French rule and its willingness to fight. Algerian Muslim society unquestionably took notice of the November 1 bombings, especially in the Constantinois of eastern Algeria, traditionally Algeria's hotbed of militant Islam and insurrection. Some joined a rebel *maquis* in the Aurès Mountains of southeastern Algeria. But most Muslims, mindful of the precedent of Sétif (when an estimated 15,000–20,000 Muslims perished in a campaign of French retaliation), concluded that fence-sitting offered the most attractive option.

Until the summer of 1955, Paris was slow to react to the growing menace in Algeria. There was a perfectly sound explanation for this – France was attempting to play a world role that far exceeded its modest means. The FLN declaration of war caught France at a bad time. Although still licking its wounds from the debacle at Dien Bien Phu and the surrender of Indochina at the Geneva Conference, Paris nevertheless maintained ambitions to garrison South Vietnam. Nationalist agitation in the French protectorates of Morocco and Tunisia captured the attention of officials, and sucked up many of its remaining forces.[7] By comparison, Algeria was quiet. On November 1, 1954, the 10th Military Division numbered only 58,000 troops and 2,300 gendarmes, responsible for a population equal to a quarter of that of the mainland and an area two-thirds the size of France, excluding the Sahara.[8] The one million *pieds noirs* were concentrated in the cities, a migration accelerated since 1945 in the Constantinois by the Sétif rebellion. Vast areas of the country, especially the remote Aurès, seldom saw a French official, and consequently reverted to a no man's land of bandits and self-sufficient communities. The relative weakness of France's presence in Algeria combined with the post-November 1954 crackdown on the FLN's Muslim rivals furnished the FLN with vital time to survive and grow.

The refusal of Muslims to enlist immediately in the cause exposed the naiveté of the FLN founders, most of whom were of rural origins, poorly educated, and innocent of the world outside Algeria. Unlike the Viet Minh, the FLN had no mass following, no coherent ideology, and no organizational structure to extend a presence throughout Algeria. Its goal of national independence, while potentially appealing to many Muslims, was vague and short on specifics, such as how to incorporate Algeria's

Algeria

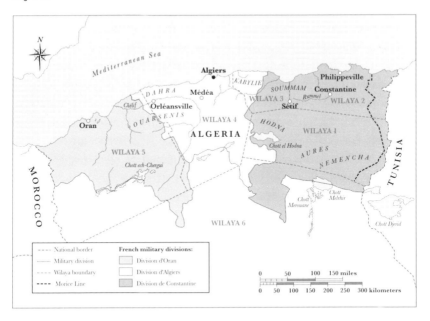

significant European and Jewish populations into an independent, Muslim-dominated republic.

On the ground, the insurgents quickly encountered the difficulties of cobbling together a movement in a sociologically diverse population with complex systems of clans, notables, clients, local customs, and even blood feuds. The assumption that logistics would take care of themselves, because "the people" would feed them, proved illusory. As a consequence, the FLN came to realize that it must impose itself on the population, with brutality if necessary.[9] Its tactics were condemned by the MNA leader Messali Hadj as "adventurist" when not suicidal, immoral, and a disservice to the cause of Algerian nationalism.[10] Even the Parti communiste Algérien, which habitually extolled armed resistance as a vehicle of social progress in occupied France, China, Indochina, and Madagascar, found the home-grown version little to their liking.[11] Only gradually did the FLN evolve a political-administrative structure called the *nizam*; a central directorate called the Comité national de la République Algérienne (CNRA), formed in 1958 in Cairo and led by the Comité de coordination et d'exécution (CCE); as well as a military force named the Armée de libération nationale (ALN), organized into regions *(wilayas)*. But even then,

French repression combined with internal feuds to decimate its cadres, keep its forces on the defensive, and prevent its regions from communicating.[12]

The French rode to the rescue by cracking down on moderate Muslims whose names peopled police files, and dissolving their organizations, at a stroke mortally wounding the FLN's in-house competition. Over time, the arbitrary brutality of French repression combined with the dislocations caused by French counterinsurgency tactics to transform a trickle of FLN sympathizers and recruits into a torrent. But this was later. In the spring of 1955, the FLN could only register disappointment that an offensive anticipated to intimidate the French and ignite a Muslim uprising against French rule seemed to have barely resonated in a Muslim population believed to be a tinderbox of rebellion. Operationally, the FLN appeared capable only of fighting a low-level insurgency that combined crop burning, attacks on isolated farms, occasional bombings, and assassinations of pro-French Muslims. A new, more spectacular tactic had to be crafted to commit the Muslim population to the rebellion.

On August 20, 1955, swarms of Muslim peasants, armed with knives and shotguns and led by the FLN, attacked Europeans in several towns in the northeast Constantinois. When the day was over, 123 lay dead and another 223 wounded. Masterminded by a militant named Zighout Youcef, the attack had been planned to coincide with the second anniversary of the exile by the French of the Sultan of Morocco. In this way, Zighout sought to link the uprising in Algeria with nationalist agitation in Morocco and Tunisia, and force the Muslim population to commit to the cause, thereby demonstrating to France and to international opinion that the French faced a war of independence, and not simply isolated attacks of "bandits and outlaws." In the process, he hoped to showcase the FLN's operational effectiveness, divert the French Army from attacks on ALN *katibas* (companies) in the Aurès, and provoke a French reaction that would make political reconciliation impossible.

Zighout had calculated well. Predictably, French retribution proved swift and brutal: with Sétif-like thoroughness, "Arab-hunting" *pied noir* "militias" seconded police and military units deployed to wipe out "centers of rebellion" in the fly-blown *mechtas* (Muslim villages) of the Constantinois and the Arab shantytowns of Philippeville. Depending on the source, between 2,000 and 12,000 Muslims were slaughtered. Zighout had succeeded beyond his wildest dreams in enlarging the gulf between Muslim and non-Muslim in Algeria. The policy of outreach to the Muslim population and reform heretofore pursued by Jacques Soustelle, Governor General of Algeria, began to unravel. 61 Muslim deputies serving in the French National Assembly condemned the repression, a first step in a progressive boycott by Muslims of French institutions of government. In January 1956, Ferhat Abbas, the symbol of Muslim accommodation, defected to the FLN, as did the conservative *oulémas* (religious scholars). The MNA began to hemorrhage cadres to the FLN in the Constantinois, although violence and rivalries between "Messalists" and the FLN continued in Algiers, the Oranie, and among Algerian migrants in France. The FLN's great fear – that moderate Muslims might be enticed by reforms into the cause of *Algérie française* – receded over the horizon. France was now at war.[13]

Activists met secretly in the Soummam Valley in Kabylia on August 20, 1956 to develop a strategy and regularize the organization tasked to carry it out. ALN structures were standardized, and the embryo of a bureaucracy began in the form of a three-man political-administrative committee at each command level to create parallel governments to collect funds and intelligence, organize logistics, call popular assemblies, give opinions on military operations, and generally control the population.[14] Many of the directives were dead on arrival because they were ignored, ill-adapted to local situations, or simply out of touch with the war's evolving dynamics. The conference also served to point out growing divisions between guerrillas in the "interior," who felt that they were bearing the brunt of the war, and those abroad, who focused on acquiring arms and publicizing the FLN cause – a gulf exacerbated by the frontier barriers. However, it is incontestable that the FLN/ALN had acquired a more coherent ideology, political goals, and political/military structure.

French Reaction

Until what became known as the "Philippeville massacres" of August 1955, French strategy had been to appease, rather than confront, Muslim nationalism in Algeria. It was a policy dictated by weakness rather than generosity. Now all of that changed. A state of emergency was declared throughout the three *départements* of Algeria, a first step in the surrender of civilian power there to the military. Service for French conscripts lengthened from 18 to 36 months in some categories; reservists were recalled; garrisons were repatriated from Indochina, Morocco, and Tunisia to bolster a wafer-thin military presence in Algeria. By 1959, almost 450,000 French troops and gendarmes had settled on Algeria, supplemented by around 200,000 Muslims in French service, commonly known as *harkis*.[15]

Nevertheless, despite a century of presence in Algeria and a long experience in counterinsurgency warfare, the French Army was slow to adapt to the terrain. The side that France turned out for war in Algeria offered what French historian Jean-Charles Jauffret calls a "two speed army" that combined conscripts scattered in isolated, morale-extinguishing posts with a "strategic reserve" of hard-hitting, largely professional companies who rushed about the country like firemen trying to localize and exterminate ALN *katibas*.[16] Initially, all divisions were under strength and under officered. Detachments returned from Indochina exhausted and depleted. With veterans declining to re-enlist and soldiers deserting at high rates, units topped up with young, inexperienced recruits.[17] Until the advent of the Challe offensives in 1959, the French lacked a culture of inter-arm cooperation, staff liaison, and what today would be called "jointness" – the ability and willingness of all services to cooperate toward a common goal. Well-equipped professionals, with their distinctive uniforms, repaid the envy of conscripts with disdain. By the time of the putsch of April 1961, the French Army was at war with itself.[18]

France's first two commanders in Algeria, Paul Cherrière and Henri Lorillot, had spent their earlier careers in command of Muslim troops. But they could do little more than attempt to isolate the Aurès and extinguish flare-ups of violence wherever they appeared. Raoul Salan, who arrived in Algeria in December 1956 in the wake of the failed invasion of Suez – meant from Paris' perspective to punish Egyptian President Gamel Abdel Nasser for his support of the FLN – imposed a whole new dynamic on the French effort. An officer of long experience in the French colonies, in French intelligence, and ultimately commander in Indochina, Salan doubled as Commander-in-Chief and Governor General to oversee a panoply of organizations tailored to extinguish rebellion.

A particularly worrisome consequence for the French government of the Indochina defeat was that it put a portion of the army in a bad mood. Most were spring-loaded to blame the Indochinese debacle on the vacillation of the Fourth Republic, the lack of US support, and the ignorance and indifference of the French people. These men found their expression and guiding idea in "*la guerre révolutionnaire*," a theory refined in 1953 by Colonel Charles Lacheroy, a controversial French intelligence officer with strong Catholic and conservative views. Based on his reading of Mao and his analysis of intelligence reports on the Viet Minh, Lacheroy concluded that the success of the Communists in Indochina lay in their use of propaganda and psychological action, and in their ability to create parallel hierarchies to control the population.

Lacheroy's theories fell like a conversion experience on a generation of professional officers humiliated by France's defeats in 1940 and 1954, and baffled by how poorly armed insurgents could defeat a modern army. *La guerre révolutionnaire* supplied an intellectual unity to a multi-pronged French strategy in Algeria. A fundamental assumption of proponents of *la guerre révolutionnaire* was that all insurgencies were part of a global Communist strategy to subvert the West. Hence, Algeria must be severed from contact with neighboring countries, through which supplies and recruits arrived, by frontier barriers. Second, the population must be segregated from the insurgents through resettlement in camps or fortified villages administered and secured by the French. Third, a plan of economic development in Algeria that became known as the Constantine Plan was to be put in place to alleviate grinding Muslim poverty. Finally, France would launch a joint military offensive to break the back of the insurgency.

Of all the French counterinsurgency tactics, that of the barriers was perhaps the most successful. After their independence in 1956, Morocco and especially Tunisia had become bases for the FLN, sources of arms supplied in part by Cairo and Communist eastern Europe, and places to train soldiers drawn from swarms of refugees fleeing the war. The Morice Line that ran from the Sahara to the sea along the common frontier between Algeria and Tunisia was the more sophisticated of the French barriers, combining electrified fences, fields of anti-personnel and "jump" mines, radar-guided artillery, and constant air surveillance. An ALN offensive, known as the "Battle of the Frontiers," launched in the first five months of 1958, proved disastrous. The ALN calculated that only 22 of every hundred men hurled at the line were able to break through, a staggering 78 percent casualty rate of killed, wounded, captured, and missing. Even these were quickly mopped up by mobile forces deployed behind lines.[19]

Resettlement, an old counterinsurgency tactic, began spontaneously in the army in the fall of 1955 to create "free fire zones." For the military, the benefits of resettlement were obvious: it weakened logistical support for the FLN; created centers of security as part of an "oil spot" of French prosperity; provided the Muslim population with access to schools, clinics, modernized housing, jobs, and commercial activities; and allowed for focused psychological action campaigns. These groupings were under the authority of Section Administrative Spéciale (SAS) officers, heirs to the old Arab Bureau, who dispensed propaganda prepared by the 5e (psyops) Bureau of the General Staff, kept a sharp eye for FLN infiltration of the camps, and organized *autodéfense* groups of *harkis* to protect these villages and act as force multipliers for regular French forces. Eventually, between two and three million Muslims, approximately half of Algeria's rural population, were displaced.[20]

Critics, however, saw resettlement as a disaster, part of a "scorched earth" policy that created zones of misery and discontent among now humiliated and unemployed peasants crowded into unsanitary camps behind barbed wire and watchtowers. In April 1959, *Le Monde* broke the story on a government report that underlined the misery and skyrocketing infant mortality in the camps, one which bolstered the FLN's case at the United Nations.[21] The government tried to respond by selling the camps as a "project for rural innovation" and creating an inspectorate to improve conditions. But few believed that the welfare of the Muslim population would take priority over the army's tactical concerns.[22] Such was the fate of the Constantine Plan, prepared under the Fourth Republic and announced by de Gaulle in October 1958. The plan's attempt to transform Algeria into an industrial center, anchored in gas and oil from the Sahara and by a massive construction program of house building, never got off the ground.[23]

Probably the greatest success from the French perspective of the "resettlement" enterprise was the recruitment of indigenous forces. Of course, this was a long tradition in every colonial empire, without which none could have existed. For France, the *harkis* served less as an effective "force multiplier," although some did engage in offensive operations with main-line units. More importantly, they became a symbol of active Muslim support for France, and diminished ALN claims to be a "national army." The reality on the ground was often very different, however. Motives for becoming a *harki* were more personal than political, propelled by clan loyalties or mere personal survival. Families sometimes placed sons in both the FLN and the *harkis* to hedge their bets. They were vulnerable to infiltration, and the French never fully trusted them. This did not save many of them from horrible reprisals at the hands of the FLN at the war's end.[24]

The FLN struggled to adapt to French counterinsurgency methods by becoming a much more ruthless, violent, even paranoid organization. While this opened the FLN/ALN to charges that it ruled through fear and intimidation, apologists countered that it was well adapted to a war fought by a community that traditionally had to survive without benefit of outside mediating forces.[25] The sad truth was that no side in this war appeared able to control the excesses of its combatants, unfortunately a frequent occurrence in an insurgency in which the political nature of war is apparent down to platoon level. In the long term, however, the war's growing brutality consolidated the FLN position by enforcing loyalty or "neutrality" among Muslims, while it discredited and undermined France's claim to hold the moral high ground.

As FLN delegates met in the Soummam valley in the summer of 1956, the French and the FLN squared off in Algiers. In many respects, the "battle of Algiers" offered the signature encounter of the war, an almost casual escalation that began as a spring strike by Muslim *lycée* students, followed by a tit-for-tat bombing campaign between the FLN and overmatched *pied noir ultras* well represented in the Algiers police. Each side brought its strategic fantasies to the contest. For Paris and the *pieds noirs*, military intimidation and repression in the form of General Jacques Massu's 10th Paratroop Division would force the Muslims back into submission. FLN operatives such as Larbi Ben M'Hidi calculated that a combination of bombs and a general strike called on January 28, 1957 to show evidence of popular support for the FLN could produce a second Dien Bien Phu, even as he ordered his troops into the teeth of *la guerre révolutionnaire*'s most formidable mechanisms of repression – psychological action, intelligence collection, and torture – at high tactical and operational cost. While Massu's paras crushed the FLN with mechanical efficiency, capturing the mastermind of the campaign, Yacef Saadi, in September 1957 and killing Ali La Pointe, the last bomber, two weeks later, the strategic payoffs for the FLN were undeniable, despite an apparent defeat for the insurgency. The battle of Algiers laid bare the racism and violence of the war for all to see.

The year 1957 proved to be a bad one for the image of the French Army. Torture and the disappearances of dissidents and detainees in military custody kick-started a heretofore sluggish antiwar movement. The FLN might be a brutal bunch, but French citizens increasingly concluded that, if their country had to descend to the level of murder and torture to win, then the game was not worth the candle.[26]

The Challe Offensive

In February 1959, the new French Commander-in-Chief in Algeria, Air Force General Maurice Challe, kicked off a new offensive; an 11th-hour surge thrown into a war that had already been forfeited. Challe coordinated a formidable offensive force able to synchronize aggressive ground and air attacks. Tracker units, known as *commandos de chasse*, made up of French and Muslim troops, combined with air reconnaissance relentlessly to track FLN *katibas* that, once located, were destroyed by helicopter-borne forces. For the FLN, who until then had basked in "liberated zones," barely bothered by French conscripts who sometimes patrolled out of their forward operating bases only to shut themselves in at night, this was the beginning of the real war. French forces – supported by mobile airfields and loyal Muslim soldiers whose numbers were doubled by Challe – deployed in an area for days, broke into mobile groups that patrolled at night, and laid ambushes on trails that heretofore had been FLN highways. Resistance only brought down a hail of artillery and napalm. Military operations were accompanied by aggressive resettlement of the local population, occupation of water sources, targeting of FLN tax collectors and political structures in towns and villages, and the shooting of livestock, especially the mules the FLN used to transport the wounded. Soon, surviving FLN *djoundi* (soldiers) were reduced to eating roots, and suffering the pangs of hunger and food poisoning.[27]

The Challe offensive cost the ALN an estimated half of its soldiers, caused a morale crisis among the ranks, and set the ALN and the GPRA at each other's throats. Nevertheless, it could not break a deeply entrenched enemy, especially as it could not be sustained. The Challe plan was a traveling circus that settled on one area, cleaned it up, and moved on. ALN *djoundi* simply buried their heavy weapons, planted mines to slow pursuit, broke into small groups, used intelligence to locate the seams of the French *ratissages* (sweeps) through which to escape, and went to ground, depending on families who set aside the "*djoundi's* portion" of each meal to feed them. Challe's sweeps could neither snuff out acts of terrorism nor prevent the FLN cells from reconstituting. Time was on their side, for from 1960, de Gaulle was dealing with a civil war of his own: one that required a redeployment of French forces to Algeria's major cities to deal with disaffected *pieds noirs* protesting at his plan for "self-determination" for Algeria.[28]

De Gaulle

Unfortunately for Paris, the French military began to succeed operationally just as France's political position in Algeria crumbled. When, in May 1958, Charles de Gaulle seized the reins of the French Republic in the wake of an unprecedented rebellion of the French military, he was greeted as France's savior. But Frenchmen disagreed on where the peril lay. For some, de Gaulle's appeal resided in his ability to corral the French Army that had taken over many civilian functions in Algeria, and its *pied noir* allies. In contrast, proponents of *Algérie française* looked to the General to preserve France's position in Algeria. Upon taking office, de Gaulle probably retained an open mind on the future of Algeria. On September 16, 1959, he promised *"autodétermination"* to Algeria. And although *"la francisation complète"* was one of the options, the fact that other options were on the table, including *"la sécession,"* was considered ominous by proponents of *Algérie française*. This made it all the more urgent for de Gaulle to reestablish the authority of the French state, beginning with the army. In December 1958, General Salan was recalled and the position of Governor General restored to civilian control, the first step in the progressive re-civilianization of the administration and police forces. The recall of the popular Massu, regarded by the *pieds noirs* as the hero of the battle of Algiers, in January 1960 provoked a week-long riot in Algiers known as *"l'insurrection des barricades."* The failure of this rebellion deprived the opposition of leadership, which was either arrested or in flight, and reinforced de Gaulle's popularity with the French.[29] De Gaulle toured garrisons in Algeria to explain the requirement for obedience and legality, and briefly opened talks with the FLN at Melun in June 1960. Outreach to the enemy was accompanied by proscriptions against torture and the recall of reservists from the legal profession to investigate the abuse of detainees. And although these measures were vigorously resisted by the military command, clearly the high tide of *la guerre révolutionnaire* had crested. In 1961, the government began to dismantle the resettlement camps, over the protests of the military, and stopped executing FLN prisoners.

De Gaulle's visit to Algeria in December 1960 witnessed widespread pro-independence demonstrations by Muslims waving FLN flags. Seeing the writing on the wall, a group of dissident officers formed an Organisation armée secrète (OAS) in Madrid in January, and began a campaign of assassination against officials, to include attempts on the life of the General himself. In April 1961, disaffected military units led by Challe and Salan seized control of Algiers and denounced de Gaulle's "government of abandonment." The French President went on the radio to forbid any soldiers to follow the orders of the putschists. With the support of only a minority of diehard professional regiments, the attempted putsch collapsed. Many of the leading proponents of *la guerre révolutionnaire* were now in prison or on the run. Politically, it was a godsend to de Gaulle, because it allowed opponents of the war to rally behind defense of the Republic.

However, not only did the war not cease, but it also spread to Europe where, from August 1958, the FLN and the MNA battled to control 350,000 Algerian workers in France. Maurice Papon was brought back from Algeria and installed as Prefect of Police in Paris to create a climate of insecurity for Algerian workers. When the FLN began to attack police and military targets in France, Papon launched a campaign of internment, summary arrests, deportations based on anti-terrorist legislation, and repression that rivaled that of the worst days of the battle of Algiers, culminating in the brutal police repression of an FLN demonstration in Paris on October 17, 1961.[30]

On March 19, 1962, after 11 days of negotiations at Evian, a ceasefire was declared. While the official war ended, violence continued. An OAS-inspired *pied noir* demonstration was brutally put down on March 26. Salan's capture, on April 30, 1962, turned the cautious exodus into a *sauve qui peut* (every man for himself) of *pieds noirs*, Jews, and Muslims who had been loyal to France from Algeria. Faced with a huge influx of refugees into France, officials began to distinguish between "Muslim" and "European" French, in effect unilaterally stripping Muslims of their French nationality, and in the process condemning many *harkis* to brutal retaliation.[31]

Conclusion

The French Army proved to be fairly innovative on an operational and tactical level in its Asian and North African theaters of conflict. But this virtue could save it in neither Indochina nor Algeria because the legitimacy of the political objective was compromised. There was no way to engage a population with a message of colonialism – with its subtext of defeat, racial and economic domination, and humiliation – at a time of growing anti-imperialism in the early Cold War years. And without a credible political message, the ability and the mechanisms for carrying out a viable pacification policy eluded the French. It might have been possible to defeat the Viet Minh or the FLN had the French attempted sooner to hand over power to moderate nationalists who would create a government favorable to French interests. But the political will to achieve this goal in the context of a weak Fourth Republic was lacking.

The insurgents in both Indochina and Algeria proved to be formidable opponents: tough minded, focused, resilient. Each was able to leverage inflexible French policy and repression, and to combine propaganda and brutality to dominate or eliminate potential internal rivals. Both insurgencies were able to appeal to the international community to compensate for their military weakness. Neighbors and sympathizers offered the insurgents support and sanctuary, without which they might not have survived, much less prevailed. Meanwhile, while there was some US support for France in Indochina, there was no such support for French goals in Algeria. In the case of Algeria, the Atlantic alliance turned its back on France's war, a policy which incidentally helped drive France from NATO's integrated military forces by the mid-1960s and, in turn, led to tempestuous Franco-American relations for decades thereafter.

Finally, French military operations, while innovative, never really eliminated the insurgents' ability to regenerate their fighting power. Indeed, off-the-shelf, heavy-handed, overly militarized strategies helped, if not to throw the population into the arms of the insurgency, then at least to create a constituency to replace those who had been killed or arrested. As in so many cases before and since, the French military seemed to be fighting war for war's sake, and to have lost sight of the fact that its organized violence should have been calculated to achieve a political objective. In the end, escalation of the conflict benefited the insurgents rather than the French, and ruptured the post-1945 French goal to remain among the rank of the Cold War powers via a revival of imperialism.[32]

6

FROM SEARCH AND DESTROY TO HEARTS AND MINDS

The Evolution of British Strategy in Malaya 1948–60

Dr Richard Stubbs

During the Malayan Emergency, which lasted from June 1948 to July 1960, the Malayan Communist Party's (MCP) armed wing, the Malayan Races Liberation Army (MRLA), and its support organization, the Min Yuen, sought to overthrow the British colonial administration and later, after independence in 1957, the Malayan government. The Emergency is well known for two reasons. First, it is an example of a government decisively defeating an insurgency. Second, it introduced the term "winning the hearts and minds" – a phrase made popular by General Sir Gerald Templer, the British High Commissioner in Malaya from 1952 to 1954 – into the counterinsurgency lexicon. This chapter examines the evolution of the British counterinsurgency strategy as it sought to come to grips with the MCP threat, and provides an evaluation of the role of the "hearts and minds" approach and its relevance for other counterinsurgency campaigns.

The Emergency began in a haphazard manner, with neither side fully prepared for an all-out insurgency. The Communists had not deployed all their forces into the jungle when a number of relatively autonomous units began an unauthorized campaign of extortion and robbery that culminated in the killing of three British planters on June 16, 1948. Public outrage at the murders forced the colonial government to declare a "State of Emergency" eventually covering the whole of the country. However, the British administration was equally as unprepared as the MCP. It lacked both solid information about the various MRLA units and a proper appreciation of the Communists' links with the ethnic Chinese community, which constituted about 38 percent of the total population of five million, and from which they drew the bulk of their support.

Over the next three years the insurgency grew in intensity. The MCP built on widespread dissatisfaction with the shortages of food, the high cost of living, the continuing corruption, and the increasing repression of labor. The Min Yuen delivered food, information, funds, and recruits to the MRLA units, and was responsible for generating propaganda materials and providing communications throughout the peninsula. The number of insurgents rose from about 2,000 in 1948 to nearly 8,000 by the end of 1951, with 10,000–15,000 regular workers in the Min Yuen and about ten times as many active adherents of one sort or another.[1] Similarly, on the government side, more battalions of the Malay Regiment were quickly formed and more British, and later Commonwealth, troops were shipped into the peninsula to increase the size of the army from 10 infantry battalions in 1948 to 19 by October 1950. The numbers in the police quickly grew from over 10,000 to nearly 17,000 (mostly Malays) in early 1950, plus 30,000 special constables (again mostly Malays). The incidence of violent clashes rose steadily over the next three years, culminating in more than 1,000 insurgents and 500 security forces killed during 1951. Civilian deaths also increased to over 500 in 1951.[2]

From 1952 onward, the government gradually gained the upper hand as the shift from a predominantly "search and destroy" approach to a new "hearts and minds" strategy began to take effect. By 1953 the 23 infantry battalions (some 30,000 armed troops, of which 22,000 were combat troops), and the 30,000 police and 41,000 special constables, in combination with the considerably augmented civil service, started to put the insurgents on the defensive.[3] During the last few weeks of 1953, the MCP leader, Chin Peng, was forced to move his headquarters across the border into Thailand. From 1953 onward, civilian casualties dropped off markedly, as did the number of security forces killed. Nevertheless, the insurgency remained a continuing problem, with estimates indicating that there were still more than 6,000 insurgents in the jungle at the beginning of 1954. But, as the government's strategy proved increasingly effective, more and more insurgents were killed or surrendered, and the numbers began to drop significantly. By the end of 1955, the estimated strength of the MRLA was down to 3,000. The granting of independence in 1957, which increased the rate of surrender, and a series of security forces' successes further reduced the MRLA to fewer than 400 by late 1958.[4] The remnants of the MCP's army were forced to join their leaders on the border area with Thailand and on July 31, 1960, the government declared victory.

The Government's Initial Search and Destroy Strategy

The government interpreted the outbreak of violence as a conspiracy by a relatively small number of armed agitators who had to be eliminated so that law and order could be restored. Senior members of the government had little appreciation of either the strength of support for the MCP insurgents within the ethnic Chinese community, or how insurgency warfare was conducted and, hence, what countermeasures might be most effective. The focus of attention was on eradicating the Communist insurgents as quickly as possible, and severely punishing all those who supported them in any way. Almost as a reflex action, the use of force to challenge law and order in Malaya was answered by a reciprocal use of even greater force by the army and police. What emerged was a policy of enforcing law and order through coercion or, in modern terms, a search and destroy policy.

The initial counterinsurgency strategy was developed by Major General C. H. Boucher, General Officer Commanding (GOC) Malaya. His approach was to use the army for large-scale "sweeps" designed to locate and trap the most active of the Communist insurgents. Boucher also held the view that the army was fighting a war, and that his soldiers should shoot to kill. The success rate of these operations was extremely low. The major effect of such mass movements of troops was to alert the insurgents, so that they were able to melt quickly into the jungle or catch the troops in ambushes. In addition, often innocent civilians fleeing the advancing soldiers were shot and killed. In one notorious incident in December 1948, 24 Chinese villagers from Batang Kali, who were being held on suspicion of aiding the insurgents, were shot by jittery British soldiers. The army appeared more at war with the Malayan population, especially the Chinese community, than as acting as its guardian and protector.

The police force, like the army, adopted an aggressive approach to searching out possible Communist insurgents and their supporters. Faced with escalating violence, the government rapidly expanded the number of recruits, nearly all of whom were drawn from the 44 percent of the population who were Malays. They were quickly put into service with the minimum of training to counter Malay suspicion of the Chinese community that had resulted from the racial clashes in the period directly after the

Japanese occupation during World War Two. To oversee the new recruits, the government sought out European officers and sergeants. Most were drafted in from Palestine, where British responsibilities were winding down. These new arrivals had no knowledge of the local languages – Malay, Chinese dialects, or Tamil – and no appreciation of the customs of the country. Many brought with them the heavy-handed approach to dealing with people that had been developed in the Palestine conflict.[5] As Harry Miller, a reporter for the *Straits Times*, recalls, this meant that they tended to the view that "every Chinese was a bandit or potential bandit and there was only one treatment for them, they were to be 'bashed around.'"[6] Indeed, the police quickly gained a reputation for brutality. Bribery and extortion also became endemic.

There were other aspects of the government's strategy that similarly had deleterious consequences for the Chinese community. Too often, after an attack by insurgents, security forces, faced with a sullen, scared Chinese population, with no understanding of Chinese ways, and with little or no useful intelligence, vented their frustrations on those nearest. In two cases in 1948, entire villages were burned to the ground, and in many other instances, large numbers of houses were destroyed. In addition, those living in areas that contained known groups of insurgents were either arrested or rounded up and put into detention camps, with a large proportion subsequently deported to China. However, towards the end of 1949, the new Communist government in China restricted deportations, making it increasingly difficult for the government to accommodate all the people they detained – the vast majority of whom were innocent bystanders.

The government fully recognized the kind of policy it was pursuing, but had little understanding of its effects on the general population. Sir Henry Gurney, the High Commissioner and therefore the leading British administrator in the country, acknowledged that the "police and army are breaking the law every day," but did not see this as a problem. His argument was that the Chinese are "notoriously inclined to lean towards whichever side frightens them more and at the moment this seems to be the government." He felt that it was crucial that the government be seen as "stronger than the bandits and inspiring greater fear."[7] However, the policy only served to alienate more and more of the Malayan-Chinese population. Faced with violence and threats from the MRLA insurgents and the Communist support organizations on the one hand, and the excessive use

The Federation of Malaya at the time of the Emergency

of force by the army and police on the other, most members of the Chinese community sought to simply keep out of trouble and survive. If they were pressed, they likely had more sympathy for the Communists. The MCP had gained considerable prestige from having fought the Japanese during the occupation, and benefited from the fact that in many Chinese families a member, or a member's friend, was linked to the Communists in one way or another. Membership in both the MRLA and, just as importantly, the Min Yuen support organizations increased markedly as Chinese sought refuge from a distant and threatening government with which they had only very limited contact, and which was generally seen as ignorant of their daily fears and needs.

For the government, the antagonism of the Chinese community was not its only problem. Malays, Indians, and Europeans (who at the time constituted 44, 10.5 and 1.5 percent of the population respectively) were also targets of the MCP, and resented the government's inability to maintain a semblance of law and order. The government, therefore, found that it was losing the support of all sections of the Malayan population. Certainly, the Malay-dominated state governments that made up the Federation were increasingly reluctant to cooperate in fighting the MCP, fearing that the concerns of the Malay community were being ignored while increased amounts of scarce resources were being channeled into the Chinese community. In addition, news of the victory of China's Communist Party in late 1949 and the British government's formal recognition of the new Chinese People's Government in January 1950 raised questions about Britain's commitment to fighting communism in Malaya. By early 1950, there was a widespread consensus that the original strategy was not working, and the situation was steadily deteriorating.

Revising the Strategy

The person chosen to try to turn the tide of the government's fortunes was Lieutenant General Sir Harold Briggs. He was brought in to fill the newly created position of Director of Operations, and was given the task of devising a revised strategy to combat the Communist threat. Towards the end of May 1950, Briggs produced what became known as the "Briggs Plan." The plan recognized the importance of eliminating the threat posed by both the MRLA and the Min Yuen support organizations. It advocated a series of measures that were designed to "dominate the populated areas" and build up "a feeling of complete security" so that people would provide the government with information about the Communists, break up the Min Yuen and thereby isolate the MRLA from their supplies of food and information, and force the MRLA to attack "us on our own ground."[8]

The Briggs Plan set out a number of key measures for achieving its goals. First, and perhaps most radical, was the idea of resettling all the rural ethnic Chinese who lived in relative isolation on land at the fringes of the jungle. They were generally referred to as "squatters" because they often lived on the land illegally and were a critical source of support and recruits for the MRLA and the Min Yuen. According to the Briggs Plan the resettlement program, and its associated regrouping of laborers on plantations and in tin mines, was to be undertaken in a systematic operation which would begin in the south of the peninsula and progress northward as the resettlement centers were completed and the squatters were moved in. An ambitious timetable was established, which proposed that the whole program would be completed by the beginning of 1952. Second, the Briggs Plan called for a substantial strengthening of the administration. Special provisions were put in place to recruit more administrators at the District Officer level. Third, Briggs established a coordinating structure that gave the civil administration, the police, and the army at all levels – federal, state, and district – a chance to meet regularly and collaborate in the implementation of government policy. Fourth, the Plan called for access roads to be built into the more isolated areas of the country, so that the police and administrators could establish a permanent presence in all populated areas. And finally, the Briggs Plan envisioned the army maintaining full control of all areas that had been cleared of the "squatters," so as to stop the MRLA from returning and reestablishing links to the population.

The resettlement and regroupment programs moved ahead at a fairly rapid pace, but with very mixed results. By December 1951 a remarkable 385,000 people had been resettled, a figure that was to reach over 570,000 squatters and landowners by the end of 1954. As a result of being moved away from their plots of land, resettled squatters were no longer able to provide a steady supply of food for the insurgents who, as a consequence, had to spend more of their time searching out alternative sources of supply. However, in the process of moving so many people in such a short time, property was destroyed and people were separated from the land they had carefully cultivated. The resulting hardship and distress turned people away from the government. Many resettlement centers ended up as squalid slums with atrocious living conditions. Sympathy for the Communists increased; there were regular reports that members of the Min Yuen were very active among newly resettled squatters, and that MRLA units entered resettlement centers virtually at will.[9]

Other aspects of the Briggs Plan also foundered. Briggs quickly became frustrated and disillusioned by the lack of a single individual with complete executive authority over the military, the police, and the civil administration. The police and the army continued to use aggressive, sometimes brutal, tactics in attempting to confront an elusive enemy. The home guard, whose function was to provide security for the resettlement centers and regrouped labor lines, was still largely composed of Malays, who were ill trained and, as a result, generally ineffective. The resettlement program as a whole was placed in jeopardy because of the government's failure to provide adequate security, and the administrative machinery continued to be undermanned and stretched to the breaking point. While in retrospect it is clear that the Briggs Plan provided some of the key foundations for what later became known as the "hearts and minds" strategy, it was much more difficult to implement than its author had envisaged.

Indeed, the last three months of 1951 proved to be a particularly dark period for the government. In early October, Gurney's car was ambushed and he was killed. A few weeks later, the MCP insurgents mounted the highest number of attacks recorded up to that point in any one-week period. The Joint Intelligence Advisory Committee reported that "the Communist potential has increased and the organization is now able still further to increase its activities."[10] As a result of the growing problems, Oliver Lyttelton, the Secretary of State for the Colonies in the newly elected Conservative government, decided to visit Malaya. Before leaving London, he was briefed and concluded that the Malayan government was "on the way to losing control of the country and soon." As he noted later, when he arrived in Malaya, he found that "[t]he situation was far worse than I had imagined: it was appalling."[11] At best, Malayans appeared destined to suffer a chronic state of insurgency warfare for years to come.

After touring the country and hearing the many different views on how to regain the initiative in the battle against the Communists, Lyttelton developed a six-point plan. First, there was a need for a unified, overall direction of the civil administration and the military forces. Second, the police should be reorganized and retrained. Third, government-run compulsory primary education was necessary to counter Communist propaganda in Communist-infiltrated schools. Fourth, resettlement areas should be given a high level of protection. Fifth, the home guard had to be reorganized and large numbers of Malayan-Chinese enlisted. And sixth, the strain on an undermanned civil service had to be alleviated. He also made the point that "[w]e have to see that our philosophy opens up to the people of Malaya the prospect of a finer and freer life than that which our enemies are trying to instill."[12] The key for Lyttelton, however, was to find someone who would be answerable directly to the Cabinet in

London, could direct both the civilian administration and the military forces, and could put his program of action into effect. The British government's choice was Lieutenant General Sir Gerald Templer, who arrived in Malaya in early February 1952.

The Hearts and Minds Strategy Implemented

Templer's personal philosophy, underpinning his approach to the campaign against the Communists, emerged a short time after his arrival in Malaya. First, he emphasized that he could win the Emergency if he could get two-thirds of the people on his side. Echoing Lyttelton, he felt that the way this could be done was by persuading the people of Malaya "that there is another and far preferable way of life and system of beliefs than that expressed in the rule of force and the law of the jungle. This way of life is not the American way of life. It is not the British way of life. It must be the Malayan way of life."[13] Equally importantly, Templer felt that people should be well treated and their grievances heard and when possible addressed – hearts and minds were to be won. Templer's evident concern with the welfare of the general public marked a significant change in the direction of the government's policy, and one which was widely welcomed by Malayans.

Second, and complementing the first point, Templer believed that it was wrong to separate the peacetime activities of government from the counterinsurgency activities. He argued forcefully that "you cannot divorce them unless you admit that the military side is the main thing which matters in the Emergency and that must be wrong – absolutely wrong."[14] He was most adamant that all government departments, no matter how far removed from the fighting they thought they were, had to be made to realize that the Emergency was their first concern. For Templer, the key to defeating the Communists lay in administrative, political, economic, cultural, spiritual, and military factors. The campaign he envisaged was to be all out and on all fronts – the counterinsurgency equivalent of "total war."

Given Templer's approach to counterinsurgency, retraining the police and the home guard was a top priority. The massive expansion of the police had been achieved without proper training. New training centers were established, where the emphasis shifted from paramilitary functions to ensuring that members of the force were well versed in basic civil police duties. Particular attention was given to ensuring that special constables received a minimum level of training and were properly supervised. Better equipment was also made available, which boosted morale. In late 1952, the government introduced Operation *Service*, which emphasized that the police were servants of the people, and that their job was to help and protect members of all communities. Retraining the home guard went along with arming units with shotguns. Armed Chinese home guard units were also formed, especially in the tin mining areas of Perak. Despite concerns on the part of some government officials, the loss of arms and ammunition to the Communists was very limited. And the 100,000 Malay and 50,000 Chinese home guard troops became invaluable in the static defense of settlements throughout the peninsula.[15]

Just as crucial for Templer as the retraining of the police and home guard was the need to increase the size and expand the skills of the civil administration. Particularly important was the filling of the many vacancies at the district level and in the resettlement centers. After appropriate training, more local recruits were inducted into the elite Malayan Civil Service and the Malayan Administrative Service, and a new category of Chinese Affairs Officers was created. In addition, a steady stream of Chinese-speaking missionaries, who had worked in China but had left when the Communists took over, were persuaded to move to Malaya to become resettlement officers. Engineers were recruited for the understaffed Public Works Department; new teachers and educational supervisors filled positions generated by the expansion of the school system; static health dispensaries were set up and manned in the resettlement centers; and mobile St John's Ambulance and Red Cross medical teams were brought in from Britain and Australia. Gradually, the government was able to provide services to a larger section of the population and, hence, extend its administrative authority over a wider area of the country.

Increased security and more administrative capacity were crucial in turning around the "new villages," as Templer decreed the resettlement centers should be called. Strict security was designed not only to protect residents of the new villages from the MRLA, but also to ensure that essential supplies such as food, medicine, and clothes were not taken from the new villages and passed on to the insurgents in their jungle bases. The provision of services and amenities for the new villages was no longer to be referred to as "after care" but as "development." The aim was to ensure that the "new life, after the initial disturbance of moving, should be more attractive than the old."[16] The government sought to provide new villages with road or rail access to the wider world; supplies of clean water; schools; community centers; basic medical care; and some agricultural land or other sources of income, such as work on rubber plantations or in tin mines. While it took a number of years to bring all the services to the approximately 500 new villages that were created, eventually most had access to essential services and amenities.

Success in effectively administering the new villages made food control and food denial policies a potent weapon, forcing the Communist insurgents onto the defensive. In places where the insurgents were known to be operating in the surrounding jungle, central cooking stations were set up and no uncooked rice was allowed to be sold. Cans of food were also punctured at the time of sale. Non-perishable food could only be moved around the country during daylight hours, and under license. With cooked rice and punctured cans of food going bad if not eaten within a few hours, it became increasingly difficult for the members of the Min Yuen support groups to smuggle food out to the armed insurgents who, as a consequence, became more concerned with mere survival and less able to operate as effective fighting units.

Food control was just one of the policies employed to keep pressure on the Min Yuen, and new villages more generally, in an attempt to get them to sever their links to the MRLA insurgents. When, after an MRLA-initiated attack, local villagers were uncooperative, officials imposed extended curfews lasting days or even weeks (often up to 22 hours per day), collective fines, and a reduction in rice rations. In some cases, those who refused to provide information were sent to detention camps. Templer's policy was to introduce these punishments with considerable fanfare, as a way of discouraging others who might be tempted to aid the Communists. In a number of well-publicized incidents he went to new villages where insurgent attacks had taken place, berated the village leaders, and imposed the collective punishments personally. However, as the hearts and minds strategy gradually evolved, these kinds of policies tended to be used less frequently.

To balance off the very real hardships imposed by food control, curfews, collective fines, detention, and restrictions on the movement of goods and people, Templer introduced the concept of "white areas." This designation meant that there were no active insurgents in the area, and that Emergency regulations – apart from those requiring residents to remain in the new villages or regroupment areas, and keeping a small home guard unit for defensive purposes – were lifted. They were viewed by senior administrators as a major incentive for people to cooperate with the government. The first "white area" was declared in September 1953, and covered 221 square miles of Malacca. By mid-1954 there were "white areas" containing over 1.3 million people, mostly along Malaya's coastline. They were gradually expanded as the insurgency subsided, and more and more people accepted the authority of the government.[17]

As Templer implemented the reforms advocated by Briggs and Lyttelton, so the government received better intelligence about the MRLA and the Min Yuen. Members of the general public were less alienated and generally reassured by the new policies. As a former Director of Military Intelligence, Templer fully understood the importance of improving the acquisition, coordination, and effective use of information about all the divisions of the MCP.[18] He brought in the second-in-command of Britain's MI5 for a one-year term to reorganize and expand the Special Branch of the police force. Increased funds were given to intelligence activities, an Intelligence (Special Branch) training school was established, and other facilities were improved. A Director of Intelligence was also appointed whose job was to oversee the analysis of such subjects as the MCP's strengths, weaknesses, and strategy, and the attitudes of various groups towards the Communists. Templer's emphasis on intelligence quickly paid off. Food denial campaigns were combined with information gleaned by Special Branch, and after some trial and error became very effective at forcing members of the MRLA and the Min Yuen to take risks that made them vulnerable to detection and capture.

Among the best sources of intelligence were surrendered enemy personnel (SEPs). Insurgents tended to surrender for different reasons, including internal friction and, after 1952, shortages of food and an increasing sense of hopelessness.[19] However, one of the key factors was the program of giving reward money to anyone providing information leading to the capture or surrender of insurgents. Propaganda distributed by the government emphasized that SEPs would be treated well, and could take advantage of the rewards program. As a result, the SEPs provided not only valuable information about individual insurgents as well as Communist policies and practices, but in later years also went back into the jungle and persuaded their former colleagues to surrender.

The increase in quantity and quality of intelligence was also integral to the military's revised tactics. As it became obvious that sweeps were unproductive, a number of battalion commanders decided to make use of small, 10–16-man patrols operating for four or five days in the jungle. Gradually, the number in each patrol was lowered and the time each spent in the jungle increased. On arrival in Malaya, all army units were put through courses in the latest techniques for patrolling the jungle at the Far East Land Forces Training Centre (FTC), or Jungle Warfare School as it became known. The FTC had been developing and refining jungle warfare techniques since the early years of the Emergency, and the training it provided was extremely valuable in ensuring an effective, and widely appreciated, approach to combating the guerrillas and cutting them off from their sources of supply in the local communities.[20] Templer also insisted on the development of a common handbook, *The Conduct of Anti-Terrorist Operations in Malaya*, which detailed best practices in terms of basic tactics, drills, and approaches to counterinsurgency jungle warfare. This handbook, which was originally written by Lieutenant Colonel Walter Walker, became the "bible" for all units of the army, as well as the police.[21] By the end of 1952, with rapidly improving intelligence, the security forces were able to frame localities where insurgents were known to be operating, flood the area with patrols, and set ambushes of their own rather than be ambushed. The MRLA was steadily pushed back onto the defensive and its numbers reduced.

Similarly, the role of air power changed over the course of the Emergency. In the early years, the RAF conducted offensive air operations such as bombing jungle targets. However, given the lack of good intelligence, these sorties were not very effective. Indeed, as the Emergency evolved, aircraft were put to a number of different uses that proved to be invaluable. Most particularly, the role shifted to intelligence gathering; the movement of troops and the evacuation of the wounded; supply drops to jungle forts set up to win over aboriginal groups and units on extended jungle patrols; and propaganda flights in which leaflets were distributed or "voice aircraft" circled over the jungle canopy broadcasting messages to known insurgent groups. While the bombing of clearly identified jungle-based targets was used when solid intelligence was developed, the instances of such operations became fewer as the Emergency wore on. It was the auxiliary tasks that the air force performed which proved to be most valuable.[22]

Efforts to win over hearts and minds were aided by the development of an increasingly effective propaganda machine, which built on Templer's personal commitment to gain the confidence of the general population, and by a program of psychological warfare.[23] Propaganda came in many forms: pamphlets and newspapers in the local languages were widely distributed; radio broadcasts became important as individuals started to buy transistor radios and receivers were placed in community centers in new villages and regroupment areas; and mobile film units toured the new villages, showing commercial films along with films specially developed by the Malayan Film Unit. Psychological warfare was geared primarily to persuading members of the MRLA to surrender. The SEPs were particularly adept in devising approaches that proved effective. Emphasis was placed on exploiting the doubts insurgents had about their mission and circumstances, and overcoming the MCP propaganda that they would be harshly treated if they fell into government hands. As the Emergency progressed, surrender rates increased markedly.

One of the main reasons why the surrender rate rose was that the introduction of elections encouraged the development of a wide range of competing political parties which eventually rendered the MCP largely irrelevant.[24] At the initiative of Gurney, municipal elections were first held in late 1951. Local democracy through "self-government from the ground up" was promoted in the new villages from 1952 onward. The first countrywide federal election was held in 1955 and ushered in a new era, with a Malay, Tunku Abdul Rahman, as the chief minister. Importantly, political parties vying for votes encouraged many, who might otherwise have turned to the MCP, to participate in Malaya's electoral arena in order to express their fears and aspirations. Moreover, the electoral success of the Alliance Party, which was made up of three parties representing the three major ethnic groups in Malaya – Malays, Chinese, and Indians – pushed for independence. This clearly undercut the MCP's original anti-colonial appeal. Indeed, after independence in 1957 the MCP rapidly became a spent force.

The hearts and minds strategy evolved over many years. While the ideas and planning that formed the foundations of the policy were set out by Gurney, Briggs, and Lyttelton, it was Templer whose energy and drive turned the various plans into action. In just over two years, he gave form and substance to the hearts and minds strategy, and established a trajectory for the government's counterinsurgency policy which was continued by his immediate successor, Sir Donald MacGillivray, and later by Tunku Abdul Rahman and his very able deputy, Tun Abdul Razak. The hearts and minds strategy, then, was a constantly evolving approach to counterinsurgency based on both an underlying philosophy of gaining the confidence of the general population and a willingness to engage in trial and error on all fronts – administrative, military, policing, social, and political.

Evaluating the Hearts and Minds Strategy

The Malayan experience in developing a successful counterinsurgency strategy raises a series of important questions. First, was the hearts and minds strategy responsible for the Malayan government's success? The clear consensus among analysts of the Emergency is that the hearts and minds strategy was indeed the key to victory. However, Karl Hack has argued that the tide was beginning to turn in the government's favor by late 1951, before Templer's arrival and the implementation of the hearts and minds approach, and that "population control" was the decisive factor in eliminating the Communist threat, with the hearts and minds strategy playing only an auxiliary role.[25] Yet Hack's argument is difficult to sustain. His reliance on statistics relating to "incidents," "clashes," and the number of Communists, civilians, and security forces killed is reminiscent of the American government's claims during the Vietnam War that it was winning because such statistics were moving in its favor. As the Americans found, such statistics mean very little. His argument that the change in MCP strategy in late 1951 was evidence that the tide had turned before Templer arrived misses the point that the Communists were set to combine a military campaign with an attempt to win over the population. Clearly, the hearts and minds strategy proved timely and critical in confronting this change in the MCP's policy. Overall, then, Hack provides little evidence to question the centrality of the hearts and minds strategy to the Malayan government's victory over the MCP.[26]

Second, to what extent is it possible to generalize from the Malayan government's success? Those who argue against making generalizations allude to three broad points.[27] They charge that the MCP was not as potent a force as it might have been. Its base of support was effectively confined to the Chinese community, which constituted less than 40 percent of the total population. This allowed the government to concentrate its efforts on one sector of the population, knowing that the other sectors were generally sympathetic. Moreover, the MCP received relatively little outside aid, with only the narrow Thai border providing a land link to the outside world. Partly as a result of this, the MRLA's firepower was severely limited. And the fight against the Japanese during the occupation had left the MCP short of good strategists and strong leaders. Another general point is that the British government was able to take full advantage of its position as a colonial power. It had administrators with a good understanding of the languages and cultures of the country; it was able to introduce reforms that a less autonomous, locally based government could not have undertaken; and it was eventually able to grant independence, which undercut the appeal of the MCP. Finally, the point is made that the British were lucky. The Korean War brought a massive inflow of wealth to the peninsula, as the prices of Malaya's two major export commodities – rubber and tin – soared. The resulting prosperity was particularly timely. It made resettlement possible, and financed much of Templer's hearts and minds strategy. Essentially, these points emphasize that each insurgency has its own unique characteristics and, as a consequence, specific policies and the way in which they are implemented in one arena cannot necessarily be transferred to another.

Yet, as the extensive theoretical literature on the principles of waging insurgency war indicates, they all have some basic features in common. Significantly, of course, the hearts and minds approach mirrors in important ways the argument made by practitioners such as T. E. Lawrence, Mao Tse-tung and Che Guevara.[28] They argue that in order to win, insurgents need the support of the general population. In other words, to defeat an insurgency, governments must sever the link between the insurgents and the people on whom they rely for support. This is exactly what Templer sought to accomplish. Indeed, Robert Thompson, in laying out his now classic "principles of counterinsurgency" asserts that "an insurgent movement is a war for the people" and that "the government must give priority to defeating the political subversion not the guerrillas."[29] In Malaya, the government initially tried to employ a military-driven, insurgent-focused search and destroy approach, but it not only failed to stamp out the MCP threat; it also alienated key sections of the population and, as a result, actually produced more recruits for the Communists' cause. The Malayan experience with the success of the hearts and minds approach strongly indicates that alienating the population cannot produce victory, but gaining the general support of the population can.

Finally, can the Malayan experience teach us anything about the way counterinsurgency strategies normally unfold? In many ways the government's initial reaction was typical of most governments facing a well-supported insurgent movement. Almost as a reflex action, what was perceived as a military threat induced a primarily military response. And indeed, such a strategy is appealing. If the insurgents have no support, they can be eliminated before the movement gains any momentum. Moreover, it is probably the best strategy for ensuring that the government does not lose the "war." The military ought to be able to control key areas of the country, including the major urban centers. Yet clearly, employing such a "not-lose" approach virtually guarantees that a government will not defeat well-supported armed insurgents. As in the initial years in Malaya, the use of force in a search and destroy strategy without accurate, detailed intelligence simply alienates large sections of the population. As a result, there will always be people willing to help supply the insurgents with money, medical supplies, food, clothing, and information; and there will always be recruits ready to replace fallen comrades as well as swell the ranks of the insurgents' support organizations. More troops using the wrong strategy simply means more alienation, more insurgents, and the inevitable call for yet more troops. As Thompson has noted, when the strategy is wrong, doubling the effort only squares the error.[30]

However, the Malayan experience demonstrates that a shift in policy from a military-driven search and destroy strategy to a comprehensive hearts and minds strategy is possible. These two approaches should not be considered as a dichotomy, but rather as two poles of a continuum. Any counterinsurgency strategy will contain elements of both strategies, although one will usually predominate at any one time. Getting any government to move down the continuum toward an out-and-out hearts and minds approach is often difficult. Senior politicians, military officials, and bureaucrats become tied to specific policies, and find it hard to admit they may be wrong. In Malaya, the shift in policy came about through a combination of factors. There was a willingness to learn from mistakes and a general culture of adaptation. This capacity for continually adjusting and refining policy was to be found not just in the military, as John Nagl points out, but even more importantly among those at the top who recognized the need to rely more heavily on the police and especially on an expanded administrative capacity that could provide much-needed services.[31] Significantly, there was a major change in personnel following the assassination of Gurney in October 1951. The governing party changed in London, and most of the top officials in Kuala Lumpur moved on and

129

were replaced. This allowed for a reassessment of the Malayan government's policy up to that point. Finally, Malaya had an effective leader in Templer, who was able to drive the new strategy forward with vigor and determination and, just as significantly, persuade people not to seek retribution against those who supported the insurgents, but to provide them with the resources that would wean them away from the MCP.

Overall, then, the Malayan Emergency represents a significant case study of how counterinsurgency can be successfully waged. While the Malayan government clearly benefited from a series of unique factors, the philosophy underlying the hearts and minds approach has relevance for almost all other counterinsurgency campaigns. The comprehensive victory enjoyed by the Malayan government provides important lessons for practitioners and theorists alike.

7

COUNTERINSURGENCY IN VIETNAM
American Organizational Culture and Learning[1]

Lieutenant Colonel John A. Nagl

The United States entered the Vietnam War with a military trained and equipped to fight a conventional war in Europe, and totally unprepared for the counterinsurgency campaign it was about to wage. The bureaucracy of the United States government was slow to adapt to the demands of counterinsurgency in Vietnam, making real changes only when it was too late – after the American public had already lost faith in the effort to create a free and democratic South Vietnam. Throughout the American experience in Vietnam, organizational learning foundered on a national vision of the object of warfare as the destruction of the enemy's forces. This concept was so deeply ingrained in America's leaders that they refused to listen to innovators who were convinced that the US counterinsurgency strategy was not just ineffective but actually counterproductive in the kind of warfare the United States faced in Vietnam. In particular, conventionally bred Army generals were not the sort to encourage new ways of winning wars, and in fact often actively discouraged innovation by their subordinates. The history of the United States in Vietnam can be seen as the history of individuals attempting to implement changes in counterinsurgency strategy and doctrine, but failing to overcome very strong organizational cultures predisposed to a conventional attrition-based doctrine.

The failed American counterinsurgency efforts in Vietnam are important, and not just because of the vast humanitarian tragedy that resulted throughout Southeast Asia as a consequence of American policies and the damage that the Vietnam War inflicted on the United States military. The Vietnam hangover resulted in an American unwillingness to think about and prepare for future counterinsurgency campaigns – a failure that led to a 40-year gap in comprehensive American counterinsurgency doctrine and contributed to the American military's lack of preparedness for fighting insurgencies in Afghanistan and Iraq after the attacks of September 11, 2001.

An Advisory Effort

The United States became involved in Vietnam even before the Viet Minh guerrillas, led by Ho Chi Minh, defeated the French in 1954 and gained independence for North Vietnam. Direct US military involvement began on August 1, 1950 with the creation of a four-man Military Assistance Advisory Group (MAAG) to the French Army; by the fall of Dien Bien Phu to the Viet Minh on May 7, 1954 the MAAG had increased to 342 advisers.

Ngo Dinh Diem, a Catholic Vietnamese nationalist, returned from exile in the United States to lead the Government of Vietnam (GVN), with US support, in 1954. The Geneva Agreement, concluded about a month later, partitioned Vietnam at the 17th parallel, with French forces withdrawing from the north and North Vietnamese forces from the south. The agreement stipulated that the issue of unification would be decided through elections in 1956. The elections never occurred, though, and the Communist insurgency recommenced in the south in October 1957. Over 400 South Vietnamese officials were assassinated over the next two years.[2]

With the French gone, the United States and the MAAG had to guide the South Vietnamese toward the defeat of the insurgency. The MAAG focused on creating a conventional military for South Vietnam. Rather than a counter-guerrilla force dedicated to providing local security, the American advisers sought to build a force that was a mirror image of the US Army, trained to fight an airmobile and mechanized war under the cover of lavish amounts of (US) firepower. In late 1959, a presidential committee to study the advisory effort questioned the MAAG's basic premise: that fighting insurgents was a "lesser included capability" of fighting a conventional war. Instead, the committee reported that:

> Tailoring a military force to the task of countering external aggression – i.e., countering another military force – entails some sacrifice of capabilities to counter internal aggression. The latter requires widespread deployment, rather than concentration. It requires small, mobile, lightly equipped units of the ranger or commando type. It requires different weapons, command systems, communications, logistics...[3]

Infiltration Routes into South Vietnam

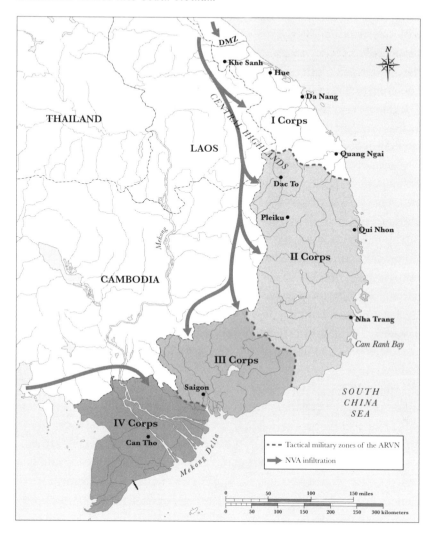

Not just a presidential committee, but the advisers themselves questioned the US Army's certainty that, by preparing to defeat a conventional invasion of South Vietnam, they were also building a capability to defeat insurgents. However, this message was not being heard at the higher levels of the MAAG. In fact, General Sam L. Meyers, deputy chief of the American military mission in South Vietnam, testified before the Senate Foreign Relations Committee in April 1959 that the guerrillas had been "gradually nibbled away until they ceased to be a major menace to the government."[4] On July 8, 1959, less than three months after this assertion, Viet Cong insurgents attacked a compound manned by a US advisory team in Bien Hoa; two American soldiers were killed by supposedly neutralized guerrillas. The attack marked the escalation of the Communist offensive against the Diem government; 110 local government leaders were assassinated in the last four months of 1959.[5] The under-resourced local militia could offer these leaders little protection against the Viet Cong, who in short order created a political vacuum in the countryside.

These reverses did not go unnoticed. When John F. Kennedy took office in January 1961, the first question he asked his aides after his inauguration was reportedly "What are we doing about guerrilla warfare?"[6] Kennedy worked very hard to get the armed forces behind his counterinsurgency program, but the Army had neither the knowledge nor the desire to change its orientation away from conventional war. It did, grudgingly, create purpose-built Special Forces to focus on unconventional war, with the attitude that doing so would inoculate the rest of the Army against that virus.

The Army attempted to create a counterinsurgency doctrine very quickly, without doing the deep analytical thinking required to come to a complete understanding of the nature of this kind of warfare. *Field Manual 100-5, Operations*, the Army's war-fighting bible, first had a chapter on counterinsurgency in 1962. However, the Army as a whole made only paper changes to its doctrine, without fully training and equipping its officers and men for the challenges they would soon face in Southeast Asia. General Earle Wheeler, later Army Chief of Staff and, under President Johnson, Chairman of the Joint Chiefs of Staff, said in a speech at Fordham University on November 7, 1962, "It is fashionable in some quarters to say that the problems in Southeast Asia are primarily political and economic rather than military. I do not agree. The essence of the problem in Vietnam is military."[7]

Military Assistance Command – Vietnam (MACV) became operational on February 8, 1962, its first commander a purely conventional warrior named Lieutenant General Paul D. Harkins. Harkins quickly demonstrated that he was unlikely to substantially modify US Army doctrine in Vietnam from its firepower-intensive focus. He was inconsiderate of the complexities involved in winning the hearts and minds of the local populace (tellingly reduced to the acronym "WHAM" during his command); in one interview, when asked about the political consequences of using napalm on villages, Harkins replied, "It really puts the fear of God into the Viet Cong. And that is what counts."[8]

By 1963, South Vietnam fielded nine infantry divisions, an airborne brigade, three Marine brigades, and one independent regiment. Like the US military on which it was modeled, the Army of the Republic of Vietnam (ARVN) was heavily reliant on helicopters and artillery support, and tended to focus on large-scale operations instead of the small-unit patrolling, ambushes, and reconnaissance activities conducive to locating insurgents.

An instructive early battle occurred at the village of Ap Bac on January 2, 1963, when some 400 Viet Cong decisively defeated more than 1,500 ARVN soldiers supported by American advisers and aircraft and South Vietnamese artillery, inflicting more than 200 casualties and downing five helicopters. The Americans and South Vietnamese had expected neither the strength nor the skill of the Viet Cong defenders and stumbled their way into a bloody defeat.[9] The battle underlined the truism that numbers and firepower are no substitute for good intelligence.

Unshakably optimistic even in the face of such setbacks, Harkins refused to acknowledge shortcomings in the ARVN, preventing the drastic changes required to provide true security in the countryside. One initiative that had been successful in the British counterinsurgency campaign in Malaya was the creation of "new villages" or "strategic hamlets," fortified villages where the government would provide economic assistance and the people would be protected from the insurgents. The hamlets were intended to create rings of security that would expand like oil spots. In Vietnam, the program was insufficiently resourced, poorly coordinated, and thus an abject failure. Territorial forces were too few and too poorly motivated to defend enough strategic hamlets to make a difference. The irony is that later evidence has shown that the North Vietnamese and Viet Cong considered well-defended hamlets to be a genuine threat to their control over the population. The official history of the North Vietnamese Army described the effect of the strategic hamlets:

> Liberated areas and areas where the masses had seized control shrank. Guerrillas from a number of villages and hamlets were forced to move to other areas or flee to our base areas. Cadre and Party members hid in rice paddies and along canal banks to wait for nightfall to enter the hamlets to contact our supporters and rebuild our armed forces.[10]

If the hamlets had been better protected through the formation of locally recruited territorial forces, they might have withstood the ensuing Viet Cong political and military efforts to eliminate this thorn in their side.

A high-level fact-finding mission, dispatched to Vietnam from Washington to assess the progress of the war effort two weeks after the battle of Ap Bac, decided that "We are winning slowly on the present thrust and...there is no compelling reason to change."[11] Meanwhile, Viet Cong terrorism grew steadily, as did repression under Diem's regime. Public discontent erupted that hot summer of 1963, after Diem and his brother Nhu brutally quelled protests led by Buddhist monks. Diem and Nhu were killed during a coup carried out with US approval on November 2, 1963. President Kennedy himself was assassinated in Dallas three weeks later, unsuccessful in his attempts to make the Army an effective instrument for counterinsurgency. Lyndon Johnson assumed the US Presidency as military juntas rose and fell in South Vietnam with alarming speed. As the truth about Diem's repression and the poor performance of the ARVN under his command came to light in the wake of the coup, General Harkins, who had been one of Diem's strongest supporters, came to be seen as a liability. Scheduled to retire in September 1964, he left Saigon three months early, turning over command to General William Westmoreland.

CIA, CIDG, and Switchback

The Central Intelligence Agency (CIA), with a much shorter and more varied institutional memory than the US Army, was correspondingly more open to experimentation in counterinsurgency techniques. The CIA developed the Civilian Irregular Defense Group (CIDG) program in the early 1960s. The experiment began in Buon Enao village in Darlac Province in November 1961. Villagers were armed, organized, and given medical and agricultural assistance under the supervision of US Army Special Forces soldiers. By April 1962, 40 villages in the province had been pacified, and the oil spot of security was continuing to spread. In July, the CIA requested another 16 Special Forces teams to join the eight who had arrived in May. By the end of the year, some 38,000 irregulars were participating in the program, and the GVN declared the province secure.

But the success of the CIDG experiment, far from initiating the learning cycle and changing US Army counterinsurgency doctrine, was instead about to be altered. General William Rosson, after an inspection tour of the program in April 1962, reported to General Maxwell Taylor,

Chairman of the Joint Chiefs of Staff, that the Special Forces were being used "improperly" and should engage in more offensive operations in keeping with the Army's "find 'em, fix 'em, and finish 'em" philosophy.[12] General Rosson's report led to a transfer of CIDG from CIA to MACV control in July 1963. The transfer, known as Operation *Switchback*, changed the nature of the program from a defensive orientation on population security to a more aggressive, offensive stance. By January 1, 1965, General Westmoreland had redefined the mission of Special Forces soldiers in Vietnam to be one of border surveillance and control, operations against infiltration routes, and operations against VC war zones and base areas. Even the official US Army History of the Special Forces describes the process as the "conventionalization" of the CIDG.[13]

The Big War

During General Westmoreland's first year as MACV commander, the performance of the ARVN declined consistently, while Viet Cong terrorist attacks increased in both frequency and effectiveness. After a bomb strike on the Brinks Hotel in Saigon fanned fears that the government might fall, General Westmoreland requested the deployment of a US Division, stating that:

> I am convinced that US troops with their energy, mobility and firepower can successfully take the fight to the VC. The main purpose of the additional deployments recommended below is to give us a substantial and hard hitting [offen]sive capability on the ground to convince the VC that they cannot win...[14]

The first American ground combat forces in Vietnam were two battalions of Marines, sent to protect logistical installations at Danang. They landed on March 8, 1965. The US military's blood was up; it was ready and willing to fight a war which it had no doubt it could win, and win quickly and decisively. Forces of the Government of Vietnam were to be relegated to a secondary role.

Westmoreland's tactics were to find the enemy and "pile on" troops supported by close air support, artillery, and even B-52 strikes. The mission was to kill as many Viet Cong and North Vietnamese Army (NVA) soldiers as possible. An important early example of the "search and destroy" tactics the United States would employ under General

Westmoreland was the battle fought by the Army's 1st Cavalry Division in the Ia Drang valley in November 1965. Immediately after the battle, Lieutenant Colonel Moore, the battalion commander, informed his higher command that US tactics and strategy were incorrect, and requested a study group be formed. His request was overruled. Moore states:

> The American Mission and the Military Assistance Command – Vietnam had not succeeded in coordinating American and South Vietnamese military operations with follow-on Vietnamese government programs to reestablish control in the newly cleared regions. If they couldn't make it work in Bong Son – where the most powerful American division available had cleared enemy forces from the countryside – how could they possibly hope to reestablish South Vietnamese control in other regions where the American military presence was much weaker?[15]

Once the Viet Cong came in contact with American firepower, they quickly changed their tactics. They began "hugging" American units, which prevented the use of close air support and artillery. This demonstrated a tactical flexibility, a willingness to admit and learn from mistakes, that US forces demonstrably lacked. Self-criticism forums were held in VC units after operations, in which officers and men admitted mistakes and denounced each other for errors in battle. The sessions not only contributed to group cohesion, but also encouraged learning of tactical and operational lessons.

The US Army's focus on firepower and attrition increased steadily for the next several years. In Operation *Masher* (later renamed *White Wing*), the 1st Cavalry Division reported 1,342 Viet Cong killed, 633 Viet Cong captured, and 1,087 suspected VC captured in Binh Dinh Province in January, February, and early March 1966 during an operation that fired 140,000 artillery rounds. As a result, according to the division's after action report, the enemy was driven from the coastal plain, and "so far as is now known, the GVN intends to reestablish a government in this area."[16] The hope that others would "hold and build" after the division had cleared was misplaced; almost exactly a year later, the 1st Cavalry Division fought again for control of Binh Dinh in Operation *Thayer II*. After thousands more artillery shells and 171 B-52 strikes, the division's official report stated that 80 percent of the population of Binh Dinh were "free from organized Vietcong control, at least temporarily. This is not to mean that they have been brought under government control...As far as political control is concerned, the AO is still a power vacuum."[17]

The US Army focused its efforts on finding and destroying the enemy, utilizing to the full its advantages in artillery, close air support, and mechanized forces. This course of action continued despite evidence that the tactics were ineffective in accomplishing strategic objectives. The metric the United States used to measure progress in counterinsurgency was the body count. The consequent emphasis on killing the enemy did not calculate the heavy costs such profligate use of firepower imposed on the security of the population and on the professional ethos of the US Army. Yet in "I Corps," the northernmost part of South Vietnam – ironically where the threat of a conventional invasion was greatest – the US Marine Corps was taking a very different tack. In contrast to Westmoreland's search and destroy strategy, Major General Lew Walt, commander of the III Marine Amphibious Force (MAF) from mid-1965 onward, applied an approach heavily tinted by the Marine Corps' organizational culture, a culture born out of a long history of fighting small wars. Walt established a coordinating council composed of the regional civilian agency heads, ARVN and US military commanders, and a Vietnamese government representative. He also integrated Marine rifle squads into Vietnamese Regional Forces platoons. These "Combined Action Platoons" lived in the villages of I Corps and focused on pacification. In the meantime, regular Marine battalions divided their time between platoon-sized patrols and civic programs. Lieutenant General Krulak, Commanding General Marine Force Pacific, made the case to Secretary of Defense McNamara that the safer roads and more secure hamlets in I Corps, while "harder to quantify," were a better measure of success than MACV Commander Westmoreland's body count: "The raw figure of VC killed...can be a dubious index of success since, if their killing is accompanied by devastation of friendly areas, we may end up having done more harm than good."[18] General Westmoreland disagreed, arguing that "I believed the Marines should have been trying to find the enemy's main forces and bring them to battle, thereby putting them on the run and reducing the threat they posed to the population."[19]

Army Chief of Staff Harold K. Johnson's decision to commission a high-level study in mid-1965 provided what was perhaps the last best chance for the Army to learn that its counterinsurgency procedures were flawed, to accept that fact at a high level within the organization, and to implement organizational and doctrinal change as a result. The Program for the Pacification and Long-Term Development of South Vietnam (PROVN) study, under the leadership of General Creighton Abrams, was tasked with "developing new courses of action to be taken in South Vietnam by the United States and its allies, which will, in conjunction with current actions, modified as necessary, lead in due time to successful accomplishment of US aims and objectives."[20] The results were striking: repudiation of the Army's current emphasis on search and destroy operations and a move toward pacification through winning the population over to the government's cause. Most notable of all is the lack of enthusiasm for false optimism as practiced by MACV. The final report of the PROVN study, submitted to the Chief of Staff of the Army in March 1966, clearly stated:

> The situation in South Vietnam has seriously deteriorated. 1966 may well be the last chance to ensure eventual success. "Victory" can only be achieved through bringing the individual Vietnamese, typically a rural peasant, to support willingly the GVN. The critical actions are those that occur at the village, district, and provincial levels. This is where the war must be fought; this is where that war and the object which lies beyond it must be won.[21]

In short, the PROVN study contended that the entire American policy since the creation of the MAAG – creating an ARVN in the mold of the US Army, equipping it with heavy weapons and helicopter support, using American troops on search and destroy missions – was flawed. The key to success in Vietnam was the creation of security forces "associated and intermingled with the people on a long-term basis" such as the CIDG under CIA control, or the USMC's Combined Action Platoons.

However, Westmoreland recommended that the PROVN study be downgraded to a "conceptual document, carrying forward the main thrusts and goals of the study" to "be presented to National Security Council for use in developing concepts, policies, and actions to improve the effectiveness of the American effort in Vietnam."[22] Thus, the Army's best chance at reforming itself was pushed upstairs to the level of the National Security Council. The PROVN study is a remarkable document, demonstrating a dispassionate appraisal of organizational effectiveness which could have led to real learning. The authors of PROVN demonstrated integrity and moral courage in presenting what were certain to be unpopular conclusions to the leaders of the Army, men who had previously written and approved the very policies their juniors were now questioning. The learning stopped at the level of COMUSMACV (Commander, US Military Assistance Command Vietnam) and the Chief of Staff of the Army, both of whom were unwilling or unable to change policies and viewpoints rooted deep in the organizational culture of the US Army.

The political and military leadership of the United States paid lip service to the importance of combined political–military efforts to defeat the rural insurgency in Vietnam, but in reality little effort was expended in this arena before 1967. There was no institution in the United States government that was organized, trained, and equipped to perform this mission, and little incentive for any existing institution to adapt to meet the need for one. The personal and very vigorous intervention of "Blowtorch" Bob Komer was instrumental in creating perhaps the most remarkable example of American institutional innovation during the Vietnam War. Komer was able to pull together all of the American civilian and military pacification programs into Civil Operations and Revolutionary Development Support (CORDS) on May 1, 1967.

CORDS was a dramatic change from "business as usual." It comprised personnel from the CIA, the US Information Agency (USIA), the US Agency for International Development (USAID), the State Department, the White House, and all of the military services. In addition to Komer, who worked directly for COMUSMACV, each of the four US Corps Commanders had a deputy for pacification. The real innovation of CORDS, however, was the placement of unified civil–military advisory teams in all 250 districts and 44 provinces. In addition to being purpose-built for the demands of counterinsurgency warfare in Vietnam and integrating civilian and military personnel at all levels to promote a combined political–military approach to problem recognition and solution, CORDS had the dramatic advantage of not being constrained by an institutional culture with preconceived ideas of how missions should be accomplished; "CORDS in effect wrote the field manual as it went along."[23]

Despite the overall positive nature of the changes CORDS inspired, one of its component programs was more questionable: the GVN's "Phung Hoang" program, called "Phoenix" by Americans. This was an effort to eliminate Viet Cong political leaders and organizers (known as the Viet Cong Infrastructure or VCI) by any means necessary. While killing large numbers of important insurgents, it did so at the cost of substantial human rights violations that lost public support among the people of both Vietnam and the US.

Tet and Vietnamization

With programs such as Phoenix beginning to have an impact in South Vietnam, the Viet Cong counterattacked. The Tet Offensive of February 1968 was a general assault by the Viet Cong that dramatically changed the course of the war. The Viet Cong infiltrated directly into South Vietnamese cities, including Hue and Saigon, and attacked the heart of the GVN's power. Although the Viet Cong were slaughtered when they emerged from their cover to fight openly (probably suffering about 40,000 killed compared to 1,100 US and 2,300 ARVN killed), their pervasive presence and numbers clearly indicated to the American people that the United States and the GVN had failed to implement an effective counterinsurgency strategy. General Westmoreland, steeped in an organizational culture which saw the battlefield as the place where wars were won and lost, was convinced that Tet had been an American victory; America disagreed. Even if the insurgents were defeated tactically in Tet, they had shown that they had not been defeated strategically, and forced the US government and public to reconsider the length and likely costs of the war. The US public decided that the effort to secure Vietnam was not worth what it now understood would be a very high cost.

General Earle Wheeler, Chairman of the Joint Chiefs of Staff, took advantage of the post-Tet air of panic in Washington to urge Westmoreland to ask for more troops. The Joint Chiefs were concerned that the already vast deployment of 525,000 men to Vietnam was stripping the United States of its defenses, and pressed President Johnson to call the reserves to active duty. Johnson and McNamara sent Westmoreland another 10,000 men without calling up the reserves, over the Joint Chiefs' protests that doing so would further weaken America's strategic depth. Wheeler returned from a visit to Saigon to brief Johnson that Westmoreland urgently needed another 200,000 troops.

President Johnson, confronted by disagreement between the civilian and military leaders of his Department of Defense, struggled with the issue of providing another 200,000 men. After conferring with a panel of prestigious former generals and politicians (the "Wise Men"), on March 22, 1968, Johnson announced that General Westmoreland would be the

Army's next Chief of Staff; on March 31, the President announced restrictions on the bombing of North Vietnam and on the number of soldiers he was sending to Vietnam (just 13,500 support troops), and further, that he would not be a candidate for re-election.

Westmoreland was replaced by General Creighton Abrams on July 1, 1968. Abrams had been an enormously successful tank battalion commander in World War Two and understood counterinsurgency very well, but even he was unable to reform the Army's approach to insurgency. Though Abrams attempted to steer the Army away from its search and destroy tactics, the Army culture was too strong even for a man of his stature. Abrams' campaign plan, approved early in 1969, acknowledged diminished public support for the war: "The realities of the American political situation indicate a need to consider time limitations in developing a strategy to 'win.'"[24] Abrams completely changed the emphasis of American strategy in his appropriately named "One War: MACV Command Overview, 1968–72," which stated:

> The key strategic thrust is to provide meaningful, continuing security for the Vietnamese people in expanding areas of increasingly effective civil authority... It is important that the command move away from the over-emphasized and often irrelevant "body count" preoccupation...In order to provide security for the population our operations must succeed in neutralizing the VCI and separating the enemy from the population. The enemy Main Forces and NVA are blind without the VCI. They cannot obtain intelligence, cannot obtain food, cannot prepare the battlefield, and cannot move "unseen."[25]

Unfortunately, Abrams' new strategy, learned at such great cost during nearly 20 years of American experience in Vietnam, ran head-on into the organizational culture of the Army, which still had little intention of changing its focus. In the words of one senior US Army officer, "I'll be damned if I permit the United States Army, its institutions, its doctrine, and its traditions to be destroyed just to win this lousy war."[26] Abrams, although aware of his subordinates' failure to change their operations in accordance with his directives, was unwilling to ruin their careers for their disobedience and was unsure that their replacements would be any more willing to pursue the campaign in a manner antithetical to everything they had been taught.

Search and destroy tactics and excessive use of firepower continued to mark the approach of most American units; they were unable to change their spots after years of a conventional approach to an unconventional war. An emphasis on air assault, armored, and mechanized operations persisted.[27] For example, Lieutenant General Julian Ewell, commander of the 9th Infantry Division and known as the "Delta Butcher," conducted Operation *Speedy Express* in 1969. Supposedly over 10,000 "insurgents" were killed, although only 748 weapons were found, a ratio that dismayed the local CORDS adviser. Lieutenant General Ewell was not replaced but instead promoted to command II Field Force in 1969–70. The Army's continuing offensive orientation was most famously displayed by Major General Melvin Zais' 101st Airborne Division in Operation *Apache Snow* in the A Shau valley from May 11–20, 1969, in an assault on Hill 937, soon to become famous as "Hamburger Hill." 56 Americans were killed and 420 wounded during the 10-day fight for a hill which was abandoned as soon as it was captured. The objective had been to engage the enemy where he was found; the hill itself had no strategic significance.[28]

The battle of Hamburger Hill captured the attention of the nation, and impelled President Nixon to visit Vietnam on July 30. While there, he announced that he had "changed General Abrams' orders so that they were consistent with the objectives of our new policies. Under the new orders, the primary mission of our troops is to enable the South Vietnamese forces to assume the full responsibility for the security of South Vietnam."[29] Thus, although Abrams was unable to change the strategy of the US Army, the President was able to bring the Army home; the number of US forces declined steadily for the next three years, as did the number of large search and destroy operations and American casualties.

The Nixon administration's plan was to turn over primary fighting responsibilities to the South Vietnamese, while the United States continued to supply material and financial assistance, including air support for the ARVN. The new policy was formally announced in Guam in July 1969, and dubbed "Vietnamization" by Secretary of Defense Melvin Laird. Under Vietnamization, Saigon rapidly increased the size of its regular and paramilitary forces. The ARVN was given improved equipment and better training, including modern rifles, tanks, and artillery. By 1975, the ARVN deployed one million men in 11 infantry divisions, one airborne division, 15 Ranger groups, 66 artillery battalions, and four armored brigades.[30] Unfortunately, while the ARVN became well armed and equipped, deficiencies remained in officer and NCO leadership. Officers were selected on the basis of loyalty to the government as much as their military prowess, and could never rival their North Vietnamese counterparts as leaders.[31] The quality of the ARVN's leadership was not helped by the fact that the American advisory effort was being scaled down even as the need for US advisers increased.

The most positive aspect of Vietnamization was the heightened emphasis placed upon pacification. Territorial militias finally received appropriate attention. Regional Forces and Popular Forces (RF/PF), locally recruited irregular forces, grew from 300,000 in 1967 to 525,000 in 1973. They bore the brunt of the combat against the Viet Cong and NVA, sustaining a higher casualty rate than the American forces or the ARVN. Because of their constant presence and knowledge of their local areas, they were clearly the best forces for securing rural villages. Dollar for dollar, RF/PFs were the most effective force for killing Viet Cong and NVA in the whole country; they absorbed only 2–4 percent of South Vietnam's war costs but accounted for 12–30 percent of all Viet Cong and NVA combat deaths.[32] Additionally, four million citizens were recruited into the People's Self-Defense Force and armed, in order to defend their own communities and back up the RF/PFs.

Three other actions also contributed to improving pacification efforts. First, Ambassador William Colby, who took over CORDS in late 1968, helped expand and decentralize the Phoenix program in order to better collect intelligence on the Viet Cong infrastructure. As a result, by 1971, the Phoenix program had led to the capture or killing of 48,000 Viet Cong.[33] Its perceived success in damaging Viet Cong command and control, would later impress American commanders thinking about how to fight in Iraq. Second, CORDS extended the "Chieu Hoi" program, which offered amnesty to Viet Cong who would surrender or serve as informants. In 1969, more Viet Cong defected (47,000) than in any other year of the war.[34] Third, the GVN finally pushed through reforms to improve the lives of the rural population. President Thieu enacted laws to redistribute land from landlords to tenant farmers, such as the 1970 "Land to the Tiller" law, which addressed some of the rural population's grievances with the government, and undercut support for the Viet Cong. It was unfortunate that the improvements in pacification only came after the US decision to withdraw.

Meanwhile, as American combat forces were being withdrawn, the NVA and Khmer Rouge insurgents in neighboring Cambodia increased their preparations for decisive attacks against South Vietnam. President Nixon ordered that their base areas be raided in early 1970. A coordinated US–ARVN attack began on May 1, 1970, which ended two months later without capturing the elusive Central Office of South Vietnam (COSVN) Headquarters. The offensive not only revealed serious shortcomings in ARVN organization and performance, but also led to widespread protests against the widening of the war in the United States. In the aftermath of tragedies such as the deaths of four student protesters at Kent State University on May 4, Congress took action to force an acceleration of the US withdrawal, and explicitly prohibited operations outside South Vietnam involving US ground forces. As a result, the February 1971 invasion of Laos ordered by President Nixon was conducted entirely by ARVN forces, without the US advisers who had played a key role in controlling American fire support for all ARVN operations for the preceding 10 years. The attack was repulsed by the NVA, displaying further weaknesses in ARVN and GVN leadership.

Taught by the US military to fight with the support of robust American artillery, armored, logistics, and helicopter resources, the ARVN had grown dependent. The ARVN had its own artillery, armor, logistical support, and helicopters, but did not have the lavish resources necessary to maintain and employ them. The ARVN still had American air power to call upon for support when the NVA launched a conventional invasion of the South on March 31, 1972; with that support the attack was defeated, although at great cost. The last American ground troops withdrew from South Vietnam in August 1972. The loss of American public support for the government's Vietnam policy in the wake of the Watergate scandal meant that when the North Vietnamese attacked again on March 10, 1975, the GVN could not count on American air support. Despite the absence of air cover, the ARVN fought gallantly in some places, such as Xuan Loc, but in others commanders as well as soldiers readily deserted. The NVA quickly broke through the South Vietnamese defenses. On April 30, 1975 Saigon fell to the NVA – 25 years to the day after President Truman had first authorized US military assistance to Indochina.

Counterinsurgency Doctrine and Learning after Vietnam

The United States failed to adapt to the demands of counterinsurgency in Vietnam because the organizational culture of its military, particularly the Army, focused on conventional warfare as its primary purpose. That misguided organizational culture continued to exert a pernicious effect after the war. In the wake of its defeat in Vietnam, the US military ignored counterinsurgency, and continued to focus on the conventional warfare that has always been its preference. An important milestone came in 1981 when Colonel Harry Summers, a professor at the Army War College, published *On Strategy: A Critical Analysis of the Vietnam War* to enthusiastic reviews from the Army's leadership. The book inaccurately argued that the reason for the Army's defeat in Vietnam had been that it focused too exclusively on counterinsurgency and not enough on conventional combat. The creation of AirLand Battle Doctrine in the 1980s took that lesson to heart, re-energizing an Army struggling to recover from the hangover of Vietnam by focusing its efforts on a conventional war with the Soviet Union. Counterinsurgency received little attention. The low-scale counterinsurgency campaign in El Salvador in the 1980s was fought almost exclusively by Special Forces soldiers, and never engaged the Army or the US Marines. Although conventional war against the Soviet Union never emerged, Saddam Hussein's invasion of Kuwait did, and the US Army and Marine Corps triumphed in the kind of war it had always wanted to fight.

After the apparent victory of *Desert Storm*, the 1990s was a confused decade for the American military, which struggled to understand what David Halberstam called "War in a Time of Peace." Even as US forces deployed to fight campaigns that included aspects of counterinsurgency in Somalia, Bosnia, and Kosovo – and as a global Islamic insurgency took root – the Army and Marines continued to prepare for conventional combat at their training centers and in their schoolhouses. The State Department and USAID also abandoned the hard-won lessons they had learned about assisting foreign governments under the harsh conditions of an insurgency. The United States focused on winning short campaigns to topple unfriendly governments without considering the more difficult tasks required to rebuild friendly ones. Thus stunningly successful invasions of Afghanistan in 2001 and of Iraq in early 2003 were triumphs without victory, as stubborn insurgencies stymied America's conventional military power.

Reflecting on the impact of Vietnam on Operation *Iraqi Freedom*, General Jack Keane stated, "We put an Army on the battlefield that I had been a part of for 37 years. It doesn't have any doctrine, nor was it educated and trained, to deal with an insurgency... After the Vietnam War, we purged ourselves of everything that had to do with irregular warfare or insurgency, because it had to do with how we lost that war. In hindsight, that was a bad decision."[35] The nation's studious avoidance of the problems implicit in counterinsurgency resulted in a national security apparatus that was unprepared in doctrine, organization, training, and equipment for the wars that it was tasked to fight in the early years of the 21st century. Instead, the Army and Marine Corps – and the other agencies of the United States government that have such an important role to play in successful counterinsurgency efforts – had to relearn lessons under fire. Tragically, those lessons had already been purchased with American and Vietnamese blood 40 years before, in another long war in a place called Vietnam.

8

RED WOLVES AND BRITISH LIONS

The Conflict in Aden

Jonathan Walker

Origins of the Conflict

The settlement of Aden, on the southwestern tip of the Arabian peninsula, was the first acquisition of Queen Victoria's reign. Procured in 1839, it became Britain's only Arab colony. Initially a coaling station on the route to India, it later became a large military base and strategic pivot between Britain's African and Far East colonies. To provide a buffer in the hinterland behind Aden township, the British entered into a series of treaties with the fierce and independent local tribes, under the umbrella of a Western and Eastern Aden Protectorate. The development of air power in the early part of the 20th century enabled the British to control this rugged and mountainous region, essentially by "proscription bombing"[1] when bribes of guns and money failed to keep the peace. This policy largely maintained the status quo until the advent of the Cold War.

In the 1950s, Britain's empire was under siege. India had become independent in 1947, depriving the empire of a large, cheap reservoir of armed forces at a time when Britain was economically pressed. Furthermore, the United States was keen to see the British Empire dismantled in oil-rich areas such as the Middle East, and events in Palestine in 1948 and in Suez in 1956 had hardly helped the British lobby in the region. Early Arab nationalism, espoused by Egypt's President, Gamal Abdel Nasser, was indulged by US policy, for as one CIA operative put it:

> If he [Nasser] had to be "anti" anything (and he did, in accordance with the principle that it's easier to rally followers against something than for something), we preferred that it be "imperialism" rather than Israel.[2]

Nasser was ready to export his brand of Arab nationalism throughout the Middle East, but first he wished to be rid of the British presence in South Arabia. In 1962, he supported an armed coup which ousted the religious ruler of the Kingdom of North Yemen, a country on the northern border of the Protectorates. There was little of value to Nasser in this backward state, now renamed the Yemen Arab Republic (YAR), but its strategic position allowed him a springboard into South Arabia. There also remained the ultimate prize of Saudi Arabia and her vast oil wealth.

Nasser's aspirations were widely shared by Arab nationalists in Aden and a number of terrorist attacks were carried out, including an attempted assassination in December 1963 of the British High Commissioner, Sir Kennedy Trevaskis. Against a background of spiraling unrest, the British government attempted to tighten up the loose treaties of the hinterland and secure them around Aden and its military base. The formation of a Federation of South Arabia in the early 1960s in place of the old Protectorates was, in the words of a leading adviser, Donal McCarthy, a "*cordon sanitaire* created to preserve the Aden military base." However, he complained that ultimately it was more like "a chastity belt – uncomfortable without necessarily preventing impregnation."[3] The retention of military bases had worked in Cyprus after independence in 1960, but President Makarios, together with his Greek and Turkish counterparts, had been minded to conclude a deal. In South Arabia, neither the belligerents nor their external sponsors were ready for any peaceful settlement. The scene was set for an insurgency, which lasted until the British withdrawal in November 1967 and involved a prolonged campaign "up-country" in the Radfan mountains, as well as a bitter urban conflict in the streets of Aden.

The Radfan Campaign

The National Liberation Front (NLF) commenced its first major campaign against the Federation in the highland region of the Radfan, a rugged and isolated area of some 400 square miles, containing numerous *wadis* (dried river beds) and *jebels* (mountains), and lying 60 miles north of Aden. Although nominally under the control of a British ally, the Amir of Dhala, the Radfan was a region of many warring clans and tribes, dominated by the fierce Qateibi, self-styled "Red Wolves of Radfan." Such tribes, for whom the possession of weapons was a birthright, had traditionally earned much of their livelihood from exacting tolls from passing caravans. A sizeable part of this booty now had to be paid into Federation coffers.

This was a financial grievance carefully exploited by the NLF, who used their bases just across the border in the Yemen Arab Republic (YAR) as safe sanctuaries. The Egyptian-backed government in this new republic was far from in control, and a British-inspired clandestine war made sure that this position would remain unchanged. Nevertheless, the border region remained highly porous for insurgents, and largely inaccessible to British and Federation troops.[4] This was in contrast to previous border experiences during the Malayan Emergency, which had proved more favorable and where not only was an agreement reached with neighboring Thailand over cross-border security, but also intelligence was widely shared between the countries' security agencies.

By late 1963, the situation in the Radfan had deteriorated, with dissident tribesmen blocking and mining the Dhala Road, a twisting and precarious track which formed the main artery connecting the Radfan to Aden. The Federation had to make a display of control over the region, and to facilitate that control an operation was devised to build a new road into the heart of the Radfan. However, roads were an anathema to the mountain tribesmen, who feared the loss of work from transporting goods by camel over the mountain passes, as well as the prospect of penetration of their isolated world. Operation *Nutcracker* commenced on January 4, 1964, and although it involved the local Federal Regular Army (FRA), its commander was a British officer (Brigadier James Lunt) and the enterprise was supported by a troop of Centurion tanks from The Queen's Royal Lancers (16/5 L) together with 3rd Regiment Royal Horse Artillery (3 RHA) and 12th Field Squadron, Royal Engineers. Despite Lunt's reservations that territory won might not be held, the expedition carved a route through hostile territory and the road was finally built. Local tribesmen were employed by day to help build the road, but at night would take to the mountaintops to snipe at the British encampments.

The problem of operating in the Radfan was the domination of heights, inherent in any mountain campaign. Picquets had to climb the 4,000 laborious feet to the top ridges or plateau, or be airlifted by the few available Belvedere or Wessex helicopters. Helicopters were a precious commodity, and were working near the extent of their air ceiling and heat tolerance. Sniping added an extra worry to pilots who spent interminable minutes hovering above ridges obscured by dust, while dropping troops or placing 105mm pack howitzers. British helicopter design was still some

Aden

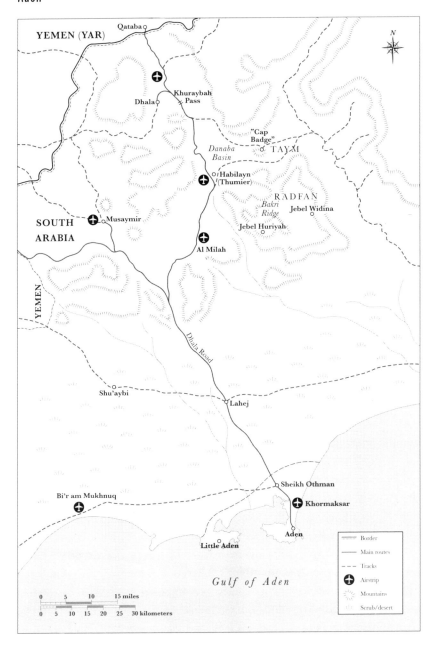

way behind the Americans and Soviets and, although the pilots displayed
great skill, there were simply never enough helicopters to reinforce British

or FRA positions under threat.[5] And with each man consuming 5 liters of water per day, many sorties were taken up with just keeping the existing picquets supplied with food, water, and ammunition. Building the road through the Wadi Taym was a great achievement, but unless the heights above it could be held on a permanent basis, control of the road would be lost. Dissidents, who could survive on little sustenance, slowly took back the high ground, tearing up the road as they went. Air support from 208 Squadron Hawker Hunters knocked out some enemy positions, but with only a 10 percent kill rate, due to the unsophisticated 25-year-old rockets as well as dust screens from previous salvoes, there was a limit to their impact. As Brigadier Lunt predicted, his FRA units became depleted and had to retire at the end of February 1964, leaving the mountains and *wadis* to the NLF and their Qateibi allies.[6]

Such was the shortage of intelligence that the British continued to see the Radfan rebellion as tribal-inspired and therefore lacking in any agenda beyond some financial grievances. There was a serious lack of human intelligence (HUMINT), as there was very little opportunity to infiltrate tribes or clans, due to their isolated villages, which had little outside human traffic. Local political officers may have had the ear of friendly clan members, but a lack of Arab-speaking British soldiers meant greater reliance on a few interpreters. This problem was aggravated by the legacy of proscription bombing, which allowed land forces to be substituted by air control. There was really no substitute for "boots on the ground" or intelligence agents out in the field.

Because of the meager intelligence, great reliance was placed on information from journalists, especially those coming out of Yemen and the border region. This was the age of new "photojournalism," with a number of large-format magazines, such as *Life* and *Paris Match*, feeding a public demand for action pictures and sometimes brutal photography from a host of post-war colonial conflicts. In South Arabia, the Army's response to the media was curious. Guidelines for officers and troops indealing with the press were few, and newsmen found they had liberal access to hotspots. Journalists have always been in a position to pick up local information, but their easy passport across South Arabia allowed more license than usual. If they chose to pass it on, such HUMINT could be extremely useful to the British forces. However, Middle East Land Forces and the British Foreign Office's Information Research Department proved less adept at public relations than their enemies.[7]

The early 1960s was the time when cheap transistor radios first became available. This new medium was used to great effect by Nasser, who promoted his nationalist message over the airwaves via the Egyptian wireless station, "Voice of the Arabs." This message reached all parts of South Arabia, so that even the most primitive and isolated tribesman now had access to anti-British propaganda. The Radfan again became the focus of dissident attacks and in April 1964, the British High Commissioner had to admit that "The Aden–Dhala Road is again unusable as the area is now under guerrilla control." In an attempt to crush the dissidents and drive them out of the Radfan, the Commander Aden Garrison, Brigadier Louis Hargroves, swiftly put together a brigade-size force. However, within Middle East Command (MEC) there was some disagreement as to the extent of the objectives, because the size of the rebel threat could not be accurately assessed.[8] The overall objective was to draw out the dissidents and kill them with superior firepower, and then destroy their crops and means of subsistence; there was certainly no talk of "hearts and minds." Whereas in Malaya there had been a campaign of forced resettlement in some areas, with the creation of new villages free of Communist influence, in South Arabia this was not possible. Tribal loyalty was too strong and ingrained to move communities, while new land meant new cultivation, and in most areas the soil was simply too arid. These limitations were further compounded by the inertia of the Colonial Service administration, which failed to foster civic action programs in the hinterland. Despite the best efforts of British political officers who worked up-country, support for projects was minimal:

> Generally speaking, the non-Arabist, frequently changing and largely administrative Colonial Service in Aden did not match the limited but active intelligence and drive of most of the Service up-country. There was practically no interchange between the Colonial Service in the field and the Colonial Service at home, and little or no first-hand knowledge of the area among politicians and public here [in London].[9]

The Abyan Cotton Scheme, which capitalized on an extremely fertile band of land running through the Fadhli and Lower Yafa'i tribal areas, was one exception. Equipped with a number of engineers, researchers, and agricultural and water specialists, the scheme grew cotton in fields fed by the rich floodwater from Wadi Bana. But this project owed more to the individual zeal of its managers than to any government direction.[10]

This lack of investment, and indeed interest, by the British Foreign Office in the hinterland hardly created an affinity between the Radfan tribes and the new Federal government. The tribes had their own rulers, customs, and justice systems without, they felt, the need for outside interference, and members of the Federal government often had little sway over events in the tribal lands.[11] However, one area that the British government had always indulged was the creation of local military formations. The four battalions of Aden Protectorate Levies (APL), firstly under army and later Royal Air Force (RAF) control, were the forerunners of the Federal Regular Army (FRA), which was created for the new Federation in 1961. The FRA was originally officered by British regulars but over the next few years there was a move to "Arabize" the 4,000-strong force. While the individual Arab soldier could be trained, and a certain esprit de corps evolved, tribal ties remained stronger than loyalty to the Federation. The NLF methodically infiltrated the FRA and the Arab Army's British Commander, Brigadier Gordon Viner, even found that the first FRA student he sent to Staff College, Camberley, turned out to be an NLF member. Yet at the time, few of the remaining British officers in the FRA voiced concerns about the loyalty of their Arab troops.

Brigadier Hargroves' "Radforce" comprised units from 45 Commando, Royal Marines (45 Cdo RM); 3rd Battalion, The Parachute Regiment (3 PARA); 1st Battalion, The East Anglian Regiment; D Squadron, 4th Royal Tank Regiment (4 RTR); and J Battery, 3rd Regiment, Royal Horse Artillery (3 RHA), together with two battalions of FRA. In order to occupy the Radfan heights, the initial objective was to capture the 3,700-foot mountain known as "Cap Badge." To do this, three companies of 45 Cdo RM would secure the Danaba basin surrounding the mountain, while B Company, 3 PARA would be parachuted onto "Cap Badge," both operations starting during the night of April 30/May 1, 1964. But disaster struck. A troop from A Squadron, 22 Special Air Service Regiment (22 SAS), who were to mark the drop zone for 3 PARA, were attacked by rebels, and the parachute drop had to be canceled.[12] Instead, 3 PARA marched by night to take "Cap Badge" from the southeast, as 45 Cdo RM scaled the southwest side of the mountain. Because of the lower temperatures during night operations, water consumption was less, but the route for both units was hard going and as dawn broke on May 5, 3 PARA found themselves in front of the rebel-held village of Al Naqil. A fierce fight ensued, in which they suffered two killed and eight wounded, but eventually they took the village and joined 45 Cdo RM on the summit of "Cap Badge."

The first objectives in the Radfan campaign having been achieved, MEC was able to reflect on the problems encountered:

> Almost invariably the time taken to get from one point to another was underestimated, even after air reconnaissance and the study of air photographs. Initially, the maps available were of poor quality, inaccurate and with few details. Eventually Commanders were considerably more cautious in their estimation of time and space problems.[13]

This admission highlighted the fact that there were still too few helicopters available. The Belvedere, while having a good capacity, needed a large, clear landing zone and was too high off the ground for quick loading and unloading, often in view of enemy snipers. And British units invariably found that the enemy kept their distance; they knew the crags, rocks, and valleys, were as light on their feet as mountain goats, and once contact was made, regularly changed positions. Consequently, British infantry units rarely captured any rebels alive, which hardly helped their already meager intelligence on enemy deployments; and the enemy left little evidence of their casualties, carting them swiftly away for burial according to Islamic custom. Frustrated by this lack of close encounter, British troops often called in air support from Hawker Hunters. This required ground-based Forward Air Controllers (FAC) and Forward Observation Officers (FOO) to mark the intended strike, but they too faced inaccessible terrain. Hunters from 43(F) or 208 Squadron would attack ground targets in pairs, diving from 3,000 feet at 500mph and releasing 3-inch rockets or short bursts of cannon fire. From that height and speed, scurrying tribesmen, already obscured by dust and rocks from previous rocket salvoes, were very difficult to hit. Consequently ammunition and rocket expenditure was increasing at an alarming rate and was cause for concern. For British units trapped by ambush or fighting in remote *wadis*, there was great incentive to call in artillery strikes. This in turn created logistical problems, as the 105mm pack howitzers manned by the horse gunners often had to be dismantled and moved over passes by camel train. Should the elusive helicopters not appear, much of the ammunition also had to be brought forward in this way.[14]

The rebel threat remained. Although the northern end of the Radfan mountains was temporarily under British control, the southern heights of the Bakri Ridge and Jebel Huriyah remained in enemy hands. As "Radforce" was only temporary, a new brigade had to be found to complete the objectives. Finding a suitable brigade from a British Army already heavily committed to emergencies in Borneo, Cyprus, and East Africa was none too easy. However, Headquarters 39 Brigade, normally based in Northern Ireland, was brought in to take command of operations in the Radfan.

On May 18, the fresh C Company, 3 PARA, led by Major Tony Ward-Booth, scaled the heights of Bakri – each man with an 80-lb pack – and as they moved forward, encountered fire from rebel positions. This time the enemy was in entrenched positions, with a network of forts and underground caves. As RAF Hunters flew in from Khormaksar airfield, they streamed rockets onto the defenders in their *sangars*.[15] The tribesmen continued to hold out, while those in the caves fought 3 PARA to the last man. Meanwhile, 3 miles to the west, 1 East Anglian, together with 2 FRA, moved along the Wadi Misrah to close the approach to the final objective, the 5,500-foot peak of Jebel Huriyah. Once the Bakri Ridge was quelled, units from 3 PARA and 45 Cdo RM abseiled down the sheer sides of the mountain into Wadi Dhubsan, a basin below Huriyah. There they encountered further resistance before they could finally control this heart of the Radfan on May 28. With the capture by the East Anglians of Jebel Huriyah on June 12 and the occupation of nearby Jebel Widina on June 27, 1964, the Radfan campaign came to a close.[16]

The Radfan heights continued to be picqueted, but the British could not afford the investment of forces required to seal the *jebels* (mountains) and *wadis*. MEC again conceded that even brigade-strength campaigns could not suppress the tribesmen, admitting that "the latest intelligence reports indicate that supplies continue to be sent from Yemen into Radfan." Indeed, a lower intensity campaign continued to be waged in the Radfan by British and FRA forces right up to British withdrawal in 1967. There were no attempts at dialogue with the rebel tribes, through fear that any deals with local sheiks would founder once the NLF re-emerged. And there was no hearts and minds campaign, such as the one that underpinned General Sir Gerald Templer's counterinsurgency operations in Malaya (see chapter 6). The British saber had been rattled in the Radfan, but as the armored and artillery units started to pull out, tribesmen in sandals, mixed with NLF cadres in combat fatigues, confidently picked their way across the mountain passes from Yemen, back into the Radfan.[17]

Urban Warfare in Aden

Part of the reason for the Radfan campaign was to wave the Federal flag, yet there was also a fear in London that the British presence in South Arabia, and thereby the Gulf region, was about to fall to revolutionary forces under "the domino effect." The US was beginning to see this effect in Southeast Asia, and elements inside the early 1960s Conservative government in Britain were determined to see off the threat. Influential lobbies outside of government, including Billy McLean and David Stirling, assisted in stalling Nasser's advance in Yemen through a clandestine war.[18] But October 1964 saw the election of a Labour government under Harold Wilson, and a change in foreign policy took place. Among government ministers there was some empathy for the nationalist cause in Britain's Dependent Territories and when it was allied to emerging trade union activity, it found more than one sympathetic ear in Westminster.[19] For while the NLF and its leader, Qatan al-Sha'abi, remained in the shadows, other nationalists such as Abdullah al-Asnag maintained a high-profile trade union mantle in an increasingly powerful movement. The expansion of Aden port, and particularly the creation of a large BP refinery across the bay at Little Aden, had drawn in large numbers of Yemeni immigrants from the north, as well as landless tribesmen from the south. This large labor force in Aden became a vociferous campaigner for union strength, which was increasingly allied with nationalist goals. While the British government seemed unwisely focused on the trade union-based nationalist forces, its position was also undermined by the attitude of the US government. In the Cyprus Emergency, the threat of a Greek war with Turkey and more importantly a conflict within NATO, had kept the US on board diplomatically. However, in 1962, the US had swiftly recognized the anti-British Yemen Republic, and seemed committed to reducing Britain's influence in the Middle East.[20]

Al-Asnag, in and out of jail, and in and out of favor with the Egyptians, nevertheless was a nationalist the Wilson government felt they could do business with. During 1965, al-Asnag helped to orchestrate industrial unrest, and as the focus moved from the Radfan to Aden town, the NLF and rival dissident groups began an assassination and terror campaign. They targeted the Aden Special Branch in an attempt to cripple intelligence gathering and were brutally successful, slaughtering 18 British and Adeni officers. Even the British government's announcement that independence would be granted to the Federation in 1968 failed to dampen the insurrection. Bomb outrages and industrial action were countered by the appointment of known nationalists and agitators to the Federal government, but to no avail. Witnesses to killings were threatened by the NLF, as were juries, so that trials collapsed and the perpetrators remained free. The dissidents capitalized on a weak and overlapping Federal security system, which had only received an overall Director of Intelligence, John Prendergast, as late as 1966. He was able to bring his skills, honed in the emergencies in the Canal Zone, Kenya, and Cyprus, to bear on an ebbing tide, but such experience was rarely lauded in the Aden Police. Lessons from previous insurgencies were hardly ever learned, as one experienced police officer recalled:

> After nearly every campaign an official report is produced, duly classified and entombed in a thousand safes. I cannot remember any of these reports being put to any practical use although once, during the Borneo Campaign, I was allowed a quick glance at a highly classified booklet on the Emergency in Cyprus. Whatever lessons were learned there were not to be divulged to anyone actually engaged in counter-insurgency.[21]

There was increasing NLF infiltration in the two main police units in Aden: these were the Aden Police, who dealt with civil matters, and the Aden Armed Police, who fulfilled a paramilitary role. A weakened civil police force was tolerant of dissident-inspired extortion or bank raids, but it was the paramilitary police unit that gave most cause for concern, with its traditional recruitment in the NLF-dominated hinterland. Consequently, sensitive information was often withheld by the High Commission and MEC, for fear of leaks, and this did little for the integration of "economic, intelligence and military units" that was deemed so important in any COIN operation.[22]

Meanwhile, in neighboring Yemen the civil war spluttered on. Egyptian and YAR troops were largely confined to the capital and lowland areas, while the Royalist rebels held on to areas in the highlands. US support for Egypt was falling away as Nasser began courting the Soviet Union and the US adopted a more pro-Zionist stance. By early 1966, the British government was still declaring a public policy of independence for the Federation, coupled with retention of the British military base and defense agreements. The Defence Secretary, Denis Healey, even confirmed in January 1966 that "Britain had no intention of reneging on her commitments in the Middle East."[23] Yet one month later, the government's representative, Lord Beswick, told aghast Federal leaders that Britain would withdraw no later than 1968, and would neither retain her military base nor accept any future defense treaties. This about-face resulted from a Government Defence Review of commitments east of Suez, but it was a devastating blow to Britain's remaining friends in South Arabia, not to mention the Gulf States.

It was no coincidence that 1966 saw an upsurge in violence in Aden with 480 reported incidents compared to 286 the previous year. This upsurge resulted in 573 military and civilian casualties, against 239 in 1965.[24] It was also a time of tumult in the revolutionaries' ranks, and as dissident groups splintered, so intelligence gathering became more difficult. Egypt brokered a new unified nationalist group called the Front for the Liberation of Occupied South Yemen (FLOSY). Despite its innocuous name, it initially contained both the NLF and groups allied to al-Asnag, but it was not long before infighting started. The NLF broke away and the rump of FLOSY flocked to al-Asnag's banner, forming a military wing in the process. After a series of gang murders, these two nationalist groups became sworn enemies and vied with each other for local and world opinion. While the NLF had a cell structure and, importantly, strived for support both in Aden town and up-country, they also infiltrated the local civil administration, police, and armed forces. FLOSY continued to be courted by the Wilson government, which even sent their "wild card," Tom Driberg, to "bash nationalist heads together," but they were backing the wrong group. FLOSY had all the right nationalist credentials – feted by the newly emerging African states, lobbied for at the United Nations, their case pursued by Amnesty International – but their franchise barely extended beyond the trade union movement in Aden. Lacking a network of tribal support, the nationalist group was just too narrow and too small for such a disparate region.

Crater

Aden was dominated by a large volcanic mass called Jebel Shamsan, and within its basin lay the township of Crater. It was accessed by a narrow pass from the port area of Ma'alla, around the head of which lay Tawahi district, home to the High Commission and the interrogation center at Fort Morbut.

Across the causeway, over the salt pans, lay Khormaksar airfield and Radfan military camp, with the township of Sheikh Othman beyond. Both Crater and Sheikh Othman were centers of dissident activity and it was here that the British Army honed its street-fighting skills. The narrow alleyways were perfect hiding places for gunmen or insurgents with Blindicide rocket launchers. The Royal Pioneer Corps did their best to block escape routes along these dark passages, but no sooner had they been completed than the dissidents demolished them. The townships were awash with illegal guns and grenades, and much patrol time was taken up searching for arms caches; some of these were hidden in mosques, but the security forces were forbidden entry. They were also barred from searching Muslim women, even if the women were suspected of carrying weapons or explosives.

The failure of British intelligence to penetrate the higher echelons of the NLF or FLOSY was not a new problem. In Palestine, some 15 years earlier, there had been similar difficulties in placing agents inside the insurgent Stern Gang, as well as protecting British and Arab Special Branch officers from assassination. Conversely, Jewish terrorist gangs had much success in infiltrating the Palestinian police, and ironically many of their more profitable deceptions involved security officers who were originally trained by SIS or SOE for operations during World War Two.[25] However, one lesson from Palestine was absorbed in Aden: that execution of terrorists was no deterrent. Even so, with little likelihood of a successful prosecution in court, through a dearth of witnesses, and with the certainty that British control was to end shortly, there were few deterrents to a grenadier or terrorist sniper.

Since the local Special Branch was crippled through losses and desertions, the security forces began to place greater reliance on interrogation, and increasing numbers of suspects were taken into the Detention Centre at al-Mansoura and the Interrogation Centre at Fort Morbut. Soldiers in Crater, exhausted by the intense Aden heat and agitated after weeks of rioting street mobs, showed little restraint in dragging local Arabs in for questioning, even in the face of the world's press. For interrogators, the cell structure of a terrorist group such as the NLF proved notoriously difficult to break into. Allegations of mistreatment at Fort Morbut soon reached both the United Nations and Amnesty International and, following lurid press reports, the British government launched an investigation in October 1966. This found irregularities but few foundations for accusations of cruelty.[26] However, the allegations would not die and Amnesty International vigorously pursued them.

Interrogation was not the most productive method for gathering intelligence; suspects, in order to obtain their release, often gave numerous false leads, which had to be followed up at the expense of more manpower.

In order to capture or eliminate terrorists operating in the crowded backstreets of Sheikh Othman or Crater, army units went undercover. Some infantry battalions had their own "Special Branch" units comprising men from reconnaissance platoons, in plain clothes and armed with either a 9mm Browning or Sterling sub-machine gun. In addition, the Special Air Service (SAS) used a tried and tested routine involving two- or four-man teams disguised as Arabs. Major Roy Farran's use of counter-gangs to fight terrorists had ended in his court martial in Palestine and the disbandment of the undercover units, but in Aden the spirit was resurrected by SAS units employing "keeni-meeni" tactics for nighttime operations. This involved SAS units, disguised as Arabs, using colleagues in plain clothes as bait. As the local terrorist grapevine started working and gunmen or grenadiers showed themselves, the "local Arabs" standing nearby would retaliate. The operation took great skill and speed, but such tactics worked better in isolated areas. In crowded areas, other friendly undercover units were likely to be operating, and there were fatal instances of "friendly fire."[27]

Mutiny

The extraordinary success of the Israelis in the Six-Day War in early June 1967, and Nasser's subsequent blaming of Britain and the US for the debacle, inflamed Arab opinion throughout the Middle East. In Aden on June 20, tensions were running high as 1st Battalion, Royal Northumberland Fusiliers (1 RNF) were handing over responsibility for Crater to 1st Battalion, Argyll and Sutherland Highlanders (1 A & SH). That morning, Arab Army apprentices had gone on the rampage just outside Crater. As the mutiny spread to Champion Lines, 10 British servicemen were killed. Alarm spread to the Aden Armed Police barracks inside Crater, where their officers, assisted by the NLF, organized a blockade and ambush. A patrol from 1 RNF had gone missing, and a mixed party of "Geordies" and "Jocks" in two Land-Rovers, led by Major John Moncur, went looking for them.[28] The Moncur party drove into the ambush, and eight men were slaughtered by gunfire; only one escaped. Meanwhile the earlier patrol, led by Second Lieutenant John Davis, who had been out of radio contact, returned to base and were ordered out straightaway to help the ambushed patrol. In attempting to keep the Arab mob at bay, they too were killed, while a helicopter circling overhead was shot down. To the dismay of their surviving comrades, permission to use the main 76mm guns of the Saladin armored cars was turned down. MEC refused to launch an attack and rescue mission into Crater. Under pressure from the British government, who feared an escalation and full-blown Arab mutiny, the British Army withdrew from Crater, and eventually received the mutilated remains of the ambushed soldiers.

Against this background, the Argylls, under the command of Lieutenant Colonel Colin Mitchell, assumed responsibility for Crater. For the next two weeks, they took up positions with other units on the mountain ridges around Crater, sniping armed insurgents inside Crater while British intelligence engaged in secret talks with contacts of both the NLF and PORF (Popular Organization of Revolutionary Forces – the armed wing of FLOSY). Although the two-week occupation of Crater was a propaganda coup for the anti-British forces, it failed to militarily benefit either the NLF or FLOSY, who spent their time attempting to eliminate each other. Eventually, permission was given on July 3 for the reoccupation of Crater by the Argylls, by which time the British had secured a number of "inside deals" on reducing tension in Crater. However, anti-British elements were probably not prepared for the implementation of "Argyll law" that followed. "Mad Mitch," as the British press christened the Argylls' commander, was not minded to give the local population the benefit of the doubt. He declared, "we're a very mean lot. We will be extremely firm and extremely keen and if anyone starts throwing grenades at us, we will kill them. It's as simple as that." This message found favor among his men, tough soldiers mainly from the central region of Scotland, who were fired up by the recent slaughter and mutilation of their comrades. A sullen attitude among the local population was met by indifference among the Jocks – with British withdrawal only months away, there was nothing left to salvage, save the pride of their regiment and the honor of a British Army seen, humiliatingly, to have handed over Crater to terrorist control. For over three months the Argylls lived inside the township, in requisitioned accommodation. This was an innovation, as previous units had lived outside, only coming into Crater for patrols or reconnaissance. Living inside the territory meant nighttime curfews could be enforced and, with over 30 manned observation posts, the enemy were uncertain as to where a patrol might emerge from. The recent withdrawal from the hinterland meant that the Argylls, unlike the majority of their predecessors, had no need to train for rural operations and could concentrate solely on urban counterinsurgency.

Lieutenant Colonel Mitchell carried out counterinsurgency operations inside Crater to reinforce army control. To "portcullis" a sector meant closing it down, blocking off escape routes, putting everyone up against a wall, and searching them. Anyone running away after being challenged to stop was shot. Such tough action was still possible inside Crater, a long way from mainland Britain, but could not be transferred to closer urban trouble spots, such as Northern Ireland. Mitchell's control even extended to the press, whom he handled deftly, though his outspoken pronouncements were at odds with some of his superiors, notably GOC Middle East Land Forces, Major General Philip Tower. Mitchell's stance was eagerly supported by the British press, who were in need of a British hero after the events of June 20, which in turn made it even harder for Tower to rein him in. Comparing Aden with subsequent British Army operations, the Argylls' battalion intelligence officer, Lieutenant David Thomson, later commented:

> There was a dramatic difference between working with the cream of the world's war correspondents in Aden and then switching to briefing the local "stringer" (with a name to make) on the streets of Belfast. In Aden you needed "officer spokesmen" while in Belfast the articulate soldier could get away with saying things that his commanding officer would have been severely reprimanded for saying.[29]

While the lid was kept on the cauldron of Crater, during September gun battles raged between NLF and FLOSY units in the nearby town of Sheikh Othman. Again, there was little incentive to risk the lives of British soldiers trying to keep apart gunmen who were as intent on killing each other as they were on killing British forces. The NLF, which had by now taken over most of the hinterland, soon gained the upper hand in urban areas. During October, their snipers continued to assassinate innocent civilians and off-duty British servicemen, right up until withdrawal.

Withdrawal

On November 29, 1967, the last British troops left South Arabia. The withdrawal was a textbook combined operation, yet its strict organization was in stark contrast to the political mess left behind. The former terrorists who comprised the new government, including its leader al-Sha'abi, were barely known to the British government, which had invested too much time on the wrong nationalists. The retreat from empire, in South Arabia at least, proved more of a scuttle. When the principle of independence is conceded before an insurgency gathers momentum, as in the Malayan campaign, this can remove one of the major planks of the insurgents' case. However, in the case of the Aden insurgency, dissident groups were already well entrenched, with a string of "battle honors" to boost their credibility, by the time the British government announced a withdrawal date. It therefore provided the dissidents with a fixed timetable. Their course was to eliminate other contenders for future government, by clandestine means or outright use of force. This not only guaranteed their succession, but was also a blatant demonstration of the successful group's military prowess. Consequently, once Britain had given a date, it scored political points in its own constituency at home, but in Aden the insurgents stepped up the level of violence against its army and civil administration. By assassinations and bomb blasts, the NLF wanted to show the Arab world and international observers that they were evicting the British by force and that it was they, and not the British, who were determining events. The other practical effect of a firm withdrawal date was that it condemned, at a stroke, all those who had worked for the British or the Federation. Donal McCarthy, Political Adviser to the Commander-in-Chief, MEC, warned that:

> Local forces, local rulers, administrators and police forces can, when the going gets rough, prove very broken reeds. They are likely to crack as soon as serious political or terrorist opposition develops. When that opposition becomes determined and violent, the first victims are those that collaborate with us, and particularly Arabs on the security side.[30]

Conclusion

The creation of a British Unified Command in Aden (known as Middle East Command or MEC) proved to be one success in a sorry story. Although it was strategically well placed to cover its command area (which it did particularly well during the 1961 Kuwait crisis), MEC could have been moved to the Gulf.[31] But that would have been politically unacceptable in an atmosphere of anti-colonialism fueled by an aggressive

Soviet Bloc. Had Nasser succeeded in Yemen, and had South Arabia fallen under his control, Saudi Arabia, with its small mercenary air force, could not have defended herself; the Gulf States could have been overtaken before they had a chance to develop their economies. The effect on the West's oil supplies can only be imagined.

Following the British withdrawal, a state of turmoil prevailed in Aden. Then, in 1969, al-Sha'abi was overthrown and the Arab world's first Marxist state came into being. The People's Democratic Republic of Yemen (PDRY) became an important Soviet naval base that was vital in assisting the brutal Mengistu Regime to take power in Ethiopia in 1974. The country also became a training ground for Middle East terrorist groups as well as underground gangs from Europe, such as the Red Brigades, Baader-Meinhof, and Euskadi Ta Askatasuna (ETA).[32]

The loss of South Arabia benefited the Soviet Bloc's Middle East designs, but the fall of the Gulf "dominoes" did not materialize. However, Britain's image had taken a battering, and friendly Arab states would view future "British guarantees" with deep skepticism. But international forums, such as the United Nations, had tilted in favor of self-determination for former colonial territories, as had the British government, and the outcome was never in doubt. That the new rulers of this part of South Arabia were even less inclined to democracy than their Federal predecessors mattered little.

The British Army coped well with conditions in the Radfan, and the SAS would make good use of its experiences in its forthcoming actions in Oman, but the porous northern border between the Radfan and Yemen had never allowed them to draw out the full complement of rebels to engage in direct, sustained combat. In the township of Aden, street-fighting skills were honed that would be useful in Northern Ireland, as were lessons in the siting of observation posts, resupply by helicopter, and the use of armored vehicles in riot control. But given that there was little appetite on the part of successive British governments, particularly the Wilson government, for a protracted conflict in Aden, a joint political–military solution was unrealistic.

9

BRITAIN'S LONGEST WAR
Northern Ireland 1967–2007

Colonel Richard Iron

Introduction

Other conflicts have been more bloody,[1] more extensive, and had more at stake, but the Northern Ireland conflict is unique: after three decades of seeming intractability, it has finally reached a peaceful conclusion.

Many books have been written recently on the Northern Ireland conflict, mostly from the viewpoint of the Provisional Irish Republican Army (PIRA), long hidden in the murky world of operational secrecy. Conversely, little has been written about the counterinsurgency, bar the odd journalistic exposé of such newsworthy subjects as Bloody Sunday or the use and abuse of informers. In official circles, security restrictions imposed an almost total ban on accounts of security force operations, to the extent that there is little in the way of public record or lessons learned from the British Army's longest and most extensive counterinsurgency campaign.[2] There is still much about the counterinsurgency operation that remains classified.

Nevertheless, the time is right for an analysis of the campaign as a whole, despite more information being available from ex-insurgent sources than counterinsurgent ones. By combining both insurgent and personal counterinsurgent experiences it is possible, for the first time, to create an understanding of how and why the conflict in Northern Ireland evolved in the way it did.

There have been a large number of insurgent and terrorist groups[3] in Northern Ireland's sad history, many active in the last 40 years. This analysis focuses on the conflict with PIRA, the most dedicated and effective of them all, and the only one that threatened the British government. Without PIRA, the Northern Ireland conflict would have been considerably shorter and less violent.

The Insurgency

Civil Rights, the Military, and Radicalization

The conflict was born out of the civil rights movement, which crossed the Atlantic in the 1960s and found resonance among the minority Catholic population of Northern Ireland who for decades had been denied equality in housing, health, and education. Electoral boundaries had been gerrymandered to enable Protestant democratic control even in areas of Catholic majority, such as Derry, the second city of Northern Ireland.[4] The civil rights movement provoked a violent backlash from Protestant extremists and in 1969 resulted in widespread disorder along ethnic interfaces across Northern Ireland. Many were displaced and took refuge within their own communities, solidifying ethnic divide.

It was against the backdrop of widespread public disorder that the British Army was first deployed in August 1969 to help the devolved Government of Northern Ireland maintain order. Initially the army was deployed to Catholic areas to safeguard them from Protestant attacks.

The political basis of the army's deployment was to support the local Government of Northern Ireland, Protestant-dominated, itself dependent on its power base in the Protestant community. As that community saw itself more at threat from civil rights and growing republicanism,[5] it exerted greater pressure on the Government of Northern Ireland to force the British Army to take action against the nascent threat of armed republicanism. Thus the army was soon seen to become primarily engaged against armed groups within the Catholic nationalist community.

By mid-1970, the great majority of the Catholic minority saw itself under attack not just from the Protestant majority but from the British Army as well. Recruitment into the newly formed PIRA grew dramatically. Catholic communities were embattled in their urban enclaves, especially in Belfast. They were under frequent attack from Protestant mobs, and armed violence escalated. The local police force, the Royal Ulster Constabulary, and its reserve force, the B Specials, were recruited largely from the Protestant community; they were widely seen as supporting the Protestant cause and being anti-Catholic. The British Army was under heavy political pressure to re-impose law and order on the Catholic communities, and conducted heavy-handed search operations and imposed curfews. This reinforced the Catholic community's sense of being under siege, and over a period of 18 months created a radicalization of Catholic communities that was to sustain the republican insurgency for much of the following 30 years.[6]

The PIRA was born in this period. The "Official" IRA, direct descendent of the IRA that fought for Irish independence in 1919–20 and again in the Irish Civil War of 1921–22, had become increasingly politicized by Marxist ideology and was no longer willing or capable of significant military action to protect Catholic enclaves. The "Provisional" IRA was thus created by men of action, with little patience for politics, who believed passionately that armed violence alone could achieve the cause of republicans: Northern Ireland detached from the United Kingdom and re-incorporated into the historic entity of a united Ireland.

At the same time, the insurgency rapidly grew in rural border areas dominated by nationalists with a long history of armed rebellion. PIRA quickly caused the collapse of policing in areas such as South Armagh, where police stations were destroyed and the improvised explosive device (IED) threat prevented police movement by road. It was only through huge effort by the army that any measure of control was maintained.

In retrospect, it was a grave mistake for the British government and its army to support a local government that was itself part of the problem. By continuing to support the local Protestant-dominated government, the British Army allowed itself to be drawn into a position of partiality, and to be seen as being pro-Protestant and anti-Catholic. This increased the perception of the Catholic community as victim, enhancing its radicalization and its support for republicanism, and clearly defining the army as its enemy. The British government dissolved the Government of Northern Ireland in March 1972 and imposed direct rule from the national government at Westminster, London, through a Secretary of State for Northern Ireland. By then, however, it was too late.

Internment and the Evolution of UK and PIRA Strategies

One example of the British Army being pressured into taking action to support the Government of Northern Ireland was the introduction of internment in March 1971. Internment was a tactic that had worked before. In the 1970s, it was a natural response to the deteriorating security situation, but it was implemented earlier than the security forces wished. As a result intelligence preparation was incomplete; many active terrorists were not arrested and continued to operate under cover.

It is commonplace today to describe internment in Northern Ireland as counterproductive.[7] Certainly its implementation was bungled. It became a major embarrassment for the British government internationally, drawing widespread condemnation from abroad. It heightened the sense of antipathy among the nationalist community. Over the four years of its operation, however, it became successful in disrupting PIRA's command structure. For example, over two months in 1974, three successive commanders of PIRA's Belfast Brigade were arrested. Those terrorists that remained at large were driven underground and had to expend much effort in evading detection and capture. Arrests were based mainly on information given by informers, which otherwise could not be used openly in a law court. Between 1971 and 1975, the level of terrorism dropped significantly.

In 1975, the Secretary of State for Northern Ireland ordered the end of internment; all terrorist suspects who could not be prosecuted were released. Terrorists were in future to be treated as ordinary criminals as part of a major new government policy of criminalization. From then on, suspects had to be prosecuted in a court of law, and although changes to the law were effected,[8] it demanded that legal standards of evidence were required for a successful prosecution.

The end of internment had even greater impact on the character of the conflict than its imposition. PIRA transformed its strategy and organization: no longer did it attempt to defeat British forces militarily, but instead adopted a long war strategy aimed at eroding the will of the British government to continue. The organization was reformed on a mainly cellular structure and designed to counter security force attempts at intelligence penetration through informers. The number of active volunteers was reduced and the organization refined. There were greater levels of control imposed by the PIRA leadership, including the development of centralized training and equipment supply. Most of its members could live openly and normally while not physically conducting operations.

For the security forces, the emphasis switched to gaining evidence for successful criminal prosecution, from either eyewitness or forensic evidence. Arrests were no longer made on intelligence: successful prosecution of terrorists was rare.

The 1981 Hunger Strike

The British government's policy of criminalizing PIRA's activities resulted in terrorist prisoners in Northern Ireland being treated as ordinary

Northern Ireland

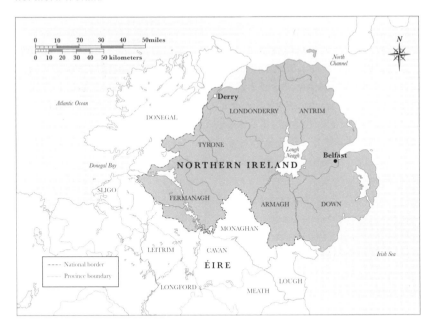

criminals and losing special status as prisoners of war. Prisoners had to wear standard prison clothing; their command structure was ignored by prison authorities; and they were expected to undertake normal prison work. This resulted in a number of internal prison protests, including the "blanket protest," in which PIRA and Irish National Liberation Army (INLA) prisoners opted for nakedness rather than wear prison uniforms, using only blankets for warmth. This extended into the "dirty protest," in which human excrement was smeared across cell walls.

Such protests radicalized republican prisoners, divorcing them from normality.[9] Their philosophy and mentality were akin to those of prisoners of war, calling prison guards "Germans," and likening themselves to inmates of World War Two POW camps. Prison restrictions on association and communication resulted in a sophisticated organization of a well-run underground communications network, based on smuggled "comms," letters written on cigarette papers, hidden through insertion in the anus, vagina, foreskin, or nostril. Comms were usually passed mouth to mouth during the greeting kiss of family and friends during prison visits. PIRA's OC in the Maze Prison[10] was in daily contact with PIRA Army Command, including Gerry Adams.

Ten PIRA and INLA prisoners starved themselves to death between May and October 1981. All were volunteers. Each death was accompanied by widespread violence and public disorder across Northern Ireland, and growing international condemnation of the United Kingdom.

Various attempts to negotiate a settlement were made. These vainly attempted to find a compromise between prisoners and the Northern Ireland Office. In the end, it was the prisoners' families who brought the hunger strike to an end. As the death toll rose and a successful resolution seemed no closer, fewer families were prepared to watch their husbands, sons, and brothers die; they began to order medical intervention as prisoners lost consciousness. PIRA was helpless to stop this family intervention, which was encouraged by the Catholic Church.

There were two unexpected outcomes of the hunger strike that were to have extraordinary impact on the future of the conflict and its eventual resolution. One was that it moved PIRA irrevocably onto a political path, parallel to the armed struggle. In a tactical move to highlight the plight of the hunger strikers, hunger striker Bobby Sands was nominated to contest, from prison, the UK parliamentary seat of Fermanagh and South Tyrone in a by-election. He died shortly after winning the seat. Subsequently, two other hunger strikers were elected to seats in the Dail, the Irish Parliament. PIRA, through its political wing Sinn Fein, has contested parliamentary seats north and south of the border ever since. This was the start of PIRA's long road to a political solution to the Northern Ireland conflict.

The other unexpected outcome is less easy to quantify, but identifiable nevertheless. It was the effect on the British government, shocked by a movement in which 10 people were prepared to starve themselves to death. This was not manipulation of innocent and ignorant foot soldiers by evil masterminds, but evidence of exceptionally strong beliefs which had to be taken seriously.

So, by a strange twist of fate, unimagined by either side at the beginning of the hunger strike, the outcome was, on the PIRA side, a move towards constitutional politics; and on the British side, a reawakening of the need for significant political process. This resulted in the Anglo–Irish Agreement in 1985, the first political admittance that the Republic of Ireland had legitimate interest in the governance of Northern Ireland. Despite its many faults, it was the start of a process that was to end the Northern Ireland conflict.

Weapons Supply, the Libyan Connection, and PIRA's "Tet Offensive"

Throughout the 1970s, most PIRA weapons came from the US. There was strong support from the Irish diaspora, both for fundraising and weapon procurement. It is estimated some 2,500 weapons were smuggled across the Atlantic, including, for a period, 300 per year stolen from the US Marine Corps (USMC) base at Camp Lejeune in North Carolina.[11] It seems little was done to stop this trade, until in 1981 personal appeals by Prime Minister Thatcher to President Reagan resulted in the FBI closing down the US arms supply network to Ireland.

After the closure of the US network, arms supply was uncertain. Overtures by President Gaddafi of Libya in 1984–85 were thus warmly received by PIRA, following the breakdown in British–Libyan relations caused by the murder of Woman Police Constable (WPC) Yvonne Fletcher in London in April 1984.[12] Three shiploads of arms totaling 150 tons, including five tons of Semtex explosive, were shipped to Ireland, and £5 million donated. The fourth shipload, on the MV *Eksund*, was the biggest, equal in size to all the others combined. But in a major success for British intelligence, not only was the shipment discovered and intercepted off the coast of France in October 1987, but also the scuttling charges on board the ship were disrupted prior to its interception.

The capture of the *Eksund* was a major defeat for PIRA. At the time PIRA's military campaign was showing little prospect of success. British security forces had been able to contain the violence to manageable levels, and the British government remained unmoved. PIRA leadership realized that something dramatic was needed to change the dynamic of the conflict: they had planned to use the massive injection of weapons to mount a major operation modeled on the 1968 Tet Offensive in Vietnam. Tet had led the American public to view that war as unwinnable, and hence to subsequent US withdrawal. PIRA planned a similar strategy for Northern Ireland: a major attack to take and hold large areas of rural Armagh, Tyrone, and Fermanagh, either to force British retreat or to provoke use of maximum force. The attack was to be spread later to Britain and Europe.[13]

This plan collapsed with the capture of the *Eksund*. Not only had PIRA lost half the weapons for its Tet Offensive, it also had to deal with the likelihood that British intelligence had discovered their plan. The offensive was called off, and with it PIRA's most ambitious military initiative. This grave disappointment increased pressure on PIRA to seek political compromise.

PIRA's Attacks on England and the Continent

Throughout the conflict, PIRA mounted bombing and shooting campaigns against British targets in Britain and Europe. In the 1970s, indiscriminate attacks against the British public proved to be counterproductive, hardening opinion against PIRA. Later there were a number of high-profile operations against the British government, including an assassination attempt on the Prime Minister in 1984 and a mortar attack on 10 Downing Street in 1991. Campaigns were also mounted against British Army targets in the 1980s, but none succeeded in changing government policy.

The most successful attacks, strategically, were those against economic targets in the early 1990s, in particular in the City of London. In April 1992 the Baltic Exchange was targeted, causing £350 million in damage. This was followed in April 1993 by another bomb, causing £1 billion in damage. In February 1996, a bomb placed near Canary Wharf caused an estimated £85 million in damage. These attacks against the UK's economy almost certainly had greater impact on the British government's negotiations than the killings of soldiers, policemen, and civilians in Northern Ireland during the same period.

The Political Process

British government policy was remarkably consistent through most of the conflict after the introduction of direct rule in 1972. This was because the bulk of the campaign was conducted during the long premiership of Margaret Thatcher from 1979 to 1991, and partly because Northern Ireland was a bipartisan issue in the British Parliament – both Conservative and Labour parties largely agreed on policy, and neither unionist nor nationalist groups were able to exploit divisions in British politics.

Margaret Thatcher's famous quote "we do not negotiate with terrorists" obscures the reality that the British government consistently negotiated with PIRA before, during, and after her premiership. Mostly this was through covert channels, frequently using Catholic priests whose role, often much maligned, was nothing short of heroic in the search for peace. Later, during the period of PIRA's ceasefires in 1994 and 1996, negotiations were held openly. By the early 1990s, channels were open at the tactical level as well; for example, in Derry, the Peace and Reconciliation Group[14] provided a conduit to avoid misunderstanding and reduce tension among the security forces, insurgent groups on both sides, and local communities.

There was great mistrust between PIRA, loyalists, and the British government. American President Bill Clinton played a significant role in bringing the protagonists together in the mid-1990s. Each side had to ensure they did not lose the support of their own power base. In the case of PIRA, the leadership had to convince the active members that they were not being sold out. To them the political process was presented as supporting the armed struggle; in reality, the situation was the opposite. The British government had to persuade the unionist majority that they had nothing to fear from negotiations; they would not be forced into a united Ireland against their will. On all sides, negotiators could be more truthful with each other than with their own constituencies. Public statements often contradicted secret negotiating positions, but each side understood the limitations within which the other operated. It was in such a climate that negotiations finally reached a conclusion with the Good Friday Agreement signed in 1998, laying out a political framework for Northern Ireland on which both republicans and unionists could agree.[15]

Although there will doubtless continue to be disagreements in Northern Ireland, they will most likely be confined to the political rather than the military sphere. It is difficult to put an end date to the insurgency: it could be 1996 when PIRA announced the final ceasefire; or the 1998 Good Friday Agreement; or it could be 2007, when Sinn Fein finally agreed to promote the Northern Ireland police force within its own community. But it is clear that the Northern Ireland conflict between the British government and PIRA is over.

Military Aspects of the Counterinsurgency Campaign

The Nature of Deterrence in Northern Ireland

One of the consequences of PIRA's long war strategy was a reluctance to accept casualties. Its increased reliance on a smaller number of better trained and trusted volunteers meant each one was a greater investment whose loss was more keenly felt than those in the mass movement of the early 1970s. Additionally, each arrest or death was a public success for the security forces that PIRA was keen to avoid.

This had a dramatic effect on the way that PIRA operated, and hence on the opposing tactics developed by the security forces. The emphasis on safety ensured that from the late 1970s, the most important part of every operational plan was a secure escape for the volunteers involved – more important than the success of the operation itself. Considerable effort was made to ensure escape routes were clear before an operation was executed. If there was any perceived threat, then the attack was aborted. With a long war strategy, there was little sense in taking a risk today when the same effect could be achieved with lower risk tomorrow.

Thus the principal approach adopted by the security forces for tackling the terrorist threat was deterrence. The emphasis was not so much on threatening the success of the operation, but threatening the following escape, thus forcing PIRA to abandon the attack. For example, the counter to PIRA shootings of army foot patrols in Belfast or Derry was not to detect or attack the sniper directly, but to develop patrol tactics that threatened escape routes from potential firing points. Thus each patrol had multiple four-man teams operating in support of each other in seemingly random patterns, so at any stage each team was protected by others behind potential firing points.[16] The aim was to make the movement of the satellite teams so unpredictable that it was almost impossible to determine where all teams were at any time and thus create uncertainty in the mind of the terrorist that his escape was secure.

The philosophy of creating uncertainty was also applied to the interdiction of PIRA resupply routes. By the early 1980s, most of the legal cross-border routes were controlled by Permanent Vehicle Check Points (PVCPs). These had an important intelligence function in monitoring cross-border movement, but also deterred the movement of weapons and munitions through searching vehicles. The volume of traffic was normally such that a 100 percent search policy was impractical, but the security forces estimated that a 5 percent chance of detection was enough to deter open movement, so only about one vehicle in 20 was searched. PVCPs were supported by patrol snap Vehicle Check Points (VCPs) to cover areas inland from, or on routes not covered by, the PVCPs. This level of deterrence forced PIRA to adopt ever more sophisticated methods for moving weapons; such sophistication involved larger numbers of people with increased planning, and heightened the vulnerability to exposure of the operation by informers and surveillance.

Attrition of PIRA terrorists reinforced deterrence. Successful operations to ambush known or discovered PIRA operations were rare – about 13 or 14 throughout the entire campaign,[17] usually carried out by Special Forces. The best known was at Loughgall on May 8, 1987, where eight terrorists died. Although infrequent, each operation had a dramatic effect, partially because the casualties were normally senior and seasoned terrorists whose loss was deeply felt within PIRA. The Special Air Service (SAS) gained an aura of invincibility; fear of compromise and ambush was never far from the minds of PIRA volunteers on active duty.

Deterrence was vitally important to the outcome of the campaign. Security force tactics were built on it; attrition supported deterrence, not the other way around. By 1992 it is estimated that in many areas, five out of six PIRA attacks were aborted due to security force activity. Terrorists who are unable to mount attacks are unproductive. Thus security force policy evolved to render the terrorist organization ineffective, not to destroy it.

Framework Operations

Within the broad operational approach of achieving deterrence, security force operations against the insurgency can be categorized as being either framework or covert operations. Framework operations were those conducted by regular military and police forces, and included patrolling, base security, searching for terrorist munitions, overt surveillance, and control of movement. Covert operations were those generally conducted by special forces, both military and police. They largely consisted of covert surveillance and agent recruitment and handling; although direct action was occasionally employed to ambush, kill, or capture terrorists engaged in operations.

For the hundreds of thousands of British soldiers who deployed to Northern Ireland over 30 years, framework operations were a way of life. It was an endless routine of patrolling, searching, guarding, and surveillance. Often it seemed a waste of time; the results in terms of insurgents killed or captured, or munitions found, were sparse. There was resentment against covert forces, whose role seemed much more glamorous. Suspicion abounded that information was being kept from the regular forces. Platoon and company commanders worked hard to maintain enthusiasm and sense of purpose, but options were limited for even the most inspiring of leaders.

The real purpose of framework operations, well done with sound tactics, is even now poorly understood. The British Army's analysis of the campaign[18] suggests that the effort put into creating and maintaining PVCPs on the border was misplaced, since the return in weapons found was minimal. This fails to recognize the real purpose of framework operations. It is to force the insurgent to do two things:

177

- *Work around the framework operation.* If he can't smuggle weapons through the border checkpoint, for example, he needs to find more difficult routes, which are potentially constrained, and open to interdiction by overt or covert patrol. In this regard, the static framework is similar to a minefield in conventional operations: by itself it will never win a battle, but in a good defensive concept it will canalize the enemy into areas where he can be interdicted.
- *Create increasing levels of sophistication.* If the easy options are closed, the insurgents are forced to adopt more complex operations. These involve more moving parts, more people, and more elements potentially to go wrong. They are also more prone to discovery, since the increased circle of knowledge may include an informer.

Anatomy of a PIRA Attack

Another consequence of PIRA's reforms of the late 1970s was the standardization of tactics, training, and doctrine in PIRA's Northern Command – the six counties that make up Northern Ireland and the three border counties in the Republic.[19] An example is the standard drill to mount what might appear to be a relatively simple urban shooting attack against a security force patrol. In fact it evolved into a sophisticated operation with multiple elements:[20]

- *Planning.* Once an opportunity for a shooting was identified, the local operational staff approved the plan and allocated resources, including the sniper and all support personnel required. PIRA quartermaster staff provided the weapon or weapons.
- *The house takeover.* Before the planned attack, a PIRA unit took over a house for the firing point. Often the house belonged to republican sympathizers, but it was made to look like a hostile takeover so the occupants would not later be pressured by the police. The sniper and the weapon were brought into the house once it was secure. The gunman personally prepared the firing point, usually in an upstairs bedroom.
- *Area surveillance.* To overcome the British Army's multiple patrolling system, PIRA used a network of surveillance to ensure there were no elements of the target patrol threatening the escape route. This network consisted normally of 3 to 6 people, arrayed around the firing point. Since this was before the era of cell phones, they communicated via CB

radio. PIRA knew the security forces monitored CB nets, but were forced to accept this since surveillance was so important. If they were unable to confirm where all the elements of an army patrol were, they aborted the attack.

- *The escape.* After the shooting, the sniper ran out of the back of the house, through the yard to the road behind. There were normally two getaway cars, hijacked earlier that day. The sniper handed the weapon to a waiting assistant who, in one of the cars, returned the weapon to a hide. The gunman was driven in the second car to a safe house where, within seconds, he was stripped and in a shower, his clothes in a washing machine; all to destroy forensic evidence from firing the weapon.

This shows the level of planning involved even for a straightforward shooting attack, one of the simplest operations in PIRA's modus operandi. It involved some 12–15 people, any of whom might have been an informer or connected with someone who was. The result was that the more PIRA attempted to improve its doctrine to overcome security force tactics, the more likely it was that the security forces were going to discover it.

Controlling the Border

Northern Ireland's border with the Republic of Ireland is about 250 miles (400km) long. Control of the border was a long-standing problem for security forces, since most PIRA training facilities, major weapons dumps, and safe areas were in the South. The border meanders through mainly farmland, and randomly dissected farms and communities. It is rarely marked or obvious. Large parts of it are in areas dominated by close-knit republican communities with long family histories of rebellion.

About 50 percent of British military forces were deployed in the rural border areas. They used completely different tactics from their urban counterparts: battalions deploying into border areas utilized traditional infantry skills of night patrolling, camouflage, ambushes, and observation posts. Movement was almost entirely by helicopter or on foot; bases were heavily fortified and under constant threat of attack. Battles with PIRA units at section or platoon strength were not unknown, sometimes lasting some 20–30 minutes with considerable expenditure of ammunition.

Although a complete physical closure of the border was mooted at various times in the 1970s and early 1980s, it was not seriously considered. Apart from the expense and manpower required to achieve closure, politically it was appreciated that any long-term solution to the problems of Northern Ireland had to include a closer relationship between North and South, not institutionalized separation.

There were 20 "approved" and 137 "unapproved" crossings. The approved crossings were controlled by the security forces who, over time, constructed major permanent installations to enable the control and search of cross-border traffic. Much effort was expended in closing unapproved crossings, but this was rarely successful since they could not be guarded and were frequently reopened by farmers whose farming was disrupted by the closure. The strategy to control the border was therefore developed to limit the movement of terrorists and their munitions; make it more difficult for them to cross the border; and gather intelligence to contribute to the total counterinsurgency effort. It was accepted that it would never be possible to prevent all terrorist cross-border movement.

Training, Lessons Learned, and Tactical Development

The foundation of the British Army's tactical success against PIRA was its training. Specialist pre-deployment training was run by the Northern Ireland Training & Advisory Team (NITAT) based near Folkestone in Kent (site of Sir John Moore's formation of the British Army's light infantry some 200 years earlier). Every unit deploying to Northern Ireland underwent a sophisticated training package specifically tailored for that battalion. A unit deploying to Belfast, for example, was given a completely different training package from one destined for South Armagh. Every instructor at NITAT was an expert, himself the veteran of several Northern Ireland operational tours, and kept up to date with frequent visits to theater.

Not only was NITAT responsible for training, it was also the mechanism for capturing and distributing tactical lessons learned, and developing new tactics. There was no Northern Ireland tactics manual; instead drills were encapsulated in loose printed *aides-mémoires* that were constantly updated by NITAT visits to all operational units in Northern Ireland. Although NITAT was officially under command of the British Army Headquarters outside Salisbury, in practice it worked directly for Headquarters Northern Ireland. Unlike many training institutions, it was never regarded as out of touch or irrelevant: it had an excellent reputation across the army for the highest standards and relevance.

Intelligence and Surveillance

It is difficult to overestimate the importance of intelligence to the conduct and outcome of the Northern Ireland conflict. The security forces expended great effort in gaining intelligence on all insurgent groups, in particular PIRA. There were multiple forms of intelligence gathering, including electronic surveillance and technical analysis of insurgent weapons. But the most important forms of intelligence in Northern Ireland were, by far, human intelligence and visual surveillance, both covert and overt.

Human Intelligence

The PIRA's long war strategy resulted in building closely knit teams with high levels of mutual trust. This is a natural dynamic among people who share experience and risk over a long period. It made it more difficult for the security forces to recruit informers, but once recruited they were highly dangerous for PIRA. From the late 1970s, PIRA started to develop a counterintelligence capability, interrogating and executing confessed informers, but this internal security unit was itself penetrated by the security forces.[21] It is likely that by the early 1990s, most elements of PIRA's organization had been penetrated to a greater or lesser degree.

Both the British Army and the police ran agents. Although they occasionally competed against each other, the separate systems were a pragmatic response to the needs and motivations of the informers themselves: some were willing to work with the army but not the police, others vice versa.

Running agents in an insurgency demands difficult decisions. To reach a position of trust and influence, an agent needs to be physically involved with terrorist operations. Thus those in the pay of the British government conducted criminal acts, probably including murder. Additionally, choices sometimes needed to be made between agents, allowing one to prosper to the detriment, and possibly death, of another. The principal criterion was protecting the greatest long-term benefit. There is an analogy with the difficult decisions made in World War Two to protect the ULTRA secret, including not acting on intelligence that could have saved many people's lives but would have jeopardized the source of that intelligence.[22] Controversy continues today over the use of informers and the extent to which the British government condoned law-breaking in the interests of the longer term counterinsurgency strategy.

Surveillance

People are creatures of habit. We like to do things we know work and are comfortable with. We only tend to change once our original pattern no longer works. Once we have found the best route to work, for example, we mostly follow that route. Policemen, soldiers, and insurgents are no different. PIRA attacks generally exploited patterns set by security forces: the murder of an off-duty policeman who always visited the same pub on Wednesday; an inadvertent pattern set by a patrol in Belfast; a routine change of security force personnel at an isolated outpost. Avoiding patterns was one of the most important lessons in counterinsurgency training.

PIRA also set patterns, and the security forces exploited these as deftly as PIRA did. Analyzing patterns was a key aspect of the security force surveillance network. This network was extensive, concentrating on the nationalist areas where most PIRA members lived and operated; it consisted of static observation posts, both in urban areas and across the most dangerous rural areas; PVCPs at border crossings and key points in Belfast and Derry; patrol sightings of known PIRA members; and covert observation of specific targets.[23]

Every soldier was an intelligence gatherer. He or she was expected to know at least 30, and preferably more than 50, suspects' faces, names, addresses, and cars from the local area. Competitions were held to improve recognition. Every time a patrol spotted a suspect, details were radioed to the operations room and input into the database. Similarly, vehicle registration numbers were input into a separate vehicle database, whether suspect or not: these totaled tens of thousands of sightings every day.

The result was two vast databases: one for people and one for vehicles. They proved particularly useful for security forces after an attack took place. Analysts checked all earlier sightings and established whether patterns were being set that correlated with earlier attacks. For example, the same elderly couple, with no known terrorist connections, who always crossed the border three to five days before an attack and never at any other time, were presumably carrying the weapon for the attack. Or the same group of two or three people, always seen together in the area of an attack a day or so before it occurred, were presumably conducting the close target reconnaissance.

Once a pattern had been recognized, it was important to exploit it to the full. It was a key indicator of PIRA's plans. What the security forces did not do was search the elderly couple or question the reconnaissance team. This would cause PIRA to change its pattern and the security forces would lose key intelligence. Instead the information was used, with other intelligence, to pre-empt or frustrate the attack in other ways.

What Did Intelligence Achieve?

The British government's intelligence attack on PIRA was undoubtedly successful, and became more successful over time. At the strategic level, the government was able to understand the nature of PIRA and its goals, enabling it to develop a political strategy for peace and create an advantage in negotiation. At the operational level, the security forces were able to pre-empt PIRA's major operations, such as its Libyan-backed version of the Tet Offensive. At the tactical level, the British Army was able to employ effective deterrence to frustrate PIRA operatives, to the extent that they were prepared to open the door to a political process.

Bringing the Conflict to an End

Accepted wisdom is that it is difficult to end an insurgency, and particularly difficult to end a long insurgency. This was not the case in Northern Ireland: the longer the insurgency continued, the more the original causes of the insurgency became irrelevant and the deeper security forces' understanding of PIRA became. Thus security forces were able to develop policies, strategies, and tactics that ushered in the peace process.

It is difficult today to determine the extent to which the Northern Ireland counterinsurgency campaign was planned at what we now recognize as the operational level. The campaign was coming to a close at about the same time as campaign planning techniques and tools were being developed. The British Army simply did not have the vocabulary to articulate a campaign plan. Nevertheless, what emerged, uncertainly and hesitantly, was an operational idea that was a mix of the conventional and the original. It had five connected elements, which today we would describe as lines of operation:

- Remove the social and economic causes of the insurgency.
- Work with successive Irish governments to evolve a political framework acceptable to both nationalist and unionist populations.
- Create and maintain a legal framework that treats insurgents as criminals; reduce their legitimacy in the eyes of the population.

- Frustrate the PIRA so that it realizes the futility of the armed struggle.
- Establish and maintain channels of communication with PIRA, whatever the cost.

The idea depended not on the defeat of the insurgent movement, but on co-opting it into the move to peace.

As the peace process evolved, there was a danger that PIRA would fracture into multiple insurgent groups, each of which would have to be dealt with separately. As it is, two splinter groups did emerge, the Continuity IRA and the Real IRA, both committed to the continuance of the armed struggle. But the vast majority of PIRA activists and their supporters were brought into the peace process by PIRA's leadership. This appears to be partly the result of the British government's realization that they needed to preserve, and sometimes strengthen, PIRA's command structure. This is counterintuitive to a soldier, where breaking an opponent's command and control is regarded as one of the most effective paths to victory; indeed, in the early stages of the insurgency it was necessary to contain the level of violence. However, from the moment it became apparent that PIRA's leadership was interested in dialogue and political process, its command structure had to be protected, not attacked.

Thus we see a strategy to protect PIRA's leadership while simultaneously frustrating its fighters, not necessarily killing them. In the end, the Northern Ireland conflict was ended not by the insurgents who were killed, but by those who lived.

10

COUNTERING THE *CHIMURENGA*

The Rhodesian Counterinsurgency Campaign 1962–80

Dr J. R. T. Wood

Introduction

Ultimately, all governments stand or fall on the consent of the governed, and all counterinsurgency campaigns depend for their success on the government securing that consent. The Rhodesian government was no exception. Governments also have to act, or abdicate. Thus, when Rhodesia's African nationalists, imbued with Marxist revolutionary theories so beloved of the national liberation movements of the day, adopted the "armed struggle" as their route to power in 1962, the Rhodesian government had no choice but to react, and was slowly drawn into countering what would become a full-blown insurgency.

Tasked to defeat the insurgency, the Rhodesian Commander of Combined Operations, Lieutenant General Peter Walls, was of the opinion that "You cannot win a war like this purely through military means. The military is merely there to maintain law and order and provide a conducive atmosphere for political development."[1] To do even this, he lacked adequate manpower, finances, and resources, and his forces had to make do with what they had. In doing so, they gained an enviable reputation as inventive and fierce exponents of counterinsurgency warfare. They would not win because as long as the Rhodesian whites, never more than 5 percent of the population, clung to power, the African population remained, at best, passive participants and did not supply the support necessary to defeat the African nationalist insurgents. Such support was forthcoming only after Ian Smith, the Rhodesian Prime Minister, accepted universal suffrage in 1978 and the subsequent election returned the moderate Bishop Abel Muzorewa as the country's first African premier in 1979. Everything then depended on Britain. Smith had rebelled against Britain and declared

Rhodesia unilaterally independent in 1965, but only Britain could transfer sovereignty. Margaret Thatcher, however, refused to recognize Muzorewa and created conditions which would ensure the accession to power of Robert Mugabe.

The Armed Struggle

Rhodesia's African nationalists chose to undertake "armed struggle" in 1962 after Joshua Nkomo's Zimbabwe African People's Union (ZAPU) had spurned the "evolution to democracy" solution offered by Sir Edgar Whitehead's Liberal government. At that moment, Rhodesia was Southern Rhodesia and part of the Federation of Rhodesia and Nyasaland. A year later, the Federation had been dismembered by Britain in her haste to divest herself of her empire. She had granted independence to the new African nationalist governments of Northern Rhodesia (now Zambia) and Nyasaland (now Malawi), both of which rejected association with white-ruled Rhodesia.

ZAPU's resort to arms and dispatch of young men for guerrilla training in Algeria, Egypt, and the Soviet Bloc reflected Nkomo's desire to be handed the reins of power in common with his fellow African nationalist leaders, Kenneth Kaunda in Zambia and Hastings Banda in Malawi. Britain, however, could not oblige Nkomo because she had never ruled Rhodesia directly and had no means to enforce her will. Southern Rhodesia had been a self-governing colony since 1923, with the right to defend herself. All Britain retained was a veto to protect African rights and, of course, sovereignty.

The African nationalists' drive for power was founded on a general desire to recover land, identity, and independence lost when Cecil John Rhodes, the founder of Rhodesia, had finessed a mining concession gained from the Ndebele king, Lobengula, into an occupation. When Lobengula attempted to thwart him, Rhodes expanded his influence through the acquisition of the very land concession that Lobengula had granted to Edouard Lippert in 1889 to undermine Rhodes' territorial ambitions. Within three years, Rhodes's British South Africa Company was at war with Lobengula, who died during a retreat to the north. In 1896, the Ndebele people in the west and the Shona-speaking people in the north and east rose in separate attempts to expel the whites. The Shona rising came to be known as the "First Chimurenga."[2] The confinement of the Africans to reserves in 1898, albeit inalienable ones, and restrictions on the purchase of outside land, did nothing to ameliorate resentment. The unequal distribution of land in 1931 between the one million Africans and the 50,000 whites did not improve the situation, particularly as the soil in the African reserves was already exhausted by traditional farming methods, and the Africans lacked the means to purchase the land set aside for them. Government attempts to conserve the soil, including de-stocking, only fostered resentment. The indefensible racial discrimination and segregation of the day exacerbated the situation. An exception was the franchise, but even that was qualified, requiring an income level above that of most Africans.

Despite these grievances, Rhodesia's African nationalists had, by the 1960s, secured only a few followers among the liberated, educated Africans living in Rhodesia's small segregated towns. The majority of the population still lived by subsistence farming, on the land, in the thrall of their traditional leaders. Indeed, to feel secure in any area, the militants resorted to deadly intimidation (and have continued to do so to this day). A rejection of such attempts at intimidation can be seen in the defiance of the African electorate in voting in the 1979 election, despite being ordered by the African nationalists to abstain, and in the willing recruits who constituted 80 percent of the Rhodesian security forces.

There had been attempts to organize African resistance in the first half of the 20th century, but militant feeling only began to grow when a post-World War Two generation came of age and grew impatient for power. The formation of a militant Youth League led to the resuscitation of the moribund African National Congress (ANC), originally founded in the 1930s. Its activities led to its banning in 1959 and its re-emergence under a succession of different names as the Whitehead government sought to curb its violent activities by increasingly harsh legislation. It emerged from another banning as ZAPU in 1962, but split in April 1963 when a group of mainly Shona-speaking intellectuals, led by the Reverend Ndabaningi Sithole and including Robert Mugabe, rejected Nkomo's leadership and formed the Zimbabwe African National Union (ZANU). Continued unrest, including internecine fighting, led to the banning of both movements in September 1964 and the preventive detention of their leaders. Both movements had, however, established external bases and sought support in Zambia and Tanzania. ZAPU strengthened ties established in the 1950s with the Soviet Bloc, while ZANU sought aid from the Chinese Communists, North Korea, Libya, and Yugoslavia, as well as from Western sympathizers, and particularly from the Scandinavians.

ZAPU's proclamation of the "armed struggle" in 1962 predated Ian Smith's rebellion against Britain on November 11, 1965. Since Rhodesia's founding, independently-minded whites had sought dominion status for Rhodesia. This quest had led them to federate with two British-controlled territories in the hope that this would increase the chances of achieving dominion status. There were, however, never enough whites for Britain even to consider entrusting the fate of the African population to them. After 1945, Britain would not and could not grant independence on terms of less than universal suffrage. Attempts by Lord Malvern, the longstanding Rhodesian prime minister, Whitehead, and Winston Field to secure dominion status were fruitless. It was galling to Rhodesians that the less-developed Zambia and Malawi should be made independent in 1964, particularly as they were virtually one-party states. In 1964 the new British Labour Prime Minister, Harold Wilson, stonewalled Ian Smith, refusing to contemplate anything less than a transfer of power to the African majority. After 18 months of frustration and insecurity, denied British money owed from the breakup of the Federation, excluded from Commonwealth conferences and committees, enduring an unofficial arms embargo, humiliated and blocked at every turn while Rhodesia's economy stalled and people began to emigrate, Ian Smith acted, declaring Rhodesia unilaterally independent.

Possessed of a margin of five seats and faced with British sentimental support for the Rhodesians, Wilson balked at asking British forces to fight their Rhodesian peers and rejected the use of force. There were also practical reasons for this decision: having been denied a port by Rhodesia's neighbors, South Africa and Portuguese-ruled Mozambique, the only one available to the British was Dar es Salaam, a thousand miles to the north along a dirt road. Instead, Wilson applied economic sanctions against Rhodesia and made them mandatory shortly thereafter by invoking Chapter Seven of the UN Charter, only the second time it had been invoked (the first was against North Korea).[3]

The Rhodesian Response

Blessed with a modern economy, Rhodesia was self-sufficient enough in everything but petroleum products and ammunition to withstand sanctions, given the willing assistance of her South African and Portuguese neighbors. The South Africans were being pilloried for their policy of apartheid and the Portuguese were still smarting over the British failure to support their protests at India's seizure of Goa.

Rhodesia also had enough experienced forces to contain the small threat posed by ZAPU and ZANU. Good police work, based on intelligence from an informer network, had already stamped out any urban threat. The insurgency was therefore confined to the rural areas, where both ZANU and ZAPU sought to secure peasant support and recruits.

Responsible for the maintenance of law and order under the Police Act, the British South Africa Police (BSAP) had 7,000 regular white and African policemen, including the paramilitary Support Unit. It was backed by a volunteer Police Reserve of 30,000 men and women of all races and the Police Reserve Air Wing. Regulars and volunteers were to be found in the Police Anti-Terrorist Unit. The intelligence effort was coordinated by the Central Intelligence Organization (CIO), which incorporated the Special Branch.

The Rhodesian Army had 5,000 regulars, the bulk of them in a white-officered African infantry battalion, the Rhodesian African Rifles (RAR) and the whites-only commando battalion of the Rhodesian Light Infantry (RLI). The remainder were distributed among a squadron of the Special Air Service (SAS) and the engineers, signals, and service corps. Backing the regulars were eight battalions of territorials and reservists of the Royal Rhodesia Regiment and the national servicemen training at its depot. All non-African males were liable for four and a half months of national service and three years of compulsory territorial service before being transferred to the reserve. There was a territorial field artillery regiment and territorials were also to be found in the engineers, signals, and service corps.

The seven-squadron Royal Rhodesian Air Force (RRAF) had 2,000 regulars flying and servicing Hunter and Vampire fighter bombers, Canberra medium bombers, DC3 Dakota transports, Alouette III helicopters and light reconnaissance and training aircraft.

The ranks of the army included veterans of the Malayan and Aden campaigns in the 1950s and 1960s, representing Rhodesian contributions to Commonwealth forces. The Rhodesian SAS squadron (commanded by Major Peter Walls) and the RAR had served in Malaya in the 1950s. In the 1960s, the re-formed SAS squadron and the RRAF served in Aden. In Malaya, the Rhodesian SAS troopers had pioneered "tree-jumping" (parachuting into unprepared landing zones). They and the RAR had been blooded in the fleeting contacts in the undergrowth and had learned the techniques of jungle warfare including small-unit tactics, cross-graining, tracking, ambushing, and inter-service cooperation. The Officer Corps had participated in the Malayan civil/military counterinsurgency structure, with its pooling of resources under a single command of the governor.[4]

In 1964, in preparation for combating the insurgency, Ian Smith took the chair of the new Security Council on which sat the service commanders and heads of relevant ministries. The Council was advised by the Counter-Insurgency Committee, also chaired by Smith, and served by the commanders, the Director, CIO, and appropriate officials. It had two subcommittees: the Operations Coordinating Committee (OCC) and the Counter-Insurgency Civil Committee. The latter, manned by the heads of appropriate ministries, planned and coordinated the civil aspects of the campaign such as the construction of roads, airfields, and protected villages. It also advised on the psychological aspects. The service commanders and the Director, CIO, who constituted the OCC, directed operations and, with the assistance of the Joint Planning Staff, evolved a common doctrine and modus operandi. They set up Joint Operations Centers (JOCs), served by army, air force, BSAP, and Special Branch senior officers, to command the all-arms effort in the field. The JOC met daily to review and plan operations and to issue a situation report (or sitrep). When operational needs dictated, the JOC could establish sub-JOCs.

Even though the services remained answerable to their individual headquarters, this command-by-consensus worked. The implementation of a JOC's plans by its disparate subordinates was not, however, always satisfactory, and the different approaches to problems produced some indecision. A major disadvantage was the dominance of immediate tactical requirements over the need to devise a national strategy. The discontent led to the creation of a Combined Operations Headquarters in March 1977, but it could never be quite like the Malayan model because Malaya had an executive governor, while Rhodesia had an elected prime minister and cabinet government. It meant that the Commander, Combined Operations, Lieutenant General Peter Walls, remained answerable to the Prime Minister and his Cabinet, and never had the free hand which Field Marshal Templer had enjoyed in Malaya.

The counterinsurgency campaign went through five phases dictated by the political situation, until the ceasefire in 1980 and the election of Mugabe.

Phase 1: 1966–72

Realizing that, with the willing help of the South Africans, Portuguese, and others, Rhodesia could survive the sanctions, Wilson sought to negotiate a settlement. Several attempts, including meeting on the warships *Tiger* and *Fearless*, however, failed, and in 1969 Ian Smith declared Rhodesia to be a republic. He immediately enacted a new constitution which aimed at racial parity of representation. This was rejected by the British and, to secure the vital international legitimacy, Smith settled with the new government of Edward Heath in 1972, only to see the settlement terms rejected by the British Pearce Commission after sampling the opinion of six percent of the African population, obtained amidst an uproar generated by the African nationalists.

In the period 1962–65, its paucity of trained manpower had restricted ZAPU's Zimbabwe People's Liberation Army (ZPRA) to a pinpricking sabotage program directed mostly at railway lines and soft targets. It was ZANU's armed wing, the Zimbabwe African National Liberation Army (ZANLA) which mounted the first incursion from Zambia into Rhodesia in April 1966, on the unsophisticated assumption that the African people would rise. ZPRA followed suit in July, sending in a small team. Another 30 small-scale and fruitless incursions followed, but at least both movements were formulating their strategies, in contrast to the Rhodesians, who were wholly reactive. ZPRA, advised by Soviet instructors, aimed to mount a conventional threat. ZANLA adopted the Maoist concept of revolution, but never progressed very far through its phases and was never capable of positional warfare.

The threat was easily contained after an initial hiccup when the Police Commissioner, Frank Barfoot, compelled by his duty to preserve law and order, called up his Police Reserve to deal with the first ZANLA incursion rather than involve the army. The somewhat inept but successful "battle of Chinoyi" (now celebrated as a national holiday) led the OCC to insist on implementing the JOC system. What aided the success thereafter was the timely notice of incursions given by informers in the ranks of ZANU and ZAPU. This was supplemented by information volunteered by rural Africans and a steady stream of press-ganged ZANLA and ZPRA deserters. Schisms within the African nationalist ranks were exploited by the CIO with disinformation and even assassination. ZPRA and its ally, the African National Congress of South Africa, also made the mistake twice, in 1967 and 1968, of establishing bases in uninhabited areas where the absence of other human tracks betrayed them. The involvement of the ANC was also a mistake as it supplied the excuse for direct South African intervention. South Africa deployed police reinforcements and supplied military hardware.

While the completeness of their defeats depressed both ZPRA and ZANLA, the Rhodesian security forces enjoyed a solid grounding in joint-service counterinsurgency actions which allowed them to hone their small-unit tactics. The four-man "stick" (half-section) emerged as the basic formation, equipped with a Belgian MAG machine gun, a radio, and three riflemen armed with the FN FAL 7.62mm rifle. Understanding the psychological importance of not harming (and therefore not antagonizing) the innocent, emphasis was laid on the accuracy of the riflemen, teaching them to attempt the single aimed round rather than the traditional "double tap." The Rhodesians developed tracking and other skills, setting up the Tracker Combat School at Kariba in 1970 and evolving the five-man tracker combat concept now being taught to the US Marines.

One mistake was to leave the intelligence requirements to the Special Branch personnel who, untrained in military intelligence, did not assist the military planning cycle. A myth has arisen, however, that the Rhodesian security forces did not expect ZANLA to take advantage of the advance of the Mozambican insurgents of Frente de Libertaçao de Moçambique (FRELIMO) to penetrate Rhodesia's northeastern border. In fact, the Rhodesians mounted Operation *Tripper* to assist the Portuguese with tracking FRELIMO and to stop ZANLA crossing the Zambezi River. The Rhodesians knew that ZANLA, albeit in small numbers, had begun to subvert the people who lived along this vulnerable border, but a lack of manpower meant the African district assistants of the Internal Affairs Department could not be protected, and intelligence on ZANLA's whereabouts began to dry up.

Another mistake was to fail to heed warnings from the army that, despite the presence of two 100-man companies of South African police, its regular component was overstretched when merely assisting the BSAP with border control. The retired former Federal Prime Minister, Sir Roy Welensky, suggested raising 10 RAR battalions, but, because the immediate threat seemed so minor and funds were short, the Treasury and the Department of Defence were fatally deaf to all pleas.

Rhodesia: ZANLA and ZPRA Operational Boundaries

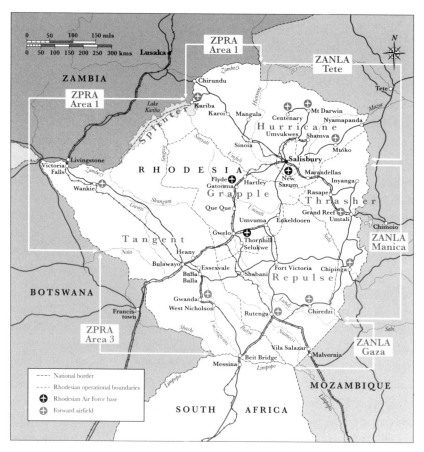

These were nevertheless good years for Rhodesians. They were winning all the battles and countering the sanctions. They were assisted in their efforts by ZANU's and ZAPU's proclaimed adherence to Marxism; this position gave credibility to the Rhodesian government's anti-Communist stance, which struck a chord in the United States and elsewhere, particularly among the conservative Arab states and Iran.

Phase 2: 1972–74

In 1972, the rejection of the Home–Smith Settlement and the success of FRELIMO against the Portuguese in Mozambique emboldened the African nationalists. ZANLA's attack on the white-owned Altena Farm in the northeastern Centenary district on December 23, 1972 opened a new phase of the war.

Having acquired sufficient finance, aid, weapons, and a growing number of young men, Herbert Chitepo, the external ZANU leader, at last adopted a telling strategy. He aimed to stretch the security forces and thereby dent white morale by forcing the mobilization of large numbers of territorials and reservists. This, he anticipated, would seriously affect industry, commerce, and agriculture. Chitepo, however, was assassinated by the CIO, sowing discord in ZANU's ranks. True to the Maoist template, ZANLA divided Rhodesia into provinces and sectors. They sought to politicize the rural people, establishing local committees, security procedures, and infiltration routes. They recruited contact men, feeders, porters, co-opted the local spirit mediums, and cached arms and ammunition. Communications were by courier and letter (a system which the Rhodesians exploited). They also planted antitank landmines in the roads, in an attempt to paralyze large areas.

The Rhodesians responded vigorously, setting up Operation *Hurricane* with its JOC at Centenary (Operation *Hurricane* endured until the ceasefire in 1980) and hunting down insurgents. The lethality of the landmines was reduced by pumping water into tires and sandbagging trucks. This prompted a rapid development of mine-protected vehicles with the aid of South Africa's Centre for Scientific and Industrial Research, the descendants of which are deployed in Iraq today. Recalling their Malayan experience, the Rhodesians moved rural Africans in the northeast into protected villages. This move was not entirely a success. The ZANLA personnel were sons of the people being moved. Furthermore, the Rhodesians deployed inadequate numbers of ill-armed Internal Affairs administrators to protect the villages instead of arming a local militia. The reason for this was the fear that unsupervised militias would be subverted. The Internal Affairs personnel were replaced in the late 1970s with the newly raised Guard Force, comprising African recruits and white national servicemen.

The Rhodesians understood the importance of psychological warfare, but were always hampered by never achieving more than the Africans' passive acceptance of the status quo. It meant that the Rhodesians could not evolve a counterinsurgency strategy, forcing them to concentrate on containment.

The vastness of the operational area and the small number of troops available demanded high mobility. The acquisition of the French Matra

151 20mm cannon enabled the Rhodesians to convert some of their Alouette III helicopters into "K-Car" gunships and to evolve the highly successful Fire Force. This unit exploited the agility of the helicopter and its troop-carrying capacity to provide a rapid reaction force which could trap and destroy the elusive enemy. The Fire Forces (three were usually deployed) comprised a K-Car carrying the army Fire Force commander and three Alouette III "G-Cars," carrying four infantrymen. Despite the small number of troops involved, the Fire Force units achieved kill rates of over 80:1.

Securing Fire Force targets was achieved by observation, patrolling, finding tracks, aerial-visual and photo reconnaissance, and intelligence. The SAS penetrated the neighboring countries to identify incoming groups, their routes and supplies. Intelligence was gleaned from villagers and captured insurgents, but much was lost through poor interrogation techniques and the use of force because the few effective Special Branch interrogators were not always available. The most successful move was the use of pseudo-gangs suggested by the ecologist Alan Savory in 1966 and advised by Ian Henderson, the Kenyan exponent of pseudo-warfare.[5] The new Selous Scouts Regiment combined army and Special Branch personnel to deploy captured-and-turned insurgents to impersonate ZANLA sections to uncover contact men, sources of food and comfort, and to pinpoint the insurgents for Fire Force.[6] The Military Intelligence Directorate (MID) was set up in 1973 to remedy the inadequacies of entirely relying on policemen to collect and interpret intelligence.

To inhibit rather than prevent cross-border movement, because Rhodesia lacked the manpower to keep the border under surveillance, a mined barrier was laid along the northern and eastern borders to harass infiltrators. It killed some 8,000 ZANLA by 1980.[7]

The success of all these measures led, by 1974, to the number of insurgents within the country being reduced to 60, all of them confined to the northeast. The insurgency was being contained but, of course, everything depended on a political settlement.

Phase 3: 1974–77

The military coup in Portugal in April 1974 robbed Rhodesia of one of her two allies and exposed her long eastern and southeastern borders to infiltration by ZANLA. At the same time, ZPRA intensified its forays from Zambia through Botswana and across the Zambezi. Rhodesia's only secure border was with South Africa. South Africa's prime minister, B. J. Vorster, however, preferred to have a compliant African government as a northern neighbor.[8] Accordingly, he withdrew his police and interrupted Rhodesian ammunition and supplies, in an attempt to force Smith to settle. The upshot was a failed ceasefire in 1974, fruitless negotiations with ZANU and ZAPU in 1975, and the intensification of the war in 1976.

ZANLA concentrated on politicizing the rural folk, by fair means or foul, while ZPRA preferred to wait. Both forces built up their strength with a growing supply of willing recruits. The intensification of the war, combined with other factors, induced white emigration and forced a recognition of political realities. Even so, the most vulnerable of whites, the farmers, remained on the land. Some 6,000 of them were still there in 1980.

The intensification provoked Rhodesian cross-border raids. These were limited to camp attacks because the Rhodesian government was fearful of world reaction and would not allow the destruction of the strategic infrastructure of the neighboring territories. It allowed, however, "hot pursuit" operations, because these were deemed legal by the Paris Pact of 1928. The first major raid was in October 1974 by the SAS against a ZPRA camp and munitions dump in southern Zambia. There followed an attack in early 1976 against ZANLA staging posts in Mozambique's Gaza Province at the Sabi-Lundi junction and Pafuri on the Limpopo. Then, in August 1976, a Selous Scouts vehicle column killed 1,200 inmates of the main ZANLA camp in the Manica Province of Mozambique. This provoked the dreaded world outcry and gave Prime Minister Vorster the excuse to pull out his helicopter pilots and enlist Kissinger (eager to help after the Angolan debacle of 1975 had led to Soviet/Cuban intrusion into southern Africa) to put pressure on Smith to concede majority rule.

The constant deployment produced battle-hardened, resourceful, and daring troops. Only able to deploy 1,400 men in the field on the average day in the 1970s, the Rhodesian forces often could not muster the classic 3:1 ratio in attack. In Operation *Dingo*, in November 1977, 165 SAS and RLI paratroops jumped into a camp complex at Chimoio, Mozambique, holding 9,000–10,000 insurgents. They killed 5,000, and then after a day's resupply, jumped into the Tembué camp deep in Mozambique's Tete Province, killing hundreds more. Psychological warfare, however, that vital ingredient of successful counterinsurgency campaigns, remained impossible until the support of the people had been won by political reform.

The Rhodesians also continued to refine their techniques in other areas. Fire Forces were strengthened with Dakotas, carrying up to 18 RLI or RAR paratroopers, and fixed-wing support, usually the Lynx (the Cessna 337G) and sometimes Hunter fighters or Canberra bombers. These aircraft were given a new range of locally produced weapons, including napalm bombs capable of precise delivery; the 1,000-lb blast Golf bomb with a meter-long fused probe to explode it on contact; and the Alpha Mk II bouncing soccer ball-sized bomb, 300 of which constituted a Canberra bomb load.[9]

The need to detect landmines produced the purely Rhodesian-invented "Pookie," the world's first mine detection vehicle, capable of finding a mine when traveling at 50mph. Between 1972 and 1980 there were 2,504 detonations of landmines (mainly Soviet TM series) by vehicles, killing 632 people and injuring 4,410. The mining of roads increased as the war intensified. In 1978, 894 mines were detonated or recovered, at the rate of 2.44 mines a day. In 1979, 2,089 mines were dealt with, at the rate of 5.72 mines a day. Between 1976 and 1980, built at a cost less than that of repairing a mine-damaged vehicle, 68 Pookies detected more than 550 landmines, saving hundreds of lives and (riding on under-inflated racing slicks) never detonating one. Twelve were damaged in ambushes by command-detonated landmines or rockets. A rocket through the armored windscreen killed the only driver to die. When ZANLA realized that the Pookie was blunting their landmine offensive, ambushes became more frequent. These were countered by arming the Pookie with the "Spider" 24-barrel 12-gauge shotgun, simultaneously covering a 270-degree arc with buckshot. The insurgents held the Spider in such awe that they began to let the Pookies through the ambushes and attacked the convoys instead.

New units were formed. The Psychological Warfare Unit attempted to fill a glaring need. The Grey Scouts Regiment exploited the capabilities of the hardy Boer pony in bush warfare.[10] The Guard Force defended the spreading protected villages and other assets. The Rhodesian Intelligence Corps (RIC) gave the army a field intelligence unit.

The Special Branch, however, retained its briefing role and continued to inhibit the planning cycle. Because of the successful marriage of army and Special Branch personnel in the Selous Scouts, it was suggested that the Selous Scouts should take over the intelligence function to provide the vital military ingredient. The Police Commissioner, however, vetoed such an intrusion into the Special Branch's prerogative.[11]

In the event, assisted by 8 Signal Squadron, which monitored radio traffic in neighboring countries, processing some 10,000 FRELIMO/Zambian signals a month, the MID gradually took responsibility for supporting the increasing external operations. What the MID neglected was counterintelligence, and failed to discover why raiding forces found some camps empty. Later, at least one member of the Special Branch frustrated assassination attempts on Mugabe, and was decorated for doing so. Elements of the Special Branch also became involved in the use of biological and chemical warfare but, although the extent was minor, it has given rise to some conjecture and some wild extrapolations.[12] Excluded from such machinations, the RIC, for its part, at least gave a military dimension to the coverage of intelligence, supplying the security forces with updated maps and research findings on a variety of military problems.

In late 1976, pressure grew to copy the Malayan precedent and have a "Director of Operations" instead of command by consensus. After initial hesitation, Smith formed, in March 1977, the Ministry of Combined Operations and appointed Lieutenant General Peter Walls as Commander, Combined Operations (ComOps). This, coupled with the increasing declaration of martial law in affected districts, produced a more coordinated effort. Walls, however, did not outrank the army commander, Lieutenant General John Hickman, and in reality was simply the chairman of the National JOC (NatJOC), a looser organization which replaced the OCC. He lacked the power to enforce his will on the NatJOC, which was further weakened by the Police Commissioner and the Director, CIO, sending deputies to it. The district administration and the BSAP continued to formulate and execute their own plans. While ComOps prepared operational orders, its intelligence staff had no evaluating role and it did not become the focus of the intelligence community to improve the strategic planning cycle. Walls sought clarification of his role, but was ignored. The overabundance of anomalies led to friction among the commanders.

The Rhodesian war effort remained reactive and lacking in a coherent strategy. Walls, nevertheless, understood that the military could still only strive to contain the war.

Phase 4: 1977–79

In late 1977, in the midst of Operation *Dingo* and fulfilling his promise to Vorster and Kissinger, Smith announced that he would negotiate with the African nationalists and accept majority rule. The upshot of those discussions was the political settlement of March 1978 and the formation of the interim government of Smith, Muzorewa, Sithole (who had been ousted from ZANU by Mugabe), and Chief Jeremiah Chirau to devise the new fully democratic constitution and prepare for the general election.

ZANU and ZAPU responded by unifying as the Patriotic Front, but their forces fought each other whenever they met. ZANLA intensified the war at great cost, with Fire Force taking a fearful toll. ZANLA also had severe logistical problems and lacked the morale, the discipline, and the training for positional warfare. ZPRA had conventional forces, but lacked a bridgehead across the Zambezi River and air support.

The increased fighting, combined with the prospect of being ruled by an African prime minister, shook the Rhodesian whites. Casualties remained light, but whites began to emigrate at the rate of 2,000 a month. Despite an infinite supply of eager African recruits, budgetary constraints and the shortage of training staff meant that the security forces could not expand fast enough to match the growth of ZANLA and ZPRA, and were soon outnumbered except at times of total mobilization.

Even so, the Rhodesian war effort improved and, with the prospect of success in the political field finally in sight, in 1978 ComOps produced a strategy with coherent goals which broke the reactive mold. This involved:

1. Protecting "Vital Asset Ground" (mines, factories, key farming areas, bridges, railways, fuel dumps, and the like).
2. Denying the insurgents the "Ground of Tactical Importance" (the African rural areas) as a base from which to mount attacks on crucial assets by:
   i. Inserting large numbers of armed auxiliaries (loyal to Muzorewa and Sithole) into these areas to assist in the reestablishment of the civil administration and to destroy the links between the insurgents and their supporters;
   ii. Using Fire Force and high-density troop operations against insurgent infested areas.
3. Preventing incursions through border control.
4. Raiding neighboring countries to disrupt ZANLA's and ZPRA's command and control; to destroy base facilities, ammunition, and food supplies; to harass reinforcements; and to hamper movement by aerial bombardment, mining, and ambushing of routes.

An addendum to this plan was CIO's decision to sponsor the anti-FRELIMO resistance movement, Resistencia National Moçambique (RNM), which began to weaken FRELIMO and allow the Rhodesians greater freedom of action against ZANLA in Mozambique.

Although many in the Rhodesian security establishment did not grasp the potential of the auxiliary forces, the 10,000 auxiliaries, deployed among the rural Africans, began to deny the insurgents the countryside. For the first time, there were forces to occupy the ground which Fire Force won. Information began to flow again from the people, and Fire Force became more deadly. The operational demands, however, were excessive. Fire Forces deployed two and three times a day. Many external air and ground attacks were mounted, even on the outskirts of Lusaka in Zambia, but economic targets remained inviolate.

MID became more effective in the analysis of intelligence, and the army was strengthened by the formation of the Rhodesia Defence Regiment to supplement the Guard Force in guarding vital points.

Phase 5: April 1979—March 1980

The election of Muzorewa in April 1979 offered the only chance for the counterinsurgency war to be won because, voting in a 62 percent poll of the newly enfranchised African population, the moderate Africans dealt ZANLA and ZPRA a stunning defeat by defying their orders to abstain. The Rhodesian security forces mobilized 60,000 men to neutralize the threat to the election. During the three days of the election, 230 insurgents were killed, and 650 overall during the month of April. The others went to ground or surrendered. The ZANLA commanders left the country for orders and for six weeks the war stood still. If Margaret Thatcher had adhered to her election promise to recognize this internationally monitored result, the insurgency could have been defeated. Instead, Thatcher reneged and the murders of Africans increased as the insurgents strove to reestablish themselves. The morale of the security forces and the public sank. At the same time, planning to rob ZANLA of victory at a decisive moment, ZPRA deployed a 3,000-strong vanguard into Rhodesia to prepare the way for its Soviet-trained, motorized, conventional army. ZANLA responded with an offensive into Matabeleland, ZPRA's heartland. Although ZANLA deployed 10,000 men into Rhodesia, including some FRELIMO volunteers, it was in dire straits due to constant Fire Force action, the external raids, the unease of the host country, and the denial of ground by the auxiliaries. The peace achieved at the Lancaster House Conference in London came none too soon for ZANLA.[13] Its real accomplishment was political. Its long campaign of intimidation ensured that Mugabe won the 1980 election.

Muzorewa could have achieved a stronger bargaining position if he had adopted a total strategy.[14] Instead, while his security forces strove to contain the situation in expectation of a political solution, his political and military aims were not tied in closely enough. He could have exerted economic pressure and threat of a conventional war on Zambia and Mozambique to cease aiding his enemies. He could have stalled to allow time for his auxiliaries and Fire Force to weaken the hold of the insurgents within the country, while his forces crippled the supply lines of ZANLA and ZPRA and the RNM kept FRELIMO at bay. The humiliation of this could have caused the fall of the FRELIMO leader, Samora Machel. The Russians might have offered some help, but Machel had seen what had happened to Angola and would have hesitated to take it. The Cubans could have intervened, but this was unlikely as they were already overextended in Angola, and South Africa would have immediately reacted. There were political dangers, but Rhodesia had demonstrated that she could withstand international pressure.

Muzorewa could have enjoyed a number of options. A separate deal with Nkomo's ZAPU would have been possible. The Lancaster House peace talks could have been stalled until the pressure on Zambia and Mozambique began to tell. Limited Western recognition might have been forthcoming to prevent a regional war. Muzorewa could have dictated the peace terms and his apparent strength would have appealed to the electorate because, like Mugabe, he could threaten the resumption of the war.

Muzorewa's external operations did contain the ZPRA threat from Zambia, by blowing bridges and leaving Zambia totally dependent on a single railway line through Rhodesia to South Africa. The raids steadily raised the odds in Mozambique to force FRELIMO to cease supporting ZANU and ZANLA. The Rhodesian forces attacked bridges in the Gaza Province to cut ZANLA's supply lines. They planned to do likewise in the Manica, Sofala, and Tete Provinces had they not been stopped. Perhaps they were stopped because the British were bent on achieving a settlement embracing all players, including Mugabe, and the South Africans wanted to woo Machel to deny their ANC safe havens. Muzorewa also weakly allowed the British to divide his delegation, while Mugabe and Nkomo delayed signing anything to gain time to build their political support within Rhodesia and recoup their losses.

Enforcing the ceasefire, the Commonwealth Monitoring Force restrained the Rhodesian forces and ostensibly confined the ZANLA and ZPRA forces to a number of assembly point camps. The British, however, ignored the presence of mostly recruits in the camps and the absence of the hard core, who remained outside among the population and ensured that Mugabe won the election. The British, with too few troops to intervene, accepted the result despite the overwhelming evidence of intimidation.

The Rhodesian forces flirted with, but rejected, the idea of a coup because only Britain could confer sovereignty. Instead they concentrated on forcing the British to reschedule the election. Lord Carrington, the British Foreign and Commonwealth Secretary, aided and abetted by Ken Flower, the Head of CIO, and P. K. Allum, the Police Commissioner, ignored the evidence of widespread intimidation supplied not only by the Rhodesian forces but also by the British monitors.[15]

In the end, the leaders of the intelligence establishment betrayed their own, perhaps for the sake of their pensions. Flower went on to serve Mugabe and his Marxist aspirations, and the CIO became a feared secret police organization rather than an intelligence agency. The war cost ZANLA and ZRPA 40,000 dead at a cost of 1,735 Rhodesian dead – a ratio of 23:1.[16] A flawed election placed Mugabe in power and, bent on the retention of power, he has ruined a once thriving state. Where once food was exported and policemen went unarmed, famine and terror stalk the land. All the Rhodesian military gained out of the failure of the counterinsurgency campaign was an enviable reputation.

11

THE ISRAEL DEFENSE FORCES AND THE *AL-AQSA INTIFADA*

When Tactical Virtuosity Meets Strategic Disappointment

Dr Sergio Catignani

Introduction

This chapter will analyze the Israel Defense Forces' (IDF) counterinsurgency strategy and campaign in the West Bank and Gaza Strip (the "Territories"), with particular reference to the *Al-Aqsa Intifada*, which began in September 2000 and petered out toward the end of 2005. The IDF achieved significant tactical success, but this did not translate into a strategic decision or victory. The IDF's campaign, in fact, until late 2004 managed to galvanize, rather than diminish, Palestinian violence. Even thereafter, Palestinian insurgent activity was only reduced, not eliminated. An important factor behind this lack of success was Israel's inability to align its political goals and overall strategy with the limited leverage the IDF could provide.

The Arab–Israeli conflict has been an enduring feature of the Middle East region since the establishment of the state of Israel in 1948. Prior to this date and particularly over the last 20 years, the Arab–Israeli conflict has manifested itself mostly as an intercommunal, rather than an inter–state, conflict between the state of Israel and the Palestinian population living in the West Bank and Gaza Strip.

Economic deprivation, deep-seated anger and frustration borne out of living under the 20-year Israeli occupation, combined with the awareness that no outside intervention was forthcoming (given the Palestinian Liberation Organization's (PLO) defeat and exile from Lebanon in the mid-1980s), led local Palestinians to take matters into their own hands. In December 1987, a spontaneous popular uprising, known as the Intifada, broke out in the Territories as a form of protest against the Israeli occupation. The low-key yet widespread nature of the violence, and the defiance shown by the Palestinian civilian population – strikes, large-scale demonstrations, barricades, and stone-throwing – proved problematic for the IDF. The highly asymmetric nature of the struggle between the local Palestinian population and the IDF enabled the Palestinians to gain widespread international sympathy. The IDF, which until then had been accustomed to conducting major conventional military warfare and counterterrorist operations with Special Forces, was unprepared to confront a civilian-based uprising.

Cases of excessive force, abuse, and innocent civilian fatalities being broadcast around the world (due to the pervasive media coverage of the uprising) eroded within Israel the national security consensus regarding the need to continue the occupation of the Territories. Until then the occupation had been inexpensive and relatively unproblematic. However, demoralization within the IDF ranks was growing, due to the IDF's inability to suppress the uprising. This contributed to ethical dilemmas and operational blunders. All of these factors, combined with the spiraling manpower and financial costs associated with the constant deployment of forces, led Israel to conclude that an exclusively military solution to the Intifada was unobtainable.

The September 1993 Oslo Peace Accords proved to be a watershed in Israeli–Palestinian relations. They were seen to be the first step toward a two-state solution to the protracted Israeli–Palestinian conflict. While Israel recognized the Palestinians' right to self-government, the Palestinian Liberation Organization (PLO), as the official representative of the Palestinians, recognized Israel's right to exist in peace and security. A five-year interim process was set up in order to gradually relinquish land, as well as internal security and administrative duties, to the newly formed Palestinian Authority, under the leadership of PLO Chairman Yasser Arafat.

However, disparity between Israel's and the Palestinian Authority's positions regarding final status issues (for example, Jerusalem, refugees, borders, etc.) precluded any lasting peace. This became only too obvious at the Camp David talks in July 2000, when Arafat rejected the best offer that Prime Minister Ehud Barak could make. Disillusionment with Arafat's lack of flexibility and (in the opinion of both Barak and US President Bill Clinton) goodwill during the final status talks led to a series of mutual recriminations.[1] In spite of further Israeli concessions during talks at Taba in December 2000, increasing Palestinian violence and Israeli reprisals led to the complete breakdown of the Oslo peace process.

The *Al-Aqsa Intifada*

According to Palestinian Authority Communications Minister Imad Falouji, Arafat decided to initiate a violent uprising, similar to the first Intifada, following the failed Camp David talks.[2] By resorting to violence, Arafat possibly sought to pressure Israel to make further concessions (as had indeed occurred at Taba) or even to "internationalize" the conflict by encouraging some form of international, rather than merely US-led, peace process and possible intervention. The purported pretext that led to the onset of large-scale violence arose from Likud opposition leader Ariel Sharon's visit to the Temple Mount on September 28, 2000.[3] Violence broke out. The Palestinian Authority took advantage of this spontaneous uprising and over the Palestinian Authority's official radio station, "Voice of Palestine," exhorted Palestinians to rise up and defend the Al-Aqsa Mosque. The *Al-Aqsa Intifada* had begun.[4]

Arafat's attempt to obtain maximum diplomatic gains by unleashing limited Palestinian violence backfired. Unorganized popular unrest gradually converged into an organized popular resistance, often involving guerrilla tactics, led by Hamas, Palestinian Islamic Jihad, and PLO-affiliated militias Fatah-Tanzim and Force-17.[5] These groups now controlled the Palestinian street and escalated the crisis.

During the first three months, while traditional riots continued to disrupt daily living in the Territories, the violence took on a decidedly different character from the first Intifada. Gunmen fired on Israeli vehicles in the Territories.[6] Israelis inside the areas under Palestinian Authority jurisdiction were assassinated, and IDF soldiers were ambushed. The placement of roadside improvised explosive devices (IEDs) on roads leading to settlements was an especially lethal tactic that accounted for numerous military and civilian casualties.

Initial IDF Reactions:"Containment Policy"

During the initial stages of the *Al-Aqsa Intifada*, when Palestinian violence was predominantly centered on rioting, the IDF functioned very efficiently and suffered no casualties; troops operated according to precise drills and under clear-cut rules of engagement. Anti-riot rules of engagement required IDF units to adopt the gradual use of non-lethal weapons, such as stun grenades, tear gas, and rubber-coated plastic bullets, which did cause harm if shot within the maximum stand-off combat ranges (100–150 meters).[7] However, once Tanzim, Hamas, and other gunmen began firing from within these rioting crowds, the IDF began returning live fire, and civilian casualties and deaths could not be avoided. Consequently, Israel was blamed for using excessive firepower against the Palestinians. IDF Head of Operations, Major General Giora Eiland, defended the IDF's conduct in a letter to the Association for Civil Rights in Israel,[8] writing:

> the Palestinians make deliberate use of children, with the clear aim of increasing the number of casualties. We have here a bizarre situation whereby the other side is actually trying to increase its casualties. There is a limit to our ability to prevent them from achieving their desired aim.[9]

Nevertheless, given the amount of ammunition used during the initial months of the *Al-Aqsa Intifada*, it is difficult to determine the extent to which the IDF was genuinely intent on limiting its retaliatory fire.[10]

Even though Barak had become disenchanted by Arafat's refusal of his offers at Camp David and Taba, he believed that an Israeli–Palestinian final status agreement could be achieved. Hence, Israeli policymakers initially decided to adopt a strategy of "containment." Such a strategy would restrain the military response and, in turn, allow negotiations to carry on. However, the IDF found it difficult to implement this policy at the operational and tactical levels. In response to increasing gunfire aimed at Israeli citizens, thruways, and neighborhoods, such as the Gilo neighborhood in southern Jerusalem, the IDF began retaliating against Palestinian areas from where the attacks were initiated with helicopter and fixed-wing air strikes, machine-gun fire, and tank main gun rounds.

The IDF set various limitations to its activities along the lines of the containment policy. For the most part, during the initial months of the *Al-Aqsa Intifada*, it did not initiate operations, but only responded to Palestinian violence. It typically did not operate within the Palestinian-controlled "A" areas in order to respect the Palestinian Authority's "sovereignty" in these areas, except when carrying out limited surgical strikes. Finally, the IDF, in principle, attempted to retaliate in proportion to the Israeli-perceived severity of the Palestinian attack. However, due to the distance that often existed between Palestinian terrorists who systematically operated from Palestinian civilian quarters and IDF units deployed outside the "A" areas, the IDF was often forced to resort to stand-off weapon attacks that, despite the fact that they mostly involved precision-guided munitions, resulted occasionally in collateral damage and civilian deaths.

The IDF was torn between curtailing such incidents, in order to avoid negative media fallout, and jeopardizing the safety of its own troops. Then-head of IDF's Armored Corps, Brigadier General Avigdor Klein, stated that:

> my mission is to prevent the Palestinians from achieving political goals through violence... And since we face numerous threats each day from terrorists willing to die, we're not going to risk the safety of our troops in attempts to look better in front of the news cameras.[11]

The IDF's Operational Assertiveness

As Palestinian violence increased, the IDF loosened its adherence to the Israeli government's containment policy. Consequently, one can argue that the IDF played a part in escalating the *Al-Aqsa Intifada* toward the end of 2000. Casualties quickly mounted on the Palestinian side. By the end of the year, 327 Palestinians had been killed and around 1,040 had been wounded.[12] While the Barak government had hoped to limit any escalation of the conflict in order to achieve a political agreement with the Palestinian Authority, the IDF General Staff had made up its mind and declared publicly that the IDF would pursue all necessary means to achieve "victory." In a widely read national newspaper, *Yediot Ahronot*, the IDF General Staff was quoted as saying, "The IDF intends to win in this encounter. It is not ready to allow the political echelon, with its contradictory orders and other considerations, to dim its victory."[13]

The disparity between Barak's and the IDF's stated strategies soured Israeli civil–military relations, but such tensions proved to be short-lived once Ariel Sharon got elected as Israel's new prime minister in February 2001. Fed up with Barak's peace concessions under fire, the Israeli population opted to elect Sharon, who was known for his hard-line stance vis-à-vis Palestinian terrorism and nationalist aspirations.

Yet, during the initial phase of the *Al-Aqsa Intifada* Arafat did make an effort, albeit a half-hearted one, to reduce the intensity of Palestinian

Figure 1 – Israeli Victims of Palestinian Suicide Terror Attacks[16]

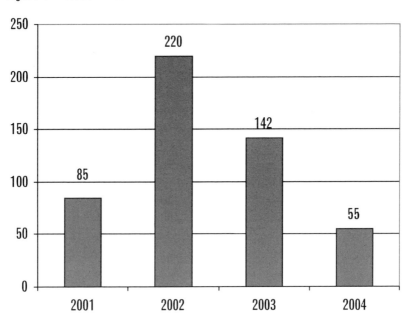

attacks, which were by late 2001 escalating beyond control due to Hamas' and the Islamic Jihad's growing participation in the conflict. The IDF, nonetheless, despite the existence of a shaky Israeli–Palestinian ceasefire agreement, carried out the targeted killing of Raed Karmi, a local Tanzim leader, in December 2001. The effect of his assassination galvanized Fatah and led it to collaborate with other terrorist groups.[14] The Al-Aqsa Martyrs Brigade declared, in fact, that as a result of the targeted killing, "the so-called cease-fire is canceled…With your assassination of Raed Karmi, you have opened hell on yourselves. You will be burned by its fire."[15] The "fire" came in 2002, in a deadly surge of terror attacks (see Figure 1).

The IDF's Second Phase of COIN: Punishing the Palestinian Authority

With the negotiations deadlocked, Israel's strategic policy changed from containment to the direct targeting of the Palestinian Authority. Israeli leaders came to see the Palestinian Authority as directly responsible for the violence perpetrated by terrorist organizations. Indeed, the Palestinian Authority supported and associated with the Fatah-affiliated Tanzim and the Al-Aqsa Martyrs Brigades, as well as Hamas and the Palestinian Islamic

Jihad.[17] The interception of major weapons shipments and the seizure of documents seriously implicated the Palestinian Authority in substantial financial, intelligence, and operational assistance of terrorist activities aimed at Israel.[18] This shattered Yasser Arafat's credibility as a peace partner.

Israel's main strategic goal during this second phase of the *Al-Aqsa Intifada* was to

> burn into the consciousness of the Palestinian side, that there is no chance
> of gaining achievements with terror and of forcing Israel to surrender...
> If this struggle ends with terror having produced achievements for the
> Palestinians we will find ourselves on a slippery slope in terms of our
> deterrence...[19]

Consequently, a much heavier military approach was adopted in order to stifle the growing Palestinian terrorist threat. Real diplomatic initiatives by now were not considered seriously.

Israel Air Force (IAF) air strikes (and sea-based strikes along the Gaza Strip) increased considerably. They mostly targeted security and governmental installations in order to punish the Palestinian Authority for supporting the uprising and terror/guerrilla campaign. While the IAF air campaign enabled Israel to degrade the Palestinian Authority's military infrastructure, it was far less successful in eliminating potential suicide bombers, which the IDF dubbed "ticking bombs." Stand-off precision weapons systems were often used in order to reduce Israeli casualties. At least until March 2002, their use enabled the IDF to retaliate against violence without violating the Palestinian Authority's areas of jurisdiction. The cost was that the Palestinians could call attention to the public display of a disproportionate level of force and accuse the IDF of being heavy-handed.

As a result of negative media exposure from such high-profile attacks, the IDF, as early as November 2000, began combining the use of air power and stand-off weapon attacks with special covert counterterrorist/guerrilla raids aimed at either arresting or eliminating suspected terrorists without having to expose the IDF to media scrutiny. These operations came to be known as "low-signature" missions.[20] Most land raids were conducted by the special *Sayerot* (reconnaissance) infantry, paratrooper, and Special Forces units. They were also carried out by the specialist *Mistar'aravim* ("to become an Arab") undercover hit squads.[21] Yet each targeted killing, whether carried out by air or by land, seemed to encourage, rather than deter, the recruitment of new volunteers and martyrs.[22] By early 2001, Hamas and Palestinian Islamic Jihad had fully resumed suicide terror bombings within Israel itself.

Coercive economic measures were also enacted in order to pressure the Palestinian Authority into restraining Palestinian militants and terrorists. These proved ineffective but were prolonged nevertheless as a means of punishing the Palestinian Authority for its collaboration with terrorist groups. Income tax was withheld indefinitely. The periodic closure of the Territories, which inhibited Palestinian workers from entering Israel, as well as the transfer of goods between the Territories and Israel, was also used as a punitive economic measure against the Palestinian Authority.

Once Palestinian terrorists began carrying out terror attacks within Israel, the closure of the Territories and the imposition of long curfews on Palestinian urban areas came to be seen as a strategic necessity in order to stop the infiltration of additional Palestinian terrorists into Israel or Israeli settlements. Access routes to various Palestinian towns were placed under the IDF's control and numerous checkpoints were established. These population control measures facilitated intelligence collection, search and arrest operations, and targeted killing missions by the IDF and the Israeli secret services (Shin Bet).

The decision to demolish housing belonging to families of terrorists was also taken. The IDF saw this as a major deterrent against further terrorist activity. A senior IDF officer said, "demolishing a house is a grave penalty for the family. It is not merely an economic blow. A home has emotional value which cannot be restored."[23] And yet, according to Zuhair Kurdi, a journalist with Hebron's *Al Amal* TV station, house demolitions and other IDF preventive or punitive measures had the opposite effect. Zuhair remarked, "the legal father of the suicide bomber is the Israeli checkpoint, while his mother is the house demolition."[24] Indeed, despite the growing use of such house demolitions, Palestinians did not really seem to be deterred from conducting further attacks on Israel (see Figure 2).

Moreover, as a result of Israel's punitive economic and the IDF's population control measures, Palestinian living standards, which were already low, deteriorated substantially. By early 2002, Palestinian areas were more dependent than ever on humanitarian aid. Although the IDF

Figure 2 – IDF House Demolitions: A Deterrent to Palestinian Suicide Bomb Attempts?[25]

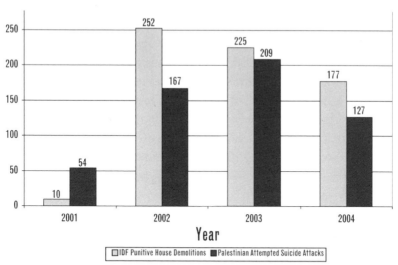

IDF Punitive House Demolitions ■Palestinian Attempted Suicide Attacks

attempted to alleviate the burgeoning humanitarian problems in the Territories by allowing the distribution of aid and the periodic lifting of curfews and closures, very often such momentary respites would be used by Palestinian terrorists to shift weapons and other materiel in or around the Territories. They would also take the opportunity to infiltrate another suicide bomber into Israel, who would then carry out an attack against Israeli civilians in buses, cafés, markets and other crowded public places.

IDF officers acknowledged that indiscriminate population control measures had negative humanitarian consequences, alienated the local civilian population, and exposed Israel to further domestic and international opprobrium. Yet on the other hand, they considered them effective at sparing Israeli lives from further suicide bombing attacks. Former Coordinator of Government Activities in the Territories, Major General Amos Gilad, highlighted this dilemma by stating that

> it is very difficult to solve this contradiction between terror, on one side, and humanitarian assistance on the other... To ease the daily life of Palestinians we must open the roads between cities, but the moment we do that, we are hit with terrorist attacks.[26]

What the IDF leaders did not fully realize was that Palestinian desperation fueled terrorist recruitment and activism.

Operation *Defensive Shield*: From Reactive to Proactive IDF Counterinsurgency

As a result of the growing lethality of Palestinian terrorism – during the first three months of 2002, over 170 Israelis were murdered in terror attacks – following the March 27, 2002 Seder (Passover meal) Night Massacre,[27] the Israeli government initiated a third stage to the conflict. In this stage, the IDF abandoned its "low-intensity" and reactive strategy, and adopted a much more proactive and aggressive posture.

Once the new Israeli government and IDF leadership came to view Israel as being in a state of war, a significant increase in the volume and intensity of the IDF's military operations occurred. Statements by various leading military and political figures reiterated what Prime Minister Sharon had affirmed in December 2001: "A war has been forced upon us... A war of terror [is] being conducted systematically, in an organized fashion and with methodical direction."[28] Israel was ready to fight Palestinian terror without any half measures.

This was particularly obvious once Israel decided to unleash the IDF onto the Territories through Operation *Defensive Shield*. According to Lieutenant General Shaul Mofaz, then Chief of Staff, the principal goals of the operation included: "neutralizing the terrorist infrastructure in the West Bank and Gaza Strip, highlighting the Palestinian Authority's involvement with terrorism, and isolating Arafat."[29] Israel also decided to conduct this major operation in order to restore its deterrent credibility, which had suffered a major blow from the IDF unilateral withdrawal from South Lebanon in May 2000. Mofaz's successor, Lieutenant General Moshe Yaalon, justified *Defensive Shield* as showing the Middle East that

> the state of Israel is already no longer considered what [Hezbollah leader] Hasan Nasrallah said in his victory speech after we withdrew from Lebanon in May 2000, "a spider web"... [They believe] Israeli society is not prepared to struggle anymore. Shed its blood and it surrenders. *Defensive Shield* substantiated that this isn't so.[30]

In this major operation, roughly 30,000 troops set about to seize weaponry, destroy weapons factories and suicide bomb workshops, arrest terrorists and their support network, eliminate potential suicide bombers, and collect crucial intelligence for the purposes of preventing future attacks. The operation took place in Palestinian West Bank towns such as Nablus, Ramallah, Bethlehem, Tul Karem, and Jenin. "Operationally, this translated into the encirclement of a city and...the entry of infantry forces [normally a brigade, sometimes two of them], supported by tanks...and by attack helicopters."[31] The encirclement of these towns was meant to deny terrorists and guerrillas an avenue of escape from IDF search operations.

Combined IDF infantry, engineer, armor, and helicopter assault units abandoned traditional linear urban assault tactics. Instead, they were able to "deploy out of contact with the enemy by selectively seizing small areas...drastically reducing exposure to enemy fire and maintaining momentum by only clearing as necessary."[32] According to the IDF's Head of Doctrine and Training, Brigadier General Gershon HaCohen, "in urban warfare we [had] to coordinate among many small teams coming from many different directions simultaneously."[33] This tactical approach was dubbed "swarming."

Units of the newly formed Field Intelligence Corps deployed at the tactical level alongside combat units and were able, among other things, to pinpoint enemy snipers and other threats in real time. With this intelligence, combat units or helicopter air cover could neutralize threats before being attacked themselves.[34] With the use of the Field Intelligence Corps, according to its commander, Brigadier General Amnon Sofrin, "the information now goes faster to the troops and we have closed the gap between intelligence and operations."[35] By using such rapid "swarm" tactics, the IDF was able to surprise and confuse Palestinian guerrilla and terrorist fighters, who were deeply embedded within the refugee camps and towns in the Territories, and who were expecting to ambush large, cumbersome IDF conventional units.

Palestinian ambushes and sniper fire were mostly circumvented by employing armored D-9 bulldozers. These generated different avenues of approach by powering through buildings, even if at the cost of collateral damage. Both circumvention and "swarm" tactics were innovations that were adopted as a result of the need to protect forces entering heavily booby-trapped areas.

Moreover, according to the Israeli Air Force Commander, Major General Dani Halutz, "[the major discovery] we made, during the last operation, was the importance of helicopters for urban fighting."[36] Up until the *Al-Aqsa Intifada*, helicopter units were not trained to fly and maneuver in urban operations. Out of necessity and through constant tactical learning and innovation, the Iraqi Air Force was able to adapt its helicopter squadrons to conduct urban operations.

Such squadrons were used in various capacities. Helicopter crews were used to coordinate closely with ground commanders who had access to real-time imagery of targets supplied by Unmanned Aerial Vehicle (UAV) units in order to guarantee that correct targets were attacked. Attack helicopters were also used to provide more accurate fire cover than that provided by tanks, thus reducing the likelihood of collateral damage and civilian casualties. Attack helicopters gradually became the weapons platform of choice for conducting targeted killings.[37]

Dealing with the Negative Media Fallout

Even though before Operation *Defensive Shield*, senior IDF officers, such as Major General Giora Eiland, had warned that "public opinion must be considered when evaluating the effectiveness of operations," the IDF's decision to ban the free movement of the press in Jenin had obvious negative public opinion repercussions.[38] By not trying to work with them, the press was left to fill "the information gap with imagination, rumor, and disinformation," according to an IDF reservist communications strategist.[39] The Palestinian Authority was only too happy to lead the media on through its tried and tested propaganda machine.

Despite subsequent IDF and United Nations (UN) reports negating the Palestinians' claims of an IDF massacre, the media was able to damage the IDF's image and legitimacy. Even though the IDF attempted thereafter to prepare its soldiers and commanders to understand the important role of the media in counterinsurgency campaigns and to deal with the media in general, other media setbacks occurred throughout the conflict, due to the IDF's overall inability to manage more carefully the media's portrayal of its operations.[40] In any case, Operation *Defensive Shield* ultimately led to the arrest of many terrorist and guerrilla suspects, the partial dismantlement of the terrorist and guerrilla infrastructure within the areas targeted, and definitely confirmed the Palestinian Authority's link with terrorist activity. But this was not enough to stop the Palestinian terror/guerrilla campaign.

Controlling the Ground: Operation *Determined Path*

Accordingly, following Operation *Defensive Shield*, the IDF entered the fourth stage of its counterinsurgency campaign, dubbed *Determined Path*. Operation *Determined Path* was aimed at regaining indefinite control on the ground of all security sensitive areas within the Territories that were known to foster terrorist activities. This would be achieved by reoccupying key Palestinian-controlled urban areas and their adjacent refugee camps. Further restrictive measures on the movement of the population were set up.

The pervasive presence of the IDF and the control of the Territories were meant to facilitate the conduct of sweeping house-to-house searches by Shin Bet operatives and IDF task forces. These units were tasked with the mission of eliminating weapons caches, weapons factories, and wanted terrorists. By early 2004, the IDF had been able to apprehend and incarcerate over 6,000 Palestinians on various terror-related charges (see Figure 3). It had also been able to "decapitate" much of the terrorist group's local spiritual and military leadership, most notably Hamas' Sheikh Yassin Mohammed and Abdel Aziz Rantisi.

Within the Gaza Strip, the IDF was involved in detecting and destroying the wide network of tunnels used to smuggle large quantities

Figure 3 — Palestinians Held in Custody by Israeli Security Services[41]

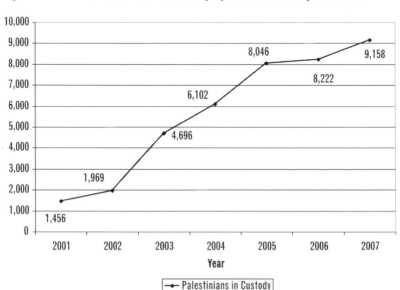

215

of weapons and explosives from Egypt into Gaza. Such underground smuggling efforts increased as the IDF's grip on land, sea, and air access routes into the Territories tightened.

Though the IDF had been effective in reducing the number of successful suicide attacks against Israeli civilian targets by mid-2004, Palestinian violence increased, particularly in the Gaza Strip, where the Intifada had become an "'over/under' conflict, with mortar shells and Qassam rockets being increasingly fired against Israeli settlements" and Israeli towns bordering the Gaza Strip, and IEDs being laid against Israeli convoys.[42]

So, while the IDF was able to reduce the phenomenon of suicide terrorism by late 2004, Palestinian insurgency had adapted itself by relying more on Gaza-based rocket and IED attacks. Such attacks increased even after the IDF decided to conduct two major operations in the Gaza Strip (Operations *Rainbow* in May 2004 and *Days of Penitence* in October 2004).

Coping with the *Al-Aqsa Intifada*

The constant operational use of both IDF regular (conscript and professional) and reservist units during the *Al-Aqsa Intifada* resulted in major cutbacks in training and weapons development programs.[43] While IDF commanders saw operational experience in the Territories as an excellent way for troops to gain "on-the-job" training and expertise, units were often sent into combat missions without the appropriate training and, in some cases, without appropriate equipment (due to the IDF's budgetary constraints). This led to various operational blunders, which occasionally cost the lives of IDF soldiers.

The IDF found itself unprepared to conduct the regular constabulary duties it had already struggled with during the first Intifada. Not much effort was put into learning and implementing the lessons from the IDF's experiences in the Territories during that period. Consequently, they had to be relearned as troops tried to conduct patrols and house searches, establish checkpoints, and operate within a largely hostile civilian population.

Nonetheless, given the IDF's need to train and adapt its forces to urban warfare and routine constabulary missions, new training schemes were adopted progressively during the conflict. They allowed forces to operate more effectively and with a greater regard towards ethical and human rights issues. For example, the IDF School of Military Law produced an ethical code of conduct, which specified 11 key rules of ethical behavior. This code was taught to both regular and reservist units through courses that offered wide-ranging role-playing exercises, addressing the characteristic predicaments that soldiers faced while serving in the Territories, particularly at checkpoints.[44] The IDF School of Leadership also held residential workshops in which combat units could discuss their moral misgivings in a protected environment between deployments. Such discussions were effective in decreasing the pressure and stress that accumulated during operations in the Territories.[45]

Furthermore, the IDF initiated a multimillion dollar program in June 2002 to upgrade its Tze'elim National Training Center in the Negev desert. These upgraded training grounds were established to give Israeli soldiers superior urban warfare training facilities. They reproduced Palestinian cities and were designed to prepare the IDF soldier for all kinds of contingencies within the Territories. As stated above, however, not all units were able to undergo decent levels of training until 2005 due to the operational tempo that the IDF was under in order to fight ongoing Palestinian violence and terrorism.

Frustration, inexperience, operational stress, and in some cases malice nonetheless played a major part in negatively influencing the behavior and conduct of some IDF units. This was particularly problematic for conscript units, who were often unable to understand the importance of avoiding unprofessional and/or abusive methods and actions that would alienate the Palestinian civilian population and incite it into adopting further violent means.[46] Pressed with the need to provide security by eliminating terrorists, collecting as much intelligence as possible, arresting individuals affiliated with terrorist groups, and pre-empting any major security threat against Israel, the IDF adopted a mostly "kinetic" approach with not much regard for a "hearts and minds" strategy.[47] Thus, quite often, continuous IDF operations, rather than lowering the level of Palestinian violence, actually raised it, at least until mid-2004. Mindful, furthermore, of the belief that Israel was fighting a war and that it was facing an existential threat in the guise of terrorism, the achievement at all costs of immediate military tactical objectives very often took precedence over the need to determine whether or not the realization of such objectives actually achieved Israel's ultimate strategic goal of obtaining "victory."[48]

By 2004, the IDF at last began to grasp that continued counterinsurgency operations, which may have yielded significant tactical achievements, did not amount to a strategic resolution to the conflict.

Indeed, in February 2004 an IDF committee, chaired by Major General Amos Yadlin, found that despite great tactical innovation and initiative Israel did not really follow a clear strategy. This was partly because coordination between the political and military echelons was lacking. It also concluded that, despite the considerable latitude for maneuver given to the IDF, it had not been able to stop the *Al-Aqsa Intifada* altogether.[49]

Unilateral Disengagement and the Security Fence

By late 2002 even Ariel Sharon had come to the realization that the IDF could not sit in the Territories and conduct counterinsurgency operations indefinitely without jeopardizing Israel's economy, the IDF's operational preparedness, and the IDF soldier's moral fiber. Sharon stated in an interview that "I do not want to have our country mobilized forever to sit in Nablus."[50] The decision to create a security barrier, which would separate Israelis from Palestinians and protect Israel from further terrorist infiltration, had already been taken in late 2001. The partial construction and operation of this security fence was, by 2003, very effective in reducing the number of successful suicide attacks in Israel and, according to some analysts, proved to be a much more effective method than Israel's targeted killing policy.[51]

Furthermore, Sharon's belief that there was no serious Palestinian peace partner led him to adopt a unilateral disengagement plan in late 2003, which would lead to the total dismantlement of Israeli settlements and withdrawal of the IDF from the Gaza Strip and limited parts of the West Bank. Unilateral disengagement was perceived as a bold and unprecedented move by Sharon, a historical champion of the Israeli settler movement. Amid considerable domestic controversy, due to opposition from right-wing parties and the settlement movement, and international upset at Israel's unilateralist approach, the disengagement plan was carried out in August 2005.

Sharon regarded such a unilateral approach as necessary. US President George W. Bush's Road Map peace plan, which was first proposed in April 2002, called for internal democratic reforms within the Palestinian Authority and for it to clamp down on terrorism. No progress had occurred on either front. By unilaterally disengaging, Sharon hoped that Israel would limit the source of friction and tension between Israeli settlers and local Palestinians, reduce the burden of the IDF tasked with protecting such settlers, and hopefully, kick-start the Road Map peace plan.

Conclusion

By ultimately adopting a military-oriented strategy vis-à-vis Palestinian terrorist groups and activities, the IDF was able by late 2004 to wear down terrorists' capabilities. Israel's strategy, though, was not able to reduce terrorist motivation and influence within the Territories. Nonetheless, Israel's choice of strategy was natural, given its perceptions of the *Al-Aqsa Intifada* as a war and the Palestinian Authority as not really wanting peace. According to the Israeli military and civilian leadership, without peace to be won gaining the hearts and minds of the Palestinian population became an almost irrelevant goal; hence Israel's preference for an overall kinetic strategy during the *Al-Aqsa Intifada*.

In a certain sense, as the well-known scholar Yaacov Bar-Siman-Tov has written, "the terrorist attacks affected the mode and intensity of Israeli security activity, but that same activity influenced Palestinian violence."[52] Israel emasculated the Palestinian Authority's security and governmental capabilities between 2000 and 2004 and prevented a significant number of Palestinian terrorist attacks. But in doing so, Israel alienated and galvanized the local Palestinian population to support further violence. By seriously eroding the Palestinian Authority's security and administrative infrastructure, as well as alienating significant portions of the Palestinian population through its heavy-handed tactics, the IDF ultimately paved the way for Hamas to gain political ground in the Territories and win the Palestinian legislative council elections in January 2006.[53]

In sum, the Israeli case study can teach us two important lessons that should be applied to future counterinsurgency scenarios. First, a kinetic, even if tactically successful, counterinsurgency campaign cannot achieve any major strategic or political dividends without carefully balancing such a campaign with clear political objectives/direction and ongoing diplomatic activity. Second, if insurgencies are viewed as "wars" by the counterinsurgent, the proclivity for employing a kinetic approach to address insurgent threats becomes stronger, as the military aspects of such conflicts are over-emphasized to the detriment of the underlying political realities. By failing to address political realities and by relying too heavily on the military to "stamp out" an insurgency, a counterinsurgency at best will be able to reduce the level of violence for a limited period until a new round of hostilities erupts. At worst, it will merely feed into the tit-for-tat escalatory process of violence that so often plagues "long wars."

12

LESSONS IN 21ST-CENTURY COUNTERINSURGENCY
Afghanistan 2001–07

Dr Daniel Marston

Introduction

When US and allied forces invaded Afghanistan and toppled the Taliban regime in 2001–02, they fundamentally misunderstood the implications of occupying a war-torn and ungoverned country. In particular, they failed to recognize the scope of local support for the Taliban, and the root causes for this support. The desire for quick solutions led to actions that encouraged an insurgency in southern and eastern Afghanistan. Additionally, they failed to prepare their forces for the possibility of conducting a prolonged counterinsurgency campaign. Ignoring the lessons of history, the United States, and to a lesser extent Australia, Great Britain, and other NATO allies, did nothing to create a viable counterinsurgency strategy or to train and equip soldiers and civilian advisers for a couple of years. As of 2007, it appeared that the principal members of the coalition had developed a better understanding of counterinsurgency theory, but applying many of its key practices – unity of effort, understanding the locals, protection of the population, and training of a viable indigenous security force – remained a challenge.

The Afghan insurgency was not primarily religious; ethnic tensions, poor governance, and economic difficulties were all rallying points for disaffected Afghans. This was particularly true for the Pashtuns, who had traditionally been politically powerful in Afghan society and suddenly found themselves disenfranchised.[1] The presence of Western military forces, which could be construed as an occupation, was an additional provocation.

Afghanistan pre-September 11, 2001

To understand the complex problems that Afghanistan faces today, it is necessary first to look back at the country's history. Afghanistan has been important to outside powers since the mid-19th century, when, because of its location, it became a buffer state in the struggle for territory between the British and Russian Empires (commonly known as "The Great Game"). After nearly 80 years of British governmental involvement, Afghanistan regained full autonomy in 1919, but part of the British legacy was a Pashtun community disgruntled by the establishment of the Durand Line, a national border that divided Pashtun ethnic territories between Afghanistan and British India (modern-day Pakistan). As the Pashtuns assumed, the location of the line was deliberately chosen to undermine the unity and political power of their community.[2]

Following a period of stability that lasted through much of the 20th century, the Afghan government was toppled by a Communist coup in 1978. This, in turn, led to a Soviet invasion in 1979, undertaken in support of the Communist uprising, and a 10-year Soviet occupation. This incursion was bitterly contested in a guerrilla campaign carried out by Afghan opposition forces commonly known as the Mujahideen. These forces received significant financial support and training from, among others, the US Central Intelligence Agency (CIA) and the Pakistan Interservice Intelligence (ISI). During this period, both the Soviet-backed government in Kabul and the Mujahideen included representation from all of Afghanistan's major ethnic groups.

The withdrawal of Soviet forces in 1989, the loss of more than 1.5 million people in the conflict, and the abandonment of Afghanistan by the West left the country in total disarray. The Soviet-backed government, led by President Najibullah, was toppled in 1992 by former Mujahideen. The coup was led by Tajik forces under the authority of Burhanuddin Rabbani and his military commander, Ahmed Shah Massoud, aided by troops loyal to the Uzbek commander in the north, General Rashid Dostum. The coup was a devastating blow to the Pashtun community, which had been the politically dominant ethnic group in Afghanistan for more than 300 years.[3]

Following the coup, the country disintegrated into a series of warlord-controlled fiefdoms. Rabbani controlled only Kabul and the northeast; the rest of the country descended into chaos, at the mercy of warlords who switched sides endlessly. The civilian population suffered the most, preyed upon by roaming bands of armed men who exacted payment as and when they saw fit. The Pashtun community struggled to remain unified, but many of the leaders from the Soviet War were considered corrupt and power-hungry, unfit to lead the community depending upon them.

The Taliban movement was born in the Pashtun tribal areas of Pakistan among Afghan refugees.[4] It garnered considerable support from its earliest days from the Pashtun communities on both sides of the border. Ahmed Rashid described in 2000 how "the Taliban had won over the unruly Pashtun south because the exhausted, war-weary population saw them as saviors and peacemakers, if not as a potential force to revive Pashtun power which had been humiliated by the Tajiks and Uzbeks."[5] However, the Taliban were more than a Pashtun political movement. Their specific aims were to restore peace, enforce Sharia law, disarm the population, and defend the integrity and Islamic character of Afghanistan. To achieve these goals, the Taliban imposed brutal punishments on those who failed to follow traditional modes of behavior and their own strict interpretation of Islam. Despite this, many people, especially in the Pashtun belt of the south and east of the country, were willing to accept such repression in exchange for stability, security, and a sense of political power.[6] The Pakistani government, military, and ISI all openly supported the Taliban from 1994 onward.

The ethnic divisions of the country were exacerbated by the Taliban's rise to power and expansion of influence west towards Herat and north towards Kabul. The Taliban were perceived as a Pashtun political movement, even though not all Pashtuns supported them.[7] Many Pashtuns feared the fundamentalist aims of the Taliban, but many more, both in Afghanistan and across the border in Pakistan, saw the Taliban as their community's best hope of unseating the Tajik and Uzbek interlopers. The fighting in Kabul during 1995 and 1996 emphasized the growing ethnic divisions, as Tajik, Uzbek, Pashtun, and Hazara killed one another. By 1996, the Taliban had swept Kandahar and seized Kabul. Massoud moved his army back into the Panjshir valley to the north. Within 24 hours of seizing Kabul, the Taliban imposed strict Islamic law, essentially excluding women and girls from society by banning them from work and education, and introducing corporal punishment for minor crimes.[8]

As the Taliban continued to expand their influence, they began to focus their attention on neutralizing specific ethnic groups. In 1998, this campaign reached a climax in Mazar-i-Sharif, where the Taliban, having captured the city, went on a two-day killing spree. Their principal targets on this occasion were the Hazaras, who are largely Shi'a Muslims and comprise much of the city's population. Estimates for noncombatant deaths in this cleansing operation range from 5,000 to 8,000.

By 2000, the lines had been drawn between the Taliban and the United Islamic Front for the Salvation of Afghanistan (also known as the Northern Alliance), which had formed in 1996. The Northern Alliance only controlled 10–15 percent of Afghanistan, but was supported by Russia, Tajikistan, Iran, and India, as against the Pakistani and Saudi Arabian support of the Taliban. The Northern Alliance was headed by Burhanuddin Rabbani; other notable members included the Tajik military commander, Massoud; the Uzbek leader, Abdul Rashid Dostum; representatives from the Hazara community; and anti-Taliban Pashtuns. The Northern Alliance's broad support reflected growing resentment of the state of affairs in Afghanistan: the endless war, the religious orthodoxy, the presence of foreign Arabs, and the corruption within the Taliban itself.[9] In the eyes of the world community, the Taliban were anathema for their views on Islam and treatment of the Afghan people.

Osama bin Laden arrived in Afghanistan to take refuge in 1996. He was allowed to build and run training camps for Al-Qaeda foreign fighters in Afghanistan; in exchange, he supported the Taliban war effort with both money and foreign troops to fight on the Taliban front lines. Despite considerable pressure from the US and the world community to deal with bin Laden and the training camps, the Taliban refused to interfere with his activities or to turn him over to outside authorities.

Two days before the attacks in the United States in 2001, two Al-Qaeda members met with General Massoud, detonated a bomb, and killed him. This action was a serious blow to the Northern Alliance, and set the stage for the next phase of combat with the Taliban.

Operations to Topple the Taliban 2001–02

Following the September 11 attacks, President George W. Bush called upon the Taliban to hand over bin Laden and any Al-Qaeda leadership based in Afghanistan. The Taliban flatly refused to accede to this request, and the US government began to make plans for an incursion into Afghanistan. The first CIA operatives arrived in areas controlled by the Northern Alliance on September 26, 2001 to discuss potential operations. The American agents advised the Northern Alliance that the main purpose of US operations in Afghanistan was to kill and capture Al-Qaeda

Afghanistan

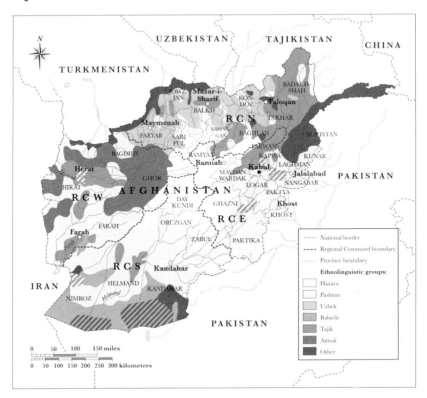

leadership. The Americans recognized, however, that they would have to contend with Taliban opposition in order to accomplish this objective, a complication which fit in nicely with the Northern Alliance's goals. The US government's mission, however, took no account of the actual political and military situation in Afghanistan at that time, in its haste to take immediate action and find the people responsible for the horrific attacks of September 11. This failure to undertake appropriate long-term planning was to have significant consequences. The principal aims of the military operation, as outlined by Secretary of Defense Donald Rumsfeld and General Richard Myers, were to force the Taliban to give up Osama bin Laden, or else suffer the consequences; this was to be accomplished by developing relations with anti-Taliban groups, and altering the military balance in favor of the Northern Alliance. Other goals were to acquire intelligence and make life difficult generally for terrorists. Last on the list was "provide humanitarian relief."[10]

Operation *Enduring Freedom* (OEF) began on Sunday, October 7, 2001, when American and British aircraft and cruise missiles struck Taliban and Al-Qaeda targets. Under cover of the bombing, Special Forces teams from the US and UK began to arrive in the country. The Special Forces teams were to provide assistance to the Northern Alliance in the north and to anti-Taliban Pashtun forces in the south. The Taliban, in response, organized themselves in large formations, which quickly began to suffer heavy losses from the ongoing coalition air strikes. The Taliban were mainly receiving reinforcements in the form of aid from Pakistan's ISI and new recruits from the Pashtun areas of the northwest frontier. In less than a month, the focus of the bombing missions had shifted to achieving strategic effects as determined by the Northern Alliance; these, in combination with Special Forces assistance, began to create victories for the Northern Alliance. By late November, Northern Alliance forces had seized Mazar-i-Sharif, Kabul, and Kunduz.[11]

The Taliban had begun to disintegrate as anti-Taliban Pashtun forces in the south, led by Hamid Karzai and coalition Special Forces, closed in on Kandahar in early December, supported by more than a thousand US Marines. The Taliban and Al-Qaeda fled the city on December 8, 2001, taking refuge in the mountainous regions of eastern Afghanistan.[12] This phase demonstrated how fragile Pashtun support for the Taliban really was, which numerous commanders failed to note in their drive to hunt down and kill Al-Qaeda and Taliban forces. Many Special Forces personnel felt that more time should have been spent trying to bolster Pashtun support to topple the Taliban, rather than relying so heavily upon the Northern Alliance,[13] and that strike operations and searches for Taliban and Al-Qaeda operatives in Pashtun communities actively alienated people who later became insurgents.

The departure of the Taliban left a political vacuum. Observers described how

anti-Taliban Pashtun leaders...failed to demonstrate cohesiveness. Commanders raced to establish their own authority, creating a patchwork of predatory, competing fiefdoms. A culture of impunity was allowed to take root in the name of stability, with abusers free to return to their old ways as long as they mouthed their allegiance to the central government.[14]

As the Taliban and Al-Qaeda headed for the hills to the east and south, the campaign in Afghanistan began to shift to more conventional-style operations. The fighting in the Tora Bora region in eastern Afghanistan in December 2001 highlighted some of the deficiencies of the Special Forces/Northern Alliance partnership. Reports had stated that Al-Qaeda and Taliban forces were heavily dug in, but a series of sweeps found little evidence to substantiate this. Some US commanders and politicians blamed a lack of motivation on the part of Northern Alliance forces, and called for more coalition troops to be deployed to the region. The US forces subsequently deployed from the 10th Mountain and 101st and 82nd Airborne Divisions did not understand counterinsurgency, never having been trained in its principles. Their sole stated mission was to find, capture, and kill Al-Qaeda and Taliban leadership.[15]

In March 2002, *Anaconda*, the first large-scale conventional operation in Afghanistan, unfolded in the eastern regions. More than 2,000 US, Afghan, British, Canadian, Australian, and New Zealand forces were airlifted into the area to destroy some 1,000 Taliban and Al-Qaeda forces. The coalition forces succeeded in killing about 500 insurgents, but most observers felt that a battle of attrition was unlikely to lead to victory.[16] As the then Director of the CIA, George Tenet, commented at the time: "You're entering into another phase here that is actually more difficult, because you're probably looking at smaller units that intend to operate against you in a classic insurgency format."[17] Some Taliban and Al-Qaeda forces dug in; some fell back towards the tribal areas of Pakistan; others retreated to the southern regions of Afghanistan, the spiritual home of the Taliban.

The nuances of this development were lost on Secretary Rumsfeld, who was looking for something else altogether. Rumsfeld, who felt that the military had not yielded enough high-level captures or kills in the mountains,[18] launched Operation *Mountain Sweep* in August 2002, led by units of the 82nd Airborne Division. This operation demonstrated how the actions of a force untrained in counterinsurgency can help perpetuate a growing insurgency. As a *Newsweek* reporter noted on October 7, 2002:

> Not long after the special forces team [who had done a proper search, demonstrating awareness of and respect for Pashtun customs] left...six paratroopers from the 82nd...were positioned outside the farmer's house, preparing to force their way in, the way they had been trained to do...The

farmer panicked and tried to run, paratrooper[s] slammed him to the ground. The soldiers frisked the women. The family was in a state of shock. The women were screaming. The farmer was in tears. He had been dishonored.[19]

In addition to misunderstanding the tactical aspects of fighting an insurgency, the coalition failed to step back and try to understand the economic and political problems facing the Pashtun community. For example, nearly all insurgents in Afghanistan were identified as Taliban, when many were just disgruntled Pashtuns. It took more than five years to recognize and acknowledge that many of the insurgents were fighting for the same reasons that have always motivated insurgents: economics, politics, perceived wrongdoing, revenge, and tribal or ethnic issues. By the time Western forces had begun to learn from their early mistakes, a great deal of damage had already been done in fueling support for and participation in the insurgency.

The Government and the Community

An insurgent movement is a war for the people. It stands to reason that government measures must be directed to restoring government authority and law and order throughout the country, so that control over the population can be regained and its support won. This cannot be done unless a high priority is given to the administrative structure of government itself, to its institutions and to the training of its personnel. Without a reasonably efficient government machine, no programs or projects, in the context of counter-insurgency, will produce the desired results.[20]

Operations from 2001 to 2004 were marked by a series of disjointed efforts to learn how to conduct counterinsurgency in Afghanistan. The coalition made some significant mistakes along the way. Primary among these was the failure to grasp that numerous local insurgencies could spark simultaneously in different parts of Afghanistan, all motivated by a lack of security and economic stability, and by the perception that the Pashtuns, by losing the Taliban, had lost a major political stake in the future of Afghanistan. The war in Iraq drew attention and resources before the counterinsurgency campaign in Afghanistan had been properly developed, and before the coalition partners understood the mission.[21]

Further complicating the situation, the Pashtuns continued to face political marginalization. In December 2001, the first interim administration was formed, headed by a Pashtun, Hamid Karzai. Despite this high-profile appointment, many Pashtuns remained concerned that the rest of the government appeared to be heavily influenced by the Panjshiri Tajiks, who were considered suspect because of their involvement with the coalition troops in the recent fighting. A Loya Jirga (literally, "great council"; traditional Pashtun/Afghan governing assembly) held in June 2002 served to reinforce Pashtun fears that the Tajiks were the true leaders of the new Afghanistan, when the latter took control of a number of key security positions within the government.[22] Ahmed Rashid described how

> since December 2001, Panjshiris [Tajiks] have dominated the army, police and intelligence services. Their power has caused widespread resentment, especially among ethnic Pashtuns...[A]t the Loya Jirga, delegates repeatedly [accused] Karzai of being held a virtual hostage of the Panjshiris.[23]

Karzai subsequently tried to respond to and address these concerns, with mixed results.

With minimal influence outside Kabul during this period, the Karzai government had difficulty reaching out to the Pashtuns. The Pashtuns expressed concern that security and reconstruction were progressing too slowly in their regions. Their feeling was that, despite having a legitimately elected president, government, and parliament, the Afghan government and the international community consistently failed to provide troops, security, and funds for reconstruction and nation-building to the Pashtun population.[24] For government in the south, Karzai relied on loyal Pashtun warlords, who did not hold the allegiance of the majority of Pashtuns, to serve as governors, police chiefs, and administrators. The warlords became visibly corrupt, involved in the drug trade, and did not deal effectively with development issues. According to Ahmed Rashid, "For the majority of the southern Pashtuns, the corruption of these warlord-governors unfortunately symbolized the intentions of the Kabul government."[25] General Karl Eikenberry, commander of the coalition forces in Afghanistan from 2005 to 2007, summed it up as follows: "the enemy we face is not particularly strong, but the institutions of the Afghan state remain relatively weak."[26]

The Insurgents

> The interlocking agendas of anti-government insurgents and self-interested spoilers are fuelling the violence…Taliban commanders are mainly driving today's violence from sanctuaries in Pakistan. However, other elements contribute, while an enabling environment of corrupt and weak government helps provide recruits…[It is] estimated that only 20% of the insurgents are ideological "Taliban." Their numbers are augmented by non-ideological recruits, including those who oppose Kabul, local leaders or the international presence for their own reasons but are happy to do so under the cover of the Taliban banner…[T]here are fluid alliances of convenience at the local level.[27]

It was common for coalition forces to refer to the insurgents consistently as "Taliban," both in theater and at home; this was a politically useful generalization, since it reinforced the perception of a direct link between the Taliban and September 11. It was a misleading generalization, however. In the first place, it implied that the Taliban were operating from a position of political power and visibility. In 2002, this was not the case, as the Taliban had lost all political primacy and was on the run. Moreover, the insurgency was not as politically or ideologically homogeneous as this terminology indicates. While many observers concur that the insurgency's radical leadership included members of the old Taliban, and received support from Al-Qaeda and foreign Islamic extremists, there is also general agreement that the vast majority of the insurgents were spurred to fighting by broken promises, lack of a stable government, blood feuds, ethnic and tribal identity, and economic considerations. One key report cited insurgents' motivations as lack of money, extreme poverty, anger, revenge, unfair treatment by Kabul, and fear of the Taliban.[28]

At least two insurgent organizations of some significance besides the Taliban have been identified: these are the Haqqani Network and Hezb-e Islami Gulbuddin. Both of these organizations were, like the Taliban, heavily Pashtun in origin. Taken together, they presented a new and interesting variation on the portrait of the insurgent as presented in classic counterinsurgency theory: instead of being members of a perpetually downtrodden underclass, the Pashtun insurgents in Afghanistan were members of a group that had recently been displaced from a position of political power and dominance within their own society.[29] Continuing in this vein, it is even more interesting to note that some commentators have asserted that the main focus, even of the Taliban leadership, was not ideological, as has commonly been portrayed, but political and economic.[30]

All three main insurgent groups of this period relied upon the vast "Pashtun belt" of the Pakistan Federal Administered Tribal Areas along the eastern border between Afghanistan and Pakistan for troops, supplies, and support. Pakistan played an important role in the insurgency campaign; despite its governmental stance of support for US and coalition forces, the reality of the Pashtun belt was its long history of resistance to government control and its close relationships with Pashtun tribes on the Afghan side of the border. The Pashtun areas of Pakistan provided safe havens for insurgent troops, and considerable scope for cross-border traffic and smuggling activities. Pakistan sent thousands of troops into the region to wage a campaign against "Taliban" forces; heavy but inconclusive fighting ensued. The campaign was a drain on Pakistani Army personnel and resources, and was very unpopular with the Pakistani population. In September 2006, the Pakistani government reached an agreement with tribal leaders to withdraw their forces. This eased the political situation inside Pakistan but greatly disappointed Pakistan's coalition allies as it allowed the Taliban to retain a considerable advantage, with sanctuaries just over the border providing volunteers, money, and intelligence. [31]

Coalition and Afghan Security Forces and Reconstruction

Sir Robert Thompson encapsulates the goals and challenges of carrying out counterinsurgency in strongholds of resistance:

> The army's role here is to clear the main insurgent units out of the area over which the government is attempting to regain control, and keep them out. Elimination of the units and the killing of insurgents is a secondary consideration at this stage. After clearing, it is the role of the police field units, supported by the regular police and civilian government departments, to hold the area, restore government authority and win the people to the side of the government.[32]

This is the essence of the "clear-hold-build" strategy, but the strategy is one that takes time, patience, money, and coordination across multiple governmental (and international non-governmental) lines of communication.

The counterinsurgency campaign in Afghanistan made significant progress from 2004 to 2007 in developing and implementing a workable military-led strategy. United States, British, and Canadian forces began carrying out counterinsurgency study days, to learn the history of counterinsurgency operations, and understand how the trial and error of past campaigns could apply to contemporary situations.

Much of this refocus on the basics of counterinsurgency came about as a result of personnel changes within the command structure of Combined Forces Command-Afghanistan (CFC-A). Lieutenant General David Barno took command of Combined Joint Task Force-180 in 2003; he recognized that the focus of the effort should be on the "Afghan" people and not the hunting down and killing of Al-Qaeda and the Taliban. He and his staff, which included British officers, created a plan for security and stability for 2004 in the southern and eastern regions of Afghanistan. Their plan had two overarching principles: "the people as the center of gravity" and "unity of purpose." Staff officers read the classic counterinsurgency theorists – Robert Thompson, David Galula, Frank Kitson – and studied key counterinsurgency campaigns of the past to gain a better understanding of counterinsurgency theory in its broadest sense.[33]

The apparatus for absorbing and disseminating lessons learned on the ground began to improve, and coordination of information among various forces began to happen. Military commanders also began to grasp that political, economic, cultural, and tribal questions might be more important than the religious motivations that had previously been considered key by both the military and politicians. Military commanders also recognized that a viable army and national police force – properly trained, officered, equipped, financed, and ethnically representative – were critical to establishing a stable and secure civil administration.

Until 2006, the two principal coalition organizations operating in Afghanistan were the US-led Operation *Enduring Freedom*'s CFC-A, and the NATO-led International Security Assistance Force (ISAF). Implementation of the Provincial Reconstruction Team (PRT) concept, created by a British officer and expanded by the United States, provided another key factor in the areas of security and reconstruction.

Operation *Enduring Freedom*
The American forces deployed on OEF were initially tasked with hunting down, capturing, and killing Al-Qaeda and Taliban operatives. By June

2003, US troop levels were at about 9,000, but were providing security for the local population to only a very limited degree. US forces generally deployed in Regional Command East, covering much of the Pakistan border from Kabul south towards Kandahar. Most of these conventional forces had not been trained in counterinsurgency, and many observers believe that they exacerbated the low-level support for the Taliban with their heavy-handed approach in the Pashtun regions. One observer commented that "the use of large sweeps has produced the alienation of the local populace, fostering mistrust and creating a further impediment to intelligence collection."[34]

The US military from 2006 onward was a changed organization, thanks to significant reforms in the system and a much greater emphasis on counterinsurgency theory, education, and training. In Afghanistan (as in Iraq), this was manifested in the strategy of clear-hold-build. As of early 2007, the US had more than 22,000 personnel deployed to Afghanistan, working in counter-terrorism, counterinsurgency, PRTs, and advisory teams to the Afghan National Army. The vast majority of these troops (17,000) came under NATO command. The troops deployed had been trained in counterinsurgency and were generally highly regarded. The US military (again, as in Iraq), created an in-theater counterinsurgency Center of Excellence for officers and troops rotating to Afghanistan to study local conditions and create plans for the implementation of a counterinsurgency strategy in their given area. The coalition partners – Great Britain, Australia, and Canada – have begun to join this program shortly after its inception.[35]

ISAF

ISAF was originally created by the United Nations Security Council in December 2001; "...in its pre-NATO configuration [it] had a vague but potentially competing mandate with OEF and possessed virtually no resources or firepower to provide significant influence in the city of Kabul, its designated area of operations."[36] Originally ISAF comprised only 4,500 troops, far fewer than the 30,000 troops generally considered necessary to secure the larger cities, but under strength because there was no way to compel member nations to supply the necessary personnel for the potentially dangerous mission.[37] NATO took command of ISAF in August 2003, and the Security Council extended its mandate outside Kabul in September. ISAF troops moved to the north in 2004 and to the west in 2005, taking over PRTs and security from US forces.

In January 2006, ISAF deployed to Regional Command South, taking over security tasks in that region from American forces. Its remit was to expand the influence of the Afghan central government, to focus on the growing counter-narcotics operations, and to contend with security issues in light of the growing Pashtun insurgency. Following this deployment and the change of command of US forces in Regional Command East in September 2006, fractures began to emerge. With ground forces moving into Pashtun areas where there had previously been minimal security, anti-coalition and Taliban forces from the border regions responded violently. This led to some NATO countries refusing to allow their troops to be deployed in volatile regions. Thus, although more than 35,000 troops have been assigned to ISAF, not all have been eligible for deployment in all areas, due either to political issues in their home nations, or to a lack of appropriate counterinsurgency training.[38] The only troops willing and able to deploy in Regional Commands East and South as of 2007 were the Americans, Australians, British, Canadians, Danes, Dutch, and Romanians. The rest of ISAF was limited to Regional Commands North and West.

Lieutenant General David Richards, commander of NATO forces in Afghanistan from July 2006 to February 2007, commented:

> Our force levels in 2006 were just sufficient to contain the insurgency. Significant capability gaps remain that restricted my ability to reinforce where the situation dictated. As a result of too few forces, we have found it difficult to maintain security where we have gained it, and we are using the ANSF [Afghan National Security Forces] more than is ideal for its development and growth...Given the nature of the insurgency we are now fighting, we should look again at force requirements and adjust as necessary.[39]

Provincial Reconstruction Teams (PRTs)

The implementation of the PRT concept in 2002 had a significant impact on the practice of counterinsurgency in Afghanistan.[40] The chief purpose of PRTs was to deliver reconstruction, governance, and security to local populations under the auspices of the Afghan central government, using combined teams of civilian and military personnel. The US led the way in the development of these systems; they were followed by other countries who developed the concept in relatively quiet areas of the country, chiefly in the north and west. By the end of 2006, ISAF had taken over command of the 27 PRTs based all over Afghanistan.

The PRTs have been generally praised, but also criticized. One of the significant flaws of the PRT program was that they initially answered to their own national governments, rather than to a central Afghan government agency. This resulted in inconsistency as to how and what services were delivered:

> The PRTs…have been hamstrung by the policy constraints of troop-contributing nations, resource limitations, and national caveats to act decisively against local thugs, drugs and official mugs. While the PRTs are mandated to help extend the authority of the central government and facilitate stability, in certain cases they have discouraged government action against spoilers because of concerns about their own security.[41]

There have also been accusations of failing to sufficiently involve local leaders in planning and implementing projects undertaken by the PRT.[42]

NATO has further developed the concept into the Afghan Development Zone (ADZ) strategy, which has been implemented in RC (Regional Command) South, particularly in Helmand and Kandahar provinces. Lieutenant General David Richards described how

> The [ADZs] – where governance, reconstruction and development are properly synchronized in areas secured by ISAF and ANSF – have flourished as a result. Among other measures, the Policy Action Group (PAG) was established to provide a mechanism for focusing government and international community efforts on key areas of the insurgency. Recently its focus has been expanded, as it is seen as an effective tool for spreading the writ of the government into all areas. For example, after the PAG met in Kandahar, ministers started to travel outside Kabul on a more frequent basis.[43]

The International Crisis Group, an internationally renowned policy research and advocacy organization, supports PAG's attempt at coordinating the efforts of the various agencies and government services: "This is promising, because institution building and listening to representations at this level are needed." It is not as optimistic, however, about the implementation of the ADZ concept:

No new money has been allocated to the ADZ...[T]here are concerns about whether those immediately outside a zone...would resent the ADZ...[The] ADZ is supply driven by the international community, dividing up a small amount of resources to do something, rather than [a] needs-led approach to tackle the insurgency comprehensively.[44]

The campaign consistently suffered from a lack of coordination among coalition partners. Each of the leading organizations had differing viewpoints about the mission's goals and how to achieve them. This affected planning, execution, and interaction. Lieutenant General David Barno, former commander, CFC-A, 2003–05, commented in 2007 that:

Twenty-six NATO PRTs are now deployed across Afghanistan, but they vary widely in size, composition, and mission – and now report through a different chain of command than do NATO's maneuver units in the same battlespace...[C]ontinual turnover of US senior leaders has made continuity of effort a recurrent challenge in this very complex fight... [S]ince mid-2005, the comprehensive US led [counterinsurgency] strategy...has been significantly altered by subsequent military and civilian leaders who held differing views. With the advent of NATO military leadership, there is today no single comprehensive strategy to guide the US, NATO, or international effort. Unity of purpose – both interagency and international – has suffered; unity of command is more fragmented...NATO's ISAF has assumed a narrow focus on the 20 percent military dimension of [counterinsurgency]. It views the remaining 80 percent non-military component of successful [counterinsurgency] operations as falling outside the purview of what is, after all, a military alliance.[45]

Afghan Forces

Proper training and build up of local indigenous forces is key to clearing and holding any contested region in a successful counterinsurgency campaign. As one southern Afghan noted: "if Afghan people come to the community, people will help them if they are doing the right thing by the community."[46] Efforts to reform and reestablish the ANA and the ANP have produced mixed results as of 2007.

The Afghan central government, ISAF, and the US have all failed to make a properly trained police force a priority in establishing a stable and secure civil administration.[47] From the perspective of the local population, the 62,000-strong ANP was nothing more than local militias and thugs, preying upon the community they were supposed to serve. Corruption was rife. The actual numbers of police were often inflated, to enable commanders to get more money. Many national police did not come from the areas where they served, which made locals less willing to cooperate with them. Many communities, given their previous experiences, were only willing to trust those from their own ethnic group in a police role. Because of these problems, the coalition began experimenting with the establishment of the Afghan National Auxiliary Police (ANAP), whose members were locally recruited.[48] The ANAP echoed the British-established Frontier Scouts, which came into being in the northwest frontier of present-day Pakistan for similar reasons in the early 20th century.

The ANA[49] had a better reputation than the ANP, but it too experienced problems.[50] Development suffered from responsibility being handed from one partner to another, or shared among several; in 2007, there were American, British, and Canadian training teams embedded with the ANA. This heterogeneity revealed differences of opinion about training and military ethos that could undermine consistent functioning.[51] Concerns were also expressed about ethnic composition; in particular, that there was not enough Pashtun representation. British officers (as well as Afghan officer cadets at Royal Military Academy Sandhurst) noted that Pashtun leaders were hesitant about Pashtuns going north to Kabul for Officer Candidate School (as opposed to Kandahar). Many Pashtuns viewed the ANA with suspicion, considering it little more than a re-branded Northern Alliance. Finally, the ANA structures had not yet been established to ensure adequate financial support and long-term economic sustainability, although there are recent signs of improvement.[52]

Helmand: A Case Study[53]

The NATO coalition presence in the southern province of Helmand was minimal before the arrival of the British 16th Air Assault Brigade in 2006 (Operation *Herrick IV*). The US had initially deployed Special Forces in the region to carry out direct action against high-level Taliban and Al-Qaeda targets and, in 2005, an American PRT was established with some coalition support. There was essentially no "Kabul-backed" regional government in the province when the British arrived; this created a number of obstacles, as Afghan governmental representatives were often not available to discuss operations or deal with reconstruction.

Initially, there was also confusion about the purpose of the mission. Senior British politicians claimed that the troops were being deployed on a Peace Support Operation to support counter-narcotic operations.[54] Meanwhile, brigade personnel[55] were working on the understanding that they were carrying out a major counterinsurgency operation that would include heavy fighting to clear areas for development and governance to take hold (ink spot/ADZ strategies).[56]

This confusion was a significant concern, as the goals of the two missions were contrary to one another. Counter-narcotics operations were, for many politicians, the most significant aspect of the mission. As of 2006, 50 percent of the Afghan government's GDP came from the production of opium, with about 12 percent of the population dependent on the opium trade for their livelihood. It was estimated that 90 percent of the world's heroin came from Afghanistan, making the narco-economy a significant problem both inside and outside Afghanistan.[57] However, many experts – military and otherwise – considered carrying out counter-narcotics operations and undertaking clear-hold-build operations to be fundamentally incompatible missions. Commentators pointed out that, until viable economic alternatives were identified and an eradication strategy developed that included confronting high-level corruption, any attempt to eradicate the opium trade was likely only to create more insurgents, while failing to solve the problem. This was a politically unpopular point of view, because it meant that implementing a counter-narcotics strategy properly was likely to involve several years' delay.

The British began moving forces into Helmand in April 2006, eventually deploying more than 3,000 troops. The 16th Air Assault Brigade served until October 2006 and was heavily involved in clearing and holding a number of locations, including Garmser, Lashkar Gah, Gereshk, Sangin, Nowzad, and Musa Qaléh. As part of the clear and hold process, the brigade established Camp Bastion and Forward Operating Bases Robinson and Price. The Canadian Task Force conducted similar operations against the Taliban in Kandahar Province. The brigade's experiences in this campaign were representative of the larger war effort: they were overstretched in deploying forces as a result of higher-level decision making, which was focused on achieving targets that were not necessarily related to what was practicable in theater. Civil–military cooperation was also lacking, due to the civilian organizations' lack of familiarity with counterinsurgency and their aversion to the dangerous environment, although recent experience shows that things are improving.

The vast majority of the 3 Battalion Parachute Regiment (3 PARA) fighting force was initially deployed in company- or platoon-sized bases in selected towns. The idea, in accord with traditional counterinsurgency thought, was to concentrate on securing population centers before spreading out further. This strategy was adopted because many commanders wanted to start small so as not to overextend their forces. In practice, the plan changed as more platoon houses were established due to higher-level decision making. This caused numerous logistical and close air support problems. The positions established by 3 PARA and other units of the brigade quickly became Taliban targets, as part of a dedicated campaign to demoralize both British troops and the British public watching from afar. What followed, in selected locations, was some of the most sustained fighting undertaken by British troops since World War Two. Even with positions located inside the towns, the intensity of the fighting and the sophistication of the Taliban's attacks severely limited British troops' ability to move out and interact with the population. Ultimately, however, the Taliban's strategy backfired, as the heavy fighting and stalwart defense of the British positions sent a message to the local people that the British were going to dig in and defend the town and people against the Taliban. The Taliban also failed in their plans to overrun positions, and paid dearly in loss of life in the attempt.

The British formed Maneuver Outreach Groups in August 2006 to provide a mobile force, working as long-range reconnaissance, interdicting supplies and insurgents, and establishing relations with the local community. The brigade also provided soldiers, NCOs, and officers for Operational Mentoring and Liaison Teams working to mentor and train ANA forces. During Operation *Herrick IV*, this effort was on a small scale, but during *Herrick V* (3rd Commando Brigade) it was expanded to a full battalion, with 45 Royal Marine Commando (45 Cdo) providing training teams.

The PRT that was set up in Lashkar Gah was compromised by insufficient provision of civilian personnel and resources. The same PRT had worked well in Regional Command North in Mazar-i-Sharif, a relatively quiet area, but Helmand was a different proposition. Both the American and British militaries found a reluctance to commit civilian personnel and money from other governmental agencies to areas still perceived as dangerous. This severely hampered the follow-up development that needed to be done in close proximity to the fighting.

Operations *Herrick IV* and *Herrick V* were clearing and holding operations; they prepared the way for the reconstruction activities that were supposed to follow, taking advantage of the newly secure environment. General Sir Frank Kitson characterized the complexities of counterinsurgency strategy as follows:

> The first thing that must be apparent when contemplating the sort of action which a government facing insurgency should take, is that there can be no such thing as a purely military solution because insurgency is not primarily a military activity. At the same time there is no such thing as a wholly political solution either, short of surrender, because the very fact that a state of insurgency exists implies that violence is involved which will have to be countered to some extent at least by the use of force.[58]

Herrick IV and *V* were largely successful militarily, but they highlighted persistent shortcomings in the coalition's counterinsurgency effort: force numbers; adequate commitment to joint civilian–military-led development; training of indigenous police and military forces; training of civilians; and coordinating security and reconstruction initiatives. Achieving the correct balance between military and political solutions is key to the success of any counterinsurgency campaign, and there appears to be some progress in this area.

Conclusion

The counterinsurgency campaign in Afghanistan was initially unsuccessful because the coalition misunderstood the potential long-term implications of its decision to send in troops; failed to recognize the scope of, and reasons for, local support of a burgeoning insurgency; and failed to understand and apply concepts of counterinsurgency, particularly in its non-military aspects. As a result of numerous initiatives undertaken between 2004 and 2007, coalition forces improved their knowledge of counterinsurgency strategy, and developed initiatives to improve its delivery. The primary vehicle for these initiatives was the PRTs and their successors, which used a combination of military and civilian resources to address problems specific to local populations, provide security and development, and in the process win the support and trust of the people. Many coalition field commanders made great strides during this period in understanding counterinsurgency and its application to both history and current events. They attempted to consider the insurgency in Afghanistan from a fresh perspective, which takes the insurgents' own views into account.[59]

As of 2007, the main problem impeding coalition forces' successful application of counterinsurgency was decentralization of responsibility. The number of different governments involved in the coalition, and as a result directly involved with the functioning of personnel involved in carrying out counterinsurgency operations, made it very difficult to implement a single, cohesive, consistent plan of action that could be applied across Afghanistan. The question of who owns the campaign plan remained unanswered: the broad outline of tasks and goals was the same for all coalition forces, but the details of implementation varied considerably. This caused ongoing problems, both with completing tasks effectively and with building relationships with the Afghan people.

Carrying out a successful counterinsurgency campaign takes a substantial amount of money, and even more importantly, a substantial amount of political will. This may include an undertaking that such a campaign could last for decades, and that casualties are inevitable in providing security and holding cleared areas. For all – military participants on the ground and civilians following through news reports – this means looking at the situation from the perspective of the local community, and remembering that a Western upbringing and perspective is not a great help, and is frequently an active detriment, to understanding the world in which the average Afghan lives.

Greater comprehension paves the way for the implementation of a true counterinsurgency strategy, one that links up all the disparate groups from within the coalition, and includes not only the Afghan government but also the community, including the community fueling the insurgency. It is critical to remember that today's so-called enemy is likely to be part of tomorrow's solution. This has always been true, throughout the history of counterinsurgency.

13

COUNTERINSURGENCY IN IRAQ
May 2003–January 2007

Dr Carter Malkasian

The United States' campaign in Iraq marked its second major counterinsurgency campaign in 40 years. The US military attempted to adapt to the situation it found in Iraq, drawing upon lessons from history and its own operations. However, in the first four years of the conflict, it could not suppress the insurgency, which prompted President George W. Bush to revise his strategy in January 2007.

The reasons behind the lack of progress from May 2003 to January 2007 may not be clear for some time, if at all. To some extent, American attempts to adapt neglected the sectarian divisions in Iraq. The key elements of the US strategy – democratization and the construction of a national (and consequently predominantly Shi'a) army – did nothing to placate the Sunni minority, who backed the insurgency and sought to preserve their political power against both the occupation and the emerging Shi'a government. This strategy did not make success impossible before 2007, but it certainly made it harder to suppress the violence.

The Outbreak of the Insurgency

The insurgency in Iraq broke out over the summer of 2003, following the coalition's lightning victory over Saddam Hussein's standing forces in March and April.[1] Sunni Arabs, who lived primarily in Baghdad and western and northern Iraq, represented the overwhelming majority of the insurgents. In general, the insurgents sought to compel the United States, viewed as an occupier, to withdraw from Iraq; and to recapture some of the political power and economic benefits that the Sunnis had lost to the Shi'a Arabs with the demise of Saddam Hussein's regime.[2] US plans for democracy promised to place the Shi'a, representing 60 percent of the population, in the most powerful political position. The large role played by exiled Shi'a leaders on the newly constructed Iraqi Governing Council (an interim advisory body), the dissolution of the old Iraqi Army (which Sunnis had largely officered), and the prohibition of members of the Ba'ath Party from working in the government (de-Ba'athification) exacerbated the Sunni feeling of marginalization. An extreme element of the insurgency, the Al-Qaeda-affiliated network of Abu Musab al Zarqawi, wanted to create their own Islamic state within Iraq that might be able to support Al-Qaeda's activities elsewhere in the region. Zarqawi purposefully targeted Shi'a in order to draw reprisals upon the Sunnis and instigate a civil war.[3] Zarqawi's network, later known as Al-Qaeda in Iraq (AQI), held the allegiance of the foreign fighters and Iraqi terrorists of most concern to the United States.

In the summer of 2003, the United States had 150,000 military personnel (in five divisions) in Iraq, which together with 13,000 personnel from the United Kingdom and other allied countries (in two divisions) formed Combined Joint Task Force 7 (CJTF-7), under the command of Lieutenant General Ricardo Sanchez. The allied forces were known as the "coalition."

Ambassador Paul Bremer controlled the Coalition Provisional Authority (CPA), which was responsible for governing Iraq and guiding its progression toward democracy, a foremost goal of the Bush administration. Many US leaders, including Bremer, believed that democracy represented a natural antidote to the extremism of Zarqawi and other terrorists. Furthermore, the most respected Shi'a religious leader, Ayatollah Ali al Sistani, with strong popular Shi'a backing, pressured Bremer to hold direct elections as soon as possible.[4]

The United States and its military were unprepared to confront the insurgency that developed. Since the end of the Vietnam War, both the US Army and Marine Corps had focused on learning rapid maneuver and combined arms in order to fight a conventional war, instead of the patrolling, bottom-up intelligence collection and minimization of force generally considered necessary for successful counterinsurgency. Training, such as at the Army's National Training Center in the California desert, dealt with defeating conventional mechanized opponents. No comprehensive doctrine existed for counterinsurgency. Expecting to fight a conventional war, the US Army fielded armored and mechanized battalions that were heavy on M1A1/M1A2 Abrams tanks and M2A2 Bradley fighting vehicles, but light on infantry (armored and mechanized battalions contained 500 to 600 personnel). Such organization made it difficult to thoroughly patrol or interact with the population. The Marines were somewhat better off: their battalions contained 900 infantry; every battalion had a team dedicated to human intelligence collection; and there had been intensive training for urban combat since the late 1990s.

Neither Major General Sanchez nor General John Abizaid, commander of Central Command, promulgated a plan to counter the insurgency. When confronted with insurgent attacks, the five US divisions reacted differently, but with a tendency toward conventional-style operations and heavy-handed tactics. Units conducted raids based on scant intelligence and applied firepower loosely. Operating north of Baghdad around Samarra and Tikrit (Salah-ah-din Province), Major General Raymond Odierno's 4th Infantry Division acquired a reputation for heavy-handedness. Instead of trying to secure the population, his commanders launched large-scale sweeps to roll up insurgents and Ba'athist leaders, fired artillery blindly to interdict insurgent activity ("harassment and interdiction fires"), purposefully detained innocents to blackmail their insurgent relatives, and leveled homes to deter people from supporting the insurgents.[5] Such actions further alienated the Sunni population. Other divisions operated in a similar pattern. In Fallujah, troops from the 82nd Airborne Division, feeling threatened, fired into mass gatherings on both April 28 and 30, 2003, killing 13 civilians and wounding 91. In November, Sanchez conducted a series of sweeps and air strikes, such as Operation *Iron Hammer*, meant to crush the insurgents. Major General Charles Swannack, the commander of the 82nd Airborne Division, said: "This is war... We're going to use a sledgehammer to crush a walnut."[6]

The operations of Major General David Petraeus' 101st Airborne Division, working in the north of Iraq (Ninewa Province), diverged from this trend. Petraeus considered securing the population to be the key to effective counterinsurgency and concentrated his entire division in Mosul, the largest population center (1.8 million) in the province. Determined to minimize harm to the population, before approving any operations he would ask his commanders, "Will this operation take more bad guys off the street than it creates by the way it is conducted?"[7] Rather than undertaking large sweeps, his troopers operated out of outposts in the heart of the city and focused on collecting detailed actionable intelligence for raids against insurgent leadership. Meanwhile, Petraeus interacted with the Sunni elements of society, even holding his own local elections to draw them into the political process. Insurgent attacks stayed low during the division's tenure. Unfortunately, the following unit boasted only a third of the 101st's manpower, and the situation deteriorated.

The one method that characterized all US operations was high-value targeting. Elite special operating forces enjoyed carte blanche to capture and kill insurgent leaders. The conventional forces let the same tactic drive their operations. Every battalion, brigade, and division developed a high-value targeting list detailing the most wanted insurgents in their area of operations. Intelligence collection assets were devoted to finding insurgent leaders.

It is worth noting that the British, who controlled the coalition forces around Basrah, Al Amarah, and An Nasiriyah, adopted a more circumspect approach than the Americans. Applying the lessons of a half-century of counterinsurgency, the British patrolled in small units, rigorously collected intelligence, and used firepower sparingly. In general, British and other Western European forces tried to maintain a light footprint in cities to avoid upsetting the locals. As early as September 2003, British generals made the development of local Iraqi forces a priority. For example, in 2004, the entire Argyll & Sutherland Battalion was dedicated to training them. Some of the first effective Iraqi units appeared in the British operating area.[8] Unfortunately, the light approach toward securing the population would later allow militias to gain control of the city, which would have negative side effects in 2007.

The First Battle of Fallujah and the Mahdi Uprising

For the most part, small-scale roadside bombings, mortar shelling, and fleeting skirmishes characterized insurgent activity in 2003. By early 2004, the insurgency was gaining strength. Poor strategic decisions made it explode.

The I Marine Expeditionary Force (I MEF) took over Al Anbar Province from the 82nd Airborne Division in March 2004. On March 31, insurgents and people in Fallujah murdered four American civilian contractors and hung their bodies from a bridge over the Euphrates. Against the advice of Major General James Mattis and Lieutenant General James Conway (the Marine commanders), the Bush administration ordered an offensive to clear Fallujah. Determined to signal their resolve, they made the decision with little consultation with the Iraqi Governing Council and allowed insufficient time (just days) to evacuate civilians, gather intelligence, and construct a public relations campaign to mitigate the negative effects of attacking a Sunni city.[9] Indeed, instructions from Sanchez, Abizaid, and Rumsfeld endorsed harsh military action, thereby de-emphasizing the importance of minimizing civilian casualties.[10] Of the four Iraqi battalions assigned to the assault, only 70 Iraqi soldiers (from the 36th Commando Battalion) accompanied the 2,000 Marines (two reinforced infantry battalions) that led the offensive, hardly lessening Sunni feelings of oppression.

The ensuing offensive ignited widespread Sunni outrage. Viewing it as an attack on their society, Sunnis poured into Fallujah from other Sunni cities. When the Marines stepped off, they encountered heavy resistance from roughly 2,000 insurgents. Insurgents coordinated mortars, volleys of rocket-propelled grenades, and machine-gun fire in defense of their positions. Marine commanders risked prohibitive casualties unless they reverted to using artillery, air strikes, and tanks as per their conventional combined arms doctrine. Such firepower was applied selectively but, nevertheless, civilians died (the Iraqi Ministry of Health estimated 220 for the first two weeks of fighting).[11] Insurgent propaganda and Arab media exploited these casualties to inflame opposition to the coalition. The coalition had no response. The Iraqi Governing Council came under tremendous pressure to stop the fighting. Sunni members threatened to resign if Bremer did not initiate ceasefire negotiations. With the democratization process in jeopardy, on April 9 the US government halted the offensive.[12] Fighting around the Marine bridgehead persisted until April 30, when Conway pulled the Marines out of the city.

At the same time that Fallujah exploded, a Shi'a uprising shook coalition control over southern Iraq and threatened to ignite a national resistance. The Shi'a did not oppose the coalition to the same extent that the Sunnis did, largely because their leaders now held power. However, most Shi'a still wanted the occupation to end. Moqtada Sadr, a radical young Shi'a cleric with a widespread following who had not been given a role in the coalition's political process, tapped into this vein. His militia, Jaysh al Mahdi, was organized around poor, young Shi'a males throughout the country. On April 4, he called the militia into the streets when Bremer shut down one of his newspapers and arrested one of his lieutenants. Thousands of Jaysh al Mahdi attacked coalition and Iraqi compounds in Najaf, An Nasiriyah, Al Kut, Baghdad, Al Amarah, and even Kirkuk. Fighting spread to Basrah, Karbala, and Hillah. Over the next few months, the coalition fought to regain control of the southern

Iraq

cities. The only exceptions were in Basrah and Al Amarah, where British patrols and British-advised Iraqi forces quelled the uprising.

As a result of the Mahdi uprising and the first battle of Fallujah, attacks throughout the country jumped from just under 200 per week in the first three months of 2004 to over 500 per week in the summer.[13] Fallujah grew into an insurgent base of operations and staging ground for attacks elsewhere in the country. Additionally, in Samarra, Ramadi, Baqubah, and Baghdad, insurgents exerted control over the population and massed in groups of 20 or more for attacks on the coalition. The insurgency enjoyed widespread popular support among the Sunni population. Sunnis perceived that the insurgents had won a great victory in Fallujah, forcing an embarrassing withdrawal upon the United States. A poll in late April 2004 found that 89 percent of Iraqis considered the coalition to be an occupying force.[14] Fighting with Jaysh al Mahdi in Najaf (the holiest Shi'a city) and Sadr City (a Shi'a neighborhood in Baghdad) temporarily ended in June, but Sadr and his forces maintained control of the two urban areas.

The breadth of violence made it abundantly clear that the coalition could not secure Iraq without more numbers. Abizaid and the American commanders had been looking to the Iraqis to supply those numbers, rather than request US reinforcements, which was not considered politically feasible and might deepen the perception of occupation among the Iraqi population. Since the dissolution of the old Iraqi Army, the coalition had focused on creating locally based forces, known as the Iraqi Civil Defense Corps (renamed the Iraqi National Guard after June 2004), to help provide security within Iraq while a new Iraqi Army was built.

Success in developing the Iraqi National Guard and other local forces depended entirely on the attitudes of the local population. National Guard battalions based on the Kurdish militia (*peshmerga*), or Shi'a militias, performed adequately. Battalions based on Sunnis did not. Disaffected from the Iraqi government and angry at the coalition, at this stage in the war, Sunnis generally sympathized with the insurgency and had no intention of fighting their fellow tribesmen or family members.

There is little doubt that the US military could have done a better job advising and training the Iraqis. Few commanders embedded advisers with local forces. Yet, at this time, even when Americans did, Sunnis remained reluctant to fight. One of Mattis' most progressive ideas was to adapt the combined action program (CAP) of the Vietnam War to Iraq. A platoon in every Marine battalion was trained to operate within an indigenous unit. Each had received a month of special training in Arabic, Arab culture, and Soviet weapons handling. Three of Mattis' seven Marine infantry battalions embedded their CAP platoon with local forces. US Special Forces also attempted to build local Sunni forces, cultivating a relationship with the warlike Albu Nimr tribe west of Ramadi. All this effort, however, yielded few results. In a quarter of all engagements, Sunni units with advisers fled or even surrendered. For example, during fighting in the town of Hit in October 2004, elements of the 503rd Iraqi National Guard Battalion, operating directly alongside Marines, fled from positions defending the city bridge.[15] Most Sunni National Guard and police forces refused to work with advisers at all, let alone contribute to coalition operations. By the end of October 2004, only two companies of the original seven National Guard battalions established in Al Anbar had not deserted or sided with the insurgency.

The failure of local forces, combined with widespread insurgent activity, caused coalition commanders to look to the Iraqi Army as the answer to their lack of numbers. Conway said at the end of that hard-fought summer: "The situation will change when Iraqi Army divisions arrive. They will engender people with a sense of nationalism. Together with an elected government, they will create stability."[16]

Stemming the Tide

On June 28, 2004, the United States granted Iraq sovereignty and created the Iraqi Interim Government under Prime Minister Ayad Allawi. Shortly thereafter, General George Casey succeeded Sanchez as the commander of Multi-National Forces, Iraq (the new coalition headquarters). Additionally, Petraeus returned to Iraq to command Multi-National Security Transition Command-Iraq (MNSTC-I) and oversee the creation of the Iraqi security forces (roughly 300,000 men), including 10 Iraqi Army divisions (roughly 120,000 men).

Casey took immediate steps to give the coalition strategy a purpose hitherto lacking. He wanted to transition authority over security in each province to the Iraqis. For this to occur, Najaf, Baghdad, Fallujah, and other centers of violence would need to be dealt with one by one. As they went about doing so, Casey and his commanders paid careful attention to the mistakes of the past year, taking much more care to tailor military action to political priorities.

The blueprint for better counterinsurgency, and what would become known as the clear-hold-build approach, took form when Sadr unleashed a second uprising in Najaf on August 6, 2004.[17] Casey and Qasim Dawood, Allawi's national security adviser, carefully balanced military and political measures to coerce Sadr into backing down. While the 11th Marine Expeditionary Unit (augmented by two US Army battalions, four Iraqi battalions, and scores of elite US snipers) battled Sadr's 1,500 fighters, Dawood negotiated with Sistani with the hope of inducing Sistani to intercede and end the fighting. Political negotiations took precedence over the military offensive, which was repeatedly stopped to placate Sistani and ensure that fighting did not endanger the sacred Imam Ali Mosque. After three weeks, Sistani marched into Najaf with thousands of his followers and Sadr agreed to disperse his militia and surrender the mosque. Allawi and Casey immediately poured $70 million in reconstruction and compensation funds into the city. Najaf would remain quiet for the next three years, and Sadr started pursuing power through political means instead of violent ones.

Next, Major General Peter Chiarelli's 1st US Cavalry Division cleaned up Jaysh al Mahdi resistance in Baghdad, and Major General John Batiste's 1st US Infantry Division reasserted presence in Samarra. The big show was Fallujah, though, where 3,000–6,000 insurgents were ensconced. Casey pressed forward only after the full support of the Iraqi Interim Government had been obtained, which took months and meant that the operation could not take place until after the US presidential elections in early November. Allawi slowed the pace of planning in order to hold extensive discussions with obstinate Fallujah leaders and other Sunni notables. These discussions exhausted all diplomatic options, placing Allawi in a stronger political position to use force.

New Marine generals, Lieutenant General John Sattler and Major General Richard Natonski, listened to Conway and Mattis about the lessons of the first battle. Measures were taken to lessen the political impact of the firepower needed to defeat so many insurgents. All civilians were encouraged through leaflets, radio announcements, and a whisper campaign to leave the city. In the event, the coalition would find only 5,000 civilians in the city out of a population of 250,000. Additionally, Sattler prepared to pre-empt insurgent propaganda with his own press releases, enabling him to take the initiative in shaping the news stories. Finally, in order to lessen the image of occupation, Sattler and Natonski, in parallel with Allawi, pressed for Iraqi Army units to accompany American forces in the assault.[18] The 1st Iraqi Intervention Force Brigade and 3rd Iraqi Army Brigade joined the 1st Marine Regiment, 7th Marine Regiment, and US Army Blackjack Brigade for the operation.

The offensive, known as Operation *Al Fajr*, kicked off on November 7, 2004, following months of air strikes on insurgent defenses and command and control nodes. Coalition tactics within Fallujah were those of a straightforward conventional battle. Four Marine infantry battalions methodically cleared out the insurgent defenders in the wake of two US Army armored battalions that spearheaded the assault. As in the first battle, the strength of insurgent defenses compelled the Marines to call in artillery fire or close air support. Marine squads aggressively cleared buildings, making use of grenades, AT-4 rocket launchers with thermobaric warheads, and, most of all, well-drilled urban combat tactics. By the end of December, the insurgent resistance had come to an end. Roughly 2,000 insurgents were killed, wounded, or detained in the course of the battle.[19]

After the battle, the coalition initiated an intensive effort to work with the leaders of Fallujah and rebuild the city. The State Department representative, Kael Weston, worked hand in hand with political and religious leaders. They built a city government and motivated the people of Fallujah to participate in the political process. Approximately 65–80 percent of the city's population participated in three electoral events of 2005. Over 2005 and 2006, the Iraqi government provided a total of $180 million in compensation for damage to homes while the coalition engaged on major water, sewage, health, and power projects. 1,000–2,000 Marines continued to operate in the city, alongside roughly 1,500 soldiers of the Iraqi Army. When sectarian violence broke out in Baghdad in 2006, Sunnis fled to Fallujah because they considered it the safest Sunni city in Iraq.

Counterinsurgency Reforms

With Baghdad and Fallujah secure, Casey turned to improving the Iraqi security forces. In late 2004, Casey conducted a review of his campaign plan. The review, guided by the counterinsurgency expert Kalev Sepp, concluded that the formation of the Iraqi Army needed to be accelerated. Nowhere was the need for more forces clearer than in Mosul, where security collapsed outright in November 2004 after one Stryker battalion was sent to Fallujah. Insurgents coordinated attacks against police stations and 5,000 police surrendered en masse, forcing the coalition to reassert its presence in the city. Rather than deploy more US forces to Iraq, the answer was thought to lie with the Iraqi Army. Najaf, Baghdad, Samarra, and Fallujah showed that, when properly advised, the predominantly Shi'a and partly Kurdish Iraqi Army would stand and fight. The planners viewed the Iraqi Army as the lynchpin of effective counterinsurgency. From their perspective, the Iraqi Army could both provide vital manpower and gather intelligence better than coalition forces. Plus, Iraqi soldiers would not be perceived as occupiers, undercutting a major cause of the insurgency. It was thought that the Iraqi Army could eventually shoulder the burden of counterinsurgency operations, allowing the coalition to withdraw. Accordingly, Casey directed coalition forces to shift their focus from fighting insurgents to training Iraqis.

The coalition and Interim Iraqi Government wanted the Iraqi Army to be a national force that integrated Kurds, Shi'a, and Sunni. Few Sunnis joined, though, and the army became mainly Shi'a. In order to accelerate Iraqi Army development, MNF-I (Casey's headquarters) created the transition team concept – 10–12 advisers embedded into every Iraqi Army battalion, brigade, and division. Additionally, Marine and Army battalions partnered with Iraqi battalions (roughly 500 soldiers) in order to assist in their operations and training. Eventually, the Iraqi battalion would operate independently, with only its advisers working with it daily.

In parallel to developing the Iraqi Army, General Casey and Ambassador Zalmay Khalilzad made every effort to ensure that the democratization process took hold. The CPA's transitional administrative law (TAL) scheduled three electoral events for 2005: the election of a transition government in January responsible for drafting the constitution; a referendum on the constitution in October; and the election of a permanent government in December. The establishment of a legitimate democratic government was considered central in cutting support for the insurgents and building cooperation across the sectarian communities.[20]

As the Iraqi Army developed and democratization pressed forward, Casey shifted his attention to securing Iraq's borders. Iraqi politicians considered this essential to stopping the flow of Sunni foreign fighters into the country; plus, according to Sepp and other counterinsurgency experts, blocking foreign assistance was part of effective counterinsurgency. The two major operations that ensued refined the clear-hold-build approach of 2004 and showcased improved US counterinsurgency techniques.

The first was the clearing of Tal Afar in September 2005 (Operation *Restoring Rights*). Tal Afar, a city of 250,000 people located 40 miles from Syria, had been used by AQI (Al-Qaeda in Iraq) as a staging ground for foreign fighters entering Iraq since early 2005. The 3rd Armored Reconnaissance Regiment (3rd ACR), under Colonel H. R. McMaster, and two brigades of the 3rd Iraqi Army Division carried out the assault on the city. McMaster had directed that civilians be evacuated from the town in order to allow his forces to use artillery and attack helicopters to overcome insurgent makeshift fortifications. Groups of perhaps hundreds of insurgents massed to counterattack the advancing US and Iraqi forces, but the Abrams tanks and Bradley fighting vehicles tore them apart.[21]

After the battle, McMaster positioned his soldiers in 29 outposts throughout the city to hold the cleared areas. From these outposts, his forces saturated Iraqi neighborhoods with patrols. Once civilians had returned to the city, the use of force was minimized. Second Battalion, 325th Airborne Infantry Regiment, killed no civilians at all, which won the appreciation of the locals. Building intelligence on insurgents was made easier through the cooperation of the significant Shi'a minority in Tal Afar.[22] Similarly, McMaster could recruit a police force because the Shi'a were willing to serve, whereas the Sunnis still considered the Iraqi Army and police to be their enemy.[23]

The second operation was the clearing of Al Qa'im (Operation *Steel Curtain*) in November 2005. After the second battle of Fallujah, insurgents affiliated with AQI had fled to Al Qa'im, a city of 200,000 that lies on the Euphrates River at the Syrian border, and turned it into a base of operations. Two reinforced Marine infantry battalions (2,500 Marines) and one Iraqi battalion (roughly 500 soldiers) cleared the city from November 5 to 16, killing roughly 100 insurgents.[24]

Like Tal Afar, the operations after the battle were more important than the battle itself. Lieutenant Colonel Dale Alford, commander of 3rd Battalion, 6th Marine Regiment, dispersed his Marines into small sub-units, integrating them thoroughly with the Iraqi Army brigade. Every platoon lived and worked with an Iraqi platoon in one of 12 outposts. The platoons conducted intensive satellite patrolling both day and night. Living close to the population generated intelligence and forced the Marines to learn how to interact with them.[25] Even more important was the determination of the Albu Mahal tribe to keep AQI out. AQI had impinged upon their traditional control over the Al Qa'im area, causing the tribe to align itself with the coalition after having fought as insurgents over the previous two years. Within three months of the completion of Operation *Steel Curtain*, the Albu Mahal had devoted 700 tribesmen to the resident Iraqi Army brigade and 400 to a newly established police force.[26]

Off the battlefield, Casey took steps to institute the lessons learned since mid-2004. These included setting up a counterinsurgency academy at Taji (just north of Baghdad) that all incoming regimental and battalion commanders had to attend for eight days. Additionally, Casey personally went to every division and brigade to brief them on his strategic vision.

In the United States, the Army and Marine Corps revamped their services' training programs. The emphasis of the Marine Corps' combined arms exercise program at Twentynine Palms, CA, and the US Army's National Training Center at Fort Irwin, CA, changed from testing units against a Soviet-style conventional opponent to testing them against insurgents. Furthermore, in 2006, the US Army set up a 60-day training program for its advisers at Fort Riley, KS. Finally, Petraeus and Mattis (now both in charge of their respective services' training establishments in the United States) together sponsored a new counterinsurgency manual (*Field Manual 3-24*) for the Army and Marine Corps that was issued in December 2006.

Secretary of State Condoleezza Rice contributed to the reforms by transferring the concept of provincial reconstruction teams (PRTs) from Afghanistan, where they had performed fairly well, to Iraq. Manned by State Department diplomats, workers from USAID, agricultural experts, and engineers, PRTs focused on providing economic assistance and developing local governmental bodies within each province.

Unfortunately, Tal Afar and Al Qa'im masked problems that still existed in US counterinsurgency. At the same time as Al Qa'im was being mopped up, Marines in Haditha killed 24 civilians after being hit with a roadside bomb. Major General Eldon Bargewell, who investigated the incident, reported:

> The most remarkable aspect of the follow-on action with regard to the civilian casualties from the [November 19] Haditha incident was the absence of virtually any kind of inquiry at any level of command into the circumstances surrounding the deaths.[27]

While this incident was extreme, the use of air strikes, the detainment of innocent civilians, the occupation of homes, and checkpoints shooting at oncoming vehicles ("escalation of force incidents") were common. A later poll by the US Army Surgeon General cited widespread attitudes within both the Marines and Army that devalued Iraqi life. Almost a third of the respondents said officers had not made it clear that harming civilians was unacceptable.[28]

Other problems existed in the counterinsurgency effort as well. Some commanders still focused on mechanized sweeps or air assaults that never held an area after it had been cleared. Some battalions were shifted from actively patrolling urban areas to operating out of large US bases, reducing their ability to work with the people.

The inconsistency of the US reform effort derived from the decentralized command and control structure developed for conventional war. Part of the doctrine was to delegate as much decision-making authority as possible to prevent any pause in operational tempo. Consequently, brigade and battalion commanders enjoyed a freedom to conduct operations as they saw fit. The system might have worked if commanders had been thoroughly trained in counterinsurgency. Instead, commanders often reverted to their conventional training and conducted operations that were too methodical or heavy-handed. The commanders that instituted real change within their units, such as Petraeus and Alford, were the ones who were more directive with their subordinates.

High-value targeting remained the one tactic truly consistent throughout the US forces. The detainment or death of a key leader undoubtedly disrupted insurgent operations. However, raids to capture insurgent leaders tended to disturb Iraqi homes and sweep up innocent Iraqis, which only increased local resentment. City council meetings regularly featured complaints about raids. Furthermore, capturing or killing an insurgent leader rarely caused insurgent operations to fall apart, even in a local area. Indeed, the killing of Zarqawi himself in an air strike on June 7, 2006 caused no discernible drop in attack levels or long-term injury to AQI's organizational abilities.

Worst of all, the centerpiece of Casey's strategy was not performing well. The US strategy depended upon the Iraqi Army taking over security duties. By early 2006, the Iraqi Army had grown to 10 divisions that actively participated in operations. Nevertheless, they could not suppress insurgent activity. This was partly because of deficiencies in their advising, training, and equipping. For example, 10–12 advisers were shown to be too few to train an Iraqi battalion plus go on tactical operations with them. On top of that, they were often reservists or national guardsmen rather than the most capable active-duty personnel. However, the real problem lay in the army's Shi'a ethnicity. In Sunni areas, the population viewed the Iraqi Army as a Shi'a occupation force and refused to provide the intelligence necessary to eradicate insurgents. Polling in 2006 found that 77–90 percent of the respondents in Al Anbar province considered the government to be illegitimate. A majority considered the Iraqi Army to be a threat.[29] Other polls obtained similar results for the Sunnis overall.[30] In Ramadi, at the height of the sweltering summer, locals refused to take free water offered by Iraqi soldiers (some angrily poured it on the ground) and did not stop insurgents from bombing mobile clinics devised by the resident army brigade to render medical care to the people.

Shi'a ethnicity also posed a problem in Shi'a or mixed areas. Some soldiers and officers had connections to Shi'a militia and many admired Sadr. Consequently, Iraqi Army units often turned a blind eye to militia attacks on Sunnis in Baghdad and Diyala Provinces, the sectarian battlegrounds. Worse, the special police commandos (later known as the National Police), the paramilitary force of the Ministry of Interior, were heavily influenced by the Badr Corps (a Shi'a militia) and actively participated in ethnic cleansing.

Civil War

The sectarian divide between the Sunni and Shi'a communities widened during 2005 as the new Iraqi government took shape. The October 2005 referendum passed a constitution allowing for federalism, which threatened to deny the Sunnis a share of oil profits, polarizing the two communities. Sunnis voted en masse in December, but as a means of maximizing political representation rather than in support of a system that promised power to the Shi'a majority. The election of a Shi'a majority in the legislative body (the Council of Representatives) left the Sunnis discontented. Polls found that the majority of Sunnis did not consider the new democratic government to be legitimate and preferred that a strong leader take charge of Iraq.[31]

On February 22, 2006, AQI bombed the Askariya (Golden) Mosque in Samarra, a Shi'a holy site. Zarqawi had long been trying to instigate sectarian violence through suicide bombings in Shi'a areas. The Golden Mosque bombing was the spark that caused the Shi'a militias – Jaysh al Mahdi and the Badr Corps – to retaliate against the Sunni community in Baghdad, murdering suspected insurgents and eventually pressing Sunnis out of mixed neighborhoods. Over 30,000 civilians fled their homes in the month after the bombing. In turn, more Sunnis took up arms to defend themselves and their families.

The US leadership did not recognize that the two pillars of its counterinsurgency strategy – democratization and developing the Iraqi Army – could not circumvent the civil war. Neither Casey nor Abizaid wanted to call for US reinforcements. They firmly believed doing so would only reinforce Iraqi dependency on the United States. Also, according to Casey, American reinforcements could inflame the insurgency. He noted "We are the rationale for the resistance and a magnet for the terrorists," and persisted with plans to start withdrawing US brigades by the end of the year.[32] The Bush administration did not object to this decision because it helped avoid domestic criticism of the war.[33]

Accordingly, Casey relied on the Iraqi Army to provide the numbers to quell sectarian violence, especially inside Baghdad. With the Iraqi Army ineffective, the coalition lost control of the capital. Shi'a militias murdered scores of Sunnis while AQI set off devastating car bombs in Shi'a neighborhoods (over 100 civilians could be killed in a single day). Lieutenant General Chiarelli, now Casey's operational commander, launched two operations to regain control of the city: Operation *Together Forward I* (June 14–July 20, 2006) and Operation *Together Forward II* (August 8–October 24, 2006). In the former, US and Iraqi soldiers set up security checkpoints, established a curfew, and increased their patrolling and high-value targeting efforts. In the latter operation, 15,000 US soldiers cleared disputed neighborhoods block by block. The role of holding the neighborhoods fell to the Iraqi Army. Incapable of gathering intelligence on Sunni insurgents and often unwilling to confront the Shi'a militias, the Iraqi soldiers could not provide security. Indeed, only 1,000 of the 4,000 Iraqi Army reinforcements even showed up.[34] On October 19, Major General William Caldwell, the coalition spokesman, acknowledged that Operation *Together Forward II* had failed. During its duration, attacks rose 22 percent.[35] Attacks on civilians by Shi'a militias and Sunni insurgents had quadrupled, with over 1,000 dying each month.[36]

The situation throughout Iraq deteriorated as well. Attacks grew from 70 per day in January 2006 to 180 per day in October. The situation was particularly bad in Al Anbar. The I Marine Expeditionary Force fought for months with hardened AQI cadres to clear Ramadi, the capital of Al Anbar, without any positive results. In Basrah, the hands-off British approach left Shi'a militias (Jaysh al Mahdi, the Badr Corps, and the Fadhila Party) vying for control of the city. The militias escalated sectarian attacks on the city's sizeable Sunni minority in the wake of the Golden Mosque bombings, largely expelling them.

Sectarian violence undermined attempts at reconciliation between the Sunni and Shi'a communities. Sunni leaders felt even more marginalized from the government. A Fallujah city leader said at a city council meeting:

> We want to participate in government but what are the results? What are the benefits? We know the results. It is total failure. We still see the killing in the streets. Baghdad is in chaos. Iran's hands are everywhere.[37]

That summer, Fallujah city leaders told Marine officers that if the United States would not act against the "Iranians," then the Sunnis must be allowed to defend themselves.[38] Indeed, 34 percent of Sunnis considered attacks on Iraqi government forces to be acceptable; only 1 percent of Shi'a felt the same way.[39] Shi'a leaders, including Prime Minister Nuri al Maliki's new government, considered militias merely a form of protection against the real threat to Iraq – the Ba'athists and AQI. The growth of the Iraqi Army (as well as the Badr Corps and Jaysh al Mahdi) and majority control over the new democratic government gave Shi'a leaders little reason to compromise. Consequently, they rejected serious attempts at political reconciliation or restraining attacks upon the Sunnis.[40]

The most promising event of 2006 was the rise of certain Sunni tribes in Al Anbar against Al-Qaeda in Iraq. This had little to do with US counterinsurgency tactics. The coalition had long been trying to motivate the tribes and traditional Sunni entities, such as the former military, to fight AQI, exemplified by the efforts of Special Forces teams and Mattis' CAP platoons. It was not until it became clear that AQI was taking over the economic and political sources of power within society that tribes, many of which had formerly been part of the insurgency, started to turn. The first had been the Albu Mahal in Al Qa'im in 2005. The tide truly turned in September 2006, though, when Shaykh Abd al Sittar Bezia Ftikhan al Rishawi openly announced the formation of a tribal movement, Sahawa Al Anbar, opposed to AQI. Sittar's movement backed local police forces. Because they were Sunni, the local community would give the police intelligence, enabling them to kill or detain more insurgents than the Iraqi Army. The number of police actively involved in operations grew from fewer than 1,000 in early 2006 to over 7,000 in early 2007. By April, the police had managed to suppress insurgent activity in Ramadi, and most of the key tribes of Al Anbar had aligned with Sittar's movement.

A New Commander and a New Strategy
The civil war forced a major change in US strategy. The republican defeat in the midterm elections, followed by the Iraq Study Group report, made it impossible for Bush to ignore the deteriorating situation. The Iraq Study

Group, a team of prominent former US policy-makers – including former Secretary of State James Baker, former Senator Lee Hamilton, and former Director of Central Intelligence Robert Gates – recommended placing greater effort in expanding and training the Iraqi security forces, particularly the Iraqi Army. The group also called for benchmarks to measure the progress of the Iraqi government toward political reconciliation, and negotiating with Iraq's neighboring countries.

Bush announced his new strategy on January 10, 2007. While he acknowledged the main recommendations of the Iraq Study Group, the focus of the new strategy was reinforcing the 140,000 US personnel in Iraq with another 20,000–25,000 in five brigade combat teams and two Marine infantry battalions, known as "the surge."

To execute the surge, Bush replaced Casey, due to leave Iraq in a few months, with Petraeus. Upon taking command on February 10, Petraeus incorporated the best lessons from Tal Afar, Al Qa'im, and the new counterinsurgency manual into the security plan for Baghdad (Operation *Fard al Qanun*). Over 50 small outposts (joint security stations) manned by Iraqi police, Iraqi Army, and US soldiers were emplaced throughout the city. His top priority was protecting the people rather than building the Iraqi Army (although that remained a critical task). In his view, the point of the surge was to create a breathing space in the violence, particularly in Baghdad, in which political reconciliation could take place. Petraeus wrote to his troops on March 19:

> Improving security for Iraq's population is…the over-riding objective of your strategy. Accomplishing this mission requires carrying out complex military operations and convincing the Iraqi people that we will not just "clear" their neighborhoods of the enemy, we will also stay and help "hold" the neighborhoods so that the "build" phase that many of their communities need can go forward.[41]

Conclusion

Nearly four years of undiminished insurgent activity forced a change in American strategy in Iraq in 2007. The United States had made a serious attempt at adapting – shown by the subordination of military offensives to political priorities, the adoption of the clear-hold-build approach, the establishment of advisory teams, and the creation of provincial reconstruction teams. Yet shortcomings remained, especially in regard to minimizing the use of force and, more importantly, adjusting to the impact of the sectarian divide. The two pillars of US strategy – democratization and the building of a national and integrated Iraqi Army – did not match the sectarian realities of Iraq. The democratization process put the Sunnis in a position in which they stood to gain more by waging war than accepting the outcome of the political process. The election of a legitimate government based on a Shi'a majority actually encouraged Sunnis to fight. Nor was the Iraqi Army, Casey's main effort, suited to maintaining stability. The sectarian divide meant that Sunnis would not provide the Iraqi Army with the intelligence necessary to suppress insurgent activity. Conversely, the army's own sectarian sympathies made it a poor instrument for keeping Shi'a militias in line.

Consequently, gaining ground between 2003 and 2007 was a matter of fundamentally reorienting the whole American strategy, not just learning new tactics or making a few wiser political decisions. This is not to say that the US war effort was doomed, but that the failure to structure strategy around the sectarian divide was a major reason for the difficulties experienced before 2007. Whether such a reorientation was a realistic option is a separate question. Abandoning democracy surely would have incurred disapproval from domestic and international political audiences, not to mention the Shi'a majority in Iraq. And placing less reliance on the Iraqi Army may not have been possible, given the small size of the US military presence and the absence of large numbers of locally recruited Sunni forces until 2006. Indeed, even during the surge, the Iraqi Army remained essential to US counterinsurgency efforts.

In terms of the larger history of counterinsurgency, Iraq highlights the effect that social or political constraints, in this case the sectarian divide, have on the success of attempts to adapt and on the kind of strategy that will be most effective. Other factors – such as the presence of a capable commander, an institutional willingness to adapt, or experience in fighting insurgencies – certainly play a role in effective counterinsurgency, but any successful strategy must conform to the social and political environment in which a conflict is ensconced.

ENDNOTES

INTRODUCTION

1. David Galula, *Counterinsurgency Warfare: Theory and Practice* (New York: Praeger, 1964), 87.
2. Ibid., 89.
3. Sir Robert Thompson, *Defeating Communist Insurgency: Experiences from Malaya and Vietnam* (New York: Praeger, 1966), 111–2.
4. Gen Sir Frank Kitson, *Low Intensity Operations: Subversion, Insurgency and Peacekeeping* (London: Faber & Faber, 1971), 95.
5. Ibid., 96.
6. Ibid., 97.

CHAPTER 1: IN AID OF THE CIVIL POWER

1. C. E. Callwell, *Small Wars: Their Principles and Practice* (London: H.M. Stationery Office, 1896), quoted in I. F. W. Becket, *Modern Insurgencies and Counter-insurgencies* (London: Routledge, 2001), 35–36.
2. On April 13, 1919, General Dyer marched 50 riflemen to the Jallianwala Bagh in Amritsar, where a mass demonstration of Punjabis opposed to British rule was taking place. He had earlier issued a proclamation forbidding demonstrations, but gave no warning to the crowd before ordering his men to open fire. The "Amritsar massacre," in which at least 380 demonstrators were killed, became a major controversy in Britain and brought Dyer's military career to an end. See Charles Townshend, *Britain's Civil Wars: Counterinsurgency in the Twentieth Century* (London: Faber & Faber, 1986), 134–9.
3. Carl von Clausewitz, trans. Howard and Paret, *On War* (Princeton, NJ: repr. 1989), ch.1, section 27.
4. Cabinet conference, July 26, 1920, (C51 (20) App.IV NA CAB 23 22).
5. Cabinet minutes, June 2, 1921, in Thomas Jones, *Whitehall Diary*, vol.III (Oxford: OUP, 1969), 73.
6. Charles Townshend, *The British Campaign in Ireland, 1919–1921: The Development of Political and Military Policies* (London: OUP, 1975), 97.
7. Douglas Duff, *Sword for Hire* (London: John Murray, 1934), 77.
8. 26th (Provisional) Brigade Instructions, 1921 (WO35 93 (1)).
9. The Lord Chancellor in the House of Lords, June 21, 1921 (45 HL Reb. 5s c690).
10. Sir Charles Gwynn, *Imperial Policing* (London: Macmillan and Co., Ltd., 1934), 8.
11. Discussed by the Cabinet over the summer of 1917 and issued on November 2 that year, the Balfour Declaration was a letter from Lord Balfour (then Foreign Secretary) to Lord Rothschild (representing the Zionist Federation).
12. The text of the Balfour Declaration is widely available; for analysis see M. Verete, "The Balfour Declaration and its Makers," *Middle Eastern Studies*, 6 (1970), and M. Levene, "The Balfour Declaration – a case of mistaken identity," *English Historical Review*, vol.107, no.422 (1992).

13. Note by Sir Charles Tegart, March 6, 1939, in the Tegart Papers, file 1, box 2, Middle East Centre Archive, St Anthony's College, Oxford.

14. Secret dispatch from the High Commissioner to the Secretary of State for the Colonies, April 19, 1925 (Chancellor papers 12/6).

15. Letter dated October 21, 1934, in *Thomas Hodgkin: Letters from Palestine 1932–36* (London: Quartet Books, 1986), 91.

16. General Staff, British Forces Palestine and Trans-Jordan, "Preliminary Notes on the Tactical Lessons of the Arab Rebellion in Palestine 1936," February 5, 1937 (WO 191 70).

17. GOC Palestine to War Office, "Operations in Palestine 1 August–31 October 1938" (WO32 9498).

18. High Commissioner for Palestine to the Secretary of State for the Colonies, October 24, 1938 (CO 93521).

19. Capt O. C. Wingate, "Appreciation of the possibilities of night movements by armed forces of the Crown with the object of putting an end to terrorism in Northern Palestine," June 5, 1938 (Bredin papers, IWM), quoted by S. Anglim, "Orde Wingate, the Iron Wall and Counter-terrorism in Palestine 1937–39," in *The Occasional – no.49* (Strategic and Combat Studies Institute, 2005), 30.

20. Ibid.

21. Ibid., 31.

22. Ibid., 32.

23. GOC Palestine to War Office, August 24, 1938 (WO 32 9497).

24. O'Connor to his wife, November 2/3, 1938, O'Connor papers, quoted in Anglim, "Orde Wingate," 39.

25. Ibid.

26. GOC Palestine to GOC 6th Division, December 1938.

27. "Oozlebarts," "Ooozabarts," or "Oozles," loosely derived from the Arabic for "friend," was a widely used, mildly contemptuous slang term amongst the security forces, not only for insurgents but for Arabs generally: a dangerous fusion.

28. Charles Townshend, "The Defence of Palestine: insurrection and public security, 1936–39," *English Historical Review,* vol. 103, no. 409 (October, 1988), 932.

29. Townshend, *Britain's Civil War,* 116.

30. Cabinet Defence Committee, "Palestine: use of the armed forces," December 19, 1946 (FO 371 52567).

31. Townshend, *Britain's Civil War,* 119.

32. R. D. Wilson, *Cordon and Search: with the 6th Airborne Division in Palestine* (Aldershot: Gale and Polden, 1949), 60.

33. Operations *Elephant* and *Hippopotamus*, the sealing off of Tel Aviv and Jerusalem under martial law in March 1947, had to be curtailed when the army became unable to assure food supplies to the inhabitants.

34. Townshend, *Britain's Civil War,* 118.

35. David Charters, *The British Army and Jewish Insurgency 1945–47* (Houndmills: Macmillan, 1987), 170.

36. H. J. Simson, *British Rule and Rebellion* (Edinburgh: Blackwell, 1938), 328.

37.   In 1937 the Palestine General Staff produced a narrative report entitled "Military Lessons of the Arab Rebellion in Palestine 1936" (WO 191 70), running to over 100 pages. It was not revised to take account of the second insurgency in 1937–39, and (as with the *Record of the Rebellion in Ireland*) did not lead to the production of a usable handbook. No attempt seems to have been made to do the same for the post-1945 Jewish insurgency.

CHAPTER 2: COUNTERINSURGENCY IN THE PHILIPPINES 1898–1954

1.   Brian McAllister Linn, *The Philippine War, 1899–1902* (Lawrence, KS: University Press of Kansas, 2000), 328.

2.   Teodoro A. Agoncillo, *The Revolt of the Masses: The Story of Bonifacio and the Katipunan* (Quezon City: University of the Philippines, 1956).

3.   Dewey's squadron consisted of four light cruisers and three gunboats. See Nathan Sargent, *Admiral Dewey and the Manila Campaign* (Washington, D.C: Naval Historical Foundation, 1947), and Robert Conroy, *The Battle of Manila Bay* (New York: Macmillan, 1968).

4.   See Margaret Leech, *In the Days of McKinley* (New York: Harper and Brothers, 1959), especially chapter 14, "Destiny in the Pacific"; and John Morgan Gates, chapter 1, "Unforeseen Problems of Victory," *Schoolbooks and Krags: The United States Army in the Philippines, 1899–1902* (Westport, CT: Greenwood, 1973).

5.   Gates, *Schoolbooks and Krags*, 218.

6.   See Anthony Short, *The Communist Insurrection in Malaya, 1948–1960* (London: Frederick Muller, 1975), and Edgar O'Ballance, *Malaya: The Communist Insurgent War* (Hamden, CT: Archon, 1966).

7.   Linn, *The Philippine War*, 213–4.

8.   Linn in *The Philippine War* is particularly critical of contemporary writers who characterize the American counterinsurgency in that struggle as brutal. See Graham Cosmas, *An Army for Empire: The United States Army and the Spanish-American War* (Columbia, MO: University of Missouri Press, 1971); James C. Bradford, ed., *Crucible of Empire: The Spanish-American War and Its Aftermath* (Annapolis, MD: Naval Institute Press, 1993); and Richard E. Welch, "American Atrocities in the Philippines: The Challenge and the Response," *Pacific Historical Review*, 43 (May 1974).

9.   Emilio Aguinaldo, *A Second Look at America* (New York: Robert Speller, 1957), 66.

10.   By far the most prominent of the generally small antiwar groups was the Anti-Imperialist League, composed mainly of Easterners and Democrats. See F. H. Harrington, "The Anti-Imperialist Movement in the United States, 1898–1900," *Mississippi Valley Historical Review*, 22 (1935), and Leech, *In the Days of McKinley*, 352 and 364.

11.   See the interesting account of this episode by Aguinaldo's principal captor in Frederick Funston, *Memories of Two Wars: Cuban and Philippine Experiences* (New York: Scribner's, 1911).

12.   Linn, *The Philippine War*, 306.

13.   Linn, *The Philippine War*, 325.

14.   Frank E. Vandiver, *Black Jack: The Life and Times of General John J. Pershing* (College Station, TX: Texas A & M University Press, 1977), 266.

15. On these events, see William B. Breuer, *Retaking the Philippines: America's Return to Corregidor and Bataan* (New York: St. Martin's, 1986); Louis Morton, *The Fall of the Philippines* (Washington, D.C: Office of the Chief of Military History, Department of the Army, 1953); and Jose Laurel, *War Memoirs* (Manila: Jose Laurel Memorial Foundation, 1962).

16. Carlos P. Romulo, *Crusade in Asia* (New York: John Day, 1955), 63.

17. A. J. Barker, *Yamashita* (New York: Ballantine, 1973).

18. These quotations from Taruc are found in his book *He Who Rides the Tiger* (New York: Praeger, 1967).

19. Edward G. Lansdale, *In the Midst of Wars: An American's Mission to Southeast Asia* (New York: Harper and Row, 1972).

20. Napoleon Valeriano and Charles T. P. Bohannan, *Counter-Guerrilla Operations: The Philippine Experience* (New York: Praeger, 1962), esp. 97–8 and 206; Uldarico S. Baclagon, *Lessons from the Huk Campaign in the Philippines* (Manila: Colcol, 1960).

21. "Dysentery and stomach ulcers from inadequate food were often serious afflictions." Taruc, *Born of the People* (Bombay, 1953: repr. Westport, CT: Greenwood, 1973), 139.

22. Benedict J. Kerkvliet, *The Huk Rebellion: A Study of Peasant Revolt in the Philippines* (Berkeley, CA: University of California Press, 1977), 238.

23. On Magsaysay's campaign and election, see Carlos P. Romulo and Marvin M. Gray, *The Magsaysay Story* (New York: John Day, 1956); Carlos P. Romulo, *Crusade in Asia* (New York: John Day, 1955); and Frances Lucille Starner, *Magsaysay and the Philippine Peasantry: The Agrarian Impact on Philippine Politics 1953–1956* (Berkeley, CA: University of California Press, 1961).

24. Boyd T. Bashore, "Dual Strategy for Limited War," in Franklin Mark Osanka, ed., *Modern Guerrilla Warfare* (New York: Free Press, 1962), 198.

25. John Keegan, "Geography is the key to military history," *Intelligence in War* (New York: Knopf, 2003), 20.

26. In the early 1960s, the French Army discovered that success in isolating the Algerian insurgents from outside aid was no guarantee of ultimate victory.

27. Chalmers Johnson, *Autopsy on People's War* (Berkeley, CA: University of California Press, 1973); and Anthony James Joes, chapter 14, "The Myth of Maoist People's War," *Resisting Rebellion: The History and Politics of Counterinsurgency* (Lexington, KY: University Press of Kentucky, 2004).

CHAPTER 3: THE FIRST OF THE BANANA WARS

1. Strictly speaking, the term "Bluejackets" refers only to enlisted men of the United States Navy, particularly when they are performing duties of a military (as opposed to a nautical or technical) nature. As used here, however, it also includes the officers assigned to landing parties.

2. US Navy, Office of Naval Intelligence, *List of Expeditions, 1901–1929*, unpublished manuscript, Navy Library, Washington, D.C; and Richard F. Grimmett, *Instances of Use of United States Armed Forces Abroad, 1798–2004* (Washington, D.C: Congressional Research Service, 2004).

3. On December 2, 1823, President James Monroe told the US Congress that he would view any attempt on the part of a European power to seize additional territory in the Western Hemisphere as "the manifestation of an

unfriendly disposition toward the United States." James Monroe, "Seventh Annual Message," in Edwin Williams, ed., *The Statesman's Manual* (New York: Edward Walker, 1854), I, 451–62.

4. Robert Tomes, *The Panama Railroad* (New York: Harper Brothers, 1855), 104.

5. Descriptions of many of these proposals can be found in *The Journal of Negro History*. These include Merline Pitre, "Frederick Douglas and the Annexation of Santo Domingo," vol. 62, no. 4 (October 1977); Myra Himelhoch, "Frederick Douglas and Haiti's Mole St. Nicholas," vol. 56, no. 3 (July 1971); Harold T. Pinkett, "Efforts to Annex Santo Domingo to the United States, 1866–1871," vol. 26, no. 1 (January 1941); and Leila Amos Pendleton, "Our New Possessions – The Danish West Indies," vol. 2, no. 3 (July 1917).

6. Harry A. Ellsworth, *One Hundred Eighty Landings of United States Marines, 1800–1934* (Washington, D.C: US Marine Corps, 1934), 46–51 and 88.

7. Alfred Thayer Mahan, *Lessons of the War with Spain* (Freeport: Books for Libraries Press, 1970), 28–30 and *The Problem of Asia* (Boston: Little Brown, 1905), 136 and 198–9.

8. Donald A. Yerxa, *Admirals and Empire, the United States Navy and the Caribbean, 1898–1945* (Columbia, SC: The University of South Carolina Press, 1991), 58–66.

9. Gerhard Wiechmann, *Die Preussische-Deutsche Marine in Lateinamerika 1866-1914, Eine Studie deutscher Kanonenbootpolitik* (Ph.D. dissertation, Carl von Ossietzky Universität, 2000); Göran Henriksson, "Den Tyska Marinen och Danska Västindien," *Krigshistorisk Tidsskrift* (April 1976); and Thomas A. Bailey, "The Lodge Corollary to the Monroe Doctrine," *Political Science Quarterly* (June 1933).

10. Seward W. Livermore, "Theodore Roosevelt, the American Navy and the Venezuela Crisis of 1902–1903," *The American Historical Review* (April 1946).

11. For descriptions of these events from Zelaya's point of view, see Nicaragua, Ministerio de Relaciones Exteriores, *Documentos Referentes a la Guerra entre Nicaragua y Honduras de 1907 y a la participación de El Salvador* (Managua: Compañía Tip. Internacional, 1907).

12. Elihu Root, *Latin America and the United States* (Cambridge: Harvard University Press, 1917), 213–6.

13. Dana G. Munro, *Intervention and Dollar Diplomacy in the Caribbean, 1900–1921* (Westport: Greenwood Press, 1980), 179.

14. Hans Schmidt, *Maverick Marine: General Smedley D. Butler and the Contradictions of American Military History* (Lexington: University Press of Kentucky, 1987), 41.

15. Munro, *Intervention and Dollar Diplomacy*, 183–5.

16. Dana G. Munro, *The Five Republics of Central America* (New York: Oxford University Press, 1919), 335–40.

17. Lowell Thomas, *Old Gimlet Eye, The Adventures of Smedley D. Butler* (New York: Farrar and Rinehart, 1981), 154–7.

18. R.O. Underwood, "United States Marine Corps Field Artillery," *The Field Artillery Journal* (April–June 1915).

19. Letter of Major Smedley D. Butler to Ethel C. P. Butler, October 5, 1912, in Anne C. Venzon, ed., *General Smedley Darlington Butler, The Letters of a Leatherneck, 1898–1931* (Westport: Praeger, 1992), 121–3.

20. See, for example, Danilo Mora Luna, "La Batalla de El Coyotepe," *El Nuevo Diario* (Managua), October 12, 2007.
21. Keith B. Bickel, *Mars Learning: The Marine Corps Development of Small Wars Doctrine, 1915–1940* (Boulder: Westview, 2001).

CHAPTER 4: FEW CARROTS AND A LOT OF STICKS

1. Hannes Heer and Klaus Naumann (eds.), *War of Extermination: The German Military in World War II 1941–1944* (New York: Berghahn Books, 2000); Norbert Müller, *Die faschistische Okkupationspolitik in den zeitweilig besetzten Gebieten der Sowjetunion (1941–1944)* (Berlin: Deutscher Verlag der Wissenschafen, 1991); and Christian Gerlach, *Kalkulierte Morde: Die deutsche Wirtschafts- und Vernichtungspolitik in Weißrußland 1941 bis 1944* (Hamburg: Hamburger Edition, 1999).
2. In World War Two, the insurgents were exclusively called "partisans" or sometimes "guerrillas." The German countermeasures traded under the term "anti-partisan operations" or "anti-partisan warfare." After a personal order from Hitler in summer 1942, it was forbidden to use the term "partisan," since it conjured up heroic connotations. Hence, in German documents the words "terrorist" or "bandit" prevailed. After World War Two the term "partisan" was replaced by "insurgent," or "guerrilla fighter."
3. See especially Trevor N. Dupuy, *A Genius for War: The German Army and General Staff, 1807–1945* (London: MacDonald and Jane's, 1977).
4. The Francs-Tireurs were ordinary French citizens organized in rifle clubs or unofficial military societies. During the Franco-Prussian War the efforts of the French government to integrate them into the regular French Army mainly failed. So the Francs-Tireurs operated mostly on their own account and harassed Prussian supply lines in the occupied territory. The German troops shot captured Francs-Tireurs on the spot. The overall military effect of the Francs-Tireurs movement was limited, but it triggered harsh German countermeasures.
5. For these events, see John Horne and Alan Kramer, *German Atrocities: A History of Denial* (New Haven and London: Yale University Press, 2001). The figure of 6,000 civilian casualties must be treated with some caution as Horne and Kramer include "combat-related" casualties.
6. Peter Lieb is currently working on a major book project on the German counterinsurgency campaign in the Ukraine in 1918. For provisional results see Peter Lieb, *A Precursor of Counter-insurgency Operations? The German Occupation of the Ukraine in 1918*, Working Paper of the European Studies Research Institute, University of Salford, 2007.
7. John A. Armstrong, (ed.), *Soviet Partisans in World War II* (Madison: University of Wisconsin Press, 1964); Alexander Hill, *The War behind the Eastern Front: The Soviet Partisan Movement in North-West Russia 1941–1944* (London and New York: Frank Cass, 2005); Leonid D. Grenkevich, *The Soviet Partisan Movement 1941–1944: A Critical Historiographical Analysis* (London: Frank Cass, 1999); Kenneth Slepyan, *Stalin's Guerrillas: Soviet Partisans in World War II* (Lawrence: University of Kansas Press, 2006).
8. Emphasis on the ideological side: Heer and Naumann, *War of Extermination*. Emphasis on the situational aspects: Klaus Jochen Arnold,

Die Wehrmacht und die Besatzungspolitik in den besetzten Gebieten der Sowjetunion: Kriegführung und Radikalisierung im "Unternehmen Barbarossa" (Berlin: Duncker & Humblot, 2005). Overview: Christian Hartmann, Johannes Hürter and Ulrike Jureit (eds.), *Verbrechen der Wehrmacht: Bilanz einer Debatte* (Munich: Verlag C. H. Beck, 2005) and Timm C. Richter, (ed.), *Krieg und Verbrechen: Situation und Intention* (Munich: Fallbeispiele, Meidenbauer Verlag, 2006).

9.   Edward B. Westermann, *Hitler's Police Battalions: Enforcing Racial War in the East* (Lawrence: University Press of Kansas, 2005).

10.   Krisztián Ungváry, "Das Beispiel der ungarischen Armee: Ideologischer Vernichtungskrieg oder militärisches Kalkül?" in Hartmann, *Verbrechen*, 98–106.

11.   Peter Lieb, "Täter aus Überzeugung? Oberst Carl von Andrian und die Judenmorde der 707. Infanteriedivision," in *Vierteljahrshefte für Zeitgeschichte 50* (2002), 523–57.

12.   For an English translation of the Kriegsgerichtsbarkeiterlass see Matthew Cooper, *The Phantom War: The German Struggle against Soviet Partisans 1941–1944* (London: MacDonald & Jane's, 1979), 167–8.

13.   For the responsibility of the Army Group and Army Commanders see Johannes Hürter, *Hitler's Heerführer: Die deutschen Oberbefehlshaber im Krieg gegen die Sowjetunion 1941/42* (Munich: Oldenbourg Verlag, 2006).

14.   Walter Manoschek, *"Serbien ist judenfrei:" Militärische Besatzungspolitik und Judenvernichtung in Serbien 1941/42* (Munich: Oldenbourg Verlag, 1993).

15.   Helmut Krausnick and Hans-Heinrich Wilhelm, *Die Truppe des Weltanschauungskrieges: Die Einsatzgruppen der Sicherheitspolizei und des SD 1938–1942* (Stuttgart: Deutsche Verlagsanstalt, 1981); Ronald Headlands, *Messages of Murder: A Study of the Reports of the Einsatzgruppen of the Security Police and the Security Service 1941–1943* (Rutherford: Fairleigh Dickinson University Press, 1992); Peter Klein, (ed.), *Die Einsatzgruppen in der bestetzten Sowjetunion 1941/42: Die Tätigkeits- und Lageberichte des Chefs der Sicherheitspolizei und des SD* (Berlin: Edition Hentrich, 1997); Martin Cüppers, *Wegbereiter der Shoah: Die Waffen-SS, der Kommandostab Reichsführer-SS und die Judenvernichtung 1939–1945* (Darmstadt: Wissenschaftliche Buchgesellschaft, 2005); and Wolfgang Curilla, *Die deutsche Ordnungspolizei und der Holocaust im Baltikum und in Weissurssland 1941–1944* (Paderborn and Munich: Schöningh, 2006).

16.   Lieb, "Tater," and Gerlach, *Kalkulierte Morde*, 609–28.

17.   Hürter, *Hitlers Heerführer*, 449–65.

18.   TsAMO (*Tsentral'nii Arkhiv Ministerstva Oborni*, Central Archive of the Ministry of Defence, Russia), 12454-411; Kommando der Heeresgruppe Mitte. Ia Nr. 6634/42 g.Kdos. v. 25.8.1942. Betr.: a) Bandenbekämpfung b) Landeseigene Verbände.

19.   Theo Schulte, *The German Army and Nazi Policies in Occupied Russia* (Oxford: Berg, 1989), 172–9.

20.   National Archives, T-501, roll 71. Korück 532. Ia Br.B.Nr. 989/42 geh.v. 7.8.1942. Betr.: Miliz.

21.   Joachim Hoffmann, *Kaukasien 1942/43: Das deutsche Heer und die Orientvölker der Sowjetunion* (Freiburg: Rombach, 1991); Joachim

ENDNOTES

Hoffmann, *Die Ostlegionen 1941–1943, Turkotataren, Kaukasier und Wolgafinnen im deutschen Heer* (Freiburg: Rombach, 1976); Joachim Hoffmann, *Die Geschichte der Wlassow-Armee* (Freiburg: Rombach, 1984); and Samuel J. Newland, *Cossacks in the German Army 1941–1945* (London: Frank Cass, 1991).

22. Alfred Streim, *Die Behandlung sowjetischer Kriegsgefangener im "Fall Barbarossa"* (Heidelberg: Müller Verlag, 1981) and Christian Streit, *Die Wehrmacht und die sowjetischen Kriegsgefangenen 1941–1945* (Bonn: Diety Verlag, 1997).

23. In the Wehrmacht the Ic (also 3rd General Staff Officer) and his staff were responsible for intelligence, propaganda and counter-sabotage. The Ia officer (also 1st General Staff Officer) was the operational officer. With his staff, he worked on the tactical and operational military planning and served as an adviser to the commander. Ia officers were normally picked from the best candidates of each General Staff course.

24. Gerlach, *Kalkulierte Morde*, 859–1055.

25. Armstrong, *Soviet Partisans*, 495.

26. TsAMO, 12454-396. Oberkommando des Heeres. Gen.St.d.H./Op Abt (I). Nr. 11058/42 geh. v. 31.8.1942. Betr.: Zusammenstellung von Jagdkommandos zur Bandenbekämpfung.

27. BA-MA (*Bundesarchiv-Militärarchiv*, Federal Military Archives, Germany), RH 26-707/3. Der Oberbefehlshaber des Heeres. Gen.St.d.H./Ausb. Abt. (Ia). Nr. 1900/41. O.K.H., den 25.10.1941. Richtlinien für Partisanenbekämpfung.

28. Armstrong, *Soviet Partisans*, 422–514.

29. Klaus Schmider, *Partisanenkrieg in Jugoslawien 1941–1944* (Hamburg: Verlag E.S. Mittler & Sohn, 2002). For these tactics it needed elite divisions such as 1st Mountain Division or 7th SS Division used to rugged terrain.

30. See, for example, the drastic order of 2nd Panzer Army in BA-MA, RH 21-2/901. PzAOK 2. Ia Nr. 338/42 g.Kdos. v. 28.5.1942. Betr.: Weisung für das Unternehmen "Vogelsang."

31. Ben Shepherd, *War in the Wild East: The German Army and Soviet Partisans* (Cambridge and London: Harvard University Press, 2004); Lieb, "Tater"; and Arnold, *Wehrmacht*.

32. This expression was coined by Alexander Dallin, *German Rule in Russia: 1941–1945: A Study of Occupation Policies* (London: Macmillan, 1957).

33. International Military Tribunal (IMT), Vol. XXXIX, Document 066-UK. Der Chef des Oberkommandos der Wehrmacht. Nr. 004870/42 g.Kdo.WFSt./Op (N). 16.12.1942. Betr.: Bandenbekämpfung.

34. According to Soviet sources, the partisan movement in Belorussia grew from 57,700 men in January 1943 to 180,000 in March 1944 (Gerlach, *Kalkulierte Morde*, 861).

35. Timm C. Richter, "Die Wehrmacht und der Partisanenkrieg in den besetzten Gebieten der Sowjetunion," in *Die Wehrmacht: Mythos und Realität*, ed. Rolf-Dieter Müller and Hans-Erich Volkmann (Munich: Oldenbourg Verlag, 1999), 837–58, here 856.

36. For example BA-MA RH 26-339/23. 339. Inf.Div. Anlage zu den B.A.V. Nr. 74/42 geh. Qu. v. 1.6.42.

37. Gerlach, *Kalkulierte Morde*, 1036–55.

38. BA-MA, RHD 6/69/2. Merkblatt 69/2. Bandenbekämpfung (Gültig für alle Waffen) from 6/5/1944.

39. See Hill, *War behind the Eastern Front*.

40. It is difficult to estimate the loss of life in the occupied areas of the Soviet Union during the German anti-partisan operations. Gerlach talks about 345,000 victims (civilians and partisans) in anti-partisan warfare for Belorussia alone (Gerlach, *Kalkulierte Morde*, 1158). This figure is based on Soviet statistics after 1945 and German contemporary documents, which often lack precision. It is also impossible to give exact figures for the loss of German lives, including local supporters. They vary between 35,000 and 65,000, according to Lutz Klinkhammer, "Der Partisanenkrieg der Wehrmacht 1941–1944," in *Wehrmacht*, edited by Müller and Volkmann, 815—36, here 822. Understandably, no number of real or alleged collaborators killed is given in Soviet figures. The quantity of the dead remains open as well as their whereabouts in the statistics. In the case of France, collaborators killed before and after the liberation almost equal the direct victims of German anti-partisan warfare.

41. Robert O. Paxton, *Vichy France: Old Guard and New Order* (New York: Knopf, 1972).

42. Eberhard Jäckel, *Frankreich in Hitlers Europa: Die deutsche Frankreichpolitik im Zweiten Weltkrieg* (Stuttgart: Deutsche Verlagsanstalt, 1968). Although this book is from the 1960s, it remains the most important analysis of German policy towards France during World War Two.

43. For the German military administration system, see Hans Umbreit, *Der deutsche Militärbefehlshaber in Frankreich 1940–1944* (Boppard am Rhein: Harald Boldt Verlag, 1968).

44. Marc Olivier Baruch, *Servir l'Etat Français: L'Administration en France de 1904 à 1944* (Paris: Fayard, 1997) and Bernd Kasten, *"Gute Franzosen": Die französische Polizei und die deutsche Besatzungsmacht im besetzten Frankreich 1940–1944* (Sigmaringen: Thorbecke, 1993).

45. Vichy France has been studied much more thoroughly than Résistance France, so there is no modern general book with a synopsis on the French resistance. For older multi-volume books see Henri Amouroux, *La Grande Histoire des Français sous l'Occupation* (1939–1945), 10 volumes (Paris: Laffont, 1976–94) and Henri Noguères, *Histoire de la Résistance en France de 1940 à 1945*, 5 volumes (Paris: Laffont, 1967–81).

46. Ahlrich Meyer, *Die deutsche Besatzung in Frankreich 1940–1944: Widerstandsbekämpfung und Judenverfolgung* (Darmstadt: Wissenschaftliche Buchgesellschaft, 2000).

47. Peter Lieb, *Konventioneller Krieg oder NS-Weltanschauungskrieg? Kriegführung und Partisanenbekämpfung in Frankreich 1943/44* (Munich: Oldenbourg Verlag, 2007), 68–70.

48. For the relation between the Maquisards and the local French population, see Harry R. Kedward, *In Search of the Maquis: Rural Resistance in Southern France 1942–1944* (Oxford: Clarendon Press, 1993).

49. Michael R. D. Foot, *SOE in France*, rev. ed. (London: Frank Cass, 2004).

50. Lieb, *Konventioneller Krieg*, 309–57.

51. For the German repression and anti-partisan warfare in France see Lieb, *Konventioneller Krieg*.

52. BA-MA, RH 19 IV/133. Ob.West. Ia/Ic Nr. 1503/44 g.Kdos. v. 8.6.1944.

53. Max Hastings, *Das Reich: Resistance and the March of the 2nd SS Panzer Division through France, June 1944* (London: Joseph, 1981).

54. Lieb, *Konventioneller Krieg*, 339–50, and Paul Dreyfus, *Vercors: Citadelle de Liberté* (Paris: Arthaud, 1997); also Michael Pearson, *Tears of Glory: The Betrayal of Vercors 1944* (London: Macmillan, 1978).

55. Dwight D. Eisenhower, *Crusade in Europe* (London: Heinemann, 1948).

56. However, it should be noted that from the territory of the *Militärbefehlshaber* in France slightly more than 60,000 French were deported between 1940 and 1944 to concentration and labor camps in Germany or Poland under the auspices of the SS. These persons were deported on account of political reasons or acts of resistance. About 40 percent perished in the camps, mainly in the last months of the war in 1945.

57. Lieb, *Konventioneller Krieg*, 412–15.

58. Yugoslavia has been omitted because it involved too many players, making it impossible to consider it sufficiently in the scope of this chapter.

59. Perry Biddiscombe, *Werwolf! The History of the National Socialist Guerrilla Movement, 1944–1946* (Toronto: University of Toronto Press, 1998); Steffen Prauser, "Mord in Rom? Der Anschlag in der Via Rasella und die deutsche Vergeltung in den Fosse Ardeatine im März 1944," in *Vierteljahrshefte für Zeitgeschichte* 50 (2002), 269–301, here 298.

60. Interview with *Le Monde* on May 3, 2001. See also his memoirs: Paul Aussaresses, *Pour la France: Services Spéciaux 1942–1954* (Monaco: Editions du Rocher, 2001).

CHAPTER 5: FRENCH IMPERIAL WARFARE 1945-62

1. Sylvie Thénault, *Histoire de la guerre d'indépendance Algérienne* (Paris: Flammarion, 2005), 19–20.

2. Ibid., 214.

3. Ibid., 32.

4. Maurice Vaïsse, "Conclusions," in Jeann-Charles Jaufret and Maurice Vaïsse, *Militaires et guerilla dans la guerre d'Algérie* (Paris: Editions Complexe, 2001), 545.

5. Raphaëlle Branche, *La Guerre d'Algérie: une histoire apaisée?* (Paris: Editions du Senil, 2005), 378.

6. Omar Carlier, "Le 1er novembre 1954 à Oran: action symbolique, histoire périphérique, et marqueur historiographique," in Charles-Robert Ageron, *La guerre d'Algérie et les Algériens 1954–1962* (Paris: Armand Colin, 1997), 8–9, 23, 25; indeed, some argue that the origins, if not the beginning of the Algerian War, can be traced to Sétif on May 8, 1945. See Branche, *La guerre d'Algérie*, 372–6.

7. Benjamin Stora, "Le Maroc et les débuts de la guerre d'Algérie (1953–1956)," in Jaufret and Vaïsse, *Militaires et guerilla*, 270–4, 281.

8. For numbers see Jean-Charles Jauffret, "Une armée a deux vitesses en Algérie (1954–1962): Réserves générales et troupes de secteur," 22; Alban Mahieu, "Les effectifs de l'armée française en Algérie (1954–1962)," 39; Jacques Frémeaux, "La gendarmerie et la guerre d'Algérie," 74, in Jaufret and Vaïsse, *Militaires et guerilla*.

9. Daho Djerbal, "Les maquis du Nord-Constantinois face aux grandes operations de ratissage du plan Challe (1959–1960)," in Jaufret and Vaïsse, *Militaires et guerilla*, 196–7.

10. Carlier, "Le 1er novembre 1954 à Oran," 18; Thénault, *Histoire*, 114.

11. Jean-Louis Planche, "De la solidarité militante à l'affrontement armé: MNA et FLN à Alger (1954–1955)," in Jaufret and Vaïsse, *Militaires et guerilla*, 229.

12. Thénault, *Histoire*, 71–4.

13. Charles-Robert Ageron, "L'insurrection du 20 août 1955 dans le Nord-Constantinois: De la résistance armée à la guerre du peuple," in Ageron, *La guerre d'Algérie et les Algériens*, 37–47; Mahfoud Kaddache, "Les tournants de la guerre de Liberation au niveau des masses populaires," in Ageron, *La guerre d'Algérie et les Algériens*, 54; on violence between Algerian nationalists, see Gilbert Meynier, "Le FLN/ALN dans les six wilâyas: étude comparée," in Jaufret and Vaïsse, *Militaires et guerilla*, 169.

14. Gilbert Meynier, "Le FLN/ALN dans les six wilâyas: étude comparée," in Jaufret and Vaïsse, *Militaires et guerilla*, 165.

15. *Harki* is a general term in this case applied to Muslims enlisted in French service, which also included *goumiers, moghazni, gardes ruraux* and *groupes d'autodéfense*. It encompassed a variety of categories of short-term enlistment, usually outside a formal military structure, although they could be placed with gendarmes, parachutists, and commandos. Dalia Kerchouche says that officially 263,000 Muslims served as *harkis* in *Mon père, ce harki* (Paris: Editions du Senil, 2003), 23. However, Sylvie Thénault says that no one really knows how many Muslims were enlisted by French commanders, often by SAS (Section Administrative Spéciale) officers to serve in home guard units, and paid by the day (*Histoire*, 259).

16. Because Algeria was considered part of metropolitan France for administrative purposes, the force mustered for that war included a majority of conscripts otherwise prohibited from serving outside the metropole. The amalgamation of conscript and professional/imperial units into one force in Algeria contributed to problems of adaptation and morale, which expressed themselves in political terms as France's exit from Algeria became evident.

17. André-Paul Comor, "L'adaptation de la Légion étrangère à la nouvelle forme de guerre," in Jaufret and Vaïsse, *Militaires et guerilla*, 61–7.

18. Jauffret, "Une armée a deux vitesses en Algérie (1954–1962)," in Jaufret and Vaïsse, *Militaires et guerilla*, 21–36.

19. Jacques Vernet, "Les barrages pendant la guerre d'Algérie," in Jaufret and Vaïsse, *Militaires et guerilla*, 256–68.

20. Some simply fled to the towns where they lived in slums. Charles-Robert Ageron, "Une dimension de la guerre d'Algerie: les 'regroupements' de populations," in Jaufret and Vaïsse, *Militaires et guerilla*, 353.

21. Michel Rocard, *Rappot sur les camps de regroupement et autres textes sur la guerre d'Algérie* (Paris: Mille et une nuites, 2003).

22. Ageron, "Une dimension de la guerre d'Algerie: les 'regroupements' de populations," in Jaufret and Vaïsse, *Militaires et guerilla*, 332–49.

23. Daniel Lefeuvre, "L'échec du plan de Constantine," in Jean-Pierre Rioux, *La guerre d'Algérie et les Français* (Paris: Fayard, 1990), 320–4.

24. Thénault, *Histoire*, 97–9, 178–9, 255–9; see also Kerchouche, *Mon père, ce harki*.

25. Thénault, *Histoire*, 88–9.
26. Thénault, *Histoire*, 150.
27. Djerbal, "Les maquis du Nord-Constantinois," in Jaufret and Vaïsse, *Militaires et guerilla*, 202–8.
28. Ibid., 202–8; Thénault, *Histoire*, 178–81.
29. Charles-Robert Ageron, "L'opinion française á travers les sondages," in Rioux, *La guerre d'Algérie et les Français*, 35.
30. Jim House and Niel Macmaster, *Paris 1961: Algerians, State Terror and Memory* (Oxford: Oxford University Press, 2006), 12–5, 31, 78–80, 122–6.
31. Todd Shepard, *The Invention of Decolonization: The Algerian War and the Remaking of France* (Ithaca, New York, and London: Cornell University Press, 2006), 239, 243.
32. Thénault, *Histoire*, 15; Vaïsse, "Conclusion," in Jaufret and Vaïsse, *Militaires et guerilla*, 550–2.

CHAPTER 6: FROM SEARCH AND DESTROY TO HEARTS AND MINDS

1. Anthony Short, *The Communist Insurrection in Malaya 1948–60* (London: Frederick Muller, 1975), 472; No. 44, Foreign Office, "Intel." February 21, 1952, CO 1022/2, Public Record Office; Rhoderick Dhu Renick, Jr., "The Emergency Regulations of Malaya: Cause and Effect," *Journal of Southeast Asian History*, 6 (September 1965), 4.
2. John Coates, *Suppressing Insurgency: An Analysis of the Malayan Emergency, 1948–54* (Boulder: Westview Press, 1992), 169; Short, *The Communist Insurrection*, 290, 507–8.
3. Coates, *Suppressing Insurgency*, 123; Richard Stubbs, *Hearts and Minds in Guerrilla Warfare: The Malayan Emergency 1948–1960* (Singapore: Oxford University Press, 1989), 157, 159.
4. Short, *The Communist Insurrection*, 350; Stubbs, *Hearts and Minds*, 125; Chin Peng, *My Side of the Story* (Singapore: Media Masters, 2003), 403.
5. For more information on the training of local police forces, see Lt Col James S. Corum, *Training Indigenous Forces in Counterinsurgency: A Tale of Two Insurgencies* (Strategic Studies Institute, 2006).
6. Harry Miller, *Menace in Malaya* (London: Harrap, 1954), 89.
7. Telegram, Gurney to the Secretary of State for the Colonies, December 19, 1948, CO 537/3758; Annex A to Minutes of the BDCC(FE), 15th Mtg., January 28, 1949, CO 537/4773, Public Record Office, UK.
8. See A. J. Stockwell, (ed.), *Malaya: Part II, The Communist Insurrection 1948–1953* (London: HMSO, 1995), 216–21 for the text of the Briggs Plan.
9. "Secret Abstracts of Intelligence for February 14–28, 1951," CO 537/7300; and Department of Labour, "Monthly Reports," August and September 1951, National Archives of Malaysia. For a review of the early years of resettlement, see Stubbs, *Hearts and Minds*, 100–27.
10. Coates, *Suppressing Insurgency*, 96.
11. Viscount Chandos (Oliver Lyttelton), *The Memoirs of Lord Chandos* (London: Bodley Head, 1962), 336.
12. See P/PM1, Chief Secretary 438/W/51, National Archives of Malaysia.
13. *Proceedings of the Federal Legislative Council*, 5th Session, March 19, 1952.

14. Verbatim Record of Templer's Speech to Division One Officers, February 9, 1952, P/PM1, Secretary to Government Y5, National Archives of Malaysia.

15. Federation of Malaya, *Annual Report*, 1954 (Kuala Lumpur Government Printer, 1955), 409; and P/PM1, Secretary to Government 32 (4/7), National Archives of Malaysia.

16. "Resettlement and the Development of New Villages in the Federation of Malaya 1952," *Proceedings of the Federal Legislative Council*, Paper No. 33. For an extended analysis of the development of the new villages see Stubbs, *Hearts and Minds*, 168–80.

17. *Proceedings of the Federal Legislative Council*, 6th Session, c.745.

18. For an overview of intelligence gathering see Leon Comber, *Malaya's Secret Police 1945–1960: The Role of the Special Branch in the Malayan Emergency* (Singapore: Institute of Southeast Asian Studies, 2007).

19. Coates, *Suppressing Insurgency*, 65.

20. See Daniel Marston, "Lost and Found in the Jungle: The Indian and British Army Jungle Warfare Doctrines for Burma, 1943–5 and the Malayan Emergency, 1948–60," in Hew Strachan, (ed.), *Big Wars and Small Wars: The British Army and the Lessons of War in the 20th Century* (London: Routledge, 2006), 97–103.

21. Coates, *Suppressing Insurgency*, 118; Marston, "Lost and Found in the Jungle," 96; and Short, *The Communist Insurrection*, 369.

22. Kumar Ramakrishna, *Emergency Propaganda: The Winning of Malayan Hearts and Minds 1948–1958* (Richmond: Curzon, 2002), 209; and Coates, *Suppressing Insurgency*, 170–2.

23. On both propaganda and psychological warfare, see Ramakrishna, *Emergency Propaganda*, and Herbert A. Friedman, "Psychological Warfare of the Malayan Emergency 1948–1960," www.psywar.org/malaya.php, accessed April 20, 2007.

24. For a full discussion of political developments see Stubbs, *Hearts and Minds*, 201–24.

25. See, for example, Karl Hack, "Screwing Down the People: The Malayan Emergency, Decolonisation and Ethnicity," in Hans Antlov and Stein Tonnesson, (eds.), *Imperial Power and Southeast Asian Nationalism 1930–1957* (Richmond: Curzon, 1995), 83–109; and Karl Hack, *Defence and Decolonisation in Southeast Asia: Britain, Malaya and Singapore 1941–1968* (Richmond: Curzon, 2001), 113–31.

26. See rebuttals of Hack's argument in Simon C. Smith, "General Templer and Counter-Insurgency in Malaya: Hearts and Minds, Intelligence, and Propaganda," *Intelligence and National Security*, 16, no.3 (Fall 2001), 60–78; and Ramakrishna, *Emergency Propaganda*, 53.

27. See, for example, Robert O. Tilman, "The Non-Lessons of the Malayan Emergency," *Asian Survey*, 6 (August 1966), 407–19.

28. For citations and discussion, see Stubbs, *Hearts and Minds*, 2–3.

29. Robert Thompson, *Defeating Communist Insurgency: Experiences from Malaya and Vietnam* (New York: Praeger, 1966), 51–7.

30. Robert Thompson, *No Exit from Vietnam* (London: Chatto and Windus, 1969), 89.

31. John A. Nagl, *Learning to Eat Soup with a Knife: Counterinsurgency Lessons from Malaya and Vietnam* (Westport, Connecticut: Praeger, 2002).

CHAPTER 7: COUNTERINSURGENCY IN VIETNAM

1. This chapter is a revised and updated version of chapters 6 and 7 of John A. Nagl, *Learning to Eat Soup with a Knife: Counterinsurgency Lessons from Malaya and Vietnam* (Westport, CT: Praeger, 2002). The author would like to thank Dr Carter Malkasian for brightening a tough week in Khalidiyah, Iraq in 2004 by stopping by for dinner, and for his assistance with this chapter in 2007 under rather more congenial circumstances.

2. Roger Hilsman, *To Move a Nation: The Politics of Foreign Policy in the Administration of John F. Kennedy* (Garden City, New York: Doubleday & Co., 1967), 525.

3. *The Pentagon Papers: The Defense Department History of United States Decisionmaking on Vietnam*, 4 volumes (Boston: Beacon Press, 1971), volume II, 435. Hereafter *PP*.

4. Hilsman, *To Move a Nation*, 419.

5. William Colby, *Lost Victory* (New York: Contemporary Books, 1989), 69.

6. Hilsman, *To Move a Nation*, 413.

7. Ibid., 426.

8. Ibid., 442.

9. Mark Moyar, *Triumph Forsaken: The Vietnam War, 1954–1965* (New York: Cambridge University Press, 2006), 186–7, 193.

10. The Military History Institute of Vietnam, *Victory in Vietnam: The Official History of the People's Army of Vietnam, 1954–1975*, trans. Merle Pribbenow, (Lawrence, KS: University Press of Kansas, 2002), 110.

11. Neil Sheehan, *A Bright Shining Lie: John Paul Vann and America in Vietnam* (New York: Vintage Books, 1988), 303.

12. Rosson and Yarborough to Decker, "Special Warfare Activities Field Inspection Visit," May 2, 1962, 6, in Andrew F. Krepinevich, Jr., *The Army and Vietnam* (Baltimore: Johns Hopkins University Press, 1985), 71.

13. Francis J. Kelly, *U.S. Army Special Forces 1961–1971* (Washington, D.C: GPO, 1973), 48.

14. *PP* III, 440.

15. Harold Moore and Joseph Galloway, *We Were Soldiers Once... And Young* (New York: Random House, 1992), 342–3.

16. 1st Cavalry Division, AAR, MASHER/WHITE WING, January 25–March 6, 1966 (April 28, 1966), 23; in Guenter Lewy, *America in Vietnam* (Oxford: Oxford University Press, 1978), 58.

17. 1st Cavalry Division (Airmobile), AAR, THAYER II, October 25, 1966–February 12, 1967 (June 25, 1967), incl. 6–5; in Lewy, *America in Vietnam*, 56–60.

18. Sheehan, *A Bright Shining Lie*, 636.

19. William Westmoreland, *A Soldier Reports* (New York: Da Capo, 1989), 165.

20. *PP* II, 501.

21. *PP* II, 576.

22. Ibid., 580.

23. Robert Komer, *Bureaucracy Does Its Thing* (Oxford: Westview, 1986), 115.

24. MACV, "Commander's Summary of the MACV Objectives Plan," 28–9, CMH; in Lewy, *America in Vietnam*, 137.

25. MACV, "One War: MACV Command Overview 1968–72," 15, CMH; in Lewy, *America in Vietnam*, 137.

26.   Brian M. Jenkins, *The Unchangeable War*, RM-6278-1-ARPA (Santa Monica, CA: The Rand Corporation, 1972), 3; in Lewy, *America in Vietnam*, 138.

27.   Lewis Sorley, "The Conduct of the War: Strategy, Doctrine, Tactics, and Policy," in Andrew Wiest, (ed.), *Rolling Thunder in a Gentle Land: The Vietnam War Revisited* (Oxford: Osprey, 2006), 188.

28.   Melvin Zais, *Battle at Dong Ap Bia (Hamburger Hill)* (Washington, D.C: Center for Military History, January 5, 1971).

29.   Address to the Nation, November 3rd, 1969, US President, *Public Papers of the Presidents of the United States: Richard Nixon 1969* (Washington, D.C., 1971).

30.   Lam Quang Thi, "The View from the Other Side of the Story: Reflections of a South Vietnamese Soldier," in Wiest, *Rolling Thunder in a Gentle Land*, 120.

31.   Mark Moyar, "Villager Attitudes During the Final Decade of the Vietnam War," Vietnam Center Symposium Paper, 1996.

32.   Thomas Thayer, *War Without Fronts* (Oxford: Westview, 1986), 164–6.

33.   Sheehan, *A Bright Shining Lie*, 732–3.

34.   J. A. Koch, *The Chieu Hoi Program in South Vietnam, 1963–1971* (Santa Monica, CA: The Rand Corporation, January 1973), vii.

35.   General Jack Keane on the Jim Lehrer *News Hour*, April 18, 2006.

CHAPTER 8: RED WOLVES AND BRITISH LIONS

1.   "Proscription bombing" aimed to destroy crops and houses while avoiding injury to women and children. Consequently, all-important tribal "face" was maintained against a British adversary who used superior firepower.

2.   Miles Copeland, *The Game Player* (London: Aurum Press, 1989), 198.

3.   Address to the Royal Air Force Historical Society, June 10, 1997, reported in *Royal Air Force Historical Society Journal*, 18, 1998. Between 1959 and 1965, 17 states, including Aden, joined the Federation. Of the four states of the Eastern Aden Protectorate, only Wahidi ever became a member, the remainder maintaining their informal ties with Britain outside the Federation.

4.   For the structure and fighting potential of the tribes, see "The Radfan" in *People's Socialist Party Background Paper* no. 4, London 1964, Yem. 3a Soc., Arab World Documentation Centre, Exeter University.

5.   Before sealed landing pads were introduced, helicopters suffered from ingesting enormous amounts of rock dust, sand, and debris found on Arabian landing strips. The Belvedere had to cease operations during the middle of the day, due to turbulence caused by excessive heat (in the Malayan campaign, the main problem was combating the effects of humidity). See Captain T. M. P. (Paddy) Stevens, "Troop Carrying Helicopters" in *Army Quarterly*, January 1958.

6.   Brigadier Charles Dunbar to Lieutenant Colonel Julian Paget, September 25, 1968, File 2/6, Dunbar Papers, Liddell Hart Centre for Military Archives, King's College, London (hereafter LHCMA); also T. Mockaitis, *British Counter-Insurgency in the Post-Imperial Era* (Manchester: Manchester University Press, 1995), 51.

7.   Bizarrely, the last GOC, Major General Philip Tower, had held the post of Director of Public Relations (Army).

8.   Press Conference, HQ MIDEAST, 3 May 1964, DEFE 13/569, National Archives (hereafter NA); also "Report on Radfan Operations," HQ MEC, December 29, 1964, DEFE 25/190, NA.

9.   Donal McCarthy to Sir Richard Beaumont, November 20, 1967, FCO 8/41, NA.

10.   For a fuller description of the scheme, see Peter Hinchcliffe et al, *Without Glory in Arabia: The British Retreat from Aden* (London: IB Taurus, 2006), 80–1. Political officers such as Stephen Day, Godfrey Meynell, Peter Hinchcliffe, and Julian Paxton loyally pursued the writ of the British High Commission with little support from the Foreign Office.

11.   Tribal leadership was a complex concept. The British wrongly assumed that there was a strict order of precedence among tribal leaders and, in the Federation, tended to promote and reward on that basis. (Simon Day to author, March 3, 2004.)

12.   For a full account of the SAS operation, see Jonathan Walker, *Aden Insurgency: The Savage War in South Arabia 1962–67* (Staplehurst: Spellmount, 2005), 98–103, 117–9.

13.   "Army Lessons from Radfan Operations," October 9, 1964, DEFE 25/190, NA.

14.   "Forward Air Controlling is not a Mystic Art," in *Globe & Laurel*, December 1965. During the Radfan campaign, air strikes resulted in 600 sorties, using 2,500 rockets and nearly 200,000 cannon rounds.

15.   As trenches could not be dug in rock-hard ground, the "sangar" was a traditional defensive position built above ground, using dry-stone walling.

16.   Brigadier G. S. Hargroves, "Operations in the Radfan," Lecture to RUSI, November 1965.

17.   C-in-C Mideast to Ministry of Defence, June 22, 1964, DEFE 13/570, NA. The issue of local ceasefires has arisen in Afghanistan, where agreements with local warlords have collapsed after the re-emergence of local Taliban. For Templer, see D. Charters, "From Palestine to Northern Ireland: British Adaption to Low Intensity Operations," in D. Charters, M. Tugwell (eds.), *Armies in Low Intensity Conflict: A Comparative Analysis* (London: Brassey's, 1989), 195.

18.   Lt Col Neil "Billy" McLean, DSO, MP, had served with Orde Wingate and in SOE during World War Two. In the 1960s he established links with various heads of state, especially in the Middle East. David Stirling founded the SAS and later coordinated ex-members for "special operations."

19.   Cabinet Minister Richard Crossman was delighted when the NLF overthrew the Federal government in 1967. See diary entry for September 5, 1967, Richard Crossman, *The Diaries of a Cabinet Minister*, vol. II (London: Hamish Hamilton, 1976).

20.   Harold Macmillan, *At the End of the Day 1961–1963* (London: Macmillan, 1973), 271.

21.   S. Hutchinson, "The Police Role in Counterinsurgency Operations," in *RUSI Journal*, December 1969.

22.   Military–police cooperation was not helped by the Brigadier General Staff's poor regard for the Commissioner of Police; see Brigadier C. Dunbar to C-in-C, March 8, 1967, 2/4 Dunbar Papers, LHCMA, King's College, London.

23. G. Balfour-Paul, *The End of Empire in the Middle East* (Cambridge: Cambridge University Press, 1991), 84–5.

24. "Statistics of Terrorism in Aden State," Annex D, Julian Paget, *Last Post: Aden 1964–1967* (London: Faber and Faber, 1969).

25. The Secret Intelligence Service (SIS) was, and is, effectively Britain's overseas intelligence agency. The Special Operations Executive (SOE) was a British wartime organization, which aimed to assist subversive activities by resistance groups in occupied countries.

26. See "The Alleged Use of Torture in Aden – The Bowen Report," DEFE 13/529, NA; also "Amnesty Report," November 11, 1966, PREM 13/1294, NA.

27. Jonathan Walker, *Aden Insurgency*, 184–5, 190–1.

28. "Geordies" and "Jocks" are nicknames for soldiers of the Royal Northumberland Fusiliers and the Argyll and Sutherland Highlanders respectively.

29. Major General David Thomson to author, April 17, 2007. The author is indebted to him for his constructive observations regarding COIN operations in Aden.

30. Donal McCarthy to Sir Richard Beaumont, November 20, 1967, FCO 8/41, NA.

31. The Unified Command comprised a Commander-in-Chief, together with a small Secretariat, and three subordinate army, navy and air force commanders of two star rank.

32. Terrorist groups with a Marxist-Leninist creed posed a constant threat for Western security agencies during the 1960s and 1970s.

CHAPTER 9: BRITAIN'S LONGEST WAR

1. Over the course of the conflict some 3,000 people were killed or died due to the insurgency, including more than 700 British soldiers.

2. For example, in the *British Army Review*, the army's quarterly house journal, the first article covering Northern Ireland did not appear until 1974, five years after the start of the operation. In the meantime, there had been numerous articles about such wide-ranging issues as the Yom Kippur War, the East German Army, and mounted camel operations.

3. Throughout the conflict, the British government described PIRA and other armed groups as "terrorists" rather than "insurgents." This was part of its strategy to criminalize PIRA and reduce its legitimacy. The definition was thus political rather than analytical. By academic standards, PIRA is best characterized as an insurgent group that used terrorist tactics.

4. The name of the historic City of Derry/Londonderry (and its eponymous county) continues to be a politically divisive issue in Northern Ireland. The city was founded during the 17th-century plantation, funded by the livery companies of London, on a previous Gaelic foundation named Doire. Hence unionists tend to call the city "Londonderry" and nationalists "Derry." This chapter uses the name "Derry" purely for issues of space.

5. The terms used to define various groups in Northern Ireland appear bewildering: republicans or nationalists sought union with Ireland and dissolution of the union with Britain. They were almost all Catholics. Unionists or loyalists sought the continued link with Britain, and were invariably Protestants.

6.   Ed Moloney, *A Secret History of the IRA* (London: Penguin Books, 2002), 74–92, describes the radicalization process, summarized on 92.

7.   General Staff Publication 71842, *Operation Banner: An Analysis of Military Operations in Northern Ireland*, 17, Para 220 describes internment thus: "Put simply, on balance and with the benefit of hindsight, it was a major mistake."

8.   For example, the right to jury trial was suspended due to widespread intimidation of juries by insurgent groups. Instead, courts consisted of a single judge.

9.   David Beresford, *Ten Men Dead* (London: Harper Collins, 1994) describes how the sense of isolation was created among prisoners.

10.   The Maze was the main prison for male terrorist prisoners in Northern Ireland, some 20 miles to the southwest of Belfast. It was built on an old RAF airbase at Long Kesh, where it replaced the "cages" built earlier to hold internees. The prison blocks were built on an "H" shape and were known in republican circles as H-Blocks.

11.   Moloney, *Secret History*, 16.

12.   Yvonne Fletcher was killed on April 17, 1984 outside the Libyan Embassy in St James Square during an anti-Gaddafi demonstration, when one of the Libyan diplomats opened fire on the crowd. Diplomatic relations between Britain and Libya were severed as a result.

13.   Moloney, *Secret History*, 21–2.

14.   A group staffed by volunteers who were themselves ex-terrorists from both unionist and republican groups, assisted by Quakers.

15.   Roger MacGinty and John Darby, *Guns and Government: The Management of the Northern Ireland Peace Process* (London: Macmillan, 2002) describes the peace process in full. A shorter and more readable analysis is the monograph by John Darby, *Northern Ireland: The Background to the Peace Process* (Cain Web Service at the University of Ulster, http://cain.ulst.ac.uk/events/peace/da).

16.   By the mid–late 1980s, NITAT was teaching that any successful PIRA attack on an army foot patrol could be blamed on poor patrolling tactics.

17.   General Staff Publication 71842, para 243.

18.   Ibid., para 708.

19.   Moloney, *Secret History*, 159–61.

20.   This description of an urban attack was provided by an informer working for the security forces. However, all elements of it became common knowledge to the security forces, since all attacks followed roughly the same pattern. Different, but equally sophisticated, tactics were used for rural shoots or IED attacks.

21.   Martin Ingram and Greg Harkin, *Stakeknife* (Dublin: O'Brien Press, 2004). Chapter 4 describes how senior figures in the counterintelligence unit were themselves British agents, in particular the agent codenamed *Stakeknife*.

22.   The most famous example was the German bombing of Coventry, the plans for which were supposedly revealed to Churchill by ULTRA. However, he could not take any action on the information, since this would reveal to the Germans that the British had cracked their codes.

23.   Very little has been written about the British Army's surveillance operation in Northern Ireland. Toby Harnden, *Bandit Country: The IRA and South*

Armagh (London: Hodder and Stoughton, 1999), 180–1 briefly mentions the role of observation posts and towers in South Armagh in reducing freedom of movement of PIRA insurgents, but does not mention the importance of understanding patterns.

CHAPTER 10: COUNTERING THE *CHIMURENGA*

1. Cited by Barbara Cole, *The Elite: Rhodesian Special Air Service: Pictorial* (Amanzimtoti: Three Knights Publishing, 1986), 62.
2. "Chimurenga" is a Shona word meaning "uprising."
3. Chapter 7 of the UN's Charter empowers it to take economic or military action against a sovereign state. The irony was that Rhodesia was not a sovereign state as Britain had not conferred sovereignty. Wilson's action was thus a misuse of this power.
4. Conversations with Brigadiers Peter Hosking and Tom Davidson and Lt Cols Mick McKenna, Brian Robinson, and Ron Reid-Daly, February 2007.
5. Ken Flower, *Serving Secretly, Rhodesia's CIO Chief on Record* (Alberton: Galago, 1987), 114.
6. See Lt Col Ron Reid-Daly, *Top Secret War* (Alberton: Galago, 1982).
7. Information given to Colonel Mike Pelham, Commander of the Rhodesian Corps of Engineers, by ZANLA commanders in 1984. (Interview with Colonel Pelham, December 7, 1995.)
8. When B. J. Vorster succeeded Hendrik Verwoerd in 1966, he sought better relations with Africa. The infiltration of Rhodesia by South African African nationalist insurgents in 1967, however, faced him with the need to defend his northern border on the Limpopo. He preferred the Zambesi as his defense line and reinforced Rhodesia with police units to halt infiltrations. After the Portuguese coup in 1974, Vorster aimed to secure compliant African neighbors in Mozambique and Rhodesia. He sincerely believed that he could achieve a peaceful, cooperative relationship with Africa despite maintaining apartheid. Accordingly, he would force Ian Smith to accept majority rule although he, Vorster, would not contemplate it at home.
9. Dudley Cowderoy and Roy Nesbit, *War in the Air: Rhodesian Air Force 1935–1980* (Alberton: Galago, 1987), 119–24; interview with Group Captain Peter Petter-Bowyer, March 24, 1992.
10. Interview with Lt Col Mick McKenna, former commander, Grey Scouts, December 7, 1995.
11. J. K. Cilliers, *Counter-Insurgency in Rhodesia* (London: Croom Helm, 1985), 226; interview with the late Captain A. R. Eastwood, circa 1982.
12. Jim Parker, *Assignment Selous Scouts: Inside Story of a Rhodesian Special Branch Officer* (Alberton: Galago, 2006), 155f.
13. Interview with Group Captain Peter Petter-Bowyer, March 24, 1992.
14. G. K. Burke, "Insurgency in Rhodesia – the Implications," *RUSI and Brassey's Defence Yearbook 1978–79* (London: 1980), 26–40.
15. Interview with Colonel John Redfern, Director, Military Intelligence, circa 1982.
16. John Cronin and Robert C. Mackenzie, "Counter-Insurgency in Southern Africa," paper delivered to the Center for Strategic and International Studies (Washington D.C., 1986).

CHAPTER 11: THE ISRAEL DEFENSE FORCES AND THE *AL-AQSA INTIFADA*

1.   See Ahron Bregman, *Elusive Peace: How the Holy Land Defeated America* (London: Penguin, 2005).

2.   See "*Al-Aqsa Intifada* Reportedly Planned in July," *Intelligence Briefs: Israel/Palestinians*, vol. 3, no. 3 (March 2001), *Middle East Intelligence Bulletin*, http://www.meib.org/articles/0103_ipb.htm, accessed May 12, 2007.

3.   As champion of the Israeli settlement movement and leader of the right-wing Likud Party, Sharon's visit on the Temple Mount during a particularly delicate phase of Israeli-Palestinian peace negotiations was perceived by Palestinians as a defiant declaration that Israel would gain sovereignty over the area following a final status agreement.

4.   This chapter will focus on the IDF's counterinsurgency campaign during the first four years of the *Al-Aqsa Intifada*, as this period comprises the most critical and violent phase of the ongoing Israeli–Palestinian conflict. For a detailed timeline of the *Al-Aqsa Intifada* see: "Middle East Timeline," *The Guardian*, http://www.guardian.co.uk/israel/Story/0,,554625,00.html, accessed June 25, 2006.

5.   On Palestinian strategy and tactics see Hillel Frisch, "Debating Palestinian Strategy in the *Al-Aqsa Intifada*," *Terrorism and Political Violence*, vol. 15, no. 2 (Summer 2003), 61–80.

6.   The Gaza settlement of Netzarim, for example, was denied vehicular access for almost three weeks in October 2000 due to Palestinian gunfire.

7.   David Eshel, "The *Al-Aqsa Intifada*: Tactics and Strategies," *Jane's Intelligence Review*, vol. 13, no. 5 (May 2001), 36–8.

8.   An independent and non-partisan organization established in 1972 to protect civil and human rights in Israel and the territories under its control.

9.   Quoted in Shaul Shay and Yoram Schweitzer, "The *Al-Aqsa Intifada*: Palestinian-Israeli Confrontation," International Institute for Counter-Terrorism (April 4, 2001), http://www.ict.org.il/apage/5363.php, accessed May 10, 2007.

10.   Col Yossi Kupperwaser, then a Central Command intelligence officer, stated that the IDF during the first months of the *Al-Aqsa Intifada* shot over 850,000 5.56mm bullets – 1.3 million bullets including the Gaza Strip. See Akiva Eldar, "Popular Misconceptions," *Ha'aretz* (June 11, 2004) and Reuven Peatzur, "More than a Million Bullets," *Ha'aretz* (June 29, 2004).

11.   Barbara Opall-Rome, "Tanks fill wider role in Israel's anti-terror war," *Defense News* (March 17, 2003).

12.   Bar-Siman-Tov et al, *The Israeli-Palestinian Violent Confrontation 2000–2004: From Conflict Resolution to Conflict Management* (Jerusalem: Jerusalem Institute for Israel Studies, 2005), 25.

13.   Ofer Shelach cited in Yoram Peri, *The Israeli Military and Israel's Palestinian Policy: From Oslo to the Al-Aqsa Intifada*, Peaceworks no. 47 (Washington, D.C: United States Institute for Peace, November 2002), 35.

14.   See Amos Harel, "MI: Arafat Steps Up Actions against Terrorist Organizations," *Ha'aretz* (January 1, 2002).

15.   "Soldier killed following terrorist's death. Al-Aksa Brigade claims shooting near Tulkarm, says cease-fire is over," *Jerusalem Post* (January 15, 2002),

http://info.jpost.com/C002/Supplements/CasualtiesOfWar/2002_01_14.html accessed February 2, 2002.

16. "Ebb and Flow: A Summary of 2004," IDF Spokesperson's Office (April 19, 2005), http://www1.idf.il/SIP_STORAGE/DOVER/files/6/37876.pdf, accessed April 19, 2005.

17. These weapons, transported on the Santorini and Karine-A merchant vessels, were intercepted by Israeli forces. See "Weapons Found on 'Karine-A' and 'Santorini,'" *War Online* (July 20, 2002), http://www.waronlineorg/en/analysis/pal_weapons.htm, accessed January 20, 2005.

18. See Clive Jones, "'One Size Fits All': Israel, Intelligence, and the *Al-Aqsa Intifada*," *Studies in Conflict and Terrorism*, vol. 26, no. 4 (July–August 2003), 273–88.

19. "Israel Chief of Staff Speaks His Mind," *IsraelBehindTheNews.com*, August 23, 2002, http://israelvisit.co.il/cgi-bin/friendly.pl?url=Aug-23-02!IDF, accessed May 1, 2007.

20. See Gal Hirsh, "On Dinosaurs and Hornets: A Critical View on Operational Moulds in Asymmetric Conflict," *RUSI Journal* (August 2003), 60–3.

21. For a detailed overview of these and other units and of their operational capabilities see www.isayeret.com.

22. See Edward H. Kaplan et al, "What Happened to Suicide Bombings in Israel? Insights from a Terror Stock Model," *Studies in Conflict and Terrorism*, vol. 28, no. 3 (May 2005), 225–35.

23. Amos Harel, "Razing terrorists' houses is effective, army says," *Ha'aretz* (December 9, 2002).

24. Matthew Gutman, "Destruction, Constructively Speaking," *Jerusalem Post* (January 9, 2003).

25. "Statistics on punitive house demolitions," Bt'Selem, http://www.btselem.org/english/Punitive_Demolitions/Statistics.asp, accessed May 22, 2005; and "Ebb and Flow: A Summary of 2004."

26. Major General Amos Gilad, "Inside the Maelstrom," *The Review*, vol. 27, no. 12 (December 2002), 13.

27. At the Hotel Park in Netanya a Hamas suicide bomber managed to kill 29 Israelis and injure another 150.

28. "Sharon Equates Intifada and Terror," *The Middle East Reporter*, vol. 101, no. 1171 (December 15, 2001), 10.

29. Shaul Mofaz, "Operation *Defensive Shield*: Lessons and Aftermath," Peacewatch no. 387, The Washington Institute for Near East Policy (Washington, D.C., June 18, 2002), www.washingtoninstitute.org/watch/Peacewatch/peacewatch2002/387.htm, accessed October 6, 2002.

30. Major General Moshe Yaalon, "On the Offensive," *The Review*, vol. 27, no. 9 (September 2002), 11.

31. Shlomo Brom, "Operation 'Defensive Shield:' An Interim Assessment," *Tel Aviv Notes*, 35 (Tel Aviv: Jaffee Center for Strategic Studies, April 11, 2002), 1.

32. Yagil Henkin, "Urban Warfare and the Lessons of Jenin," *Azure*, vol. 15 (Summer 2003), http://www.shalem.org.il/azure/15-henkin.htm, accessed May 23, 2003.

33. Barbara Opall-Rome, "Israel Redefines Tactics," *Defense News* (June 16, 2002).

34. David Eshel, "Israel Hones Intelligence Operations to Counter Intifada," *Jane's Intelligence Review*, vol. 14, no. 10 (October 2002), 24.

35. Steve Rodan, "IDF Steps Up Intelligence War against Palestinians," *Jane's Defence Weekly*, vol. 35, no. 2 (January 2001), 19.

36. Robert Wall and David A. Fulghum, "IAF to Modify Helos to Fight in Cities," *Aviation Week & Space Technology*, vol. 156, no. 19 (May 13, 2002), 27.

37. Ibid.

38. Barbara Opall-Rome, "Israeli leaders to move to combat negative perceptions," *Defense News* (July 22, 2001).

39. Hirsh Goodman and Jonathan Cummings, *The Battle of Jenin: A Case Study in Israel's Communications Strategy, Memorandum No. 63* (Tel Aviv: Jaffee Center for Strategic Studies, January 2003), 22.

40. See Baruch Nevo and Yael Shur, *The IDF and the Press During Hostilities* (Jerusalem: The Israel Democracy Institute, 2003).

41. "Statistics on Palestinians in the custody of the Israeli security forces," Bt'Selem, http://www.btselem.org/eng/statistics/Detainees_and_Prisoners.asp, accessed May 15, 2007.

42. See Arieh O'Sullivan, "IDF: 44% Fall in Terror Victims," *Jerusalem Post* (December 30, 2004).

43. See Sergio Catignani, "Israel Defence Forces Organizational Changes in an Era of Budgetary Cutbacks," *The RUSI Journal*, vol. 149, no. 5 (October 2004), 72–6.

44. See Amos Guiora, "Balancing IDF Checkpoints and International Law: Teaching the IDF Code of Conduct," *Jerusalem Issue Brief*, no.3 (Institute of Contemporary Affairs, November 19, 2003), http://www.jcpa.org/brief/brief3-8.htm, accessed November 11, 2004.

45. Lt Col Timna Shmueli, Head of IDF School of Leadership Development, interview with author (Netanya, Israel, August 19, 2004).

46. For soldiers' personal accounts of abusive and unprofessional actions carried out by IDF units in the Territories see *Testimonial Booklet No. 2, Breaking the Silence*, http://www.shovrimshtika.org/public/ptihabeesh-englishforweb.pdf, accessed April 3, 2007.

47. A "kinetic" military operation is one that primarily uses firepower to achieve its objectives as opposed to psychological or media-led strategies.

48. See Sergio Catignani, "The Strategic Impasse in Low-Intensity Conflicts: The Gap between Israeli Counter-Insurgency Strategy and Tactics during the *Al-Aqsa Intifada*," *Journal of Strategic Studies*, vol. 28, no. 1 (February 2005), 57–75.

49. See Amos Harel and Avi Yissacharoff, *The Seventh War: How We Won and Why We Lost the War with the Palestinians* (Jerusalem: Gefen Publishing, 2004), 328 (in Hebrew).

50. Caroline B. Glick, "Sharon: No Military Solution to the War with the Palestinians," *Jerusalem Post* (September 26, 2002).

51. See Robert J. Brym and Bader Araj, "Suicide Bombing as Strategy and Interaction: The Case of the Second Intifada," *Social Forces*, vol. 84, no. 4 (June 2006), 1969–86.

52.   Yaacov Bar-Siman-Tov, *The Israeli-Palestinian Violent Confrontation*, 52.
53.   While the IDF's activities encouraged Palestinian radicalization, one cannot discount the fact that the PLO's rampant corruption played an important part in encouraging support for Hamas, to its detriment.

CHAPTER 12: LESSONS IN 21ST CENTURY COUNTERINSURGENCY

1.   In 2006, Anthony Cordesman, a defense policy analyst with the Center for Strategic and International Studies (CSIS), visited Afghanistan. In the briefing paper produced after his trip, he identified the following weaknesses in the central government at that time: 1. Continuing tension between the government in Kabul and regional groups. 2. Lack of qualified officials; lack of depth in actual government. 3. Corruption and nepotism. 4. Impact of dependence on narco-economy, backlash against it. 5. Weakness, corruption and ineffectiveness of justice system and police. 6. Pashtun tensions with other groups. 7. Resentment of modernization and reform. 8. Poor quality of governance; failure to provide effective services and presence in field (water, roads, schools, health and security). 9. Critical infrastructure and water problems. 10. Lack of economic progress and reform, scale of aid program, and government activity. See Anthony Cordesman, "Winning in Afghanistan: How to Face the Rising Threat," CSIS, December 12, 2006.
2.   Pashtuns comprise 40–45 percent of the population of Afghanistan; Tajiks 25–28 percent; and Hazaras and Uzbeks about 9 percent each.
3.   See Ahmed Rashid, *Taliban: The Story of the Afghan Warlords* (Oxford: Pan Books, 2001), 21.
4.   For detailed discussion of the Taliban, see William Maley, (ed.), *Fundamentalism Reborn? Afghanistan and the Taliban* (London: C Hurst, 1998); Peter Marsden, *The Taliban: War, Religion and the New Order in Afghanistan* (London: Zed Books, 1998); and Rashid, *Taliban*.
5.   Rashid, *Taliban*, 35.
6.   See Rashid, *Taliban*, for a key discussion of the Taliban's rise to power.
7.   The Taliban's Pashtun support came mostly from the Durrani tribe. The Ghizalis, from the eastern part of Afghanistan, included many Mujahideen veterans. They were included in the Pashtun sweep north, but their concerns about the Taliban's religious motivations meant that their support was generally considered weak.
8.   Rashid, *Taliban*, 3–50.
9.   Ibid., 79–80.
10.   Bob Woodward, *Bush at War* (New York: Simon & Schuster, 2002), 201–2.
11.   Hy S. Rothstein, *Afghanistan & the Troubled Future of Unconventional Warfare* (Annapolis, MD: Naval Institute Press, 2006), 11–13.
12.   Rothstein, 13–14. For an in-depth discussion of the role of firepower, air power, and Special Forces during this period, see Stephen Biddle, "Afghanistan and the Future of War: Implications for Army and Defense Policy," (Carlisle, PA: Strategic Studies Institute (SSI), 2002). For a more detailed discussion of this phase, as well as follow-on operations, see *Operation Enduring Freedom: The US Army in Afghanistan* (US Army Center of Military History, 2006).
13.   Discussions with American and British Special Forces, 2005–07.

14. International Crisis Group (ICG), "Countering Afghanistan's Insurgency: No Quick Fixes" (November 2, 2006), http://www.crisisgroup.org/home/index.cfm?id=4485, 3.

15. Discussions with American officers, 2005–07. One officer, who had served as a liaison officer at the Royal Military Academy Sandhurst, gave lectures on his experiences in Afghanistan and Iraq. He emphasized that he had never been trained or even read material dealing with counterinsurgency prior to operations in Afghanistan.

16. For detailed discussion of the operation, see Stephen Biddle, "Afghanistan and the Future of Warfare;" also Sean Naylor, *Not a Good Day to Die* (New York: Penguin, 2005).

17. M. Evans, "Marines to Face Guerrilla Warfare as Taliban Fighters Change Tactics," *The Times* (March 21, 2002).

18. Rothstein, 143.

19. Colin Soloway, *Newsweek* (October 7, 2002). See also Lt Gen David Barno, "Fighting the Other War: Counterinsurgency Strategy in Afghanistan, 2003–2005," *Military Review* (September–October 2007), 32–33.

20. Sir Robert Thompson, *Defeating Communist Insurgency: Experiences from Malaya and Vietnam* (New York: Praeger, 1966).

21. Conversations with coalition military and civilian officials, 2006–07.

22. ICG, "Afghanistan: The Problem of Pashtun Alienation" (August 5, 2003), http://www.crisisgroup.org/home/index.cfm?id=1641&l=1, 2–3.

23. Ahmed Rashid, "Slow Western Aid Could Undermine Afghan Stability," *Eurasia Insight* (July 18, 2002).

24. Sean Maloney, "Afghanistan Four Years On: An Assessment," *Parameters* (Fall 2005), 23.

25. Ahmed Rashid, "Taliban's Second Coming," BBC (May 31, 2005).

26. ICG, "Countering," 4.

27. Ibid., p. 8.

28. The Senlis Council, "Countering the Insurgency in Afghanistan: Losing Friends and Making Enemies" (February 2007), http://www.senliscouncil.net/modules/publications/018_publication/The_Report, 40–2.

29. For further exploration of this concept, see Steve Metz and Ray Millen, "Insurgency and Counterinsurgency in the 21st Century: Reconceptualizing Threat and Response" (Carlisle Barracks, PA: SSI, November 2004), 2–3, http://www.strategicstudiesinstitute.army.mil/pubs/display.cfm?pubID=586.

30. Ali Jalali, "The Future of Afghanistan," *Parameters* (2006), 8 and Senlis, "Countering," 42.

31. See Joshua Hammer, "After Musharraf," *Atlantic Monthly* (October 2007).

32. Thompson, 106.

33. See Lt Gen David Barno, "Fighting the Other War."

34. Rothstein, 111; also see Rashid, ICG generally, and others for more detailed discussion of this issue. Many US officers have also commented on this.

35. Interviews with NATO and US military personnel, 2005–07.

36. Maloney, "Afghanistan Four Years On," 25.

37. ICG, "Countering," 3.

38. Meetings with many members of ISAF confirm lack of training.

39. Lt Gen David Richards, *NATO Review* (Spring 2007),
http://www.nato.int/docu/review/2007/issue1/english/art1.html
40. It is not a wholly new idea as it has its roots in the CORDS program in
Vietnam and can also be linked to the SAS formations in Algeria. Many
articles have been written describing the history and development of the
PRTS in RUSI, IISS, *Parameters*, *Military Review*, and United States
Institute of Peace. See also Major Andrew Roe, "To Create a Stable
Afghanistan: Provisional Reconstruction Teams, Good Governance, and a
Splash of History," *Military Review* (November–December 2005).
41. Jalali, "The Future of Afghanistan," 6.
42. Barnett Rubin, "Afghanistan's Uncertain Transition from Turmoil to
Normalcy," *Council on Foreign Relations*, CSR no. 12 (March 2006), 19.
43. Richards, http://www.nato.int/docu/review/2007/issue1/english/art1.html.
44. ICG, "Countering," 21.
45. Barno, *Fighting the Other War*, 43.
46. ICG, "Countering," 15.
47. See ICG, Cordesman, and Jalali for more discussion.
48. Conversations with British and Canadian officers as well as ICG,
"Countering," 17.
49. See Ali Jalali, "Rebuilding Afghanistan's National Army," *Parameters*
(2002) for a good background to the history of the army in Afghanistan pre-
1996, and for the early efforts of raising the ANA. See ICG, "Countering,"
Cordesman, and Maloney for more discussion of current state of affairs.
50. Maloney, "Afghanistan Four Years On," 25.
51. Officer and NCO education and training were key to this development. As
of 2007, the US was in charge of a four-year "War College" for so-called
"high flyers" in Afghanistan. The British were in charge of the six-month
platoon commanders' course for the vast majority of the army.
52. Conversations with American, Australian, British, and Canadian military
personnel, 2006–07.
53. The following information comes from various conversations with the
British veterans of *Herrick IV*.
54. See Peter van Ham and Jurrit Kamminga, "Poppies for Peace: Reforming
Afghanistan's Opium Industry," *Washington Quarterly* (Winter 2006–07);
Senlis Council, "Helmand at War," and ICG, "Countering."
55. 3 PARA carried out counterinsurgency study days to understand the
complexity of the issues they were facing. They also carried out additional
training before deployment.
56. Conversations with British Army personnel, 2006–07.
57. Peter von Ham and Jurrit Kamminga, "Poppies for Peace."
58. Gen Sir Frank Kitson, *Bunch of Five* (London: Faber and Faber, 1977), 283.
59. Discussions with American, British, and Canadian officers and units, 2006–07.

CHAPTER 13: COUNTERINSURGENCY IN IRAQ

1. For information on the conventional war, see Michael Gordon and Bernard
Trainor, *Cobra II: The Inside Story of the Invasion and Occupation of Iraq*
(New York: Pantheon Books, 2006).

2. For background on the history of Iraq, including its sectarian divisions, see Phebe Marr, *The Modern History of Iraq* (Boulder, CO: Westview Press, 2004).

3. Zarqawi letter, www.cpa-iraq.org/transcripts/20040212_zarqawi_full.html.

4. L. Paul Bremer, *My Year in Iraq: The Struggle to Build a Future of Hope* (New York: Simon & Schuster, 2006), 213, 302, 330, and Bob Woodward, *State of Denial: Bush at War, Part III* (New York: Simon & Schuster, 2006), 229.

5. Thomas Ricks, *Fiasco: The American Military Adventure in Iraq* (New York: Penguin, 2006), 233–4, 283. "Clash of Cultures Fuels Low-Level War of Increasing Animosity," *London Financial Times* (June 2, 2003).

6. Alissa Rubin and Patrick McDonnell, "U.S. Gunships Target Insurgents in Iraq Amid Copter Crash Inquiry," *Los Angeles Times* (November 19, 2003).

7. David Petraeus, "Learning Counterinsurgency: Observations from Soldiering in Iraq," *Military Review* (October 2006), 48.

8. Discussion with Maj Gen Andrew Graham, Camp Victory, September 8, 2004, and Multi-National Division Southeast, Basrah, November 30, 2004.

9. Bremer, *My Year in Iraq*, 317.

10. Address by Lt Gen Ricardo Sanchez, Camp Fallujah, April 3, 2004, and I MEF Brief to Gen John Abizaid, Camp Fallujah, April 9, 2004.

11. Camp Fallujah, I MEF Refugee Planning Meeting, April 20, 2004.

12. Bremer, *My Year in Iraq*, 326–7, 333–4.

13. Report to Congress, "Measuring Stability and Security in Iraq" (Washington, D.C., July 2005), 6.

14. ICRSS Poll, April 20–29, 2004.

15. Discussions with 1st Battalion, 23rd Marine Regiments, Camp Al Asad, October 31, 2004.

16. Meeting with Lt Gen James Conway and Lt Gen John Sattler, Camp Fallujah, September 10, 2004.

17. Again, the fighting spread to other cities. British battalions in Basrah and Al Amarah experienced heavy fighting putting down the uprising, having to conduct air strikes and patrol in Warrior fighting vehicles and Challenger 2 tanks to deal with the militia attacks.

18. Fallujah Confirmation Brief to Gen Casey and Lt Gen Metz, Camp Fallujah, November 5, 2004.

19. For further information see John Sattler and Daniel Wilson, "Operation Al Fajr: The Battle of Fallujah – Part II," *Marine Corps Gazette* (July 2005), 12–24, and Bing West, *No True Glory: A Frontline Account of the Battle for Fallujah* (New York: Bantam Books, 2005).

20. Ambassador Zalmay Khalilzad, press release, October 26, 2005, and speech on Iraq's Constitution, August 1, 2005.

21. George Packer, "The Lesson of Tal Afar," *New Yorker*, vol. 82, no. 8 (April 10, 2006).

22. Chris Gibson, "Battlefield Victories and Strategic Success: The Path Forward in Iraq," *Military Review* (September–October 2006), 50–5.

23. H. R. McMaster, Georgetown University, December 2006.

24. Discussions with 3rd Battalion, 6th Marine Regiment (3/6), Camp Al Qa'im, February 21, 2006.

25. Ibid.

26. Discussions with 3/6, Camp Al Qa'im, February 21, 2006, and with 3rd Brigade, 7th Iraqi Brigade military transition team, Camp Al Asad, July 15, 2006.

27. Josh White, "Report on Haditha Condemns Marines," *Washington Post* (April 21, 2007).

28. Mental Health Advisory Team IV Final Report, Office of the Surgeon General, US Army Medical Command (November 17, 2006), 35.

29. Al Anbar Survey 11: September/October 2006 (October 2006); Al Anbar Survey 7: May 2006, Lincoln Group Survey Report (June 10, 2006).

30. World Public Opinion Poll, www.worldpublicopinion.org (January 2–5, 2006). 75% of Sunnis had little confidence in the Iraqi Army according to Iraq Poll 2007, BBC, ABC News, ARD German TV, *USA Today* (March 2007).

31. World Public Opinion Poll; Iraq Poll, BBC, ABC News, ARD German TV, *USA Today* (March 2007).

32. Gen George Casey, Brief to I Marine Expeditionary Force, Camp Fallujah, March 18, 2006.

33. Brief to the Commandant of the Marine Corps, Camp Fallujah, April 11, 2006.

34. Solomon Moore and Julian Barnes, "Many Iraqi Troops are No-Shows in Baghdad," *Los Angeles Times* (September 23, 2006).

35. John Burns, "U.S. Says Violence in Baghdad Rises, Foiling Campaign," *New York Times* (October 2, 2006).

36. Lt Gen Michael Maples, DIA Testimony to the Senate Armed Services Committee (Washington, D.C., November 15, 2006).

37. Fallujah City Council Meeting, Mayor's Complex, July 25, 2006.

38. Discussion with Fallujah city leaders, Fallujah CMOC, August 1, 2006.

39. Iraq Poll, BBC, ABC News, ARD German TV, *USA Today* (March 2007).

40. Vali Nasr, "When the Shiites Rise," *Foreign Affairs* (July/August 2006).

41. General David Petraeus, Note to Troops (March 19, 2007).

BIBLIOGRAPHY

CHAPTER 1: IN AID OF THE CIVIL POWER

Bowden, Tom, *The Breakdown of Public Security* (London: Sage, 1977)

Charters, David, *The British Army and the Jewish Insurgency 1945–47* (Houndmills, Basingstoke: Macmillan Press in association with King's College, London, 1989)

Cohen, Michael, *Palestine: Retreat from the Mandate. The Making of British Policy 1936–1945* (London: P. Elek, 1978)

Gwynn, Sir Charles, *Imperial Policing* (London: Macmillan and Co., Ltd., 1934)

Hoffman, Bruce, *The Failure of British Military Strategy within Palestine 1939–1947* (Ramat-Gan, Israel: Bar-Ilan University Press, 1983)

Mockaitis, Thomas, *British Counterinsurgency, 1919–60* (Houndmills, Basingstoke, Hampshire: Macmillan, in association with King's College, London, 1990)

Seith, Andrew, "Ireland and Insurgency: the Lessons of History," *Small Wars and Insurgencies,* vol. 2, no. 2 (1991), 299–322

Shepherd, Naomi, *Ploughing Sand: British Rule in Palestine* (London: John Murray, 1999)

Simson, H., *British Rule, and Rebellion* (Edinburgh and London: W. Blackwood & Sons, 1937)

Townshend, Charles, *The British Campaign in Ireland 1919–1921* (London and New York: Oxford University Press, 1975)

Townshend, Charles, "The Irish Insurgency 1918–21: the Military Problem," in R. Haycock, (ed.), *Regular Armies and Insurgency* (London: Croom Helm, 1979)

Townshend, Charles, *Britain's Civil Wars: Counterinsurgency in the Twentieth Century* (London and Boston: Faber and Faber, 1986)

Townshend, Charles, "The Defence of Palestine: Insurrection and Public Security, 1936–39," *English Historical Review,* vol. 103, no. 409 (1988)

CHAPTER 2: COUNTERINSURGENCY IN THE PHILIPPINES, 1898-1954

Funston, Frederick, *Memories of Two Wars* (London: Constable and Company, 1912)

Gates, John M. *Schoolbooks and Krags: The United States Army in the Philippines, 1899–1902* (Westport, CT: Greenwood Press, 1973)

Kerkvliet, Benedict J., *The Huk Rebellion: A Study of Peasant Revolt in the Philippines* (Berkeley, CA: University of California Press, 1977)

Lansdale, Edward G., *In the Midst of Wars: An American's Mission to Southeast Asia* (New York: Harper and Row, 1972)

Linn, Brian McAllister, *The United States Army and Counterinsurgency in the Philippine War, 1899–1902* (Chapel Hill, NC: University of North Carolina Press, 1989)

Linn, Brian McAllister, *The Philippine War, 1899–1902* (Lawrence, KS: University Press of Kansas, 2000)

May, Glenn A., *Battle for Batangas: A Philippine Province at War* (Quezon City: New Day Press, 1993)

Romulo, Carlos P., *Crusade in Asia* (New York: John Day, 1955)

Smith, Robert R., *The Hukbalahap Insurgency: Economic, Political and Military Factors* (Washington, D.C: The Chief of the Office of Military History, 1963)

Taruc, Luis., *He Who Rides the Tiger* (New York: Praeger, 1967)

CHAPTER 3: THE FIRST OF THE BANANA WARS

Bickel, Keith B., *Mars Learning: The Marine Corps Development of Small Wars Doctrine, 1915–1940* (Boulder: Westview, 2001)

Ellsworth, Harry A., *One Hundred Eighty Landings of United States Marines, 1800–1934* (Washington, D.C: US Marine Corps, 1934)

Grimmett, Richard F., *Instances of Use of United States Armed Forces Abroad, 1798–2004* (Washington, D.C: Congressional Research Service, 2004)

Langley, Lester D., *The Banana Wars: United States Intervention in the Caribbean, 1898–1934* (Lexington: University Press of Kentucky, 1983)

Livermore, Seward W., "Theodore Roosevelt, the American Navy and the Venezuela Crisis of 1902–1903," *The American Historical Review* (April 1946)

Mahan, Alfred Thayer, *Lessons of the War with Spain* (Freeport: Books for Libraries Press, 1970)

Mahan, Alfred Thayer, *The Problem of Asia* (Boston: Little Brown, 1905)

Munro, Dana G., *The Five Republics of Central America* (New York: Oxford University Press, 1919)

Root, Elihu, *Latin America and the United States* (Cambridge: Harvard University Press, 1917)

Thomas, Lowell, *Old Gimlet Eye, The Adventures of Smedley D. Butler* (New York: Farrar and Rinehart, 1981)

Yerxa, Donald A., *Admirals and Empire, the United States Navy and the Caribbean, 1898–1945* (Columbia, SC: The University of South Carolina Press, 1991)

CHAPTER 4: FEW CARROTS AND A LOT OF STICKS

Armstrong, John A., (ed.), *Soviet Partisans in World War II* (Madison: The University of Wisconsin Press, 1964)

Gerlach, Christian, *Kalkulierte Morde: Die deutsche Wirtschafts- und Vernichtungspolitik in Weißrussland 1941 bis 1944* (Hamburg: Hamburger Edition, 1999)

Hesse, Erich, *Der sowjetrussische Partisanenkrieg im Spiegel deutscher Kampfanweisungen*, 2nd edition (Göttingen: Musterschmidt Verlag, 1993)

Hill, Alexander, *The War behind the Eastern Front: The Soviet Partisan Movement in North-West Russia 1941–1944* (London and New York: Frank Cass, 2005)

Hürter, Johannes, *Hitlers Heerführer: Die deutschen Oberbefehlshaber im Krieg gegen die Sowjetunion 1941/42* (Munich: Oldenbourg Verlag, 2006)

Kedward, Harry R., *In Search of the Maquis: Rural Resistance in Southern France 1942–1944* (Oxford: Clarendon Press, 1993)

Lieb, Peter, *Konventioneller Krieg oder NS-Weltanschauungskrieg? Kriegführung und Partisanenbekämpfung in Frankreich 1943/44* (Munich: Oldenbourg Verlag, 2007)

Militärgeschichtliches Forschungsamt (Research Institute for Military History), (ed.), *Germany and the Second World War* (Oxford: Clarendon Press, 1990)

Schulte, Theo, *The German Army and Nazi Policies in Occupied Russia* (Oxford: Berg, 1989)

Shepard, Ben, *War in the Wild East: The German Army and Soviet Partisans* (Cambridge, MA, and London: Harvard University Press, 2004)

CHAPTER 5: FRENCH IMPERIAL WARFARE 1945-62

Ageron, Charles-Robert, *La guerre d'Algérie et les Algériens 1954–1962* (Paris: Armand Colin, 1997)

Branche, Raphaëlle, *La Guerre d'Algérie: une histoire apaisée?* (Paris: Editions du Senil, 2005)

Dalloz, Jacques, *The War in Indochina 1945–1954* (London: Rowand and Littlefield, 1990)

Fleury, Georges, *La guerre d'Indochine* (Paris: Perrin, 2003)

Gras, Gen Yves, *Histoire de la guerre d'Indochine* (Paris: Plon 1979)

Harbi, Mohammed, and Stora, Benjamin, *La guerre d'Algérie 1954–2000: La fin de l'amnésie* (Paris: Robert Laffont, 2004)

Horne, Alistair, *A Savage War of Peace: Algeria 1954–1962* (London: Macmillan, 1977)

House, Jim, and Macmaster, Niel, *Paris 1961: Algerians, State Terror and Memory* (Oxford: Oxford University Press, 2006)

Jaufret, Jean-Charles, and Vaïsse, Maurice, *Militaires et guerilla dans la guerre d'Algérie* (Paris: Editions Complexe, 2001)

Kerchouche, Dalia, *Mon père, ce harki* (Paris: Editions du Senil, 2003)

Paret, Peter, *French Revolutionary Warfare from Indochina to Algeria: The Analysis of a Political and Military Doctrine* (New York: Praeger, 1964)

Porch, Douglas, *The French Foreign Legion: A Complete History* (London: Macmillan, 1991)

Rioux, Jean-Pierre, *La guerre d'Algérie et les Français* (Paris: Fayard, 1990)

Thénault, Sylvie, *Histoire de la guerre d'indépendance Algérienne* (Paris: Flammarion, 2005)

Windrow, Martin, *The Last Valley: Dien Bien Phu and the French Defeat in Indochina* (New York: Da Capo Press: 2006)

CHAPTER 6: FROM SEARCH AND DESTROY TO HEARTS AND MINDS

Barber, Noel, *The War of the Running Dogs: How Malaya Defeated the Communist Guerrillas, 1948–60* (London: Collins, 1971)

Chin, C. C. and Hack, Karl, (eds.), *Dialogues with Chin Peng: New Light on the Malayan Communist Party* (Singapore: Singapore University Press, 2004)

Chin, Peng, *My Side of the Story* (Singapore: Media Masters, 2003)

Cloake, John, *Templer: Tiger of Malaya: The Life of Field Marshal Sir Gerald Templer* (London: Harrap, 1985)

Clutterbuck, Richard L., *The Long Long War: Counterinsurgency in Malaya and Vietnam* (New York: Praeger, 1966)

Coates, John, *Suppressing Insurgency: An Analysis of the Malayan Emergency, 1948–54* (Boulder: Westview Press, 1992)

Mackay, David, *The Malayan Emergency 1948–60: The Domino That Stood* (London: Brassey's, 1997)

Nagl, John A., *Learning to Eat Soup with a Knife: Counterinsurgency Lessons from Malaya and Vietnam* (Westport, CT: Praeger, 2002)

Pye, Lucian W., *Guerrilla Communism in Malaya: Its Social and Political Meaning* (Princeton, NJ: Princeton University Press, 1956)

Ramakrishna, Kumar., *Emergency Propaganda: The Winning of Malayan Hearts and Minds 1948–1958* (Richmond, VA: Curzon, 2002)

Short, Anthony, *The Communist Insurrection in Malaya 1948–60* (London: Frederick Muller, 1975), republished as *In Pursuit of Mountain Rats: The Communist Insurrection in Malaya* (Singapore: Cultured Lotus, 2000)

Stewart, Brian, *Smashing Terrorism in the Malayan Emergency: The Vital Contribution of the Police* (Subang Jaya, Selangor: Pelanduk Publications, 2004)

Stockwell, A. J., (ed.), *Malaya: Part II, The Communist Insurrection 1948–1953* (London: HMSO, 1995)

Stubbs, Richard, *Hearts and Minds in Guerrilla Warfare: The Malayan Emergency 1948–1960* (Singapore: Oxford University Press, 1989; repr. Marshall Cavendish, 2004)

Thompson, Robert, *Defeating Communist Insurgency: Experiences from Malaya and Vietnam* (London: Chatto and Windus, 1966)

CHAPTER 7: COUNTERINSURGENCY IN VIETNAM

Blaufarb, Douglas S., *The Counterinsurgency Era: U.S. Doctrine and Performance 1950 to the Present* (New York: The Free Press, 1977)

Gelb, Leslie H., with Betts, Richard K., *The Irony of Vietnam: The System Worked* (Washington, D.C: Brookings, 1979)

Halberstam, David, *The Best and the Brightest* (New York: Fawcett Crest, 1972)

Halberstam, David, *War in a Time of Peace* (New York: Bloomsbury Publishing, 2003)

Karnow, Stanley, *Vietnam: A History* (New York: Viking, 1983)

Komer, Robert W., *Bureaucracy at War* (Oxford: Westview, 1986)

Krepinevich, Andrew, *The Army and Vietnam* (Baltimore: Johns Hopkins University Press, 1986)

Lewy, Guenter, *America in Vietnam* (Oxford: Oxford University Press, 1978)

Moore, Harold G., and Galloway, Joseph, *We Were Soldiers Once... And Young* (New York: Random House, 1992)

Moyar, Mark, *Triumph Forsaken: The Vietnam War, 1954–1965* (Cambridge: Cambridge University Press, 2006)

Nagl, John A., *Learning to Eat Soup with a Knife: Counterinsurgency Lessons from Malaya and Vietnam* (Westport, CT: Praeger, 2002)

Race, Jeffrey, *War Comes to Long An: Revolutionary Conflict in a Vietnamese Province* (Berkeley, CA: University of California Press, 1972)

Sheehan, Neil, et al, (eds.), *A Bright Shining Lie: John Paul Vann and America in Vietnam* (New York: Vintage Books, 1988)

Sheehan, Neil, et al, (eds.), *The Pentagon Papers* (The *New York Times* Edition) (New York: Bantam, 1971)

Sorley, Lewis, *A Better War: The Unexamined Victories and Final Tragedy of America's Last Years in Vietnam* (New York: Harvest Books, 2007)

Summers, Harry R., *On Strategy: A Critical Analysis of the Vietnam War* (Novato, CA: Presidio, 1981)

Tilford, Earl, *Crosswinds: The Air Force's Setup in Vietnam* (College Station, TX: Texas A & M University Press, 1993)

Westmoreland, William C., *A Soldier Reports* (New York: Da Capo, 1989)

CHAPTER 8: RED WOLVES AND BRITISH LIONS

Darby, Phillip, *British Defence Policy, East of Suez 1947–68* (London: Oxford University Press, 1973)

Hinchcliffe, Peter, Ducker, John, and Holt, Maria, *Without Glory in Arabia: The British Retreat from Aden* (London: IB Tauris, 2006)

Lackner, Helen, *PDR Yemen: Outpost of Socialist Development in Arabia* (London: Ithaca Press, 1985)

Ledger, David, *Shifting Sands: The British in South Arabia* (London: Peninsular Publishing, 1983)

Lee, Air Chief Marshal Sir David, *Flight from the Middle East – A History of the Royal Air Force in the Middle East* (London: HMSO, 1980)

Lord, Cliff, and Birtles, David. *The Armed Forces of Aden 1839–1967* (Solihull: Helion, 2000)

Mitchell, Lt Col Colin, *Having Been a Soldier* (London: Hamish Hamilton, 1969)

Paget, Julian, *Last Post: Aden 1964–1967* (London: Faber & Faber, 1969)

Pridham, B. R., (ed.), *Contemporary Yemen: Politics and Historical Background* (London: Croom Helm, 1984)

Verrier, Anthony, *Through the Looking-Glass: British Foreign Policy in an Age of Illusions* (New York: W. W. Norton, 1983)

Walker, Jonathan, *Aden Insurgency: The Savage War in South Arabia* (Staplehurst: Spellmount, 2005)

CHAPTER 9: BRITAIN'S LONGEST WAR

Beresford, David, *Ten Men Dead* (London: Harper Collins, 1994)

Bowyer Bell, J., *The Secret Army: The IRA*, rev. 3rd edition (Dublin: Poolbeg, 1998)

O'Brien, Brendan. *The Long War – The IRA and Sinn Féin from Armed Struggle to Peace Talks* (Dublin: O'Brien Press, 1995)

Bruce, Steve, *The Red Hand: Loyalist Paramilitaries in Northern Ireland* (Oxford: Oxford University Press, 1992)

Coogan, Tim Pat, *The Troubles* (London: Random House, 1996)

Dillon, Martin, *25 Years of Terror – the IRA's War against the British* (London: Bantam, 1996)

English, Richard, *Armed Struggle: The History of the IRA* (London: Macmillan, 2004)

Geraghty, Tony, *The Irish War* (London: HarperCollins, 2000)

Harnden, Toby, *Bandit Country: The IRA and South Armagh* (London: Hodder and Stoughton, 1999)

Ingram, Martin, and Harkin, Greg, *Stakeknife* (Dublin: O'Brien Press, 2004)

MacGinty, Roger, and Darby, John, *Guns and Government: The Management of the Northern Ireland Peace Process* (London: Macmillan, 2002)

McKittrick, David et al, *Lost Lives: The stories of the men, women and children who died as a result of the Northern Ireland troubles* (London: Mainstream Publishing Company, 1999)

Mallie, Eamonn, and Bishop, Patrick, *The Provisional IRA* (London: Heinemann, 1987)

Moloney, Ed, *A Secret History of the IRA* (London: Penguin Books, 2002)

Myers, Kevin, *Watching the Door: A Memoir 1971–1978* (Dublin: Lilliput Press, 2006)

Taylor, Peter, *Provos – the IRA and Sinn Féin* (London: Bloomsbury, 1997)

Toolis, Kevin, *Rebel Hearts – Journeys within the IRA's Soul* (London: Picador, 1995)

UK Ministry of Defence, *Operation Banner: An Analysis of Military Operations in Northern Ireland* (General Staff Publication 71842, 2006)

CHAPTER 10: COUNTERING THE *CHIMURENGA*

Cilliers, J. K., *Counter-Insurgency in Rhodesia* (London: Croom Helm, 1985)

Cocks, Chris, *Fire Force: One Man's War in the Rhodesian Light Infantry* (Johannesburg: 30 Degrees South Publishers, 2006)

Cole, Barbara, *The Elite: The Story of the Rhodesian Special Air Service* (Amanzimtoti, South Africa: Three Knights Publishing, 1984)

Cowderoy, Dudley, and Nesbit, Roy, *War in the Air: Rhodesian Air Force 1935–1980* (Alberton: Galago, 1987)

Godwin, Peter, and Hancock, Ian, *'Rhodesians Never Die': The Impact of War and Political Change on White Rhodesia: 1970–1980* (Oxford: Oxford University Press, 1993)

McAleese, Peter, *No Mean Soldier* (London: Orion, 1993)

Martin, David, and Johnson, Phyllis, *The Struggle for Zimbabwe, The Chimurenga War* (Harare: Zimbabwe Publishing House, 1981)

Parker, Jim, *Assignment Selous Scouts: Inside Story of a Rhodesian Special Branch Officer* (Alberton: Galago, 2006)

Petter-Bowyer, P. J. H., *Winds of Destruction* (Johannesburg: 30 Degrees South Publishers, 2005)

Reid-Daly, Ron, *Top Secret War* (Alberton: Galago, 1982)

Smith, Ian Douglas, *The Great Betrayal* (London: Blake Publishing, 1997)

Venter, Al J., (ed.), *Challenge: Southern Africa within the African Revolutionary Context* (Johannesburg: Ashanti Publishing, 1989)

Wood, J. R. T., *The War Diaries of André Dennison* (Gibraltar: Ashanti Publishing, 1989)

Wood, J. R. T., *So Far and No Further! Rhodesia's Bid for Independence During the Retreat from Empire, 1959–1965* (Johannesburg: 30 Degrees South Publishers, 2006)

BIBLIOGRAPHY

CHAPTER 11: THE ISRAEL DEFENSE FORCES AND THE *AL-AQSA INTIFADA*

O'Balance, Edgar, *The Palestinian Intifada* (London: Macmillan Press, 1998)

Bar-Siman-Tov, Yaacov et al, *The Israeli-Palestinian Violent Confrontation 2000–2004: From Conflict Resolution to Conflict Management* (Jerusalem: Jerusalem Institute for Israel Studies, 2005)

Bregman, Ahron, *Elusive Peace: How the Holy Land Defeated America* (London: Penguin, 2005)

Catignani, Sergio, "Israel Defence Forces Organizational Changes in an Era of Budgetary Cutbacks," *The RUSI Journal*, vol. 149, no. 5 (October 2004)

Catignani, Sergio, "The Strategic Impasse in Low-Intensity Conflicts: The Gap between Israeli Counter-Insurgency Strategy and Tactics during the *Al-Aqsa Intifada*," *Journal of Strategic Studies*, vol. 28, no. 1 (February 2005), 57–75

Eshel, David, "The *Al-Aqsa Intifada*: Tactics and Strategies," *Jane's Intelligence Review*, vol. 13, no. 5 (May 2001)

Eshel, David, "Israel Refines its Pre-Emptive Approach to Counterterrorism," *Jane's Intelligence Review*, vol. 19, no. 2 (September 2002)

Goodman, Hirsh, and Cummings, Jonathan, *The Battle of Jenin: A Case Study in Israel's Communications Strategy,* Memorandum no. 63 (Tel Aviv: Jaffee Center for Strategic Studies, January 2003)

Harel, Amos, and Yissacharoff, Avi, *The Seventh War: How We Won and Why We Lost the War with the Palestinians* (Jerusalem: Gefen Publishing, 2004); in Hebrew

Horowitz, Dan, and Lissak, Moshe, *Trouble in Utopia: The Overburdened Polity of Israel* (New York: SUNY Press, 1989)

Jones, Clive, "'One Size Fits All': Israel, Intelligence, and the *Al-Aqsa Intifada*," *Studies in Conflict and Terrorism*, vol. 26, no. 4 (July–August 2003), 273–88

Nevo, Baruch, and Shur, Yael, *The IDF and the Press During Hostilities* (Jerusalem: The Israel Democracy Institute, 2003)

Opall-Rome, Barbara, "Israel redefines tactics," *Defense News* (June 16, 2002)

Sandler, Shmuel, and Frisch, Hillel, *Israel, the Palestinians and the West Bank: A Study in Intercommunal Conflict* (Toronto: Lexington Books, 1984)

Shalev, Aryeh, *The Intifada: Causes and Effects, Jaffee Centre for Strategic Studies Study 16* (Oxford: Westview Press, 1991)

Shay, Shaul, and Schweitzer, Yoram, "The *Al-Aqsa Intifada*: Palestinian-Israeli Confrontation," April 4, 2001, *International Institute for Counter-Terrorism*, <http://www.ict.org.il/apage/5363.php>

Sinai, Joshua, "Intifada Drives Both Sides to Radical Arms," *Jane's Intelligence Review*, vol. 13, no. 5 (May 2001)

CHAPTER 12: LESSONS IN 21ST CENTURY COUNTERINSURGENCY

Barno, Lt Gen David, "Fighting the Other War: Counterinsurgency Strategy in Afghanistan, 2003–2005," *Military Review* (September–October 2007)

Biddle, Stephen, "Afghanistan and the Future of War: Implications for Army and Defense Policy," (Carlisle, PA: Strategic Studies Institute, 2002)

Caroe, Olaf, *Pathans* (London: Macmillan, 1958)

van Ham, Peter, and Kamminga, Jurrit, "Poppies for Peace: Reforming Afghanistan's Opium Industry," *Washington Quarterly* (Winter 2006–07)

International Crisis Group, "Countering Afghanistan's Insurgency: No Quick Fixes" (November 2, 2006)

International Crisis Group, "Afghanistan: The Problem of Pashtun Alienation" (August 5, 2003), http://www.crisisgroup.org/home/index.cfm?id=1641&l=1

Jalali, Ali, "The Future of Afghanistan," *Parameters* (2006)

Jalali, Ali, "Rebuilding Afghanistan's National Army," *Parameters* (2002)

Maley, William, (ed.), *Fundamentalism Reborn? Afghanistan and the Taliban* (London: C. Hurst, 1998)

Maloney, Sean, "Afghanistan Four Years On: An Assessment," *Parameters* (Fall 2005)

Marsden, Peter, *The Taliban: War, Religion and the New Order in Afghanistan* (London: Zed Books, 1998)

Masters, John, *Bugles and a Tiger: A Personal Adventure* (London: M. Joseph, 1956)

Metz, Steve. and Millen, Ray, "Insurgency and Counterinsurgency in the 21st Century: Reconceptualizing Threat and Response" (Carlisle Barracks, PA: SSI, November 2004)

Naylor, Sean, *Not a Good Day to Die* (New York: Penguin, 2005)

Operation Enduring Freedom: The US Army in Afghanistan (US Army Center of Military History, 2006)

Rashid, Ahmed, *Taliban: The Story of the Afghan Warlords* (Oxford: Pan Books, 2001)

Ridgway, Richard, *Indian Army Handbooks: Pathans* (Calcutta: Government of India, 1910)

Roe, Maj Andrew, "To Create a Stable Afghanistan: Provisional Reconstruction Teams, Good Governance, and a Splash of History," *Military Review* (November–December 2005)

Rothstein, Hy S., *Afghanistan & the Troubled Future of Unconventional Warfare* (Annapolis, MD: Naval Institute Press, 2006)

Senlis Council, "Countering the Insurgency in Afghanistan: Losing Friends and Making Enemies" (February 2007), http://www.senliscouncil.net/modules/publications/018_publication/The_Report

Senlis Council, "Helmand at War," http://www.senliscouncil.net/modules/publications/010_publication

Woodward, Bob, *Bush at War* (New York: Simon & Schuster, 2002)

CHAPTER 13: COUNTERINSURGENCY IN IRAQ

Alwyn-Foster, Nigel, "Changing the Army for Counterinsurgency," *Military Review*, vol. 85, no. 6 (November–December 2005), 2–15

Batatu, Hanna, *The Old Social Classes and the Revolutionary Movements of Iraq: A Study of Iraq's Old Landed and Commercial Classes and of its Communists, Ba'athists and Free Officers* (London: Saqi, 2004)

Biddle, Stephen, "Seeing Baghdad, Thinking Saigon," *Foreign Affairs*, vol. 85, no. 2 (March/April 2006), 2–14

Chiarelli, Peter and Michaelis, Patrick, "Winning the Peace: The Requirement for Full-Spectrum Operations," *Military Review* (July–August 2005), 4–17

BIBLIOGRAPHY

Diamond, Larry, *Squandered Victory: The American Occupation and the Bungled Effort to Bring Democracy to Iraq* (New York: Times Books, 2005)

Fearon, James, "Iraq's Civil War," *Foreign Affairs*, vol. 86, no. 2 (March/April 2007), 2–15

The Iraq Study Group Report, United States Institute for Peace (December 2006)

Mahnken, Thomas, and Keaney, Thomas, (eds). *War in Iraq* (London: Routledge, 2007)

Packer, George, "The Lesson of Tal Afar," *The New Yorker*, vol. 82, no. 8 (April 10, 2006)

Ricks, Thomas, *Fiasco: The American Military Adventure in Iraq* (New York: Penguin, 2006)

Sattler, John, and Wilson, Daniel, "Operation Al Fajr: The Battle of Fallujah – Part II," *Marine Corps Gazette* (July 2005), 12–24

Shadid, Anthony, *Night Draws Near: Iraq's People in the Shadow of America's War* (New York: Picador, 2006)

Stewart, Rory, *Prince of the Marshes: And Other Occupational Hazards of a Year in Iraq* (Orlando, FL: Harcourt, 2006)

The U.S. Army/Marine Corps Counterinsurgency Field Manual (Chicago, IL: University of Chicago Press, 2007)

Woodward, Bob, *State of Denial: Bush at War, Part III* (New York: Simon & Schuster, 2006)

al-Zarqawi letter, www.cpa-iraq.org/transcripts/20040212_zarqawi_full.html

INDEX

References to maps and graphs are shown in **bold**

A Shau valley 144
Abd el-Kader 101
Abdel Aziz Rantisi 215
Abizaid, Gen John 242, 245, 247, 255–256
Abrams, Gen Creighton 17, 140–141, 143, 144
Abyan Cotton Scheme 154–155
Acheson, Dean 53
Adams, Gerry 171
Aden, conflict in 149–166, **152**
    Crater 160–162, 163–164
    interrogations 161–162
    mutiny 162–164
    origins 149–150
    Radfan campaign 150–158, 166
    urban warfare 158–160
    withdrawal 164–165
Aden, Tawahi district 160
Aden Armed Police 159, 162
Aden Police 159
Aden Protectorate Levies (APL) 155
Aden Special Branch 158–159, 161
Afghan Development Zone (ADZ) strategy 234–235
Afghan forces 235–236
Afghan government (Kabul) 221, 228, 229, 236, 240
Afghan National Army (ANA) 235, 236, 238
Afghan National Auxiliary Police (ANAP) 236
Afghan National Police (ANP) 235, 236
Afghan National Security Forces (ANSF) 233, 234
Afghanistan (2001–07) 132, 147, 220–240, **224**
    Camp Bastion 237
    coalition and Afghan security forces and reconstruction 230–236
        Afghan forces 235–236
        ISAF 231, 232–233, 234, 235, 236
        Operation *Enduring Freedom* 225, 231–232
        Provincial Reconstruction Teams (PRTs) 231, 232, 233–235, 236, 238, 239–240
    the community and the government 227–228
    Forward Operating Bases Robinson and Price 237
    the government and the community 227–228
    Helmand: a case study 236–239
    the insurgents 229–230
    operations to topple the Taliban (2001–02) 223–227
    opium trade 237
    pre-September 11, 2001 221–223
    reconstruction 231, 232, 233–235, 236, 238, 239–240
Afghanistan, Soviet invasion of 221
African National Congress (ANC) 187, 191–192, 201
African nationalists, Rhodesian 185, 186, 187, 191, 193, 198
Aguinaldo, Emilio 37, 38–39, 40, 41, 43, 44, 45, 46, 47, 53, 54
Ahmed Rashid 222, 228
Ahmed Shah Massoud, Gen. 221, 223
aircraft
    Cessna 337G "Lynx" 197
    Boeing B-52 Stratofortress 137, 138
    de Havilland Vampire 189
    Douglas DC-3 Dakota 189, 197
    English Electric Canberra 189, 197
    Hawker Hunter 153, 156, 157, 189, 197
    helicopters
        Aérospatiale Alouette III 189, 195
        attack 214
        Bristol Belvedere 151–153, 156
        Westland Wessex 151–153
    Junkers 52: 96
    in Malayan Emergency 125
    Unmanned Aerial Vehicle (UAV) 214
AirLand Battle Doctrine 147
Al Amarah 245, 246
Al Anbar province 248, 254, 256, 257
Al-Aqsa Intifada 205–206, 207, 209, 219
    coping with 216–218
Al-Aqsa Martyrs Brigade 208
al-Asnag, Abdullah 158, 160
al Maliki, Nuri 257
al-Mansoura Detention Center, Aden 161

Al Naqil 156
Al-Qaeda 223–224, 225, 226, 229, 231, 236, 242
Al-Qaeda in Iraq (AQI) 242, 251, 252, 254, 255, 256, 257
Al Qa'im 252, 253, 257, 258
al-Qassam, Shayzh Izz al din 29–30
al-Sha'abi, Qatan 158, 165, 166
al Sistani, Ayatollah Ali 242, 248–249
al Zarqawi, Abu Musab 242, 254, 255
Albu Mahal tribe 252, 257
Albu Nimr tribe 247
Alford, Lt Col Dale 252, 254
Algeria 82–83, 90, 91, 100–112, **102**
    barriers as COIN tactics 106
    Challe offensive 105, 109
    de Gaulle 110–111
    "free fire zones" 106
    French reaction 104–108
    Military Division, 10th 101
    resettlement 106–107
Algerian Communist Party (Parti communiste Algérien) 102
Algerian Muslims 100, 101–102, 103–104, 107, 108, 110, 111
Algerian nationalists 100 *see also* Front de Libération Nationale
Algiers 111
Algiers, "battle" of (1956) 108, 110
Allawi, Ayad 248, 249
Allenby, Gen Edmund 27
Alliance Party (Malaya) 126
Allum, P. K. 202
Alps, French 86
Altena Farm 193–194
America, Central 55, 56, 57, 58, 59, 61–62, 68
American Civil War (1861–65) 56
American War of Independence (1775–83) 55
Amnesty International 160, 161
amphibious vehicles, Alaska "weasels" and Mississippi "alligators" 98–99
Amritsar, action at (1919) 20
Anglo-Irish Agreement (1985) 172
Anglo-Irish Treaty (1921) 26
Anglo-Irish War (1913–22) 21–26, 35
Angola 196, 201
Ap Bac 135, 136
Arab Army apprentices 162
Arab Committee, Higher 30, 33
Arab-Israeli conflict 203, 204
Arafat, Yasser 204, 205, 206, 207–208, 209, 212
Armée de libération nationale (ALN) 102, 104, 106, 107, 108, 109
    katibas (companies) 103, 105
armored cars, Saladin 163
armored fighting vehicles, M2A2 Bradley 242, 252
Aufsichtsverwaltung (Supervision administration) 84
Aurès Mountains 101, 103, 105
Aussaresses, Gen 90
Ayad Allawi 248, 249

Baader-Meinhof gang 166
Ba'ath Party 242, 243, 257
Bac Can 96
Badr Corps 255, 256, 257
Baghdad 241, 246, 248, 249, 250, 255, 256, 258
    Sadr City 247
Baja California 58
Baker, James 258
Bakri Ridge 157
Balfour Declaration (1917) 27
Baltic Exchange 174
banana wars, first 55–69 *see also* Nicaragua
Banda, Hastings 186
Bank, Aaron 90
Bao Dai 96, 98
Baqubah 246
Bar-Siman-Tov, Yaacov 219
Barak, Ehud 204, 206, 207
Barfoot, Frank 191
Bargewell, Maj Gen Eldon 253
Barno, Lt Gen David 231, 235
base aéroterrestre (air-land base) 98, 99

Basrah 245, 246, 256
Bataan Death March 47
Batang Kali 115
Batiste, Maj Gen John 249
Bedouin "Oozlebarts" 32
Belfast 164, 176, 180, 182
Belgium 72
Bell, Brig Gen 43
Belorussia 75, 76, 77
Beswick, Lord 160
Bevollmächtigter der Bandenkampfverbände
  (Plenipotentiary of the Bandit Combat
  Formations) 79
Bien Hoa 134
bin Laden, Osama 223, 224
Binh Dinh Province 138–139
Birkenhead, Lord 26
"Black and Tans" 23, 24, 28, 29
Bloody Sunday 167
Bluefields, Nicaragua 64, 65, 69
Boer War, Second (1899–1902) 19–20, 42
Bolshevik insurgency 72, 73, 74
"bombing, proscription" 149, 153
Bong Son 138
Boucher, Maj Gen C. H. 115
Bremer, Paul 17, 242, 245
Briggs, Lt Gen Sir Harold 118, 119, 124, 126
"Briggs Plan" 118–119, 120
Bristol riots (1831) 20
Britain and modern armed resistance movements 19–36
British Army
  in Aden 151, 152–153, 155–156, 157, 161, 162–163,
    164–165, 166
  Air Assault Brigade, 16th 236, 237–238
  Argyll and Sutherland Bn 244
  Argyll and Sutherland Highlanders, 1st Bn (1 A & SH)
    162, 163–164
  Brigade, 16th 32
  Brigade, HQ 39: 157
  East Anglian Regiment 155, 157
  in Iraq 244, 246
  in Ireland (1913–22) 21, 22, 24, 26, 36
  Irish Command, General Staff of 26
  in Malaya 114, 116–117, 119–120, 125
  Maneuver Outreach Groups 238
  Middle East Command (MEC) 154, 156, 157, 159, 163,
    165–166
  Middle East Land Forces 153
  in Northern Ireland 167, 168, 169, 176–178, 180, 181,
    183
  Northern Ireland Training & Advisory Team (NITAT)
    180
  Operational Mentoring and Liaison Teams 238
  in Palestine 30, 31, 32–33, 36
    Special Night Squads (SNS) 31, 32
  Parachute Regiment, 3rd Bn (3 PARA) 155–156, 157,
    238
  Queen's Royal Lancers (15/5 L) 151
  "Radforce" 155–156, 157
  Royal Engineers, 12th Field Squadron 151
  Royal Horse Artillery, 3rd Regiment, J Battery (3 RHA)
    155
  Royal Northumberland Fusiliers, 1st Bn (1 RNF)
    162–163
  Royal Pioneer Corps 161
  Royal Tank Regiment, 4th (4 RTR) 155
  Special Air Service 162, 176, 177
  Special Air Service Regiment, 22, A Squadron (22 SAS)
    155
British Colonial Service 154
British Gendarmerie (Palestine) 28, 30
British South Africa Company 186
British South Africa Police (BSAP) 189, 198
  Central Intelligence Organization (CIO) 189, 191, 193,
    200, 202
  Police Anti-Terrorist Unit 189
  Police Reserve 189, 191
  Police Reserve Air Wing 189
  Special Branch 189, 192, 195, 197, 198
  Support Unit 189
British Special Forces 225, 226 see also British Army,
  Special Air Service

British strategy in Malaya, evolution of see Malaya,
  evolution of British strategy in
Bryan, William Jennings 44
bulldozers, armored D-9 213
Buon Enao 136
Burhanuddin Rabbani 221, 223
Bush, President George W. 223, 241, 256, 258
  Road Map peace plan (2002) 218
Butler, Maj Smedley D. 64, 66

Caldwell, Maj Gen William 256
Callwell, C. E. 13, 19
Cambodia 93, 95, 145–146
Camp David talks (2000) 204, 205, 206
Canadian Task Force 237
Cao Bang 97
"Cap Badge" mountain 155–156
Caracas 60
Caribbean Sea 55, 56, 57, 58, 59, 60, 61
Carpentier, Gen Marcel 97
Carrington, Lord 202
Casey, Gen George 248, 249, 250, 251, 252–253, 254,
  255–256, 258, 259
Catholics, Northern Ireland 168–169
Catignani, Dr Sergio 8, 203–219
Central Intelligence Agency (CIA) 136, 137, 140, 149, 221,
  223–224
Central Security Committee (Palestine) 35
Centre for Scientific and Industrial Research (South Africa) 194
Challe, Gen Maurice 109, 111
Challe offensives (1959) 105, 109
Chancery Court 25
Charters, David 35
Cherrière, Paul 105
Chiang Kai-shek 53
Chiarelli, Lt Gen Peter 249, 256
Chimoio, Mozambique 196
"Chimurenga, First" 186 see also Rhodesian
  counterinsurgency campaign
Chin Peng 114
Chinese Affairs Officers (in Malaya) 122
Chinese Communists 97, 116, 118
Chinese community in Malaya 113–114, 115–117,
  118–119, 127
Chinese nationalists 93
"Chinoyi, battle of" (1966) 191
Chirau, Chief Jeremiah 199
Chitepo, Herbert 194
Churchill, Winston 28, 29
CIA (Central Intelligence Agency) 136, 137, 140, 149, 221,
  223–224
CIDG (Civilian Irregular Defense Group) 136, 137, 140
Civil Operations and Revolutionary Development Support
  (CORDS) 141, 145
  "Chieu Hoi" program 145
civil power, in aid of 19–36
civil rights movement 168
Civilian Irregular Defense Group (CIDG) 136, 137, 140
Clausewitz, Karl von 20
Clinton, President Bill 175, 204
Coalition Provisional Authority (CPA) (Iraq) 242, 251
Cochinchina 93, 96, 99
Cogny, Gen René 99
Colby, William E. 90, 145
Cold War (1945–90) 92
Collins, Michael 23, 26
Colón 57
Combined Forces Command-Afghanistan (CFC-A) 231
Combined Joint Task Force 7 (CJTF-7) 242
Combined Joint Task Force-180 231
Comité de coordination et d'exécution (CCE) 102
Comité de la République Algérienne (CNRA) 102
Commonwealth Monitoring Force 202
Communist partisan movement 70
Communist Party 77, 82 see also Algerian Communist
  Party; French Communist Party; Malayan Communist
  Party; Philippine Communist Party
Communists 70, 75, 106 see also Chinese communists
Conduct of Anti-Terrorist Operations in Malaya, The 125
Constantine Plan 106, 107
Constantinois 101, 103, 104
Conway, Lt. Gen. James 244, 245, 248, 249

Corinto 65, 66
Cork 24, 25
Corregidor, battle of (1944) 47
counterinsurgency, history behind 13
counterinsurgency, ideas of 13–15
counterinsurgency campaigns, themes for examining the
  history of 16–18
Counterinsurgency Warfare: Theory and Practice 13–14
Coyotepe, battle of (1912) 67–68
Crater, Aden 160–162, 163–164
Culebra, Puerto Rico 58
Cumann na mBan 21–22
Cyprus 150
Cyprus Emergency 158, 159

d'Argenlieu, Adm Thierry 93
Dail Eirann 21, 22, 24
Danaba basin 155
Danish West Indies 56, 58
Dar es Salaam 188
Davis, 2Lt John 162–163
Dawood, Qasim 248
de Castries, Col Christian 99
de Gaulle, Charles 84, 100, 107, 109, 110–111
de Lattre de Tassigny, Gen Jean 97–98, 99
Defeating Communist Insurgency 14–15
Defence of the Realm Act (DORA) (1914) 22
Defence Order in Council (Palestine/Israel) 35
Derry (Londonderry) 168, 174, 176, 182
"desert zones" 80, 82
Dewey, Cdre George 39
Dhala, Amir of 150
Dhala Road 151, 154
Díaz, President Adolfo 65, 68
Dien Bien Phu, battle of (1954) 99–100, 101, 132
Dill, Lt Gen Sir John 30
Dominican Republic 56, 60–61, 69
Dowbiggin 29
Driberg, Tom 160
Dublin 24, 25, 26
  "Bloody Sunday" 25
Dublin District General Officer Commanding (GOC) 24, 25
Durand Line 221
Dyer, Gen. 20

Eikenberry, Gen Karl 228
Eiland, Maj. Gen Giora 206, 214
Eisenhower, Gen Dwight D. 88–89
Eksund, MV 173
El Coyotepe hill 67, 68
El Salvador 62, 147
Estrada, Juan J. 63–64, 65
ETA (Euskadi Ta Askatasuna) 166
Evetts, Brig John 31, 32
Evian accords (1962) 100, 111
Ewell, Lt Gen Julian 144

Fadhila Party 256
Fallujah 243, 246, 248, 249, 250, 256–257
Fallujah, first battle of (2004) 244–245, 246, 247
Fallujah, second battle of (2004) 249–250
Far East Land Forces Training Centre (FTC – Jungle Warfare
  School) 125
Farran, Maj Roy 162
Fatah-Tanzim 205, 206, 208
Fearless, HMS 191
Federal Party (Philippines) 43
Federal Regular Army (FRA) (Aden) 151, 152–153, 155, 157
  2nd Bn. 157
Fenians 22, 23
Fergusson, Bernard 34
Ferhat Abbas 104
Field, Winston 188
Field Manual 3–24 (US Army/USMC) 253, 258
Field Manual 100–5, Operations (US Army) 134
Filipinos 37, 38, 39, 40–41, 42, 43, 44, 45, 47, 54
Filipinos, Christian 46
Filipinos, "ilustrados" 38, 46, 54
Fletcher, WPC Yvonne 173
Florida Straits 55, 56
Flower, Ken 202
Force-17 205

Forces Françaises d'Interieur (FFI) 84, 86, 87, 88–89
Foreign Legion 95
Foreign Office (British) 155
  Information Research Department 153
Fort Morbut Interrogation Center, Aden 160, 161
Fourth Republic 92, 93, 105, 112, 107
France, FLN attacks in 111
France, Occupied, German anti-partisan warfare in
  (1943–44) 83–89, 85
France in early days of World War One 72
Franco-Prussian War (1870–71) 72
Francs-Tireurs ("Free-Shooters") 72, 74
Francs-Tireurs et Partisans Français (FTPF - French
  Free-Shooters and Partisans) 84
French, Free 84
French Army
  in Algeria 100, 103, 104–105, 108, 110, 111
  Bureau of the General Staff, 5e (psyops) 107
  commandos de chasse 109
  groupes mobiles (GM – mechanized infantry battalions)
    98–99
    GM 100: 100
  in Indochina 91, 92, 93, 94–95, 96, 97, 98, 111
  Military Assistance Advisory Group (MAAG) (Vietnam)
    132, 133
  Muslims (*harkis*) 105, 107, 111
  North African units 93, 94–95
  Parachute Division, 10th 108
  paratroops 96
  Section Administrative Spéciale (SAS) officers 107
  Senegalese units 94–95
  Vietnamese battalions 98
French Communist Party (PCF) 84, 85, 96, 97
French government (Paris) 91–92, 93, 96–97, 99, 101, 104,
    105 *see also* Vichy government
French imperial warfare (1945–62) 91–112
  Algeria 100–112, **102**
    barriers as COIN tactics 106
    Challe offensive 105, 109
    de Gaulle 110–111
    "free fire zones" 106
    French reaction 104–108
    Military Division, 10th 101
    resettlement 106–107
  Indochina 92–100, **94**, 111–112
    1950–53 97–99
    the endgame 99–100, 101
    the first phase 92–97
  wars of decolonization 92
French Militia (Milice Française) 86
French Résistance 84, 86–87, 88, 90, 93 *see also*
    Maquis/Maquisards
French *troupes de marine* 95
Frente de Libertaçao de Moçambique (FRELIMO) 192,
    193, 198, 200, 201
Front de Libération Nationale (FLN) 91–92, 100, 101, 102,
    103, 104, 105, 106, 107–108, 109, 110, 111, 112
  katibas (companies) 109
Front for the Liberation of Occupied South Yemen (FLOSY)
    160, 161, 163, 164
Frontier Scouts 236
"Frontiers, Battle of the" (1958) 106
Funston, Frederick 41

Gaddafi, President 173
Galula, Col David 13–14, 231
Gates, Robert 258
Gaullists 84
Gaza Strip 203, 209, 215–216, 218
Geneva Agreement (1954) 132
Geneva conference (1953) 99, 100, 101
German anti-partisan operations in World War One 72–74
German anti-partisan warfare in World War Two 70–72,
    74–90
  in Occupied France (1943–44) 83–89, 85
  in the Soviet Union (1941–44) 71, 74–83
German Armed Forces High Command *see* OKW
German Army (Reichswehr) 72, 73 *see also* Wehrmacht
German Freikorps ("Freecorps") 74
German police 70, 75, 76, 79
Germany, rise of, as global naval power 57, 58
Germany and Venezuelan Claims Crisis 60

Giap, Vo Nguyen 95–96, 97, 98, 99, 100
Gilad, Maj Gen Amos 211
Goa 189
Good Friday Agreement (1998) 175
Government of Ireland Bill/Act (GIA) (1920) 22, 26
Granada, Nicaragua 65, 66, 67
Guantánamo Bay 58
Gudmundsson, Maj Bruce, USMCR (Ret.) 8, 55–69
Guéret 87
Guevara, Che (Ernesto) 51, 128
Gulf of Fonseca 62, 63
Gulf of Mexico 55, 56
Gulf States 166
Gurney, Sir Henry 116, 120, 126, 129
Gwynn, Sir Charles 13, 27, 28, 32, 34

Hack, Karl 127
HaCohen, Brig Gen Gershon 213
Haditha 253
Haining, Lt Gen Robert 31, 32
Haiphong 93
Haiti 57, 69
Halberstam, David 147
Halutz, Maj Gen Dani 213–214
Hamas 205, 206, 208, 210, 215, 219
"Hamburger Hill", battle of (Hill 937) 144
Hamid Karzai 225, 228
Hamilton, Lee 258
Hanoi 92, 97
    Politburo 44
Haqqani Network 229
Hargroves, Brig Louis 154, 155
Harkins, Lt Gen Paul D. 134–135, 136
Hasan Nasrallah 212
Hazaras 222–223
Healey, Denis 160
"hearts and minds" strategy see "winning hearts and
    minds" strategy
Heath, Edward 191
Henderson, Ian 195
Heydrich, SS-Obergruppenführer Reinhard 76
Hezb-e Islami Gulbuddin 229
Hickman, Lt Gen John 198
Hill 937 ("Hamburger Hill") 144
Himmler, Heinrich 79, 81
Hispaniola 56, 58
Hit 247–248
Hitler, Adolf 81, 82, 85
Ho Chi Minh 53, 92, 93, 95, 96, 97, 99, 132
Hoa Binh 98
Höherer SS- und Polizeiführer (Higher SS and Police Leader)
    85
Holocaust 76, 77
Home-Smith Settlement (1972) 193
Honduras 61–62
Hué 99, 142
Huks, the (later People's Liberation Army) 37, 48–50, 51,
    52, 53, 54
Hussein, Saddam 147, 241

Ia Drang valley 138
Imad Falouji 205
Imperial Policing 13, 27, 28
India 149
Indochina War (1946–54) 92–100, 94, 111–112 see also
    Vietnam
    1950–53 97–99
    the endgame 99–100, 101
    the first phase 92–97
intelligence, human (HUMINT) 153, 161, 181
International Crisis Group 234–235
International Security Assistance Force (ISAF) 231,
    232–233, 234, 235, 236
Intifada 203–204, 205, 216, 216 see also Al-Aqsa Intifada
Iraq 132, 147
Iraq, counterinsurgency in (May 2003–January 2007)
    241–259, 246
    civil war 255–257
    counterinsurgency reforms 250–255
    Fallujah, first battle of 244–248
    insurgency, outbreak of 241–244
    Mahdi Uprising 244–248

a new commander 257–258
a new strategy 257–258
stemming the tide 248–250
Iraq Petroleum Company 31
Iraq Study Group 257–258
Iraqi Air Force 214
Iraqi Army 247, 248, 249, 250–251, 252, 254–255, 256,
    257, 258, 259
    Iraqi Army Brigade, 3rd 249
    Iraqi Army Division, 3rd 251
    Iraqi Intervention Force Brigade, 1st 249
Iraqi Civil Defense Corps 247 see also Iraqi National Guard
Iraqi forces 244, 245, 246
Iraqi Governing Council 242, 244, 245
Iraqi Interim Government 248, 249, 250, 251, 255
Iraqi National Guard 247–248
    503rd Bn 247–248
Iraqi National Police 255, 257, 258
Iraqi security forces 248, 250
Ireland 21–27, 35, 36, see also Northern Ireland
Ireland, Home Rule for 22, 23
Irgun Zvai Leumi (IZL) 33, 34
Irish National Liberation Army (INLA) 171, 172
Irish Republican Army (IRA) 21, 23, 24, 25–26
    Continuity IRA 184
    "flying columns" (Active Service Units) 24, 26
    "Official" IRA 169
    Provisional IRA see Provisional Irish Republican Army
    Real IRA 184
Irish Republican Brotherhood 22, 23
Irish Volunteers 21 see also Irish Republican Army
Iron, Col Richard, OBE 8, 167–184
ISAF (International Security Assistance Force) 231,
    232–233, 234, 235, 236
Israel Air Force (IAF) 209, 213–214
Israel Defense Forces (IDF)
    Armored Corps 207
    Field Intelligence Corps 213
    General Staff 207
    paratrooper units 209
    Sayerot (reconnaissance) infantry 209
    School of Leadership 217
    School of Military Law code of conduct 216–217
    Special Forces 204, 209
    Tze'elim National Training Center 217
    undercover hit squads, Mistar'aravim 209
Israel Defense Forces and the Al-Aqsa Intifada 203–219
    Al-Aqsa Intifada 205–206, 207, 209
        coping with 216–218
    "Containment Policy" 205–207
    controlling the ground 215–216
    IDF COIN, from reactive to proactive 212–214
    IDF house demolitions 210, 211
    IDF reactions, initial 205–207
    IDF's operational awareness 207–208
    IDF's second phase of COIN 208–212
    Israeli victims of Palestinian suicide terror attacks 208,
        208, 211
    media fallout, negative, dealing with 214
    Operation Defensive Shield 212–214
    Operation Determined Path 215–216
    Palestinians held in custody by Israeli security services
        215, 215
    punishing the Palestinian Authority 208–212
    security fence 218
    unilateral disengagement 218
Israeli-Arab conflict 203, 204 see also Palestine; Palestinian
    entries
Israeli government 207
Israeli secret services (Shin Bet) 210, 215

Jaffa 30
Japan, rise of, as global naval power 57, 58
Japanese occupation of the Philippines (1942–44) 47–48, 53
Jauffret, Jean-Charles 105
Jebel Huriyah 157
Jebel Shamsan 160
Jebel Widna 157
"Jedburghs" 86, 90
Jerusalem 27, 34
    Al-Aqsa Mosque 205
    Gilo neighborhood 206

King David Hotel 34
Temple Mount 205
Jews 70, 75, 76–77, 84, 85, 86
Joes, Prof Anthony James 9, 37–54
Johnson, Harold K. 139
Johnson, President Lyndon B. 136, 142–143
Joint Chiefs of Staff (US) 142
Joint Intelligence Advisory Committee (British) 120
Jungle Warfare School (Far East Land Forces Training Centre – FTC) 125
Jura, French 86

Kabul 221, 222, 225, 229, 232, 236
Afghan government in 221, 228, 229, 236, 240
Kaminski, Bronislav 78
Kandahar 225
Karzai, Hamid 225, 228
Katipunan 38, 40–41
Kaunda, Kenneth 186
Keane, Gen Jack 147–148
Kennedy, John F. 134, 136
Kent State University 146
Khalilzad, Zalmay 251
Khmer Rouge 145–146
Khormaksar airfield 157, 161
King's Regulations 20
Kissinger, Henry 196, 198
Kitson, Gen Sir Frank 13, 15, 231, 239
Klein, Brig Gen Avigdor 207
Komer, "Blowtorch" Bob 141
Korean War (1950–53) 97, 99, 128
Kriegsgerichtbarkeitserlass decree 75–76
Krulak, Lt Gen. 139
Kunduz 225
Kuomintang armies 53
Kurdi, Zuhair 210
Kuwait 147

"la guerre révolutionnaire" theory 105–106, 108, 110, 111
La Pointe, Ali 108
Lacheroy, Col Charles 105–106
Laden, Osama bin 223, 224
Laird, Melvin 144
Lancaster House Conference 201
"Land to the Tiller" law (1970) (South Vietnam) 145
Lang Son 99
Lansdale, Col Edward, USAF 50
Laos, invasion of 146
Larbi Ben M'Hidi 108
Lashkar Gah 238
Laurel, Jose 48
Lawrence, T. E. 128
Le Monde 107
Learning to Eat Soup with a Knife... 13, 17
Leclerc de Hauteclocque, Gen. 92, 93
León 65
Leyte Gulf, battle of (1944) 47–48
Libya 173
Lieb, Dr Peter 8–9, 70–90
Life 153
Lippert, Edouard 186
Little Aden 158
Lloyd George, David 22, 24, 25
Lobengula (Ndebele king) 186
Lokot 77
London bombings 174
Londonderry (Derry) 168, 174, 176, 182
Lorillot, Henri 105
Loughgall 176
Low Intensity Operations 15
Loya Jirga ("great council") 228
Luce, R/Adm Stephen B. 57
Lunt, Brig James 151, 153
Luzon 39, 41, 48
Lyttleton, Oliver 120, 121, 124, 126

Ma'alla, Aden 160
Machel, Samora 201
Magellan, Ferdinand 38
Magsaysay, Ramon 50–51, 52, 53, 54
Mahan, Capt Alfred Thayer 57
Mahdi, Jaysh al 245–246, 247, 249, 255, 256, 257

Makarios, President 150
Malawi (formerly Nyasaland) 186, 188
Malay Regiment 114
Malaya 17
Chinese community 113–114, 115–117, 118–119, 127
Malaya, evolution of British strategy in (1948–60) 113–130, **117**
air operations 125
government's initial search and destroy strategy 115–118
hearts and minds strategy, evaluating 127–130
hearts and minds strategy implemented 121–127
intelligence in 124
"new villages" 122–123, 154
psychological warfare 126
revising the strategy 118–121
surrendered enemy personnel (SEPs) 124, 126
"white areas" 123–124
Malayan Administrative Service 122
Malayan Civil Service 122
Malayan Communist Party (MCP) 113, 114–115, 117, 119, 120, 121, 122, 123, 124, 126, 127, 128, 130
Malayan Emergency 151, 165, 189–190 see also Malaya, evolution of British strategy in
Malayan Film Unit 126
Malayan government 115–121, 129–130
Malayan home guard 120, 122, 123–124
Chinese units 122
Malayan police 114, 115–117, 119–120, 121–122
Malayan Public Works Department 122
Malayan Races Liberation Army (MRLA) 113, 114–115, 116, 117–119, 122, 123, 124, 125, 126, 128
Maliki, Nuri al 257
Malkasian, Dr Carter 9, 241–259
Malvern, Lord 188
Managua 65, 66, 67, 68
Manila 38, 39, 44, 48, 49
Manila Bay, battle of (1898) 39
Mao Tse-tung 49, 53, 96, 106, 128
Maquis/Maquisards 86–87, 88 see also French Résistance
Marshall, Gen George 52–53
Marshall Plan 52
Marston, Dr Daniel 10, 220–240
Masaya, Nicaragua 66, 67, 68
Massoud, Gen Ahmed Shah 221, 223
Massu, Gen Jacques 108, 110
Mattis, Maj Gen James 244, 247, 249, 253, 257
Mazar-i-Sharif 222–223, 225, 238
Maze Prison 171
MacArthur, Gen Arthur 42, 45
MacArthur, Gen Douglas 48
McCarthy, Donal 150, 165
MacGillivray, Sir Donald 126
McKinley, President William 39, 44, 45
McLean, Billy 158
McMaster, Col H. R. 251, 252
McNamara, Robert 142
Macready, Gen Nevil 23, 25
Mena, Luis 65, 66
Mengistu Regime 166
Menista rebels 65, 66
Merkblatt 69/2 Bandenbekämpfung (Instructions 69/2 Bandit Combat) 89
Messali Hadj 102
Mexican Navy 62
Mexico 56, 62, 68–69
Meyers, Gen Sam L. 133
Milice Française (French Militia) 86
Militärbefehlshaber in Frankreich (Military Commander in France) 85
Military Assistance Command - Vietnam (MACV) 134, 137, 138, 140
Miliz (Militia) 78
Miller, Harry 116
Min Yuen 113, 114, 117–119, 123, 124
Mindanao 38, 45
mine detection vehicle, "Pookie" 197
mine-protected vehicles 194
missionaries, Chinese-speaking 122
Mitchell, Lt Col Colin "Mad Mitch" 163, 164
Mofaz, Lt Gen Shaul 212
Moncur, Maj John 162
Monroe, President James 55
"Monroe Doctrine" 55, 56, 57, 58

Montgomery, Bernard 32, 33, 34, 35, 36
Moore, Sir John 180
Moore, Lt Col 138
Moqtada Sadr 245, 247, 248, 249, 255
Morice Line 106
Moro people 38, 45–46
Morocco 106
Mosquito Coast 61, 63, 64, 65 *see also* Nicaragua
Mosul 243, 250
Mouvement nationalist Algérienne (MNA) 100, 102, 104, 111
Mozambique 196, 200, 201
Mugabe, Robert 186, 187, 190, 198, 199, 201–202
Mujahideen 221
Multi-National Forces-Iraq (MNF-I) 248, 251
Multi-National Security Transition Command-Iraq (MNSTC-I) 248
Muslims
   Algerian 100, 101–102, 103–104, 107, 108, 110, 111
   in French Army (*harkis*) 105, 107, 111
   Shi'a Arabs 241–242, 245, 250, 251, 252, 254, 255, 256, 257, 259
   Sunni Arabs 241, 242, 243, 245, 246–247, 250, 251, 252, 254, 255, 256, 257, 259
Muzorewa, Bishop Abel 185, 186, 199, 200, 201
Myers, Gen Richard 224

Na San 98
Nacionalista Party (Philippines) 51, 52
Nagl, Lt Col John A. 10, 13, 17, 129, 131–148
Najaf 245, 247, 248–249, 250
   Imam Ali Mosque 249
Najibullah, President 221
Nasser, President Gamal Abdel 105, 149–150, 154, 158, 159, 162, 166
National Liberation Front (NLF) (Aden) 150, 151, 153, 155, 157–158, 159, 160, 161, 162, 163, 164, 165
NATO (North Atlantic Treaty Organization) 52, 112, 220, 232, 233, 234, 235, 236
   International Security Assistance Force (ISAF) 231, 232–233, 234, 235, 236
Natonski, Maj Gen Richard 248
"navalism" 57–58
Navarre, Gen Henri 99
Ndebele people 186
Newsweek 226–227
Ngo Dinh Diem 132, 134, 136
Ngo Dinh Nhu 136
Nicaragua (1909–12) 61–69
   the fighting 62, 63–65, 69
   the rebellion 65–68, 69
Nicaraguan soldiers 68
Nixon, President Richard M. 144, 146
nizam political administrative structure 102
Nkomo, Joshua 186, 201–202
NKVD 77
Normandy landings (1944) 87
North Atlantic Treaty Organization *see* NATO
North Vietnamese Army (NVA) 135, 137, 143, 145–146
North Yemen 150
Northern Alliance (United Islamic Front for the Salvation of Afghanistan) 223, 224, 225, 226, 236
Northern Ireland 167–184, **171**
   bringing the conflict to an end 183–184
   Government 168, 169
   the insurgency 168–175
      border crossings 179–180
      civil rights 168–169
      evolution of UK and PIRA strategies 169–170
      hunger strike (1981) 170–172
      internment 169–170
      the Libyan connection 173
      the military 168–169
      PIRA's attacks on England and the Continent 174
      PIRA's "Tet Offensive" 173
      political process 174–175
      radicalization 168–169
      weapons supply 173
   intelligence 181
      what it achieved 183
   military aspects of the COIN campaign 175–180
      controlling the border 179–180
      deterrence in NI, nature of 175–177

framework operations 177–178
   lessons learned 180
   PIRA attack, anatomy of 178–179
   tactical development 180
   training 180
  surveillance 182–183

OAS (Organisation armée secrète) 100, 110–111
Oberbefehlshaber (Supreme Commander West) 87
O'Connor, Richard 32
Odierno, Maj Gen Raymond 243
Office of Strategic Services (OSS) 86
OKH (Oberkommando des Heeres – High Command of the German Army) 79–80, 82
OKW (Oberkommando der Wehrmacht – High Command of the German Armed Forces) 76, 81, 82, 85, 87
Olympia, USS 39
On Strategy: A Critical Analysis of the Vietnam War 147
"One War: MACV Command Overview, 1968–72" 143
"Oozlebarts" 32
Operation
   Agatha 34
   Al Fajr 249
   Anaconda 226
   Apache Snow 144
   Bamberg 80
   Barbarossa 74, 75, 76
   Days of Penitence 216
   Defensive Shield 212–214
   Desert Storm 147
   Determined Path 215–216
   Dingo 196, 198
   Elephant 34, 35
   Enduring Freedom (OEF) 225, 231–232
   Fard al Qanun 258
   Hannover 80
   Herrick IV 236, 238, 239
   Herrick V 238, 239
   Hippopotamus 34, 35
   Hurricane 194
   Iraqi Freedom 147
   Iron Hammer 243
   Lea 96, 97
   Masher (later *White Wing*) 138
   Mountain Sweep 226
   München 80
   Nutcracker 151
   Rainbow 216
   Restoring Rights 251
   Service 122
   Speedy Express 144
   Steel Curtain 252
   Sumpffieber (Marsh Fever) 76
   Switchback 137
   Thayer II 138
   Together Forward I/II 256
   Tripper 192
   Vogelsang 80
   White Wing 138
   Zigeunerbaron (Gypsy Baron) 81
   Zitadelle (Citadel) 81
Oradour-sur-Glane 88
Organisation armée secrète (OAS) 100, 110–111
Osama bin Laden 223, 224
Oslo Peace Accords (1993) 204, 205
OSS (Office of Strategic Services) 86
Ostland 79
Otis, Gen Elwell S. 39, 41, 43, 44
Oyonnax 87

Pacific Railway of Nicaragua 65, 66
Pakistan 230
Pakistan Administered Tribal Areas 230
Pakistan Interservice Intelligence (ISI) 221, 222, 225
Pakistani Army 230
Palestine 27–35, 36, 161 *see also* Israel(i) *entries*
   Occupied Enemy Territory Administration (South) (OETA(S)) 27–28
Palestinian Authority 204, 205, 206, 207, 208–212, 214, 219
Palestinian Gendarmerie (cavalry) 28
Palestinian High Commissioner 29, 30, 31, 33, 35
Palestinian Islamic Jihad 205, 208–209, 210

Palestinian Liberation Organization (PLO) 203, 204
Palestinian police 28, 29–30, 33, 34
Palestinians 203–204, 205, 206–207, 209, 210, 213, 214, 215, 216, 217, 218, 219
Panama Canal 58, 61
plans for 56, 57, 58
Panama Railroad 56, 57
Panjshiri Tajiks 228
Papon, Maurice 111
Paris, FLN demonstration 111
Paris, French government in 91–92, 93, 96–97, 99, 101, 104, 105 see also Vichy government
Paris Match 153
Paris Pact (1928) 196
partisan war in the Occupied Soviet Union (1941–44) 71, 74–83
partisan warfare against Germany in World War Two see German anti-partisan warfare in World War Two
Pashtuns 220, 221, 222, 223, 225, 227, 228, 229, 230, 232, 233, 236
Patriotic Front (Rhodesia) 199
Peace and Reconciliation Group (Northern Ireland) 174
Pearce Commission 191
People's Army Against Japan see Huks, the
People's Self-Defense Force (South Vietnam) 145
Percival, A. E. 26–27
Pershing, Capt John "Black Jack" 46
Pétain, Marshal Philippe 83
Petraeus, Maj Gen David 243, 248, 253, 254, 258
Philippeville 103
Philippeville "massacres" (1955) 104
Philippine Army 50, 51, 52
Battalion Combat Teams 50–51
Philippine Communist Party 49, 51
Philippine Constabulary 49, 53
Philippines, counter insurgency in (1898–1954) 37–54
American counterinsurgency (1899–1902) 37, 38–47
counterinsurgent victory 46–47
fighting the Moros 45–46
food shortage 42
guerrilla war 41–43
"policy of attraction" 42, 44, 47
war at home 44–45
Huk rebellion (1946–54) 37, 47–54
the Huks 37, 48–50
Magsaysay defeats the Huks 50–51
Magsaysay to presidency 52–53
why the Huks lost 53–54
Philippines, Spanish 37–38, 40
pieds noirs 100, 101, 103, 108, 109, 110, 111
Plateau de Glières, Savoy 87
Police Mobile Force (Palestine) 33
Policy Action Group (PAG) (Afghanistan) 234
Popular Organization of Revolutionary Forces (PORF) (Aden) 163
Porch, Prof Douglas 10, 91–112
Port-au-Prince 57
Portuguese 189, 190
Potsdam Agreement (1945) 93
Prendergast, John 159
Program for the Pacification and Long-Term Development of South Vietnam (PROVN) study 140–141
Protestants, Northern Ireland 168
Provincial Reconstruction Team (PRT) concept 231, 232, 233–235, 236, 238, 239–240, 253
Provisional Irish Republican Army (PIRA) 167, 168, 169, 170, 171, 172, 173, 174, 175–177, 179, 181, 182, 183, 184
attack, anatomy of 178–179
Belfast Brigade 170
Northern Command 178
psychological warfare in Malayan Emergency 126

Qateibi tribe ("Red Wolves of Radfan") 150, 153
Quezon, President Manuel 47
widow and daughter 50
Quirino, President Elpidio 49, 50, 52, 53

Rabbani, Burhanuddin 221, 223
Radfan camp, Aden 161
Radfan campaign 150–158, 166
Raed Karmi 208
Rahman, Tunku Abdul 126

Ramadi 246, 255, 256
Rashid Dostum, Gen Abdul 221
Red Army 77, 82
Red Brigades 166
Red Cross 122
Red River Delta 93, 96
Regional Forces and Popular Forces (RF/PF) (South Vietnam) 145
Reichskommissariate Ostland 79, 81, 82
Security Division 74–75
Reichskommissariate Ukraine 79
Security Division 74–75
Resistencia National Moçambique (RNM) 200, 201
Restoration of Order in Ireland Act (ROIA) (1920) 22, 24
Révolution nationale 83
Rhodes, Cecil John 186
Rhodesia 18
Centenary district 193–194
Rhodesian African nationalists 185, 186, 187, 191, 193, 198
Rhodesian Air Force, Royal (RRAF) 189
Rhodesian Army 189
Fire Forces 195, 197, 199, 200, 201
Grey Scouts Regiment 197
Psychological Warfare Unit 197
Rhodesia Defence Regiment 200
Rhodesian African Rifles (RAR) 189–190, 192, 197
Rhodesian Intelligence Corps (RIC) 197, 198
Rhodesian Light Infantry (RLI) 189, 196, 197
Royal Rhodesia Regiment 189
Selous Scouts Regiment 195, 196, 197
Signal Squadron, 8: 198
Special Air Service squadron 189–190, 195, 196
Tracker Combat School 192
Rhodesian counterinsurgency campaign (1962–80) 185–202, 193
the armed struggle 186–188
Combined Operations HQ 190
Counter-Insurgency Civil Committee 190
Counter-Insurgency Committee 190
Joint Operations Centers (JOCs) 190, 191, 194
Operations Coordinating Committee (OCC) 190, 191, 198
Rhodesian response 188–202
Phase 1 (1966–72) 191–193
Phase 2 (1972–74) 193–195
Phase 3 (1974–77) 195–198
Phase 4 (1977–79) 198–200
Phase 5 (April 1979–March 1980) 200–202
Security Council 190
Rhodesian government 185, 193
Ministry of Combined Operations 198, 199–200
Rhodesian Guard Force 194, 197, 200
Rhodesian Internal Affairs Department 192, 194
Rhodesian Military Intelligence Directorate (MID) 195, 197, 200
Rice, Condoleezza 253
Richards, Lt Gen David 233, 234
Roosevelt, President Theodore 45, 60, 62
"Roosevelt Corollary to the Monroe Doctrine" 60
Rosson, Gen William 136–137
Route Coloniale 4 (RC4) 97
Roxas, Manuel 48, 49
Royal Air Force
43(F) Squadron 156
208 Squadron 153, 156
Royal Irish Constabulary (RIC) 22–24
Auxiliary Division 23–24, 25
"Temporary Cadets" 23
Weekly Summary 23
Royal Marines
Commando, 45 (45 Cdo RM) 155, 156, 157, 238
Commando Brigade, 3rd 238
Royal Navy 57–58
Royal Ulster Constabulary (RUC) 168
B Specials 168
Rumsfeld, Donald 224, 226, 245
Russo-Japanese War (1904–05) 58

Saddam Hussein 147, 241
Sadr, Moqtada 245, 247, 248, 249, 255
Sahawa Al Anbar 257
Saigon 92, 142, 144, 146
Brinks Hotel 137

St Amand 87
St John's Ambulance 122
Salan, Gen Raoul 98, 105, 110, 111
Samar island 45
Samarra 246, 249, 250
    Askariya (Golden) Mosque 255, 256
Sanchez, Lt Gen Ricardo 242, 243, 245, 248
Sands, Bobby 172
Santo Domingo 56
Sattler, Lt Gen John 249
Saudi Arabia 166
Savory, Alan 195
Schmidt, Genobst Rudolf 78
sectarian divides 16
Seder Night Massacre (2002) 212
Selbstverwaltungsbezirk (Local Self-Government District) 78
Semtex explosive 173
Sepp, Kalev 250, 251
September 11, 2001 attacks 132, 224, 229
Serbia 76
Service du Travail Obligatoire (STO – Obligatory Labor
    Service) 86
Service Spéciaux 90
Sétif uprising (1945) 101, 103
Sharon, Ariel 18, 205, 207, 212, 218
Sheikh Othman, Aden 161, 162, 164
Shi'a Arabs 241–242, 245, 250, 251, 252, 254, 255, 256,
    257, 259
Shona-speaking people 186, 187
Sicherheitspolizei und Sicherheitsdienst (Sipo/SD) (Security
    Police and Security Service) 76, 85–86, 88
    Einsatzgruppen 76
Simpson, Brig. 35
Sinn Fein Party 21, 22, 23, 25, 26, 172, 175
Sistani, Ayatollah Ali al 242, 248–249
Sithole, Rev Ndabaningi 187, 199
Sittar Bezia Ftikhan al Rishawi, Shaykh Abd al 257
Six-Day War (1967) 162
Small Wars 13, 19
Small Wars Manual 13
Smith, Ian 185–186, 187, 188, 190, 191, 196, 198, 199
SOE (Special Operations Executive) 86
Sofrin, Brig Gen Amnon 213
Soummam Valley, Kabylia 104, 108
Soustelle, Jacques 104
South Africa 192, 195–196 *see also* Boer War, Second
South African police 192
South Africans 189–190
South Arabia, Federation of 150, 151, 153, 154, 159–160,
    164–165, 166
South Armagh 169
Southerland, Adm William H. 66
Soviet invasion of Afghanistan 221
Soviet Union, Occupied, partisan war in (1941–44) 71, 74–83
Spanish-American War (1898) 39, 58
Spanish Philippines 37–38, 40 *see also* Philippine(s) *entries*
Special Operations Executive (SOE) 86
Spicer, Col R. G. B. 29
SS 79, 88
    brigades 76
SS-Panzerdivision "Das Reich", 2nd 87–88
Stalin, Josef 77, 99
Stern Gang 161
Stirling, David 158
Straits Times 116
Stubbs, Dr Richard 11, 113–130
Summers, Col Harry 147
Sunni Arabs 241, 242, 243, 245, 246–247, 250, 251, 252,
    254, 255, 256, 257, 259
Supernumerary Police (Jewish) 30, 31, 34
Swannack, Maj Gen Charles 243

Taba talks (2000) 205, 206
Taft, President William Howard 45, 61, 62
Tagalog people 38, 41, 54
Taji COIN academy 252
Tajiks 221, 222, 223, 228
Tal Afar 251–252, 253, 258
Taliban 16, 220, 222, 223, 224, 225, 226, 227, 229, 230,
    231, 232, 233, 236, 237
tanks, Centurion 151
tanks, M1A1/M1A2 Abrams 242, 252

Tanzim 205, 206, 208
Taruc, Luis 48, 49, 50, 52
Taylor, Gen Maxwell 136–137
Tegart, Sir Charles 30–31
Tel Aviv 34
Templer, Field Marshal Sir Gerald 113, 121, 122, 123, 124,
    125–126, 127, 128, 130, 157, 190
Tenet, George 226
Tet Offensive (1968) 142, 173, 183
Thatcher, Margaret 173, 174, 186, 200
Thieu, President 145
Thompson, Sir Robert 13, 14–15, 128, 129, 230, 231
Thomson, Lt David 164
Tiger, HMS 191
Tito, Marshal 89
Tonkin 93, 95, 96, 97, 99
Tonkin delta 93, 95, 96, 97, 99
Tora Bora 226
Tower, Maj Gen Philip 164
Townshend, Prof Charles 11, 19–36
Trans-Jordan Frontier Force 28–29
Trevaskis, Sir Kennedy 150
Truman, President Harry 52, 146
Tudor, Gen Henry 23
Tulle 87, 88
Tun Abdul Razak 127
Tunisia 106
Tunku Abdul Rahman 126

Ukraine 72–73
Ukrainian government 73
United Nations 107, 161, 166, 214
United Nations Charter, Chapter Seven 188
United Nations Security Council 232
United States Agency for International Development
    (USAID) 141, 147
United States and the Philippines 37, 38–47
United States and Vietnam War *see* Vietnam,
    counterinsurgency in
United States Army 147–148, 242–243
    in Afghanistan 226–227, 231–232
    Airborne Division, 82nd 226–227, 243, 244
    Airborne Division, 101st 144, 226, 243–244
    Airborne Infantry Regiment, 325th, 2nd Bn 252
    Armored Reconnaissance Regiment, 3rd (3rd ACR) 251, 252
    Blackjack Brigade 249
    Cavalry Division, 1st 138, 249
    Field Manual 3–24 253, 258
    Field Manual 100–5, Operations 134
    Infantry, Ninth 45
    Infantry Division, 1st 249
    Infantry Division, 4th 243
    Infantry Division, 9th 144
    in Iraq 249, 251, 252 *see also* United States forces in Iraq
    Mountain Division, 10th 226
    National Training Center 242, 253
    in the Philippines *see* Philippines, counterinsurgency in:
        American counterinsurgency
    Special Forces 136–137 *see also* United States Special
        Forces
    training program 253
    and Vietnam 131, 133, 134, 137, 138, 139–140, 143, 144,
        147 *see also* Military Assistance Command Vietnam
United States forces in Iraq 241, 242, 243–244, 245, 247,
    249, 251, 252, 253–254, 258
United States Marine Corps 13, 62–63, 147, 148
    in Afghanistan 225, 242, 243
    Camp Lejeune, NC 173
    "Combined Action Platoons" (CAP) 139, 140, 247, 257
    in Iraq 250, 252, 253, 258
    Marine Expeditionary Force, I (I MEF) 244, 245, 256
    Marine Expeditionary Unit, 11th 248
    Marine Regiment, 1st 249, 250
    Marine Regiment, 6th, 3rd Bn 252
    Marine Regiment, 7th 249, 250
    training program 253
    in Vietnam 137, 139
United States Marine Corps in Nicaragua (1909–12) 62–69
    the fighting 62, 64–65, 69
    the rebellion 65, 66–68, 69
United States Navy
    Asiatic Squadron 39

Bluejackets 55, 67
in the Caribbean 55, 57, 60, 62, 63, 64
in the Philippines 39, 41
West India Squadron ("Mosquito Fleet") 55
United States Special Forces 134, 136–137, 147, 225, 226, 236, 244, 247
United States State Department 141, 147
Uzbeks 221, 222

Vehicle Check Points (VCPs) 176
Vehicle Check Points, Permanent (PVCPs) 176, 177, 182
vehicles see also tanks
amphibious, Alaska "weasels" and Mississippi "alligators" 98–99
armored cars, Saladin 163
armored fighting vehicles, M2A2 Bradley 242, 252
bulldozers, armored D-9 213
mine detection, "Pookie" 197
mine-protected 194
Venezuela 60
Venezuelan Claims Crisis (1902–03) 60
Veracruz 68–69
Vercors mountain massif 88
Versailles, Treaty of (1919) 73
Vichy France 83
Vichy government 83, 86
Viet Cong (VC) 134, 135, 136, 137, 138, 142, 145
Viet Cong Infrastructure (VCI) 141–142, 143
Viet Minh 53, 91–92, 93, 95–96, 97, 98, 99, 106, 112, 132
Vietnam 82–83, 93 see also Indochina War
Vietnam, Army of the Republic of (ARVN) 135, 136, 137, 139, 140, 144–145, 146
Vietnam, counterinsurgency in 131–148
an advisory effort 132–136
the big war 137–142
CIA 136–137, 140, 149
CIDG 136–137, 140
COIN doctrine and learning after 146–148
infiltration routes into South Vietnam 133
"new villages" 135–136
"strategic hamlets" 135–136
Switchback 136–137
Tet Offensive 142, 173, 183
Vietnamization 98, 144, 145
Vietnam, Government of (GVN) 132, 136, 137, 138, 142, 145, 146
"Phung Hoang/Phoenix" program 141, 142, 145
Vietnamese 95
Vietnamese Army, North (NVA) 135, 137, 143, 145–146
"Vietnamization" 98, 144, 145
Viner, Brig Gordon 155
"Voice of Palestine" radio station 205
"Voice of the Arabs" radio station 154
Volkswehr (People's Defense) 78
Vorster, B. J. 196, 198

Wadi Dhubsan 157
Wadi Misrah 157
Wadi Taym 153
Wagner, Gen. Eduard 76
Walker, Jonathan 11, 149–166
Walker, Lt Col Walter 125
Walls, Lt Gen Peter 185, 189, 190, 198
Walt, Maj Gen Lew 139
Ward-Booth, Maj Tony 157
Wauchope, Sir Arthur 30
weapons
bombs, Alpha II bouncing 197
bombs, Golf 1,000-lb blast 197
cannon, Matra 151 20mm 194–195
explosive, Semtex 173
explosive devices, improvised (IEDs) 169, 205, 216
field guns, 3-inch 67
grenades, stun 206
guns, 1-pounder 67
howitzers, 105mm pack 151
landmines, antitank 194, 197
machine guns, Colt 66, 67
machine guns, MAG 192
machine guns, rifle-caliber 67
mortars 216
napalm bombs 134–135, 197

pistols, US Army .38 cal. 46
plastic bullets, rubber-coated 206
rifles, bolt-action magazine 67
rifles, FN FAL 7.62mm 192
rocket launchers, AT-4 250
rocket launchers, Blindicide 161
rockets, Qassam 216
shotguns, "Spider" 24-barrel 12-gauge 197
sub-machine guns, Browning 9mm 162
sub-machine guns, Sterling 162
tear gas 206
Wehrdörfer (fortified villages) project 82–83
Wehrmacht 70, 73 see also German Army; SS
Army, 9th 81
Army Group Center 74, 80, 82
Security Divisions 74, 75
Army Group North: Security Divisions 74, 75
Army Group South: Security Divisions 74, 75
"cauldron" operations 79–80, 81
Feldkommandanturen (Field Garrison HQ) 83–84
Infantry Division, 707th 75, 77
Jagdkommandos (hunting detachments) 79
Landesschützenbataillone (Territorial Battalions) 75
in Occupied France 83
Osttruppen (Eastern troops) 78
Panzer Army, 2nd 79, 81
Reserve Division, 157th 86–87
Security Divisions 74–75
Selbstschutz (self-protection) units 78
in the Soviet Union 76, 77–78
Welensky, Sir Roy 192
Weltanschauungskrieg (ideological war) concept 76
West Bank 203, 213, 218
Westmoreland, Gen William 17, 136, 137–138, 139, 140, 142–143
Weston, Kael 250
Wheeler, Gen Earle 134, 142
Whitehead, Sir Edgar 186, 187, 188
Wickham, Sir Charles 33
Wilson, Harold 158, 160, 166, 188, 191
Wingate, Capt Orde 31, 32, 33–34
"winning hearts and minds" strategy 113, 121–127, 134
evaluating 127–130
Wood, Dr J. R. T. 12, 185–202
Wood, Gen Leonard 45–46
World War One, German anti-partisan operations in 72–74
World War Two, German anti-partisan warfare in 70–72, 74–90
in Occupied France (1943–44) 83–89, 85
in the Soviet Union (1941–44) 71, 74–83

Xuan Loc 146

Yaalon, Lt Gen Moshe 212
Yacef Saadi 108
Yadlin, Maj Gen Amos 218
Yamashita, Lt Gen 48
Yasser Arafat 204, 205, 206, 207–208, 209, 212
Yassin Mohammed, Sheikh 215
Yediot Ahronot 207
Yemen, People's Democratic Republic of (PDRY) 166
Yemen Arab Republic 150, 151, 157, 158, 159, 166
Yemeni immigrants 158
Yugoslavia 89

Zais, Maj Gen Melvin 144
Zambia (formerly Northern Rhodesia) 186, 188, 196, 200, 201
Zarqawi, Abu Musab al 242, 254, 255
Zelaya, José Santos 61–62, 63, 64, 65, 68
Zeledón, Benjamin 65–67, 68
Zeledónistas 67, 68
Zighout Youcef 103
Zimbabwe see Rhodesian counterinsurgency campaign
Zimbabwe African National Liberation Army (ZANLA) 191, 192, 193, 193–194, 195, 196, 197, 199, 200, 201, 202
Zimbabwe African National Union (ZANU) 187–188, 189, 191, 193, 194, 196, 199, 201
Zimbabwe African People's Union (ZAPU) 186, 187, 188, 189, 191, 193, 196, 199, 201
Zimbabwe People's Liberation Army (ZPRA) 191–192, 193, 195, 196, 199, 200, 201, 202
Zionism/Zionists 29, 32, 33, 34
Zuhair Kurdi 210